Church–state relations have undergone a number of changes during the seven decades of the existence of the Soviet Union. In the 1920s the state was politically and financially weak and its edicts often ignored, but the 1930s saw the beginning of an era of systematic anti-religious persecution. There was some relaxation in the last decade of Stalin's rule, but under Khrushchev, the pressure on the church was again stepped up. In the Brezhnev period this was moderated to a policy of slow strangulation, and Gorbachev's leadership saw a thorough liberalisation and re-legitimation of religion. This book brings together fifteen of the West's leading scholars of religion in the USSR, and provides the most comprehensive analysis of the subject yet undertaken. Bringing much hitherto unknown material to light, the authors discuss the policy apparatus, programmes of atheisation and socialisation, cults and sects, and the world of Christianity.

Religious policy
in the Soviet Union

Religious policy
in the Soviet Union

EDITED BY

Sabrina Petra Ramet

Associate Professor of International Studies
University of Washington

CAMBRIDGE
UNIVERSITY PRESS

Published by the Press Syndicate of the University of Cambridge
The Pitt Building, Trumpington Street, Cambridge CB2 1RP
40 West 20th Street, New York, NY 10011-4211, USA
10 Stamford Road, Oakleigh, Victoria 3166, Australia

First published 1993

Printed and bound in Great Britain by
Woolnough Bookbinding Ltd, Irthlingborough, Northamptonshire

A catalogue record for this book is available from the British Library

Library of Congress cataloguing in publication data

Religious policy in the Soviet Union/edited by Sabrina Petra Ramet.
p.   cm.
Includes index.
ISBN 0-521-41643-4 (hard)
1. Church and state – Soviet Union – History – 1917–   2. Soviet
Union – Religion – 1917–   I. Ramet, Sabrina P., 1949–
BR936.R47   1992
261.7′0947 – dc20 91-39817 CIP

ISBN 0 521 41643 4 hardback

For Jack Dull, friend:
You helped to get me through
a difficult year

Contents

Notes on contributors

SABRINA PETRA RAMET is an Associate Professor of International Studies, University of Washington. Born in London, England, she was educated at Stanford University (in philosophy) and received her doctorate in political science from UCLA in 1981. She is the author of five books: *Nationalism and Federalism in Yugoslavia, 1963–1983* (Indiana University Press, 1984; 2nd edn, covering the years 1962–1991, published in 1992); *Cross and Commissar: The Politics of Religion in Eastern Europe and the USSR* (Indiana University Press, 1987); *The Soviet–Syrian Relationship since 1955: A Troubled Alliance* (Westview Press, 1990); *Social Currents in Eastern Europe: The Sources and Meaning of the Great Transformation* (Duke University Press, 1991); and *Balkan Babel: Politics, Culture and Religion in Yugoslavia* (Westview Press 1992). She is also the editor of six books besides this one, and has authored more than 60 published journal articles and book chapters. She has received numerous awards, including a Fulbright–Hays Fellowship, a Kennan Institute Research Grant, three short-term IREX grants, and, in 1990, a UW Jackson School Award for Outstanding Service to Students.

JOHN ANDERSON was born in Gravesend, England, and studied at the London School of Economics (where he completed his doctorate), and Moscow State University. He is the author of numerous chapters and articles on religion in the Soviet Union and Eastern Europe, published in *Religion in Communist Lands*, *Soviet Jewish Affairs*, and *Soviet Studies*, and is at present completing a book on the shaping of Soviet religious policy from Khrushchev to Gorbachev. He is currently lecturer in international relations at the University of St. Andrews, having previously taught Soviet and East European politics at the London School of Economics and Edinburgh University.

OXANA ANTIC was born in Taganrog, on the Soviet Azov Sea. She is presently a researcher at Radio Free Europe/Radio Liberty in Munich, Germany. In addition to her regular contributions to Radio Liberty's *Report on the USSR*, she delivers lectures on the situation of churches in the Soviet Union, the moral and spiritual crisis, and the role of Russian women. Her poems and short stories have been published in two anthologies: *Spurensuche* (1989) and *Morgenrot im Nebel* (1991). She contributed a chapter to *Eastern Christianity and Politics in the Twentieth Century* (1988).

MARJORIE MANDELSTAM BALZER, born in Washington DC, teaches in the Sociology and Russian Area Studies departments of Georgetown University. She is editor of the journal *Soviet Anthropology and Archeology*, and of the books *Shamanism: Soviet Studies of Traditional Religion in Siberia and Central Asia* (1990); and *Russian Traditional Culture* (1991). She has held post-doctoral research appointments at Harvard, Columbia, and the Wilson Centre's Kennan Institute. Using data from several years of fieldwork in the Soviet Union, she has written on western and eastern Siberian peoples and nationalities issues for *American Anthropologist*, *Slavic Review*, *Journal of Soviet Nationalities*, *Arctic Anthropology*, *Social Science and Medicine*, and *Canadian Slavonic Review*. Forthcoming books include *The Tenacity of Ethnicity*, and *Siberian Women's Lives: Yakut-Sakha Autobiographies*.

JOHN DUNSTAN was born near Truro, Cornwall, England. He is Senior Lecturer in Soviet Education at the Centre for Russian and East European Studies, University of Birmingham, and was, until recently, the Centre's deputy director. He is the author of *Paths to Excellence and the Soviet School* (1978) and of *V. N. Soroka-Rosinsky, Soviet Teacher, in Fact and Fiction* (1991), and editor of *Soviet Education under Scrutiny* (1987) and *Soviet Education under Perestroika* (1992). He is the former editor of *Soviet Education Study Bulletin*, and has contributed articles to *Soviet Studies*, *Compare*, and *Pädagogik und Schule in Ost und West*. He co-founded and has chaired the UK Study Group on Soviet Education.

JANE ELLIS was born in Liverpool, England, and graduated in Russian language and literature from Birmingham University. She has worked since then at Keston College, England, where she is currently senior researcher. She is also former editor (1981–6) of *Religion in Communist Lands*, to which she has contributed several articles. She is the author of *The Russian Orthodox Church: A Contemporary History* (1986) and editor of *Religious Minorities in the Soviet Union* (4th edn, 1984). She has also translated three books from Russian: *An Early Soviet Saint: The Life of Father Zachariah* (1976), *Letters from Moscow*, by Father Gleb Yakunin and Lev Regelson (1978), and *Three Generations of Suffering*, by Georgi Vins (1979), and has contributed chapters to *Religious Liberty in the Soviet Union* (1976), *Eastern Christianity and Politics in the Twentieth Century* (1988), and *Candle in the Wind* (1989).

J. A. (HANS) HEBLY was born in the Netherlands and received his doctorate in theology from Utrecht University. From 1949 to 1951 he was an ecumenical fieldworker in the Cimade (in Paris), and from 1951 to 1970 served as a minister in the Dutch Reformed Church. Since 1970, he has been a staff member of the Interacademic Institute for Missiological and Ecumenical Research, in Utrecht, Netherlands, of which he is currently director. He is the author of *The Russians and the World Council of Churches* (1978), *The New Confession of Faith of the Evangelical Christian Baptists* (1983, in Dutch), *Eastbound Ecumenism* (1986), and other books.

LARRY E. HOLMES was born in Chicago, Illinois, in 1942. He is currently Professor of History at the University of South Alabama, where he has taught since 1968. His publications on Soviet historical scholarship and on Soviet schools have appeared in *Slavic Review*, *History of Education Quarterly*, and *Sovetskaia pedagogika*. In 1991, Indiana University Press published his *The Kremlin and the Schoolhouse: Reforming Education in Soviet Russia, 1917–1931*. Holmes has received several grants from the International Research and Exchanges Board and the Kennan Institute for Advanced Russian Studies.

SAMUEL A. KLIGER was born in Brichany, Moldavia. He is the chair of the International Research Institute on Values Changes, a scientific society incorporated in New York. He is also Senior Researcher for the Book Institute of the All-Union Book Chamber in Moscow. He completed his doctoral studies at the Academy of the Sciences in Moscow, and specialises in research methodology and social structure.

ANATOLII LEVITIN-KRASNOV was born in Russia in 1915, and spent seven years in a Soviet prison during the Stalin era. After his rehabilitation in 1956, he began to write essays criticising the suppression of religion in his country. In 1974, he was allowed to emigrate, and moved to Lucerne, Switzerland. Subsequently, he authored two classic works dealing with the Renovationist Church: *Ocherki po istorii russkoi tserkovnoi smuty* (co-authored with Vadim

Savrov, Kusnacht, Switzerland, 1977) and *Likhie gody, 1925–1941* (Paris, 1977). He also wrote a biography of Orthodox Bishop Vvedenskii. He died on 5 April 1991.

OTTO LUCHTERHANDT was born in Celle/Hannover, in Germany, and studied at the Universities of Freiburg, Bonn, and Hamburg, receiving his Doctor of Jurisprudence from Bonn in 1975. He is currently Professor of Public Law and Eastern Law at the University of Hamburg. His principal publications are: *Der Sowjetstaat und die Russisch-Orthodoxe Kirche* (Cologne, 1976) and *UN-Menschenrechtskonvention-Sowjetrecht-Sowjet-wirklichkeit. Ein kritischer Vergleich* (1980). His many articles dealing with human rights and religious freedom in Eastern Europe and the Balkans have been published in various journals.

WALTER SAWATSKY (born in Altona, Manitoba, Canada) is Associate Professor of Church History, Associated Mennonite Biblical Seminaries, and also East–West Consultant for the Mennonite Central Committee. He is the author of *Soviet Evangelicals since World War Two* (1981), and has contributed chapters to *Religion and Modernization in the Soviet Union* (1978), *Religion in Communist Societies* (1982), and *Mennonites in Russia* (1990). His articles have appeared in *Religion in Communist Lands, OPREE, Journal of Church and State,* and other journals.

MYROSLAW TATARYN was born in Manchester, England, and came to Canada in 1963. An ordained Ukrainian Catholic priest, he received his Master of Divinity from Toronto School of Theology in 1981, and was ordained in Rome that same year. He has had various pastoral assignments in different parts of southern Ontario, and, since 1988, has served as executive director of St Sophia Religious Association of Ukrainian Catholics (a charitable organisation). He has been deeply involved with his church's recent resurgence in the USSR, and is currently completing his Doctor of Theology degree at St Michael's College, Toronto, where he also lectures. His articles have appeared in *Journal of Ecumenical Studies, Religion in Communist Lands, Sobornost'*, and other journals.

PAUL H. DE VRIES, born in Grand Rapids, Michigan, is president of the International Research Institute on Values Changes, based in New York city. He also holds the chair in ethics and the marketplace at King's College in New York. He completed doctoral studies in philosophy at the University of Virginia and specialises in applied ethics. He is author of *The Taming of the Shrewd* (published in February 1992).

PHILIP WALTERS was born in Cambridge, England, and is head of research at Keston College and a former research fellow (1976–9) at Cambridge University. He has written current affairs talks for the BBC and has edited the journal *Religion in Communist Lands*. He is editor of *Light Through the Curtain* (1985) and *World Christianity: Eastern Europe* (1989). His articles have appeared in *Religion in Communist Lands*, *Soviet Studies*, *Slavonic Review*, and other journals. He has contributed chapters to *Eastern Christianity and Politics in the Twentieth Century* (1988), *Candle in the Wind* (1989), and *Christianity and Russian Culture in Soviet Society* (1990).

Preface

This is a book about religious policy and policy makers in the USSR. Its purpose is to shed light on the thinking, goals, assumptions, methods, and instruments of policy. The essays collected herein embrace a wide range of subjects, covering both historical and contemporary themes. Several chapters examine the institutions and mechanics of Soviet religious policy, especially Otto Luchterhandt's chapter on the Council of Religious Affairs. Jane Ellis' chapter on Kharchev's revelations, and John Dunstan's chapter on education. Other chapters concentrate rather on policy decisions and actions, trying to account for changes and stabilities in the evolution of Soviet religious policy. These include Philip Walters' chapter, along with Larry Holmes' chapter on schools and religion in the period 1917–41, John Anderson's chapter on women and religious policy, and my own chapter on the Gorbachev era. Still other chapters focus on the perspectives and drives of the religious organisations themselves, such as Oxana Antic's chapter on modern cults, Jan Hebly's chapter on the Russian Orthodox Church and ecumenism, Myroslaw Tataryn's chapter on the re-emergence of the Greek-Rite Catholic Church in Ukraine, and Marjorie Balzer's chapter on religion in Yakutia. The contribution by Samuel Kliger and Paul de Vries takes a different road, drawing upon extensive interview data to examine values and normative attitudes among Soviet people. Finally, Anatolii Levitin-Krasnov's chapter on the Living Church re-examines some of the long-standing controversies surrounding this regime-backed schismatic movement. Taken collectively, these chapters cover a wide-ranging array of subjects, many of them hitherto neglected in the past.

It is by now a stock phrase to say that the questions raised in a particular field are as important as the answers. In practice, of course, some answers are more important than others, and some answers are more important than some questions. But, where the latter are concerned, those which are most useful are those which organise the material coherently and which take us closer to the inner spirit of the subject. Such questions would include: What were Gorbachev's ultimate goals in his religious policy? How was Soviet religious policy related to policies in other spheres? Why were the Greek-Rite Catholics, suppressed for more than 40 years, granted legalisation in 1989? What do the structures and procedures of the Council for Religious Affairs tell us about Soviet religious policy? How did changes in Soviet sociological assessments of religion correlate with changes in Soviet religious policy?

It is fashionable nowadays to question whether communism has any future, and the ambiguous term 'post-communism' has come into vogue. For a while, the old leaders in some countries (eg., the USSR, Bulgaria, Albania) held onto their positions even as the entire power structure was being transformed all around them. The tidal wave that overthrew communism achieved its first successes in what was then called the German Democratic Republic, as well as Poland, and Czechoslovakia. The transition to pluralism took longer in the other East European countries, as well as in the Soviet Union itself.

As dramatic as the changes are, however, Gorbachev's reforms, and for that matter, his vision, did not spring *ex nihilo*; nor did they unfold in a void. The system in which his reforms worked was a system built on certain assumptions and which continued to reflect the residue of those assumptions, even where they were being abandoned. This was certainly the case until summer 1991; until then, neither the CPSU monopoly nor the nomenklatura system had been abandoned, corruption and the resistance of middle-level officials remained problems despite Gorbachev's efforts to overcome them, and the notion that there should be an office for religious affairs in the first place seemed not to be questioned. The system bequeathed to Gorbachev set the agenda for reform, it conditioned the assumptions about what were the central issues, it set the limits to reform (though these limits have expanded steadily over time).

This book was launched at the end of 1986, when I was living in Washington DC, and when the direction of Gorbachev's reforms in the religious sphere, not to mention how long he would survive in office, was not yet clear. The book was essentially complete only three years later, and was later revised and updated in late 1990 and early 1991. The 14 chapters assembled in this book therefore reflect reality as it was in December 1990 or January 1991. Three chapters were subsequently updated slightly, to reflect the post-coup changes and the fall of Gorbachev, but without the possibility of a substantial expansion of the text. The epilogue was added in January 1992 in order to take some account of the impact of the intervening changes.

I am deeply indebted to Margaret Brown for translating Otto Luchterhandt's chapter from German and to George E. Rennar for translating Anatolii Levitin-Krasnov's chapter from Russian. The data included in the appendix was originally collected for inclusion as a supplement to my own chapter (2), but, given its general utility, I have decided to place it in a separate appendix.

Sabrina Petra Ramet

PART I

Introduction

∘ 1 ∘

A survey of Soviet religious policy

PHILIP WALTERS

The first 70 years of Soviet power saw a sustained offensive against religion on a scale unprecedented in history. Millions suffered and died. There is a great deal of descriptive and anecdotal material about these sufferings readily available, and I do not propose to reproduce much of it here. My task in this chapter is to present the frame of reference within which the anti-religious offensive took place, showing what the legal and constitutional situation was, what was actual policy at any given time (the two only rarely match), or (more often) the failure of the various strategies and tactics.

The CPSU has always been dedicated to promoting the disappearance of religion, but the formation and execution of a religious policy has usually been subordinate to, and influenced by, other constantly changing political, economic, and social considerations. Any attempt to subdivide Soviet religious policy into successive chronological phases tends, therefore, to be contentious, since exceptions to the general norm at any date are always to be found, and within any chosen phase there are policy modifications and even reversals. Nevertheless, just this kind of chronological approach is what I propose to attempt. Within each chronological section I shall first consider official policy towards religious institutions and towards individual believers, showing where toleration ended and discrimination began; and then I shall look at what efforts were being made in the field of anti-religious education and propaganda.

Before moving on to the chronological survey, however, I shall briefly consider some of the basic motives which have influenced those responsible for shaping Soviet religious policy, and the institutional framework within which such policy was developed. As archives begin to open up in the Soviet Union, there will soon be a wealth of hitherto inaccessible material to shed new light on all aspects of this complex subject. Good work has already been done by scholars including

3

Professor Bohdan Bociurkiw. Most of what follows in this introduction is a summary of his findings.[1]

A fundamental tenet of Marxism–Leninism is that religion will ultimately disappear. If it began to seem unlikely to do so, the authorities would naturally adopt measures to promote its disappearance, since its continued presence was a rebuke to the claims of the ideology. The above impulse was reinforced when the system developed into full totalitarianism (in the USSR, from the late 1920s): the internal compulsion of such a system demanded the liquidation of any social institution (not just religious) which was not under its complete control.

Within this general context, there were two basic, and to some extent conflicting, trends amongst those responsible for formulating specific policies. The 'fundamentalists' were found primarily in the Party's Agitation and Propaganda organisation and in the *Komsomol*; and the 'pragmatists' amongst those in the party and state executive apparatus, and also in the secret police, who generally realised that religious believers could be more easily controlled when allowed a (limited) legal existence rather than being driven underground. Each trend held sway at different times; and their policies were further modified by considerations of the changing party line in such fields as internal and external security, agricultural and industrial policy, policy towards the nationalities, and foreign affairs.

What of the institutional structure within which decisions were made and implemented? It can be assumed that major policy decisions were taken at the level of the Party's Politburo and the Council of Ministers; but the information on which such decisions were based would have surfaced through a variety of institutions which would have made their own interpretations, selections and recommendations. Let us look at some of these institutions.

From 1918, the implementation of religious policy was divided up amongst various agencies. Within the Commissariat of Justice, a subdivision which later became known as the Department of Cults was charged with overall supervision. The Commissariat of Internal Affairs was charged with more direct administration. The *Cheka* – the first in a series of secret police organisations – was made responsible for combating possible subversion by surveillance and infiltration. A special department in the Commissariat of Enlightenment, under the guidance of the Party's Agitation and Propaganda department, was made responsible for anti-religious propaganda. *Ad hoc* bodies were also set up to see particular projects through – for example, the 1922 committee on the confiscation of church treasures.

In 1922 a standing Commission, known informally as the 'Antireligious Commission', was established at Central Committee level. Headed by Emel'yan Yaroslavsky, it was to function as an overall co-ordinating body throughout the 1920s.

In 1924, the Department of Cults was abolished. Its successor, the Secretariat (later Permanent Commission) for the Affairs of Cults, involved a more active role for the OGPU and later the NKVD (successors to the *cheka*, i.e. the secret police) throughout the 1930s.

In 1925 Yaroslavsky was appointed head of a new mass atheistic organisation set up under the auspices of the Agitation and Propaganda department of the Central Committee: the League of Atheists (in 1929 renamed the League of Militant Atheists). This body was quietly dissolved early in the Second World War, to be replaced after the War by the *Znanie* Society.

With the reversal of religious policy at this time, two new bodies were set up: the Council for the Affairs of the Russian Orthodox Church (CAROC) in 1943 and the Council for the Affairs of Religious Cults (CARC) in 1944. They had all-Union powers and their purpose was officially to facilitate contacts between the churches and the government. In fact they turned out to be well adapted to facilitating both direct infiltration of church structures by the security organs, and the authorities' control over church activity. This became their chief function under Khrushchev. In 1965 the two Councils were merged into the single Council for Religious Affairs (CRA), which continued to play the same role well into the Gorbachev era.

1917–1920

This was a period of acute crisis: would the fledgling Bolshevik state survive? There was revolution and civil war, and, in response, War Communism, with all its privations. There was also real revolutionary zeal amongst the Bolsheviks and those they inspired. One element in this was a genuine hostility towards religion, particularly as institutionalised in the Russian Orthodox Church. For decades before the Revolution, the progressive intelligentsia had been alienated from the church, and during the last years of the Empire churchgoing had actually been declining, particularly in the cities. In the immediate post-Revolutionary years, it was indeed the conscious policy of the Bolsheviks to direct their anti-religious activity virtually exclusively against the Orthodox Church; but this did not mean that other denominations and confessions were immune from sporadic attacks by anti-religious enthusiasts.[2]

The priority for the Bolsheviks at this time, then, was to seize the wealth and possessions of the Orthodox Church and to remove all public institutions from its sphere of influence. The Decree of 23 January 1918 deprived the Orthodox Church of its status as a legal person, of the right to own property, and of the right to teach religion in schools. The Constitution of the same year deprived clergy of the right to elect, or be elected to, any Soviet organs of government or administration, and allowed them to own land only after the claims of agricultural workers had been satisfied. This determined effort to disestablish and dispossess the Orthodox Church was a total success. The immediate result was that the church's wealth and material resources were available to the new government.

The above measures were accompanied by bloody terror against Orthodox clergy, which began promptly after the October seizure of power, and which impelled Patriarch Tikhon, a few days before the Decree of 23 January 1918, to anathematise the Bolsheviks. Further terror followed. Dozens of bishops and thousands of priests, monks, nuns, and laymen were arrested or murdered. There were many pretexts: alleged collaboration with the enemy during the Civil War; anti-Bolshevik comments in sermons; resistance to the nationalisation of church property. As has been noted, non-Orthodox believers also suffered, but as it were incidentally, as part of the general Red Terror: while the campaign against the Orthodox was centrally co-ordinated, measures against believers of other denominations were, by and large, local initiatives.

If party zealots believed that a few months of violent persecution would serve to turn religious believers away from the faith, however, they were soon proved wrong. Similarly unsuccessful, from the point of view of the authorities, was the effort to combat religious ideas by means of education and propaganda.[3]

Anti-religious propaganda was quickly centralised under party control. The People's Commissariat of Enlightenment, set up in November 1917, produced a special department, the Chief Administration for Political Enlightenment (*Glavpolitprosvet*), which in 1920 became part of the Agitation and Propaganda Department of the Central Committee of the Party. It based its work on Article 13 of the Programme of the RCP, adopted at the 8th Party Congress in 1919. This article called for anti-religious propaganda in addition to a simple separation of church and state; but it also warned against insulting believers' feelings and thereby encouraging their fanaticism – a sign that some at least in authority were realising that persecution was counter-productive. One of the recurrent features of subsequent Soviet religious policy was to be that periods of anti-religious violence would regularly be followed by warnings similar to the above heralding periods of relative moderation.

The first professional Soviet atheist journal, *Revolyutsiya i tserkov'*, appeared in 1919. Like other types of anti-religious endeavour, anti-religious literature was aimed at the Orthodox. Protestants tended to be portrayed as hardworking and loyal; although lacking the correct ideological equipment, they were nevertheless held to be contributing objectively to the building of socialism. Muslims too were depicted as essentially loyal to the new Soviet state.

From the earliest years the authorities made efforts to undermine traditional cultural ties with religion. They tried to persuade citizens to observe secular holidays and festivals rather than religious ones, and to substitute secular civil ceremonies for religious rites of passage: religious baptisms, marriages, and funerals were deprived of legal significance.

At this time it was still legal to conduct religious as well as anti-religious propaganda. Public debates took place in which atheist spokespersons pitted themselves against religious apologists. These encounters normally did more harm than good to the atheist cause, and the authorities began to discourage them from 1921 (although they were not actually illegal until 1929).

By 1920, a rise in churchgoing amongst ordinary citizens was being noted. While the institutional attack on the Orthodox Church had been a success for the new regime, the accompanying effort to dissuade people from belief was already turning out a failure.

1921–1928

At the end of the Civil War the Bolsheviks judged it essential to provide an opportunity for economic and social recuperation. The New Economic Policy (NEP) was launched at the 10th Party Congress in March 1921 and continued until 1928. A degree of private enterprise was allowed, the arts flourished, and citizens enjoyed a freedom of expression not to be repeated until the Gorbachev era.

During this period it became apparent that the government's religious policy had not yet resolved itself into one generally accepted strategy. The fluctuations in policy reflected not only genuine disagreements about the effectiveness of particular tactics, but also aspects of the power struggle amongst the Soviet leaders which Trotsky eventually lost.[4]

The 10th Party Congress in 1921 issued a resolution calling for a comprehensive programme of anti-religious propaganda amongst the workers, using the mass media, films, books, lectures, and similar instruments of enlightenment. In August 1921 a plenary meeting of the Central Committee issued an eleven-point instruction on how to interpret and apply Article 13 of the Party Programme adopted in 1919. It made a distinction between uneducated and educated believers. The former could be admitted to the Party if, despite being believers, they had proved their devotion to communism. Anti-religious work was conceived as a long-term educative process rather than as 'destructive and negative'. The instruction was clearly in line with the general ideology of NEP, and reflected the views of such men as Emel'yan Yaroslavsky, who at the 10th Party Congress in 1921 was appointed a member of the all-powerful Central Committee Secretariat (already under the control of Stalin, who a year later became its General Secretary), rather than those of Trotsky who tended to dismiss religion as a matter of superstition, and who held that a few sharp shocks administered against religious institutions would soon persuade the masses to embrace atheism. It was Trotsky who in 1921 was in favour of having Patriarch Tikhon shot, against the advice of Lenin who feared the danger consequent on creating such a prominent martyr.

It was also Trotsky who termed the religious policy which did in fact theoretically prevail an 'ecclesiastical NEP'.[5] It was necessary to make concessions to private enterprises which would ultimately have no place in a socialist economic order; in the same way, although religion was still said to be ideologically incompatible with communism, it was necessary to conciliate practising believers.

At least at the start of this period, the government's anti-religious activity was still directed primarily against the Russian Orthodox Church. Two separate strategies were pursued: the first was the so-called 'church valuables' campaign, and the second was the promotion of the Renovationist schism.

The 'church valuables' campaign was a struggle with the church on ground of the government's own choosing. The authorities required churches to hand over their valuables to be sold to aid those starving in the widespread famines which followed the Civil War. Church leaders, priests and laity were in general willing to do so, but resisted when consecrated vessels were in question.

Early 1922 saw the campaign in full spate. Figures have been quoted to demonstrate that the government expected to raise at best only a tiny proportion of the total sum to be used to aid the starving from the sale of the seized church treasures.[6] The campaign was as much as anything else the exploitation by the government of a chance to make an example of the church. The authorities expected resistance from the faithful, which would in turn give them an opportunity to visit heavy penalties on the resisters. In the course of searches in churches and monasteries, items could be discovered, or be said to have been discovered, which would discredit or incriminate the faithful.[7]

It was actually Trotsky who was in charge of effecting church policy at this time, and the 'church valuables' campaign bears some of the characteristics of his 'short, sharp shock' mentality. Certainly the campaign can hardly be said to have corresponded to the spirit of the instruction of August 1921. Incidentally, it should be noted that Lenin himself had no scruples about using violence against believers when he was convinced the effects would be positive – witness his secret instruction relating to unrest in the town of Shuya in March–April 1922.[8]

Intensified campaigns against heterodoxy in many areas of endeavour made themselves felt during 1922. Responsibility for these has been ascribed to Trotsky and other 'left' communists who were afraid that the spirit of NEP might endanger the whole revolution. Amongst other efforts, there was an intensive anti-religious propaganda campaign which began in the spring of 1922. Nadezhda Krupskaya, Lenin's wife, has been quoted as deploring the excesses involved – tearing crosses off children's necks, shooting at ikons.[9]

It is clear, then, that there were differences at the highest level over anti-religious strategy, and that the onset of NEP made these differences more manifest.

A number of legislative measures further restricting religious activity were introduced at this time. In December 1922 church sermons were subjected to censorship. At the same time religious organisations were restricted to performing religious services, and were prohibited from organising mutual aid funds, co-operatives, or youth and women's groups. In 1923 private religious instruction for children, permitted in the 1918 legislation, was restricted to groups of no more than three minors at a time.

It was in 1922 that the government began co-ordinating the second part of its strategy to defeat the Orthodox Church: the promotion of a schism.[10] In May 1922 a group of self-styled church reformers, known collectively as the 'Renovationists', were able to stage a coup and take over the leadership of the church. Some of the Renovationists were self-seeking careerists, and some were men of pure ideals; but all of them were ready to give positive endorsement to the political and social aims of communism, and at this particular juncture were

prepared to use the issue of church valuables to oppose and supplant
the Orthodox Church leadership.

It has been suggested by some that the renovationist coup was
Trotsky's idea; others have doubted that he was behind the strategy,
since it seems hard to reconcile it with his disdain for subtle long-term
policies in the field of religion. It is arguable, however, that it offered
something to the advocates of both short- and long-term anti-religious
strategies. The short-term strategists would be relying on the continuing effectiveness of the church valuables purge, and would be prepared
to accept the help of a group of 'renovationist' clergy in pursuing it;
while the long-term strategists would welcome the chance of putting in
place a church leadership which had expressed its positive support for
the Soviet experiment, and would therefore presumably find it difficult
to offer coherent resistance to a long-term programme of atheist education and institutional attrition. It may be symptomatic of the tactical
manoeuvring going on amongst the Soviet leadership that responsibility for seeing the coup through to a successful conclusion was transferred from the Commissariat of Justice to the GPU.

Patriarch Tikhon was by this time under arrest, and the Renovationists were able to set up a High Church Administration (VTsU).
One particular group of Renovationists, the 'Living Church' (*Zhivaya
tserkov'*) group led by one Vladimir Dmitrievich Krasnitsky, soon
achieved prominence. Krasnitsky's aim was to secure the rights, both
political and economic, within the church of the 'white' parish clergy.
His writings are couched in combative terms reminiscent of much
contemporary secular revolutionary propaganda. The 'Living Church'
group set about attacking 'counter-revolution' in the parishes and
dioceses. The methods employed included denunciation, and shortly
opponents of the 'Living Church', both lay and clerical, began to
experience arrest and exile. In all this the 'Living Church' co-operated
closely with the GPU.

The long-awaited trial of Patriarch Tikhon was announced for 11
April 1923, but did not take place. The new date was 24 April; but this
too passed without developments. The Renovationists held a Council
(*Sobor*) between 29 April and 9 May, which was judged a triumph.
Finally on 26 June came devastating news: Tikhon had been released,
and had renounced his former anti-Soviet stance. Obviously there had
been a change in government policy over the previous two months.

The persecution of the Orthodox Church, and in particular the
treatment of Patriarch Tikhon, had for some time been attracting
critical comment from abroad. The 'Living Church' was being widely
dismissed by foreign observers as a tool of the Soviet government. On

8 May 1923 the Curzon Ultimatum formalised the misgivings of the British government, noting persecution of religion as one of the factors hindering the establishment of proper relations between Britain and the USSR.

The Curzon Ultimatum was not of course the direct cause of the change in anti-religious tactics, however. From the very beginning of May a significant reduction in anti-religious propaganda had already been noticeable: this was particularly striking after the hysterical anti-Christmas and anti-Easter propaganda campaigns. The central press virtually stopped publishing anti-religious articles. Directives from the Central Committee during May and June were concerned with putting a brake on the arbitrary closure of churches.

The cause of all these developments is to be found in the deliberations of the 12th Party Congress of 17–25 April 1923. The Congress had considered a background document on the work of the Central Committee in the field of anti-religious propaganda, which noted both the success of the campaign to seize church valuables and the effectiveness of the 'Living Church' in confounding reactionary clergy and winning over the believing masses. The positive tone of this document contrasted sharply with the tone of the opening report by Zinoviev on the work of the Central Committee on 17 April. 'We have gone too far,' he asserted, 'much too far . . . We need serious anti-religious propaganda, we need serious preparation in schools and appropriate education of young people.'[11]

The background document is Trotskyist in tone. Since January 1923, however, Trotsky had been increasingly isolated in the Politburo; and, in late 1922, according to Trotsky, Stalin had succeeded in appointing Yaroslavsky as Trotsky's deputy in the department of anti-religious propaganda.[12] Now at the 12th Party Congress, those who followed Zinoviev in urging the necessity to conciliate the peasantry were also expressing their opposition to Trotsky.

A special section of the resolutions of this Congress was devoted to anti-religious agitation and propaganda. The resolutions pointed out that the conditions which Marx identified as giving rise to religious feelings had not yet been eradicated, and that therefore propaganda must continue, but that crude methods and coarse mockery which would offend believers and increase their fanaticism must be avoided. Increasing economic difficulties were making themselves felt – they led to strikes during the summer of 1923 – and it was now seen as essential to work to strengthen the 'link' between the proletariat and the peasantry in the interest of NEP, and to rally and unite rather than estrange and divide. By now, the Soviet authorities had had time to

appreciate the fact that the 'Living Church' held no appeal for the
peasant masses, and that it no longer made sense for the government
to commit itself to the support of the Renovationists. The type of anti-
religious activity recommended by the Congress bore all the hallmarks
of the Yaroslavsky school.

Conciliation of the peasantry remained the central element in party
policy from 1923 to 1925, and this was also a period of more toleration
for the Patriarchal Church as an institution. As far as the Renovationist Church was concerned, the government was now attempting to
effect a reconciliation between it and the Patriarchal Church in such a
way that the latter would be forced to accept a leadership which would
do what it was told. The aim was now a form of *hidden* schism: the
infiltration of Trojan horses within that church to which the believing
population had demonstrated its continuing allegiance.

For the rest of the period we are considering the government continued to pursue this policy, at the same time growing increasingly
disillusioned with the Renovationist Church, particularly after 1927,
when Tikhon's successor, Sergii, issued on behalf of the Russian
Orthodox Church his 'Declaration of Loyalty' to the Soviet Motherland, 'whose joys and successes are our joys and successes, and whose
setbacks are our setbacks'.[13]

It was generally agreed amongst the Soviet leadership that concessions on the economic front during NEP meant the need for greater
vigilance on the ideological front. At this time a significant proportion
of the creative intelligentsia were in any case genuinely committed
atheists, and anti-religious art and literature found a natural place in
the culturally fertile years of NEP. After the 10th Party Congress in
1921 the Communist Youth League (the *Komsomol*) was also mobilised
into anti-religious activity, organising films, plays, parades and satirical demonstrations. This function was later to become the preserve of
the League of Militant Atheists founded in 1925 under the leadership
of Yaroslavsky. From 1922 several specifically atheist periodicals
began to make their appearance: *Ateist*; the first *Nauka i religiya*;
Bezbozhnik u stanka; and *Bezbozhnik*, edited by Yaroslavsky; also the
ideological journal *Pod znamenem marksizma*. In 1924 a state publishing
house for anti-religious literature was set up.[14]

So far we have been considering government policy towards the
Orthodox Church: in the early 1920s it still bore the brunt of the
attack. Persecution of other denominations did, however, begin to
increase from about 1925. It is probable that, as the persecution and
schism took their toll on Orthodox churchgoing and parish life, the
vacuum began to be filled by the Protestant sects which, with their

non-hierarchical structure, were more flexible and more difficult to control, and that these signs of resilience and even revival alarmed the authorities. Official publications ceased to maintain that Protestants and Bolsheviks were working towards the same social goals. 1927 also saw the start of an intensive anti-Muslim campaign: up to this point they had been treated very leniently. The campaign was fought on the issue of emancipation of women: as in the 'church valuables' campaign the government succeeded in fighting on ground of its own choosing, and was easily able to put the believers in a bad light. From 1928 mosques began to be closed down and pressure exerted on clergy to limit their pastoral activities.

1929–39

This decade saw the most savage persecution of religion in the entire Soviet period.[15] By 1929 Stalin had consolidated his supremacy and was in a position to begin eliminating his ideological opponents. In the area of religious policy specifically, it was at the Second Congress of the League of Militant Atheists in June 1929 that Yaroslavsky gained final ascendancy over both the 'leftists' and the 'rightists' with whom he had been struggling since 1925 and was free to follow, at Stalin's behest, an anti-religious policy which exceeded in severity anything even the 'leftists' had envisaged. At this congress the League of Militant Atheists was given extensive powers by the CPSU Central Committee to launch a campaign to destroy religion.

New laws had already confirmed a very restricted role for the churches in Soviet society. Several laws passed in 1928 and 1929 forbade 'non-working elements' (including clergy) to join co-operative or collective farms, discriminated against clergy in the area of housing, and deprived them of social security rights. The Law on Religious Associations of 8 April 1929, which remained in force until October 1990, limited the rights of religious believers to the performance of religious services in registered buildings, and made almost every other kind of religious witness or activity illegal: conducting evangelistic activity or religious education, producing and distributing religious literature, organising communal activities for believers, raising money for social or charitable purposes. An amendment to the Constitution withdrew the right of citizens to conduct religious propaganda. The five-day working week was introduced, which meant that Sunday was no longer automatically a holiday.

The law of 1929 also confirmed the important concept of 'registration'. In any locality a group of at least twenty adults (a '*dvadtsatka*') who wanted to form a religious association were allowed to apply for permission to register as such. They also needed to secure a registered building in which to hold their services. If they failed in either endeavour, for whatever reason, they were not a legal group and could not legally practise. It is worth noting that these *local* associations were the only religious administrative structures recognised by Soviet law until 1990: no *central* co-ordinating organs had any legal status.

Clergy were subjected to increased financial discrimination. After the end of NEP, taxes on those engaged in private enterprise were raised to crippling levels. By a decree of the Council of People's Commissars in May 1929, clergy were placed in this category alongside private peasants and shopkeepers. The tax situation for the clergy remained critical until after 1936, when the new Constitution no longer distinguished between 'working' and 'non-working' citizens. Taxes on clergy were then somewhat reduced, and they were given back the right to vote.

During the 1930s, anti-religious agitation and propaganda was decentralised, partly no doubt in order that it should take on the appearance of a spontaneous effort by the masses, rather than a government initiative. Local public and voluntary organisations – the *Komsomol*, the Young Pioneers, workers' Clubs and, of course, the League of Militant Atheists – were encouraged to undertake a whole range of anti-religious initiatives: promoting the observance of the five-day working week, ensuring that priests did not visit believers in their homes, supervising the setting-up of cells of the League of Militant Atheists in the army. Public lampoons and blasphemous parades, recalling the early 1920s, were resumed from 1928.[16]

The entire educational system felt the incursion of official atheism. During the 1920s the government had insisted only that lessons in schools should be non-religious, but from 1929 it pressed for the introduction of positively anti-religious material. Higher educational institutions were purged of believers in 1929, and anti-religious departments began to be established there on the initiative of the League of Militant Atheists. Atheist universities began to be founded; there were eighty-four by 1931.

One of the main activities of the League of Militant Atheists was the publication of massive quantities of anti-religious literature, comprising regular journals and newspapers as well as books and pamphlets. The number of printed pages rose from 12 million in 1927 to 800 million in 1930.[17]

All these legislative and publicistic efforts were, however, only incidental to the events of the 1930s. During this period religion was, quite simply, to be eliminated by means of violence. With the end of NEP came the start of forced collectivisation in 1929, and with it the terror, which encompassed *kulaks* and class enemies of all kinds, including bishops, priests, and lay believers, who were arrested, shot and sent to labour camps. Churches were closed down, destroyed, converted to other uses. The League of Militant Atheists apparently adopted a five-year plan in 1932 aimed at the total eradication of religion by 1937. The stages were clearly envisaged: in 1932–3 all external signs of religion were to be destroyed, and in 1933–4 all religious pictures and books in private hands; in 1934–5 the whole population, particularly the young, were to be exposed to intense atheist propaganda; in 1935–6 any places of worship still open were to be destroyed; in 1936–7 the remnants of religion were to be rooted out of their last refuges.[18]

It was not only the Orthodox who were being persecuted now: all religious denominations suffered alike. An editorial in *Pravda* of 25 December 1928 fiercely attacked religion. Amongst other allegations it made was that the sectarians had been collaborating with the Trotsky-ists, and from now on no distinction was made amongst Orthodox, 'sectarians' and Muslims as enemies of socialism.

The first year of collectivisation brought a bad press from abroad, where mass public prayers were said in several countries on behalf of the persecuted church. Stalin's response was his *Pravda* article 'Dizzy with Success' of 15 March 1930 in which he called for a slower tempo in collectivisation and condemned the use of force. What this interven-tion meant in practice was that for the rest of the 1930s the terror went on secretly.

The result is that, as far as the 1930s are concerned, 'detailed and systematic information on terror . . . is lacking. All we have is multiple individual stories retold by witnesses and survivors.' Basing their accounts of the period on this fragmented anecdotal material, experts seldom agree in the details of their chronology. Pospielovsky notes a '1930–3 lull' in religious persecution, followed in 1934 by the start of a 'new wave . . . including mass arrests and closure of urban churches', while for Struve 'the years 1932–3 marked the culminating point of the campaign against religion, and after 1934 government pressure was relaxed'. Struve sees the period of relaxation as continuing until 1936, but already by the end of that year notes 'premonitory signs of the drastic purges of 1937–40, which were to obliterate the hard-won gains of this brief period of thaw'; Pospielovsky, on the other hand, discerns signs of a more tolerant attitude emerging from 1937 and resulting in a noticeable easing of persecution from 1939.[19]

There was indeed some diminution in the activities of the League of Militant Atheists after 1937. As an institution it seems to have fallen out of favour with Stalin. Was this because the League had conspicuously failed to achieve the triumph of atheism? It was becoming apparent that, despite the almost complete institutional destruction of religion, two thirds of the rural and one third of the urban population still identified themselves as religious believers, as Yaroslavsky himself noted at the time of the 1937 census, which contained a question on religious belief and which was never published.[20] Or was it because the League had, in fact, been so successful in wiping out all visible religious activity? In these circumstances Stalin, with his chronic suspicion of autonomous organisations, especially successful ones, may have decided it was time to neutralise the League of Militant Atheists in its turn.

Part of the explanation for the impressionistic chronology of the 1930s must obviously be that circumstances differed from region to region and even from town to town. Taking the decade as a whole, however, there can be no doubt that individual believers and religious institutions of all kinds suffered more radically than at any other time in the Soviet period. By the end of the decade, visible religious life had been virtually destroyed. Out of the 50,000 Orthodox churches in the Russian Empire on the eve of the Revolution only a few hundred remained open. However, as we have seen, the majority of the population still considered themselves religious believers.

1940–53

It was the Second World War which catalysed a totally new relationship between the Soviet government and the major religious denominations as institutions in Soviet society.[21] The 1927 declaration of loyalty of Metropolitan Sergii, ignored by the government during the 1930s, now seemed to be reflected at long last in government policy. Persecution of believers for their faith almost ceased for much of the period we are considering. However, there was no change in the law of 1929, and all improvements in the lot of believers were pragmatic concessions. There was also no point at which propaganda directed against religious faith ceased altogether, and for much of this period it continued fairly intensively.

From September 1939 to the summer of 1940 the USSR, profitting by the Nazi–Soviet pact, annexed territory in the west. With this territory came 20 million Christians with their church life intact. At this time mass persecution of believers throughout the Soviet Union virtually came to an end, and steps were even taken to avoid giving unnecessary offence to believers: for example, the five-day week was replaced once again by the seven-day week from 1940.

The reversal of Soviet fortunes in 1941, when Hitler violated the Nazi–Soviet pact and invaded the USSR, only helped consolidate the fortunes of the churches. Before even Stalin had addressed the Soviet people at this hour of national emergency, Metropolitan Sergii, seizing his chance to act in the spirit of his 1927 declaration, called on the faithful to defend the Motherland. Within two years Stalin had received the Orthodox leaders in the Kremlin and had put in train a series of concessions designed to normalise the institutional life of the churches. The Council for the Affairs of the Russian Orthodox Church (CAROC) and the Council for the Affairs of Religious Cults (CARC) were set up in 1943 and 1944 respectively. The Orthodox Church was allowed to elect a Patriarch, establish a central administrative structure, reopen churches, monasteries and seminaries and start printing religious literature. Similar concessions were made to the other major religious denominations. The Muslims were allowed to open academies and to print the Koran, and several groups were given permission to go on pilgrimage to Mecca.

In return for these concessions the major religious bodies were expected to continue their patriotic efforts, encouraging the population to resist the aggressor. After the war the Soviet government saw other areas opening up in which the churches could continue to be of assistance in an ancillary capacity at a time when the Soviet state was emerging from its self-imposed isolation and beginning to play an international role. In the immediate post-war years, the Orthodox Church was encouraged to consolidate Soviet territorial gains in Eastern Europe by trying to extend its own hegemony over the various orthodox churches there (most importantly in Romania, Bulgaria and Serbia). All the major denominations soon began playing the international role they continued to play until the late 1980s: their spokespersons would appear at international conferences devoted to 'peace', where they would speak out in apparently autonomous endorsement of Soviet policies as essentially 'peaceful' and incidentally take any opportunity to rebut suggestions that religious believers were treated as second-class citizens in the Soviet Union.[22]

While all this was going on, a certain amount of persecution of believers was quietly resumed, indicating that limits to permissible religious witness within the borders of the Soviet Union were still definitely recognised.[23] Throughout the period we are considering there was continuing pressure on bishops and clergy who refused to endorse the declaration of loyalty of Metropolitan (later Patriarch)

Sergii. Some of those who eventually found themselves able to declare their loyalty to Sergii's successor Aleksii (from 1945) were nevertheless compelled to finish their labour camp sentences, and many stayed there until Stalin's death. There was also persecution of any clergy who showed particular zeal in inspiring their congregations to witness energetically to their faith; and we have evidence that lay believers who organised unofficial religious discussion groups, or who produced *samizdat* ('do it yourself' unofficial) religious literature, were similarly punished. As the Soviet troops began to reconquer territory taken by the Nazis from 1941, priests and bishops in these areas were regularly arrested, accused of collaboration with the occupying German forces. In 1946, the Ukrainian Catholic Church was declared illegal, and Ukrainian Catholic priests joined the ranks of the persecuted. In anti-religious propaganda a new enemy was identified: the Vatican and its alleged international subversive activities. Finally, after the War specific attacks were launched against the Jews as 'bourgeois nationalists' and 'rootless cosmopolitans'. In 1948 all Jewish social organisations and Yiddish publications were shut down.

For the broad mass of the believing population, however, anti-religious activity until the death of Stalin was confined to words, and even this largely ceased during the time of the Nazi invasion. Three months after the invasion, in September 1941, the last anti-religious periodical was closed down; but in September 1944, when victory over Germany was beyond doubt, the Central Committee issued a decree calling for renewed efforts in scientific–educational propaganda. In 1947 membership of the *Komsomol* and employment in the teaching profession were both declared incompatible with religious belief. In the same year the Society for the Dissemination of Political and Scientific Knowledge (the *Znanie* Society) was founded as the successor to the League of Militant Atheists, which had been quietly dissolved at some point after 1941. *Znanie* was broader in scope than the League of Militant Atheists, and adopted a subtler approach. As well as atheist propagandists it included genuine scholars and scientists amongst its active members, and the presence of the latter tended to confer respectability on the former. *Znanie* remained the most important institution operating in the anti-religious field. It was organised like the CPSU itself at both central and local levels. In 1950 the Soviet press reviewed the achievements of the renewed anti-religious propaganda campaign, and called yet again for its intensification. Along with the traditional attack on religion as unscientific and harmful to the believing individual, there were new elements reflecting Stalin's isolationist nationalism. Attacks on churches with centres outside the

USSR, and especially on the Vatican, were particularly virulent; and there was a good deal about alleged western imperialism being carried on under the guise of religion.

In the last years of Stalin's rule, then, life for ordinary religious believers and the churches settled down at a level of humdrum difficulty. The immense improvements and material gains of the 1940s were consolidated, but no new concessions were forthcoming. In particular, the government remained deeply suspicious of any attempts by believers to witness actively to their faith in their everyday life. The quantity of anti-religious propaganda was increasing again slowly but steadily.

1953–9

Stalin's death in 1953 was followed by half a decade of transition, a struggle for power between Khrushchev and his rivals. Dramatic liberalising measures in many spheres of political and social life reflected Khrushchev's own inclinations, but also represented the only possible alternative to the stagnating Stalinism of the post-war years. Fresh winds were blowing, but they stirred up new uncertainties. In the area of religious policy, there were contradictory signs.

In 1954 two Central Committee resolutions on religious policy appeared which, to a large extent, contradicted each other. That of 7 July noted that ever larger numbers of citizens were attending church services and called on the Ministry of Education, the *Komsomol*, and the Trade Unions to intensify anti-religious propaganda. That of 10 November, however, criticised arbitrariness and the use of slander and libel against believers. Between the two came the 'Hundred Days Campaign', a burst of violent but shortlived anti-religious activity which brought back unwelcome memories of the 1930s.[24] Some have argued that the campaign was an initiative by Khrushchev's rival, Malenkov; but others have argued that it was Khrushchev himself who was behind the campaign and, indeed, the author of the 7 July decree, and that a growth in religious practices had made him aware that his liberalisations in the political and social sphere required increased vigilance on the ideological front. Those who hold Khrushchev responsible are surely vindicated by the events of 1959–64. But for the moment, Khrushchev's own anti-religious zeal was tempered by political necessity, and the years 1955–7 were probably the easiest for believers since just after the end of the Second World War. The pace of concessions, which had slowed markedly in the last six years of Stalin's rule, accelerated again. The reopening of churches began, and some new ones even were built. More students were admitted to theological seminaries. Bishops of the younger generation began to be consecrated.

Already from 1957, however, when Khrushchev began the final consolidation of his power with the defeat of the 'Anti-Party Group', signs of his increasing influence on religious policy were discernible. It was in 1957 that the Academy of Sciences began to publish its scholarly *Ezhegodnik Muzeya Istorii Religii i Ateizma*, and anti-religious propaganda in general began to increase.

1959–64

These five years saw an anti-religious campaign of a ferocity unprecedented since the 1930s.[25] It seems to have come as a traumatic shock to the religious believers of the Soviet Union, who, like most Soviet citizens and observers abroad, had been too taken up with the novelties of Khrushchev's political and social liberalisation to pay much heed to hints of negative developments on the religious front.

As on the previous occasion when Soviet religious policy had been radically altered (in the early 1940s) there was no corresponding formal alteration in the law of 1929. The new policy was facilitated by decisions at Party Congresses, and put into effect through decrees, many of which remained secret, and oral instructions, leading to a whole gamut of selective discriminatory practices known as *'administrirovanie'*. The fact that the concessions they had enjoyed for nearly twenty years had no basis in legality and could easily be withdrawn was brought home to believers with traumatic force. In fact, Khrushchev and his apologists claimed that what they were doing was simply applying the existing law as it had been intended. In March 1961 a decree 'On the Strict Observance of the Laws on Religious Cults' issued by CAROC and CARC reinvoked the letter of the 1929 law, for example explicitly banning the churches from raising money for charitable purposes, and aimed to ensure closer government control over parish councils. This decree interpreted the 1929 law particularly strictly, and the modifications it envisaged were confirmed by the Supreme Soviet when, in December 1962, it altered about half the articles of the 1929 law. It was at this time that CAROC and CARC were given more explicit powers of control and interference in church life. These renewed efforts to restrict the activities of the churches were, of course, in the spirit of early Stalinist practice, just as they were in line with 'Leninist' practices of the early 1920s. Khrushchev's spokesmen tended to blame the tolerant religious policies of the later

Stalin on the dictator's abuse of 'Leninist legality'. It is salutary to consider that, while in Gorbachev's Soviet Union the Chairman of the Council for Religious Affairs, laying the foundation stone for the first church to be built in Moscow since the Revolution, could speak of his act as 'the incarnation of Leninist principles', those same principles were invoked thirty years earlier to justify a new campaign involving the mass closure of places of worship.

The campaign began with the monasteries as obvious visible symbols of religious life, as places of pilgrimage and of real spiritual sustenance to the people, and as legally the weakest link of the church (unlike local congregations, they were not separately registered as religious associations – indeed their existence was not recognised at all by the 1929 law).[26] At the end of 1958 three instructions from the Council of Ministers cancelled tax exemptions on monastic property introduced in 1945 and called for measures to cut their size and number. In 1959 there were 69 monasteries; by 1965 there were 17. At the same time, churches were closed (the number of Orthodox churches fell from 22,000 to 7,000 during the period in question) and the number of clergy reduced, by deregistration of priests, reduction of intake in seminaries, forced retirement, imprisonment, exile, and other means (Orthodox clergy fell from 30,000 to 6,000). Five of the eight existing Orthodox seminaries were closed down. The provisions of the 1929 law were strictly enforced: pilgrimages and even services outside church walls were forbidden; children under 18 were banned from attending church services; any citizens requesting a baptism, marriage or funeral in church were required to record their identities.

As part of the process of limitation of believers' activities, the major denominations were put under pressure to introduce modifications in their own internal legislation. The Orthodox Church was compelled to change its own statutes in 1961, *inter alia* depriving the priest of control over his own parish council, of which he now became merely an employee. The Baptist leadership was impelled to issue new statutes, and sent a 'Letter of Instruction' to its parishes in 1960 introducing a range of restrictions on freedom of worship and witness. This move led directly to the split in the Baptist church when the '*initsiativniki*' broke away to form their own Union.[27]

Under Stalin, the requirement that each individual congregation must register itself before being allowed to function had been used fairly simply as a means of controlling the number of congregations. Under Khrushchev, registration began to be used as a means whereby conditions could be imposed on a congregation. During the 1960s congregations of '*initsiativniki*' were regularly refused registration, even if they sought it, on the grounds that they must first agree to observe the same conditions as those already agreed to by 'official' Baptist congregations.[28]

While all these measures were being taken against religious premises and institutions, individual believers came under increasing moral and administrative pressure. The *Komsomol*, the branches of the *Znanie* society, and the trade unions appointed atheists to do personal work with known believers at their places of work or education. If they failed, the believers were criticised at public meetings. Then followed administrative harassment – reduction in pay, blocking of promotion, expulsion, barring from higher education. Cases began to come to light of parents who were bringing their children up as believers being deprived of their parental rights.[29]

Atheist propaganda reached a new peak of intensity under Khrushchev. It was directed at the mass market, and was characterised by crudity and shallowness. Those responsible for producing it were largely ignorant of the inner significance of religious faith, preferring to caricature its external forms. There was no stimulus to creative excellence in anti-religious work from artists or intellectuals since, in contrast with their forebears in the 1920s, they now tended to be indifferent to atheism or positively attracted to religion.

The resolution of July 1954 had called for a new mass-circulation atheist monthly, but this did not appear until 1959, published by the *Znanie* society under the title *Nauka i religiya*. It resembled the old *Bezbozhnik* in the slanderous nature of its material. A resolution of the Plenum of the Central Committee on 9 January 1960, 'On the Tasks of Party Propaganda in Modern Times', constituted an uncompromising call, and made no mention of the need to avoid offending the sensibilities of believers. In general the propaganda of the period portrayed individual believers as fools, and slandered the clergy as criminals, deviants and alcoholics. From the end of the 1950s, anti-religious articles began to appear regularly in the secular Soviet press for the first time – another sign of the desire to reach as wide an audience as possible. By the same token, the years of the Khrushchev anti-religious drive saw the start – and the peak – of anti-religious film making.

In the 1930s Stalin's response to adverse comment from abroad was to conduct his terror in conditions of secrecy. The Soviet Union was a closed society. After the Second World War, this policy of isolation gave way to one of much more active Soviet involvement on the world scene; details about Khrushchev's anti-religious campaign, which came as such a shock to religious believers in the Soviet Union, were nevertheless still slow to impinge on the consciousness of the world, and, when they did become known, were known only in partial or distorted form. That this should be so was in large part owing to the specific role the churches were by then obliged to play in the world at large, speaking out favourably on conditions for religious believers in the USSR. The Russian Orthodox Church joined the World Council of Churches in 1961, at the height of Khrushchev's campaign, but amid the general rejoicing not a word was heard from church spokepersons about renewed tribulations at home.[30]

1964–79

The Khrushchev anti-religious campaign represented the last concerted effort made to eradicate religion in the Soviet Union. In the Brezhnev era, which was characterised increasingly by unprincipled pragmatism and a weary cynicism, policy towards religion altered its nature. The assumption now had to be made that religion was not going to die out, and that the various religious institutions would remain as a significant presence in Soviet society for the foreseeable future. Khrushchev had been fond of proclaiming precise dates by which full communism would be achieved in the Soviet Union: presumably by then religion would have been extinguished. Under Brezhnev such predictions were no longer made. The present stage, 'developed socialism', could continue indefinitely. Towards religion the policy became one of 'divide and rule' – of granting concessions to registered congregations and even whole denominations, while dealing harshly with unregistered and dissident groups. As in the late 1930s, the perception was growing that severe persecution had simply driven believers underground rather than eliminate them altogether. There was also increasing evidence that in a climate of growing awareness of the importance of human rights, fostered by Khrushchev's liberalisations in various fields, the sufferings of religious believers were evoking sympathy amongst the non-believers in the population.

As far as legislation on religion is concerned, the Brezhnev period saw gradual codification and clarification of the relevant laws, taking into account the confusing tangle of administrative decrees promulgated since the early 1960s under Khrushchev. An article in the January 1965 issue of *Sovetskoye gosudarstvo i pravo* described administrative measures, such as those used by Khrushchev against religion, as improper and counterproductive. A revised version of the law of 1929 was announced in July 1975. It is apparent that the changes now made public corresponded closely to the alterations made secretly to the 1929 law in 1962. The revised law of 1975 defined for the first time the

field of competence of the Council for Religious Affairs. It was now
legally accorded regulatory powers over all kinds of religious matters
which it had possessed *de facto* since 1962. The 1975 law made it more
difficult for religious associations to register themselves: all power in
this area was put into the hands of the Council for Religious Affairs,
rather than left to the local Soviet. In general, the law circumscribed
more closely than hitherto the range of legal religious activity, but, in
doing so, largely confirmed what had in fact been the practice since
1962.[31]

Anti-religious education and propaganda continued during the
period we are considering, but efforts were now made both to
centralise it and to render it more 'objective' – which principally
meant integrating it with the findings of sociologists. Responsibility for
anti-religious work, under the overall control of the Agitation and
Propaganda department of the Central Committee, was transferred
from the Academy of Sciences to the Academy of Social Sciences. The
latter began publishing *Voprosy nauchnogo ateizma*. Anti-religious
material became once again the preserve of specialist journals, and it
no longer pervaded the secular press to the same extent as it had under
Khrushchev. Articles by religious apostates and personal testimonies
virtually disappeared, and slanderous personal attacks on individual
believers and clergy were more selective, generally preceding the
arrest and trial of specific prominent dissenters. Efforts were made to
give anti-religious publications a more responsible and attractive
appearance. The January 1965 issue of *Nauka i religiya* came out in a
new format, while the Ukrainian equivalent changed its name from
Voiovnychyi ateist ('Militant Atheist') to *Lyudina i svit* ('Man and the
World'). There was a persistent tendency to try to create 'dialogue'
between believers and unbelievers on the pages of the atheist press. A
'letter from the editor' published in the March 1965 issue of *Nauka i
religiya* attacked those who would characterise believers as scoundrels
or deviants: they are loyal citizens, who deserve respect, and the way
forward must be through dialogue. There was of course a logical
problem at the centre of this effort: in order to have a real dialogue you
have to concede that the other side is intellectually respectable; and
this was never conceded throughout the Brezhnev period. Religious
beliefs continued to be represented as fundamentally mistaken.
Another problem besetting the inauguration of dialogue was the relative intellectual barrenness of atheist theory: since the 1920s, as
already observed, few if any of the creative intelligentsia have been
convinced atheists or willing to champion the atheist cause.

It should, of course, be remembered that, although atheist propaganda changed its focus and character after Khrushchev, it never showed any signs of ceasing. From time to time during the Brezhnev era the Central Committee felt it necessary to call for increased ideological vigilance. In July 1971, for example, it issued a resolution 'On strengthening the Atheist Education of the Population', partly no doubt in response to the ideologically unsettling events of 1968 in Czechoslovakia, and in the context both of the subsequent clampdown on dissent in the USSR (1971–3) and of the new climate of international *détente* which was rendering the Soviet leaders especially sensitive to the danger of subversion from abroad.

As noted above, practical policies towards religious believers and religious associations from the mid-1960s were governed by the realistic perception that religion is here to stay. A central tendency was therefore to show favour to lukewarm clergy and passive believers in a bid to minimise as far as possible the effects of religious ideas on society. In this context it is instructive to read the so-called 'Furov Report', a secret report by an official of the Council for Religious Affairs on the contemporary situation of the Russian Orthodox Church which reached the West in the 1970s.[32] It is clear that the CRA was exercising control over appointments to the higher ranks of the clergy, and surveillance over the sermons and activities of clergy down to the level of parish priest. 'If a priest gives sermons', says the report 'they . . . must contain no political or social issues or examples'. It is clear from the report that some types of hierarch were more acceptable to the authorities than others. The report divides them into three roughly equal categories. Those who were most acceptable to the authorities were those who did the minimum to encourage the growth of the faith, but who were prepared to travel abroad and speak in favour of Soviet policies both at home (particularly the guaranteeing of religious freedom) and abroad (particularly the securing of world peace). The clergy who were more or less unacceptable were those whose priorities were the reverse of these.

'Loyal' clergy and religious associations which were prepared to limit their activities to worship in a registered building would be given concessions denied to more active or militant groups of believers. The working out of this policy can be seen most clearly in regard to the Baptists.[33] The '*initsiativniki*', or those Baptists who refused to accept 'voluntary' restrictions on their witness, also became known as 'unregistered' Baptists, because, by and large, they refused to accept the conditions attaching to registration; meanwhile the Soviet authorities were able to point to the 'advantages' enjoyed by their more 'law-abiding' brethren to show how 'religious freedom' could indeed be guaranteed to loyal Soviet citizens who happened to be believers. There is plenty of evidence, at the same time, to show that the presence of a vocal dissident minority such as the '*initsiativniki*', in fact, induced the authorities to offer more concessions to the 'official' church than might otherwise have been the case, and it is readily arguable that the presence of such a minority would conduce in the end to the benefit of the whole denomination. Thus for example the Congresses of the 'official' Baptist Union in the 1970s saw much freer and more genuine debate than any of the Councils of the Russian Orthodox Church during the Soviet period. As another example we may take the opening of churches. While some 40 Orthodox churches were reopened in the period 1977 to 1983, some 170 churches were reopened for the numerically much smaller 'official' Baptists in the period 1974 to 1980.

During the Khrushchev anti-religious campaign all believers – young or old, educated or uneducated, lay or clergy – suffered persecution equally. Persecution continued during the Brezhnev period, but more discriminately, reflecting the two-pronged policy towards religion just described. By and large the uneducated and the elderly were allowed to attend church without suffering criticism or abuse; only the most active clergy tended to find themselves in trouble with the authorities. The weight of the authorities' wrath was reserved for religious activists, particularly evangelicals, who were concerned with producing religious literature unofficially, organising religious education for children, and so on; and for the young, the educated, and those in responsible administrative positions who showed any kind of active interest in religion or religious rights.

At the same time, there was no sign that the authorities were prepared to concede high visibility to any religious body, even the Russian Orthodox Church, within Soviet society. In this area there was no return to the policies of the later Stalinist period. The high profile for the churches was reserved for their travels and activities abroad and for their work in hosting lavish international peace conferences. They were not allowed, however, to increase their social base. Official publishing of religious literature was severely limited. None of the monasteries or seminaries closed by Khrushchev was reopened, and only a minimal number of churches. By the early 1980s the number of working Orthodox churches was still virtually the same as it was in 1964 at the fall of Khrushchev.

1979–85

This period was marked by a significant intensification of the struggle against dissent in all fields, including religious dissent. From the mid-1970s the pace of proliferation of all kinds of unofficial religious activity had been accelerating, particularly in the major cities and amongst educated young people. Some of this activity was part of the continuing search for spiritual values amongst young people disenchanted with the dead official ideology; while an increasing proportion was related to the defence of religious rights and human rights in general, an area of activity which was given a specific boost by the Soviet Union's signing of the Helsinki Final Act in 1975.

There were various milestones on the road to a harsher treatment of religious dissent from 1979. The amended Law on Religious Associations of 1975, as we have seen, incorporated certain more restrictive provisions; the new Constitution of 1977 no longer spoke simply of 'anti-religious' propaganda as a citizen's right, but more specifically of 'atheist' propaganda, implying that it should have much more positive content; and a Central Committee resolution of 26 April 1979 was entitled 'On Further Improvements in Ideological and Politico-Educational Work'.

Arrests of human rights activists began in 1978, and of prominent religious activists in 1979. The number of religious believers known to be in prison or labour camp for their faith rose from 180 in 1979 to 411 in 1985. It is likely that in the course of the hidden power struggle which marked Brezhnev's declining years the ideological hardliners, including the head of the KGB, Andropov, attained a position where they were able to begin to put their policies into effect. When Brezhnev was succeeded by Andropov in 1982 the process continued, now as part of a campaign aimed explicitly at corruption and stagnation to which many of Brezhnev's old cronies fell victim. Two and a half years before Gorbachev, Andropov was initiating his own brand of '*perestroika*' designed to reform the corrupt Soviet system before it was too late. Where Andropov's '*perestroika*' differed from Gorbachev's was in its attitude towards ideological pluralism.[34] Dissidents as well as criminals and corrupt bureaucrats felt the effect of the new puritanism.

By the time of Chernenko's brief tenure of office (1984–5) it was nevertheless obvious that there were going to have to be major initiatives on the ideological front, and that these would have to go beyond a simple reassertion of the old formulae if the Soviet population were to be convinced of the need for hard work and discipline, and motivated to respond. The Brezhnev 'years of stagnation' had bred a generation of young people steeped in cynicism and materialism. The vast majority were simply not interested in ideology; but those who were seeking to discover a moral framework for their lives were overwhelmingly attracted to religion. The arrests of hundreds of activists had stifled their voice, but had, of course, provided no alternative answers.

Meanwhile a great symbolic event was approaching: the celebration of the Millennium of Christianity in Russia in 1988. The two powerful adversaries, church and state, were circling warily, each waiting for the other to move. At the outset the state was hardly willing to make any mention of the impending event, seeking to play down its importance; but ideological spokesmen felt bound to refute regular claims by religious figures concerning the important role played by Russian Orthodoxy in the development of Russian cultural, social, and even political life over the centuries. Bankrupt though Marxism–Leninism apparently was as an ideology capable of providing answers to the fundamental problems of life, there was equally apparently still no possibility that this official ideology could concede any kind of positive role to religious ideas either in the historical past or in the present day.[35]

Notes

1 See Bohdan R. Bociurkiw, 'The Shaping of Soviet Religious Policy', *Problems of Communism*, May–June 1973, pp. 37–51; and 'The Formulation of Religious Policy in the Soviet Union', *Journal of Church and State*, 28:3, Autumn 1986, pp. 423–38.

2 A number of studies cover this period. They include: Johannes Chrysostomus, *Kirchengeschichte Russlands der neuesten Zeit*, 3 vols., Munich, 1965, 1966, 1968; J.S. Curtiss, *The Russian Church and the Soviet State, 1917–1950*, Gloucester, Mass., 1965; Alexander Kischkowsky, *Die Sowjetische Religionspolitik und die Russisch–Orthodoxe Kirche*, 2nd edn., Munich, 1960; Walter Kolarz, *Religion in the Soviet Union*, London and New York, 1961; Otto Luchterhandt, *Der Sowjetstaat und die Russisch–Orthodoxe Kirche*, Cologne, 1976; Dimitry V. Pospielovsky, *A History of Soviet Atheism in Theory and Practice, and the Believer*, 3 vols., Macmillan, 1987, 1988, 1988; and *The Russian Church under the Soviet Regime 1917–1982*, 2 vols., St Vladimir's Seminary Press, New York, 1984; Matthew Spinka, *The Church in Soviet Russia*, Oxford University Press, 1956; Nikita Struve, *Christians in Contemporary Russia*, London, 1967.

3 See David E. Powell, *Antireligious Propaganda in the Soviet Union*, MIT Press, Cambridge, Mass., and London, England, 1975; and William van den Bercken, *Ideology and Atheism in the Soviet Union*, Mouton de Gruyter, Berlin, New York, 1989.

4 See Joan Delaney, 'The Origins of Soviet Antireligious Organisations', in

Richard H. Marshall (ed.), *Aspects of Religion in the Soviet Union 1917–1967*, University of Chicago Press, 1971, pp. 103–39; Dimitry Pospielovsky, *A History of Marxist–Leninist Atheism and Soviet Anti-Religious Policies (A History of Soviet Atheism, II)*; and M.B.B., 'Der misslungene Versuch zur Vernichtung der Russisch–Orthodoxen Kirche in den Jahren 1922–1923 und die Niederlage des linken Kommunismus', *Ostkirchliche Studien*, 22:2/3, September 1973, pp. 105–49.

5 See L. Trotsky, *Literatura i revolyutsiya*, 1923, p. 29.

6 M.B.B., 'Der misslungene Versuch zur Vernichtung', pp. 127–31.

7 See reports in the Renovationists' journal *Zhivaya Tserkov'*, for example issue No. 3, June 1922, p. 3.

8 This secret instruction was published in Russian in *Vestnik Russkogo Khristianskogo Dvizheniya*, 68, 1970, and in English translation in *Religion in Communist Lands*, 7:1, Spring 1979. It has never been included in Lenin's collected works, and Soviet ideologists have always denied its authenticity. In 1990 it was, however, published in the Soviet press (in the youth journal *Sobesednik* and in *Izvestiya TsK KPSS*: see Radio Liberty *Report on the USSR*, 4 May 1990). See also Pospielovsky, *The Russian Church*, I, pp. 93–6.

9 M.B.B., 'Der misslungene Versuch zur Vernichtung . . .', pp. 109, 131. See also Kischkowsky, *Die Sowjetische Religionspolitik* . . . , p. 48. For Krupskaya's reaction, see N. Krupskaya, *Leninskiye ustanovki v oblasti kul'tury*, Moscow, 1934, p. 198.

10 For an insider's view of the history of the schism, see Anatolii Levitin and Vadim Shavrov, *Ocherki po istorii russkoi tserkovnoi smuty*, Glaube in der 2 Welt, Küsnacht, Switzerland, 1978. See also the chapter in the present volume by Anatolii Levitin-Krasnov.

11 *Stenograficheskii otchet 12 s"ezda*, Moscow, 1968, p. 44. See M.B.B., 'Der misslungene Versuch zur Vernichtung', pp. 136–7.

12 E.H. Carr, *The Interregnum 1923–1924*, Pelican, 1969, p. 26.

13 Sergii's declaration and its implications are dealt with in most of the books cited in note 2. See also William C. Fletcher, *A Study in Survival: The Church in Russia 1927–1943*, London, 1965. For a critical assessment of the implications of Sergi's declaration, see Lev Regel'son, *Tragediya russkoi tserkvi 1917–1945*, YMCA Press, Paris, 1977.

14 Powell, *Antireligious Propaganda*, p. 35.

15 See the works cited in footnote 2; also Fletcher, *A Study in Survival*.

16 See Powell, *Antireligious Propaganda*, Pospielovsky, *Soviet Anti-Religious Campaigns and Persecutions (A History of Soviet Atheism, II)*.

17 Pospielovsky, *A History of Marxist–Leninist Atheism*, p. 62.

18 Struve, *Christians in Contemporary Russia*, p. 54; Kischkowsky, *Die Sowjetische Religionspolitik*, p. 62.

19 Pospielovsky, *A History of Marxist–Leninist Atheism*, pp. 63–4, 65–6; Struve, *Christians in Contemporary Russia*, pp. 55–6.

20 William C. Fletcher, *Soviet Believers*, Regent's Park, Kansas, 1981, pp. 211–12.

21 See Wassilij Alexeev, 'The Russian Orthodox Church 1927–1945: Repres-

sion and Revival', *Religion in Communist Lands*, 7:1, Spring 1979, pp. 29–34; Bohdan R. Bociurkiw, 'Church–State Relations in the USSR', in M. Hayward and W.C. Fletcher (eds.), *Religion and the Soviet State*, London, 1969, pp. 71–104; William B. Stroyen, *Communist Russia and the Russian Orthodox Church 1943–1962*, Washington DC, 1967; Philip Walters, 'The Russian Orthodox Church 1945–1959', *Religion in Communist Lands*, 8:3, Autumn 1980, pp. 218–24.

22 See Philip Walters, 'The Seamless Robe: the Russian Orthodox Church as a "Transmission Belt",' in David A. Charters and Maurice A.J. Tugwell (eds.), *Deception Operations: Studies in the East–West Context*, Brasseys (UK), London, 1990, pp. 85–115.

23 Pospielovsky, *Soviet Anti-Religious Campaigns*, pp. 91–7.

24 See Joan Delaney Grossman, 'Khrushchev's Anti-Religious Policy and the Campaign of 1954', *Soviet Studies*, 24:3, 1972–3, pp. 374–86.

25 See Michael Bourdeaux, 'The Black Quinquennium: the Russian Orthodox Church 1959–1964', *Religion in Communist Lands*, 9:1–2, Spring 1981, pp. 18–27; Donald A. Lowrie and William C. Fletcher, 'Khrushchev's Religious Policy, 1959–64', in Richard H. Marshall (ed.), *Aspects of Religion*, pp. 131–55.

26 Pospielovsky, *A History of Marxist–Leninist Atheism*, pp. 82 ff.

27 Walter Sawatsky, *Soviet Evangelicals Since World War II*, Herald Press, Kitchener Ontario and Scottdale Pennsylvania, 1981.

28 Michael Rowe, 'Soviet Policy Towards Evangelicals', *Religion in Communist Lands*, 7:1, Spring 1979, pp. 4–12.

29 See Michael Bourdeaux, *Patriarch and Prophets*, London, 1970, p. 169.

30 See Philip Walters, 'The Seamless Robe', p. 91; Michael Bourdeaux, 'The Russian Church, Religious Liberty and the World Council of Churches', *Religion in Communist Lands*, 13:1, Spring 1985, pp. 4–27, here p. 5.

31 See Walter Sawatsky, 'The New Soviet Law on Religion', *Religion in Communist Lands*, 4:2, Summer 1976, pp. 4–10; and 'Secret Soviet Lawbook on Religion', *Religion in Communist Lands*, 4:4, Winter 1976, pp. 24–34.

32 See Philip Walters, 'The Russian Orthodox Church', in Pedro Ramet (ed.), *Eastern Christianity and Politics in the Twentieth Century*, Duke University Press, Durham and London, 1988, p. 83.

33 See Sawatsky, *Soviet Evangelicals*.

34 See Paul D. Steeves, 'The June 1983 Plenum and the Post-Brezhnev Antireligious Campaign', *Journal of Church and State*, 28:3, Autumn 1986, pp. 439–57.

35 Since this chapter was completed events have moved faster than anyone predicted. For the most accessible summary of developments to the summer of 1990, see Michael Bourdeaux, *Gorbachev, Glasnost and the Gospel*, Hodder and Stoughton, London, 1990.

· 2 ·

Religious policy in the era of Gorbachev

SABRINA PETRA RAMET

In May 1990, after some four years of discussion and delay, the draft of a new law on religious organisations was read to the USSR Supreme Soviet. It was passed into law on 26 September 1990.[1] Initially intra-elite disagreement was said to have accounted for repeated delays. But the delays also had a propitious side-effect, in that they allowed the Gorbachev regime to make incremental changes in *de facto* religious policy, without making the changes official, *de jure*, all at once. In this way, changes in practice helped to prepare the way for changes in legislation. As passed, the law granted religious organisation full legal status, permitted religious education in public schools (after regular school hours), allowed religious organisations to own their places of worship and other property, allowed them to import literature from abroad and to engage in charitable activity, and equalised the tax structure for clergy (which had previously been higher than for ordinary citizens). It also guaranteed freedom of worship, forbade the government to interfere in religious activities, and ended the seventy-year-old policy of officially backed atheism, proscribing discrimination on the basis of religious belief. In fact, under the new law, the government was barred from financing either atheist work or religious activities. Religious property rights were also guaranteed in a new Soviet law on property ownership, the draft text of which was published in *Pravda* in November 1989. Article 21 dealt with the property of religious organisations and specified:

Religious organizations may own buildings, religious objects, production and social facilities, charitable operations, money, and other assets essential to their activities. Religious organizations are entitled to own assets purchased, built, or produced by them using their own resources, donated by believers, or handed over by the state or other persons, or acquired in other ways specified in law.[2]

31

A separate law on press and the media (passed on 20 June 1990) established that religious organisations have the right to publish their own materials, including periodicals.[3]

Even though there were at least three alternative drafts of the law on religious organisations in existence by 1988, it was not until the end of 1989 that officials reached agreement on a unified draft to place on the work agenda of the Supreme Soviet. And even at that stage, there continued to be problems. Interviewed by *Izvestiia* on 10 October, Fedor Burlatsky, head of a subcommittee of the Supreme Soviet's commission on international affairs, revealed that bureaucratic infighting (thought to be emanating from within the Central Committee) was holding up passage.[4]

But the law was only the formal, juridical aspect of a much broader *perestroika* in the religious sphere, the chief components of which were: the restoration of dignity to religious affiliation; the steady normalisation of the legal status of hitherto proscribed religious organisations; the restoration of confiscated church facilities and the grant of permission to construct new churches, register new parishes, and expand publication possibilities; and the opening up of contacts with foreign religious organisations and persons. The purpose of this *perestroika* in the religious sphere was to contribute to Gorbachev's broader effort to establish some kind of social consensus, and to achieve a partial legitimation of communist party rule. (Complete legitimation would have required that the party win in open and free elections; partial legitimation would have required only that its policies meet with broad public approval.) By early 1991, Gorbachev's *perestroika* seemed to have failed, and the attempted legitimation to have sunk. By that time, however, the relegitimation of religious life had acquired a force of its own, and it had become inconceivable that there could be any attempt to turn back the clock now.

Yet there were obstacles in the path from the beginning. Middle-level and lower-level functionaries repeatedly obstructed, or tried to obstruct, more liberal policies in the first years of Gorbachev's rule, i.e., 1985–8, and some looked to Egor Ligachev to restore the old ways. In some communities, believers who met all the legal requirements for the registration of a parish, found their applications arbitrarily rejected by local officials. But *Moscow News* and other liberal publications sprang to the defence of these believers, arguing that the law must be respected by all concerned, including by officials.

Phases in Gorbachev's religious policy

Since Gorbachev's accession to power in March 1985, there have been four phases in the evolution of Soviet religious policy.

The first phase ran from March 1985 until December 1986. During this phase there were few signs of liberalisation; on the contrary, Gorbachev himself made a speech in Tashkent in November 1986 in which he endorsed 'a determined and pitiless combat against religious manifestations' in Central Asia.[5] The announcement in summer 1986 that new religious legislation was in preparation was, however, an important signal of change. But there were actually few real concessions made at this stage – the major exception being the release of some incarcerated believers, including the Ukrainian Catholic lay activist Iosyf Terelia in July 1986.

The second phase began with the publication of an article by Soviet poet Yevgeni Yevtushenko in *Komsomol'skaia Pravda* in December 1986. Arguing that if church and state are separate, atheism cannot be an official ideology, Yevtushenko went on to praise religion as the ultimate source of both morality and culture and to call for the publication, by state publishing houses, of the Bible.[6] During this phase there began the gradual rehabilitation of religion as a healthy force – signalled above all in the publication of certain groundbreaking interviews in the Soviet press. In September 1987, for instance, *Literaturnaia gazeta* carried an interview with academician Dimitry Likhachev, which criticised the state for interfering in normal church affairs.[7] Later, *Literaturnaia gazeta* published a series of articles examining the Ten Commandments and holding them up as essential as a moral basis for civilised society.[8]

It was also during this second phase that the atheist monthly *Nauka i religiia* published a table of statistics for religious organisations for the years 1961–86.[9] Much of the data had been previously unpublished in the USSR, and the release of the data was thus symptomatic of the extension of Gorbachev's policy of *glasnost* to the area of religion.

Two highpoints of this phase came in 1988. On 29 April 1988, Gorbachev received Patriarch Pimen and other members of the Russian Orthodox Church synod for a formal meeting, in what was the first such meeting since 4 September 1943, when Stalin had received three senior prelates of the church. Richly symbolic, the meeting implied a commitment to improve conditions for the church.

The second highpoint came in June 1988, with the elaborate celebration of the millennium of the Christianisation of Kievan Rus. Official festivities took place 5–16 June in Moscow and Kiev, with additional celebrations in Leningrad and Riga. Representatives of all the Orthodox churches and major Christian communities from around the world attended the events. The millennial celebrations, televised and amply reported in the Soviet press, contributed to the prestige of the church. These celebrations represented both a rehabilitation of the church as a *social* institution (hence, not just the 'private affair of the individual', as Lenin had claimed), and a celebration of *national* (Russian) culture and of the church's contribution to it. In both regards, the celebrations reflected a decisive break with earlier state policy in the sphere of religion and nationalism.[10]

During the second phase, the Russian Orthodox Church was, by a considerable margin, the primary beneficiary of policy liberalisation. For example, of the 1,306 new religious congregations registered by the CRA between 1985 and 1988, 838 were Russian Orthodox congregations.[11] And although leading regime spokesmen, such as Kharchev, increasingly said that the question of the legal status of the Greek-Rite Catholic Church (Uniate) in Ukraine was a question for the Uniates to work out with the Russian Orthodox Church, in practice local officials seemed, at that stage, to be overtly favouring the Russian Orthodox Church against both its Ukrainian Catholic and Ukrainian Orthodox competitors. Applications for registration from the latter congregations were repeatedly turned down. And, in February 1989, there were reports that the local militia had been mobilised in the Ukrainian village of Hrabivka to compel the local residents to sign a petition requesting the opening of an Orthodox church in the village. A padlocked church, which had been used by Greek-Rite Catholics, was to be reopened as an Orthodox church. January 6 witnessed the spectacle of some 100 militia and KGB forces arriving at the village in order to open the church 'by force'.[12] Authorities seemed to be promoting the opening of *Orthodox* churches in Ukraine in an effort to pre-empt a Uniate revival, and, beginning in 1987, scores of Russian Orthodox churches were opened in the western regions of Ukraine, in such districts as Lviv, Ternopil, and Ivano-Frankivsk. Indeed, of the 723 Orthodox churches opened or reopened in the course of 1988, 200 were in Ukraine.[13] N. Kolesnik, chair of the Ukrainian Council for Religious Affairs, placed his interpretation on these developments, arguing that, 'In hundreds of statements, signed by tens of thousands of citizens living in the regions indicated, there is a request to register precisely an Orthodox society, and not that of some other religion.'[14]

The Georgian Orthodox Church was also an early beneficiary of the change of wind. A number of monasteries were returned to that church, permission was given for the church to open an ecclesiastical academy in Tbilisi in September 1988, new Georgian Orthodox parishes were registered, and 50,000 copies of the Bible in modern Georgian were scheduled for publication in 1989.[15]

For other faiths, concessions were either few (as for the Roman Catholics, Pentecostals, and Jews) or nonexistent (as in the case of Greek-Rite Catholics, unofficial Baptists, and Hare Krishnas).

This situation began to change around spring 1988, with the deepening of liberalisation and the gradual extension of religious *perestroika* to all groups, including those which had seemed least likely to benefit. This represented the third phase in the evolution of Gorbachev's religious policy. The return of Vilnius cathedral to the Roman Catholic Church in October 1988, the legalisation of the Hare Krishna community in May 1988, and the opening of a Buddhist monastery in eastern Siberia,[16] were symptoms of this transformation.

If, as I believe, Gorbachev hoped to achieve a 'partial' legitimation for his regime, and, in the religious sphere, to normalise church–state relations by depoliticising them and sanctioning all legitimate religious behaviours, then the registration of the Greek-Rite Catholic Church must be considered to have become more important for Gorbachev than for the pope himself. Kharchev, by then no longer chair of the CRA, hinted at this in an address to the Third World Congress on Religious Liberty in London on 24 July 1989. 'We all know that the [Berlin] wall must go', he said, 'and that the Uniate Church must be allowed to register, but pulling down the wall immediately would have unpredictable consequences.'[17] Asked if the Uniate Church would be allowed to register, he diplomatically declined to answer. But a few months later, on December 1, Gorbachev came to Rome to meet the pope, and the relegalisation of the Uniate Church became only a question of time.

The relegalisation of the Ukrainian Greek-Rite Catholic Church (in December 1989) inevitably encouraged the reopening of the question of the fate of other banned national churches, specifically the Ukrainian Orthodox and Belorussian Orthodox Churches. In fact, on 9 February 1990, Radio Kiev announced the reconstitution of the Ukrainian Autonomous Orthodox Church 'in canonical union with the patriarch' of Moscow, and the re-establishment of the Belorussian Orthodox Church took place about the same time. Radio Kiev promised the opening of a Ukrainian-language seminary, Ukrainian-language liturgy, and the honouring of specifically Ukrainian traditions in the church. However, *The Ukrainian Weekly*, an *émigré* newspaper, expressed skepticism, noting that the Ukrainian Autonomous Orthodox Church was not going to be allowed to re-establish an executive *sobor* of hierarchy, clergy, and laity, in accordance with a centuries-old tradition. It was going to be governed rather by a five-member episcopal synod consisting of the highest-ranking bishops of the church, operating under the veto of the Moscow patriarch. Consequently, the Ukrainian Autonomous Orthodox Church would enjoy not autocephaly, but only a measure of autonomy within the body of the Russian Orthodox Church.[18]

But, as early as August 1989, the Lviv parish of the Church of Saints Peter and Paul threw off the jurisdiction of the Moscow Patriarchate and announced its adherence to a hitherto non-existent Ukrainian *Autocephalous* Orthodox Church, thus reviving a religious body suppressed by Stalin in 1930 and again during the Second World War. Since its re-emergence in 1989, the Ukrainian Autocephalous Orthodox Church was officially registered (in October 1990) and campaigned for the return of church buildings, especially the ancient cathedral of St Sophia in Kiev. As a result of these developments, Ukraine has ended up with two local Orthodox churches: an Autonomous church subordinated to Moscow, and an Autocephalous church with its head (Patriarch Mstyslav) in Ukraine.

Similarly, among the Muslims, the new policy line emerged in this phase, with Uzbek First Secretary P.N. Nishanov advising party members in February 1989 to refrain from 'bureaucratic' approaches to religion, and to be more sensitive to centuries-old customs and traditions.[19]

The normalisation of church–state relations necessarily entailed that all regulations be open and published. In line with this, the CRA decided, in spring 1989, to annul the secret regulations adopted between 1961 and 1983 which governed its activity. These secret regulations were all of a restrictive nature. Under a 1961 instruction, for example, officials had been counselled to take the strictest possible interpretation of the 1929 Law on Religious Associations and certain denominations (the Jehovah's Witnesses, the Pentecostals, the True Orthodox, and the Reform Adventists) specifically had been excluded from possible registration.[20]

The passage and publication of the new law on religious organisations signalled the inception of a fourth phase. This fourth phase, had it not been for the declared secession of the Baltic states, the breakdown of political order in the USSR generally, and the collapse of the entire economy, would have, at a broader level, constituted the realisation of Gorbachev's ultimate goal. The emphasis in this phase was on legality, procedural predictability, and an end to arbitrary decisions by local officials, the normalisation of religious life (in the sense that clandestine work will become ever less important, perhaps to the point of disappearing altogether, and that churches will find they are able to engage in an ever wider range of activities, such as, for example, charity and voluntary work in hospitals). The CRA decision in March 1989 that believers may be schoolteachers,[21] was an important step in the direction of ending believers' second-class status. Obviously, the authorities had gradually come to appreciate that the discriminatory treatment of believers was politically counterproductive and economically inefficient.

Some developments in late 1989 adumbrated the inception of this fourth phase. First, the suppression of religious education gradually withered away. In Latvia, a number of Lutheran churches quietly reintroduced Sunday schools, even though technically they were still against the law. The Latvian newspaper *Padomju Jaunatne* [*Soviet Youth*] endorsed this process, calling for the full legalisation of Sunday schools.[22] This, in turn, encouraged other churches to follow suit. Further, in October 1989, the Baptist community held its first month-long Bible course in Moscow, with twenty participants from all over the USSR. A second month-long course was conducted by the Baptists in January 1990, while an 'Open University' course in theology was scheduled to be offered in autumn 1990 under the auspices of the Soviet Academy of Sciences.[23]

Second, the exclusion of the churches from the media was a thing of the past already by summer 1989. On 9 July 1989, Lithuanian television broadcast the first religious programme in the USSR, and TASS announced that it would become a regular feature on Sundays.[24] Subsequently, in November 1989, Latvian religious leaders reached an agreement with state officials permitting the churches to broadcast religious programmes on Latvian radio and television. The chief denominations in Latvia are the Lutheran, Catholic, and Orthodox churches.[25]

And third, in the area of taxation, the first steps were taken to end the punitive taxation of clergy in 1989. Since 1981, clergy had had to endure tax rates of up to 69 per cent, while persons in the state sector were taxed a maximum of 13 per cent. In summer 1989, the republic of Estonia unilaterally decided to abolish the special rate for clergy, effective September 1, and announced that clergy and other employees of religious organisations would henceforth be taxed at the same rate as factory and office workers.[26] Subsequently, in mid-September, an Orthodox priest in the RSFSR went to court for refusing to pay income tax for eighteen months, on the grounds that the higher rate for clergy was discriminatory. Although the court decided against him and

ordered him to pay back taxes, the mere fact that he made this protest
was a clue that pressure was building for the eventual elimination of
the special tax-rate throughout the USSR.[27]

The Russian Orthodox Church

In March 1988, addressing an episcopal conference of the Russian
Orthodox Church in Moscow, Patriarch Pimen declared, 'We are
witnesses of and participants in a particularly beneficial process in the
history of our country, when literally every aspect of our society's life is
being renewed and imbued with fresh spirit and content. Moral values
are gaining special importance. The children of our Church, citizens of
the Soviet Union, are accepting the *perestroika* with enthusiasm and are
actively helping to implement it.'[28] He had good reason for his
enthusiasm, since the Russian Orthodox Church had directly and
concretely benefited from *perestroika*. In the first four years of Gorbachev's rule, more than 1,700 Russian Orthodox churches were
opened or reopened, and several monasteries were returned to the
church, including the Optina Pustyn' monastery in Kaluga oblast, the
Tolgskoi Bozhiei Materi monastery in Yaroslavl, the Novo-
Golutvinsky monastery in Kolomna, and the Monastery of the Caves,
Pecherskaya Lavra, in Kiev. And, in May 1989, *Izvestiia* reported
plans for the construction of a mammoth new cathedral in Moscow,
which will accommodate 10,000 worshippers and include a conference
hall for international ecclesiastical conferences.[29] When one compares
the church's present 9,734 churches and 35 monasteries and convents
(as of late 1989), with the more than 50,000 churches and 1,000
monasteries of which it disposed before the Revolution,[30] it is clear that
the church is a long way from rebuilding its previous strength. But the
scope of Gorbachev's changes should not be underestimated either.

In Moldavia alone, the Russian Orthodox Church was able to register 265 new parishes in 1988, and, in April 1989, the Council of
Ministers of the Moldavian Republic decided to return the large
cathedral in Kishinev to the church.[31]

The publishing activity of the church also expanded in the Gorbachev era. In 1988, the church's central Publishing Department
became the owner of four new buildings. In April 1989, the Moscow
Patriarchate launched an eight-page weekly newspaper, *Moskovsky
tserkovnyi vestnik*, dealing with theological, social, and cultural issues
relating to the church. The paper has a print-run of 50,000 copies. The
church also published a jubilee edition of the Bible in Russian
(100,000 copies), a Russian prayer book (75,000 copies), and a

Ukrainian translation of the New Testament. And agreements were reached to import 150,000 copies of the *Bible Commentary* in Russian. In addition to this, the Soviet government paper *Izvestiia* started regular reportage of Russian Orthodox Church news.[32]

In spring 1988 the Soviet authorities let it be known that religious organisations were free to resume charitable work. As early as June 1988, a special Ecclesiastical Council summoned by the Patriarchate resolved that the church had a *duty* to perform charitable works, and subsequently sent bishops on study tours to the United States, to learn how to set up and organise their charitable activities. The Council also declared that priests – and not the state-approved committees which had performed this function up to now – have the right to administer their parishes.[33]

About the same time, Soviet television broadcast portions of the Russian Orthodox Easter service – the first time this had been done in the USSR. In April 1991, Soviet television went further and broadcast live the entire Easter service at the Epiphany Cathedral, a service prominently attended by RSFSR President Boris Yeltsin and Soviet Prime Minister Valentin Pavlov.[34] Only a few months earlier, Christmas had been declared a state holiday.

Clergy of the church said that they felt respected, at last, and were treated with a new respect not just by the officials, but by ordinary citizens too. Religious processions could be carried out in public more easily. And there was a gathering consensus that religion in general, and Russian Orthodoxy in particular, had something positive to contribute to Soviet society. In such circumstances, it was not incongruous to see Fr. Gleb Yakunin, long imprisoned for his staunch faith, joining two other priests to create a Church and *Perestroika* Society, whose main purpose was to support Gorbachev's religious policy.[35] Ironically, the new freedom which Fr. Yakunin welcomed also encouraged him to join five other priests of the Diocese of Omsk and Tyumen in announcing, at the end of November 1989, that they were transferring their allegiance from the Moscow Patriarchate to the Russian Orthodox Church Abroad, headquartered in New York.[36]

Since Gorbachev's accession to power, thus, the Russian Orthodox Church has begun a modest recovery. As of late 1989, it had 8,100 priests, 2,443 readers, 70 dioceses, 19 teaching establishments, 3,948 theological students, and, as already noted, 9,734 open churches and 35 monasteries and convents.[37]

The Islamic community

As already mentioned, the Islamic community did not benefit from Gorbachev's new policies as quickly as did the Russian Orthodox Church. The deeply ingrained prejudice felt by Russians toward the Muslim minority, together with the much stronger equation of Muslim religious identity with Muslim ethnic identity,[38] are surely among the more important factors which retarded the extension of liberalisation to Central Asia. Another factor, certainly during the lifetime of Iran's Ayatollah Khomeini, was fear of the spread of Islamic fundamentalism among the Soviet Muslim population. 'What is Khomeini's dream?', *Literaturnaia gazeta* asked in January 1988. 'It is that the Islamic revolution be victorious throughout the whole Muslim world, from Morocco in the West to Indonesia in the East.'[39]

But then, in December 1988, a mosque in Lenkoran, Azerbaijan, was returned to the Islamic community, 50 years after it had been confiscated.[40] Subsequently other mosques were reopened in Azerbaijan, including in the towns of Bine, Keshly, in Nefteshala, etc. There were more than 600 mosques functioning with official permission in the USSR as a whole in 1987, compared with 200 at the end of the Brezhnev era. Of this number, 69 had been built between 1977 and 1983.[41] There had been some 26,279 mosques functioning openly in the tsarist empire in 1912.[42] In Azerbaijan alone, there were some 2,000 mosques open in 1917, vs. 55 in 1990.

In March 1989, Muslims were allowed to open a two-year preparatory school for imams and muezzins in Ufa, in the Bashkir ASSR. It was said to be the only educational establishment of its kind in the USSR, offering courses on reading the Koran, Islamic jurisprudence, calligraphy, popular medicine, Arabic, and English.[43] An Islamic college was opened in 1990, in Tajikistan, with 25 students enrolled for the first year.[44] About the same time, new mosques were opened in three Tajik cities – Isfara, Kabadien, and Ura-Tube – and Islamic religious books were published in larger print-runs in Arabic and Tajik.[45] Meanwhile, in summer 1989, the Muslim community became involved in charitable activity for the first time.[46]

With perhaps as many as 45 million believers, Islam was the second largest faith in the USSR (after the 50-million strong Russian Orthodox Church), and the major faith of most of the peoples of Central Asia. The reports which have come to light so far, and which I have cited above, largely concern improvements for believers in the Bashkir ASSR and in the Republic of Azerbaijan. In addition, in March 1989, a group of Muslims in the village of Nizhny Dzhengutai, in Dagestan, seized possession of a former mosque and forced the authorities to negotiate. A month later, several hundred people tried to storm the official headquarters of the Spiritual Board of Muslims of Northern Caucasia, in the town of Makhachkala. They demanded land for the erection of a new mosque and the removal of the local mufti; the authorities gave in to these demands.[47] In February 1990, the Kazakh party elite bowed to pressure from Kazakh Muslim clergy and authorised the establishment of a Kazakh muftiate independent of the Spiritual Board in Tashkent. This new muftiate is headed by Ratbek-haji-Nysanbai-uli. The Kazakh party hoped that this structural innovation would enable it to channel the Islamic revival into paths supportive of the party.[48]

In the past five or so years, there has been a new development. Beginning arguably with the anti-Russian riots in Alma Ata in December 1986, there has been a revival of anti-Russian sentiment, combined with a new determination to drive the Russians out of Central Asia. Islamic fundamentalism colours this reawakening of feeling, and is centred on a Rebirth Movement which claims to have about 10,000 members (as of January 1991).[49] Anonymous sources[50] also allege that many Uzbeks talk of using violence and terror to drive all non-Muslims out of their republic. The underground Sufi movement remains strong, and some Sufis are said to have criticised Soviet socialisation of the young as early as the late 1960s. In addition, in some areas in Central Asia, there has recently been a resurgence of Wahhabism, a Sunni sect that wants to restore the pristine purity of Islam 'as it once was'.[51]

The Catholic Church

The third largest religious body in the USSR is the Catholic Church, which embraces up to 10 million believers in its Roman and Greek rites.[52] The chief centres for Catholicism in the USSR are the Ukraine (Greek-rite) and Lithuania (Roman rite), although there are also large concentrations of Catholics in Belorussia and Latvia, and active parishes altogether in 11 of the 15 union republics. The situation of the Greek-Rite Catholic Church was unique in that it had been completely proscribed since 1946; although not the only religious organisation denied legal status, it was by far the largest church forced underground. It maintained bishops, clergy, and an underground press (*Chronicle of the Catholic Church in Ukraine*), and maintained a practice of conducting services in church buildings which had been closed by the authorities ('padlocked churches'). The authorities tried for years alternatively to suppress the Uniates or to buy them out with offers of legality in exchange for breaking with Rome. But the Uniates survived and periodically submitted petitions for legalisation to the authorities.

As recently as May 1989, a Ukrainian Catholic priest (Fr. Mikhailo Havriliv) was arrested for holding Easter services in several Ukrainian villages (on 30 April). But beginning in mid-1988, there were various hints that the legalisation of the Uniates might be only a question of time. In June 1989, Aleksandr Berkov, a Soviet legal expert from the Institute of State and Law of the USSR Academy of Sciences, indicated that the question would have to be taken up in connection with the new legislation on religious associations. Subsequently, the English-language newspaper, *Moscow News*, carried an interesting exchange between Metropolitan Filaret of Kiev and Galicia, and Sergei Filatov, a research associate of the Institute of the USA and Canada in Moscow. The former, an exarch of the Russian Orthodox Church in Ukraine, repeated the hackneyed line that the pseudo-synod of Lviv (1946), which incorporated the Ukrainian Catholic Church into the Russian Orthodox Church, had represented the authentic will of the faithful and charged that advocates of ecclesiastical restoration were an 'insignificant group' linked with 'nationalistic elements'. Filatov rebutted Filaret's arguments, and urged the return of the Cathedral of St Yura in Lviv to the Ukrainian Catholics.[53]

By June 1989, Ukrainian Catholics were participating openly and publicly in liturgical services in many towns in western Ukraine. On 18 June, for example, some 100,000 faithful took part in services in Ivano-Frankivsk. There was no interference from the authorities.[54] On 29 October 1989, Ukrainian Catholics seized the Church of the Transfiguration in Lviv, and in the course of the next month, more than 50 local churches transferred their allegiance from the Moscow Patriarchate to the Vatican. On 26 November, on the eve of Gorbachev's meeting with the pope, more than 100,000 Ukrainian Catholics gathered on the streets of Lviv, in order to maintain pressure on the authorities. Subsequently, on 1 December, the day that Gorbachev arrived in Rome, officials in Ukraine announced that they would officially register congregations of the Ukrainian Greek-Rite Catholic Church – thus ending four decades of illegality.[55]

For the Russian Orthodox Church, the loss of the Uniate parishes came as a severe psychological and material blow. Russian Orthodox Irinei of Lvov and Drogobych, reacted in a fashion typical of Russian prelates, observing:

The situation is tense. I'm grieved by the activities of Ukrainian Catholics. They have experienced quite a lot themselves, and therefore must realize our feelings and apprehensions. The new situation poses hard problems to the clergy and believers of our diocese, one of the biggest in the country.[56]

The Catholic Church established a joint commission with the Orthodox Church on the 'Normalization of Relations Between the Orthodox and Catholics of the Eastern Rite in Western Ukraine', with the participation of two Vatican delegates: Archbishop Miroslav Marusyn, secretary of the Congregation for Eastern Churches, and Archbishop Stephen Sulyk, metropolitan of Ukrainian Catholics in the United States. Although the establishment of this commission was in itself a propitious development, the talks ran into trouble when the Vatican and Ukrainian Catholic delegations raised the subject of the return of the Cathedral of St George in Lviv to the Catholic Church, and the Orthodox delegation threatened to break off the talks.[57] On 6 April, however, the Lviv City Council cut through this Gordian knot and voted to return the Cathedral of St George to the Catholics.[58] By April 1990, the Ukrainian Catholic Church numbered more than 1,000 priests; and religious orders – including the Basilian fathers and the Redemptorists – were functioning openly.[59] In March 1991, Myroslav Cardinal Lubachivsky, primate of the church, returned to Ukraine after 53 years in exile.[60]

As these developments were taking place, the Catholic Church was also making important gains in other regions. In Lithuania, the Queen of Peace Church in Klaipeda and the Cathedral in Vilnius were returned to the church, and the theological seminary in Telsiai was allowed to reopen on 5 September 1989, after being closed for 43 years.[61] In both Lithuania and Latvia, new church journals were given permission to begin publication in early 1989. And in Lithuania, All Souls' Day (November 1) and Christmas Day were declared legal holidays, effective in 1989.[62] Soviet leaders also allowed Lithuanian Bishop Julijonas Steponavicius to return to Vilnius from *de facto* exile to another parish, and allowed the Vatican to appoint bishops for all six of Lithuania's dioceses, as well as a bishop for the Belorussian capital of Minsk – the first time Belorussia has had a bishop or apostolic administrator since 1927. On 5 September 1989, the church was allowed to reopen its seminary at Telsiai, in Lithuania.[63] Now Bishop Kondrusiewicz of Minsk says he wants to see a seminary open in Belorussia. Elsewhere in the USSR, the Catholic presence is weaker. There is, for example, only one priest assigned to serve all German Catholics living in Kirghizia.[64]

Other groups

There were some 1.5 million Jews reported as living in the USSR at the time of the last census, but with the recent flood of emigrants to Israel – as of December 1990, at a rate of 3,000–3,500 Soviet Jews per day[65] – Judaism may or may not still be the fourth largest faith in the USSR. It is, certainly, the fastest-declining faith in the USSR, as emigration steadily diminishes their number. In 1989, more than 71,000 Jews left the USSR (as contrasted with 914 in 1986, about 8,000 in 1987, and 18,965 in 1988), and the Israeli government talked of absorbing as many as 750,000 Soviet Jews over the subsequent six years.[66] More than 184,000 Soviet Jews moved to Israel in 1990, and at this writing, Israeli officials expect the arrival of another 400,000 Soviet Jews during 1991.[67] All of this has obvious consequences for the Jewish presence in the USSR. But meanwhile, in legal terms, the situation of Soviet Jews began improving. Soviet authorities permitted the opening of a Judaic Studies Centre (for the training of rabbis and teachers) in Moscow in February 1989. Two Jewish bulletins were also launched in Ukraine: *The Information Bulletin of the Chernivsti Jewish Society Cultural Fund*, edited by Iosyp Zisels, a member of the Ukrainian Helsinki Union; and *News of Jewish Organizations of Ukraine*, launched in Kiev in September 1989. A Jewish cultural centre was opened in Tallinn, Estonia, in May 1988. But, as recently as November 1989, there were only 100 synagogues in the entire USSR,[68] and the prospects for opening new ones, in a time of tidal emigration, are dim.

This tidal emigration comes, in part, as a response to the revival of anti-Semitism in the USSR. *Molodaia gvardiia, Nash sovremennik*, and other mass periodicals have published anti-Jewish articles, and the expression of anti-Jewish sentiment has proven to be riskfree. K.V. Ostashvili, leader of a faction in the anti-Semitic organisation Pamyat, told *Izmailovskii vestnik*, 'A Zionist-influenced commercial–financial mafia is operating in our country. It is taking over the spiritual and economic life of the country and making a dash for power.' He claimed that Jews are '[overrepresented] in all areas of government and public life.'[69] Anti-Semitism feeds on crises, and, rather than facing crises honestly and braving a complex analysis, the anti-Semite retreats to the reassuringly superficial simplicities of group hatred.

Yes, always these Jews, as though there were nobody else in this world. The Jews live everywhere, own the capital, live like parasites throughout the world, emigrate freely from country to country and are always depicted as the most unfortunate nation. . . . It is enough to read the 'Protocols of the Elders of Zion' to realize who created this situation. However, not all Zionists are Jews and not all Jews are Zionists. This is why we are not anti-Semitic.[70]

By contrast, the fastest-growing religious organisation is the Hare Krishna, which had only 3,000 adherents when it finally achieved legalisation in May 1988, but which had more than 100,000 by the end of 1990; in fact, today, there are more than 200 Krishna groups across what used to be the USSR from the Baltics to Vladivostok.[71] Among Protestants, many churches benefited from *perestroika*. The Lutheran Church won a number of concessions, including the right to elevate Latvian Haralds Kalnins to serve as bishop for the German Lutherans in the USSR;[72] the right to publish a theological journal in Latvian (*Cels*, edited by Janis Liepins);[73] permission to publish several newspapers and magazines, as well as a new Estonian edition of the New Testament (the first since the annexation of Estonia, and the product of co-operation between Estonia's Lutherans and Baptists);[74] permission to launch a new intensive six-month course in theology, for the training of assistant pastors in Latvia;[75] permission to open a theological seminary for German Lutherans (in Riga);[76] and the return of the Lutheran cathedral in Riga.[77] In addition, two Latvians – Lutheran pastor Juris Rubenis and philosopher Ilmars Latkovskis – were able to start publication of an ecumenical newspaper in spring 1989. Called *Svetdienas Rits* (*Sunday Morning*), the first issue had a print-run of 30,000 copies.[78]

The Lutheran Church in Latvia started showing a new resilience. At a General Synod in Riga, 11–12 April 1989, Lutheran clergymen and other delegates from Latvian congregations voted to dismiss Archbishop Eriks Mesters and the entire Consistory. Mesters, in particular, was viewed as having been too submissive to the political authorities. In his place, the Synod elected fifty-three-year-old Karlis Gailitis, a member of Latvia's Rebirth and Renewal Movement. The Synod also passed a resolution calling for the annulment of the Molotov–Ribbentrop pact and the independence of Latvia, and endorsing the work of the Latvian Popular Front and the Latvian National Independence Movement with regard to religious freedom.[79] In Estonia, the Lutheran Church started to show sudden strength. Several thousand people joined the church within a matter of months.[80]

Soviet Baptists, particularly the so-called 'official Baptists' (who have registered with the authorities), have also made gains under *perestroika*. These gains have included the opening of a church facility in Luga (near Leningrad) in autumn 1988,[81] the holding of a national Baptist youth conference in April 1989 (the first since the 1920s),[82] the

possibility to undertake voluntary hospital work as a charitable
activity,[83] and permission to publish a new *Information Bulletin* (effective
March 1989).[84] I have already mentioned the Bible courses launched
by the Baptists in late 1989. As in the case of the Lutherans, liberalisation encouraged some Baptists to become more outspoken. Specifically, about 500 former members of the official Baptist Church in
Estonia formed an unofficial 'Word of Life' Church in early 1988, with
followers in Tallinn, Tartu, and Parnu. Two-hundred and thirty-two
members of the church signed a petition, addressed to Presidents
Reagan and Gorbachev, renouncing their Soviet citizenship and
requesting permission to emigrate.[85]

And finally, the Seventh Day Adventists were able to open a theological training institute, to register some nineteen communities in
Moldavia, and to establish a publishing house at the Adventist centre
in Zaoksky, near Tula.

In addition to these churches, several other smaller organisations
have established footholds in the USSR. These include the Baha'i
World Faith (with about 1,000 adherents at the end of 1990), the
Mormon Church (granted official registration late in 1990), and the
Unification Church, whose founder, the Revd Sun Myung Moon, was
described by *Moscow News* in April 1990 – not without a touch of irony
– as 'one of the most brilliant anti-Communists in the world'.[86] There
has also been a new interest in faith healers, ESP, UFOs, astrology,
clairvoyants, mental telepathy, out-of-body experiences, and even
'abominable' snowmen. Far from being symptomatic of religious or
spiritual revival *per se*, however, these latter phenomena are indicative
rather of the breakdown of the former position of the traditional
churches, and the opening up of new possibilities in conditions of
urbanisation and mass communication.

Conclusion

I have already argued that it is doubtful that Gorbachev knew from
the beginning exactly where religious policy was heading. His religious
policy, accordingly, emerged on the basis of an underlying commitment to liberalisation, modulated through a sequence of *ad hoc* adjustments and *ad hoc* responses to problems.

If one compares the chief demands of religious activists in the 1970s
and 1980s with Gorbachev's policy responses and innovations, the
parallelism is striking. Religious activists demanded, for example, the
release of incarcerated priests and other persons imprisoned for their
faith; Gorbachev authorised the steady release of prisoners of faith,

closed some of the prison camps, and opened up the Perm prison camp to a French film crew.

Religious activists demanded the return of confiscated churches and an end to restrictions on church construction; Gorbachev allowed the return of various churches, mosques, and temples to the various faiths, and has ended restrictions on church construction.

Religious activists demanded the relegalisation of the Greek-Rite Catholic Church in Ukraine; this was granted at the end of 1989, in what was surely one of Gorbachev's most surprising moves overall. As of 16 January 1990, there were approximately 600 parishes in Ukraine openly functioning as Greek Catholic parishes. Another 700 congregations had filed applications for registration.

Religious activists demanded the normalisation of the hierarchical structure (where the Catholic Church was concerned). With new appointments in Lithuania, Latvia, and Belorussia, the return of Bishops Sladkevicius and Steponavicius to their dioceses, and the re-emergence of the Church in Ukraine, this was, in great part, accomplished.

Religious activists demanded the opening of new seminaries, rabbinical centres, medresas for the training of Islamic elders, etc., and the lifting of the quota system. As already noted, this has been granted to all the religious organisations.

Religious activists demanded legal permission to publish mass periodicals for believers. As already noted, two such periodicals (one in Lithuanian, one in Latvian) were launched in early 1989. There have been others where other religious groups have been concerned.

Religious activists demanded access to Soviet television. And on 9 July 1989, the first religious programme was shown on Lithuanian television.[87]

And religious activists demanded an end to mandatory atheism classes in the schools and the introduction of religious instruction on an elective basis. This, too, has been achieved as of early 1991.

The changes unleashed in religious policy by Gorbachev were part of a much larger process of change and rethinking, and the purposes served by changes in this sphere were closely related to the purposes served by changes in other spheres. In brief, Gorbachev hoped, until the proclaimed secession of the Baltic states incited him to retrench in late 1990, to obtain the partial legitimation of Soviet rule, to modernise the system and the society, and to make the Soviet Union more efficient by opening the doors to various kinds of pluralisation. In a signed statement issued on the eve of his encounter with the pope, Gorbachev said,

We have changed our attitude on some matters, such as religion, which admittedly we used to treat in a simplistic manner. Now we not only proceed from the assumption that no one should interfere in matters of the individual's conscience. We also say that the moral values that religion generated and embodied for centuries can help in the work of renewal in our country.[88]

Pluralisation and relegitimation of religion are not the only fruit of this opening up, however. The loosening of strictures has also unleashed a new epidemic of chauvinism, which has manifested itself at various levels. *Pamyat*, the notorious anti-Semitic organisation which came into prominence early in Gorbachev's rule, is only the best known. Islamic fundamentalism, anti-sect violence by Georgian nationalists at the instigation of Georgian Orthodox clergy,[89] and a renewed hatred between Orthodox and Catholics in Ukraine,[90] are among other signs of this new chauvinism.

At the same time, relegitimation of the churches' role as social institutions, especially in times of national chaos, has inevitably brought the churches into politics. The Latvian Lutheran Church, the Lithuanian Catholic Church,[91] and the Georgian Orthodox Church all endorsed their republics' aspirations for independence. A Christian Democratic Party was founded in Moscow in August 1989; and Orthodox clergy were elected deputies in the Russian parliament as well as members of working committees of the USSR Supreme Soviet.

Finally, I would like to close with four general observations about the process of *perestroika* in the religious sphere.

First, the process tended to snowball. It is, as I have already indicated, quite doubtful whether Gorbachev originally intended to carry his reforms as far as they actually went, even during the course of his term of office; but each new concession and freedom encouraged believers to seek additional concessions and freedoms. For example, the Ukrainian and Belorussian Orthodox churches, about which almost everyone seemed to have forgotten, revived themselves in 1989, and, in February 1990, Russian Orthodox Metropolitan Filaret of Kiev announced that these two long-submerged churches would be resurrected, as autonomous branches of the Russian Church. But even then, as already mentioned, Ukrainian autocephalists continued to press for relegalisation, and Ukraine has ended up with two rival 'Ukrainian Orthodox' churches.

Second, the process very quickly led to a complete reversal of the status of religion. Where, prior to Gorbachev, church membership bore a certain social stigma in official circles, necessarily affecting popular expressions of attitudes regarding the church, officials increasingly found it useful to show their links with the church – for example, in Gorbachev's admission that he was baptised, and in Russian President Boris Yeltsin's attendance at Easter services in 1991. Accordingly, a 1990 survey in the Moscow region found that more people trusted the church than any other institution: 64 per cent trusted the church, vs. 56 per cent for the armed forces, 54 per cent for the Green Movement, and only 5.4 per cent for the communist party.[92]

Third, the process necessarily involved legislative overhaul. New prerogatives and freedoms require institutional and procedural safeguards. Since legislative reform in one sphere is organically connected with legislative reform in other spheres, the pace of change in the religious sphere has been to a large part dependent on the pace of change more broadly.

And fourth, just as the repression and constriction of religion tended to politicise religion, deepening the linkage between religion and nationalism and encouraging churches to become involved in forms of dissent, by the same virtue, processes of relaxation and liberalisation were supposed to work in the opposite direction – partly depoliticising religion, slackening the bonds with nationalism, partly for tautological reasons and partly for natural, substantive reasons, drawing the churches away from illegal forms of activity and into legal forms of protest and social criticism. Religion, I have argued repeatedly over the years, is inherently political, and the bonds between religion and nationalism/national culture are often very deep: liberalisation will not change these facts. But Gorbachev's *perestroika* in the religious sphere will have a lasting impact on religious life in the former Soviet republics, an impact which the collapse of the Soviet Union is unlikely to reverse.

Notes

1 *Izvestiia* (5 June 1990), as cited in *Keston News Service*, no. 352 (14 June 1990), p. 5; and Otto Luchterhandt, 'The Council for Religious Affairs', below.
2 *Pravda* (18 November 1989).
3 *Keston News Service*, no. 353 (28 June 1990), p. 15.
4 *Ibid.*, no. 337 (2 November 1989), p. 10.
5 AFP (Paris, 28 November 1986), in Foreign Broadcast Information Service (FBIS), *Daily Report* (Soviet Union), 1 December 1986, p. R6.
6 *Komsomol'skaia Pravda* (10 December 1986), p. 2.
7 *Literaturnaia gazeta* (9 September 1987), p. 2.
8 *Süddeutsche Zeitung* (Munich), 26–7 January 1991, p. 11.
9 *Nauka i Religiia*, no. 11 (November 1987), pp. 21–3.
10 For further discussion, see Pedro Ramet (ed.), *Religion and Nationalism in*

Soviet and East European Politics, Revised edn (Durham, NC: Duke University Press, 1989).

11 *Keston News Service*, no. 343 (8 February 1990), citing the January 1990 issue of *Nauka i religiia*.
12 *Ibid.*, no. 319 (16 February 1989), p. 4.
13 According to N. Kolesnik, chair of the Ukrainian Council for Religious Affairs, as cited in *Keston News Service*, no. 321 (16 March 1989), p. 8.
14 Quoted in *ibid.*, p. 9.
15 *Ibid.*, no. 307 (25 August 1988), p. 14.
16 *Süddeutsche Zeitung* (27–8 October 1990), p. 6.
17 Quoted in Mark Beeching, 'Kharchev Discusses Draft Law on Religious Freedom', *Radio Liberty: Report on the USSR* (4 August 1989), p. 3.
18 *The Ukrainian Weekly* (Jersey City, 18 March 1990), p. 6.
19 *Keston News Service*, no. 321 (16 March 1989), p. 10.
20 *Ibid.*, no. 323 (13 April 1989), p. 2.
21 *Ibid.*, no. 322 (30 March 1989), p. 9.
22 *Keston News Service*, no. 329 (6 July 1989), p. 5.
23 *Ibid.*, no. 344 (22 February 1990), p. 10.
24 *Ibid.*, no. 330 (20 July 1989), p. 7.
25 TASS (17 November 1989), in FBIS, *Daily Report* (Soviet Union), 20 November 1989, p. 89.
26 *Keston News Service*, no. 333 (7 August 1989), pp. 7–8.
27 Keston College writes, 'Fr. Gleb Yakunin, giving evidence at the trial [of Fr Nikolai Gainov], said that higher clergy such as Patriarch Pimen, members of the Holy Synod, and clergy working in the Department of External Church Relations of the Church are taxed as ordinary workers at the normal rate. He said that by giving privileges to them, the state was robbing the lower clergy.' *Keston News Service*, no. 336 (19 October 1989), p. 6.
28 Quoted in *Journal of the Moscow Patriarchate* (1988), no. 6, p. 4.
29 *Keston News Service*, no. 327 (8 June 1989), p. 11; and Emily Pyle, 'Moscow Patriarchate Brings Out New Weekly Publication', in *Radio Liberty: Report on the USSR* (21 July 1989), p. 13.
30 Emily Pyle, 'Prospects for a Third Wave of Russian Monasticism', in *Radio Liberty: Report on the USSR* (4 August 1989), p. 5; and *Keston News Service*, no. 339 (30 November 1989), p. 7. See also D. Pospielovsky, 'Podvig very v ateisticheskom Gosudarstve', in *Grani*, 42:147 (1988).
31 TASS (28 April 1989), in FBIS, *Daily Report* (Soviet Union), 8 May 1989, p. 76.
32 *Journal of the Moscow Patriarchate* (1988), no. 6, p. 7; *Keston News Service*, no. 329 (6 July 1989), p. 6; and Pyle, 'Moscow Patriarchate', p. 12.
33 *New York Times* (10 June 1988), p. 3; and *Neue Zürcher Zeitung* (12–13 June 1988), p. 3.
34 *Daily Telegraph* (London), 8 April 1991, p. 11.
35 *Pravoslavlje* (Belgrade, 1 May 1989), p. 4.
36 For a discussion of this organisation, see Oxana Antic, 'The Russian

Orthodox Church Abroad', in Pedro Ramet (ed.), *Eastern Christianity and Politics in the Twentieth Century* (Durham, NC: Duke University Press, 1988).

37 *Keston News Service*, no. 339 (30 November 1989), p. 7.

38 See James Critchlow, 'Islam and Nationalism in Soviet Central Asia', in Ramet (ed.), *Religion and Nationalism*.

39 *Literaturnaia gazeta* (13 January 1988), p. 14.

40 *Keston News Service*, no. 317 (19 January 1989), p. 15.

41 *Muslims in the USSR* (13 January 1987), cited in Yasin Aslan, 'Mosques Reopened in Azerbaijan', in *Radio Liberty: Report on the USSR* (10 February 1989), p. 16.

42 *The Guardian of Liberty (Nemzetör)* (Munich), September–October 1989, p. 8.

43 *Keston News Service*, no. 325 (11 May 1989), p. 19.

44 *Ibid.*, no. 356 (9 August 1990), p. 8.

45 TASS (6 March 1989), in FBIS, *Daily Report* (Soviet Union), 14 March 1989, p. 79.

46 *Keston News Service*, no. 330 (20 July 1989), p. 10.

47 *Ibid.*, no. 331 (3 August 1989), p. 12.

48 Martha Brill Olcott, '*Perestroyka* in Kazakhstan', in *Problems of Communism*, 39:4 (July–August 1990), pp. 70–1.

49 *Süddeutsche Zeitung* (12–13 January 1991), p. 7.

50 Cited in *News Network International* (10 July 1989), p. 23.

51 Yaacov Ro'i, 'The Islamic Influence on Nationalism in Soviet Central Asia', in *Problems of Communism*, 39:4 (July–August 1990), p. 52. See also Andreas Kappeler, Gerhard Simon, and Georg Brunner (eds.), *Die Muslime in der Sowjetunion und in Jugoslawien* (Cologne: Markus Publishing House, 1989).

52 See Roman Solchanyk and Ivan Hvat, 'The Catholic Church in the Soviet Union', in Pedro Ramet (ed.), *Catholicism and Politics in Communist Societies* (Durham, NC: Duke University Press, 1990).

53 *Keston News Service*, no. 331 (3 August 1989), p. 7.

54 *Ibid.*, no. 329 (6 July 1989), p. 4.

55 Moscow World Service (4 November 1989), in FBIS, *Daily Report* (Soviet Union), 7 November 1989, p. 68; and *New York Times* (2 December 1989), p. 8.

56 Quoted in *Moscow News* (7–14 January 1990), p. 13.

57 *The Ukrainian Weekly* (Jersey City, NJ), 18 March 1990, pp. 1, 10.

58 *Ibid.* (15 April 1990), p. 11.

59 *Keston News Service*, no. 347 (5 April 1990), p. 8.

60 See report in *National Catholic Reporter* (12 April 1991), p. 5.

61 *Keston News Service*, no. 335 (5 October 1989), p. 6.

62 TASS (18 October 1989), trans. in FBIS, *Daily Report* (Soviet Union), 20 October 1989, p. 56; and Moscow Domestic Service (22 October 1989), trans. in FBIS, *Daily Report* (Soviet Union), 24 October 1989, p. 64.

63 *Keston News Service*, no. 335 (5 October 1989), p. 6.

64 *Frankfurter Allgemeine* (11 December 1990), p. 8.
65 *International Herald Tribune* (Paris), 22–3 December 1990, p. 5.
66 *New York Times* (14 December 1989), p. A1; and Zvi Gitelman, 'Glasnost, Perestroika and Antisemitism', in *Foreign Affairs*, 70:2 (Spring 1991), p. 155.
67 *Ibid.* (9 January 1991), p. A1.
68 Oxana Antic, 'The Situation of Religious Jews in the USSR: 1987–1989', in Radio Liberty, *Report on the USSR* (24 November 1989), p. 8.
69 *Izmailovskii Vestnik*, no. 2 (1990), p. 3, as quoted in Gitelman, 'Glasnost', p. 149.
70 Dimitry Vasilev, a leader of Pamyat, in interview with *La Repubblica* (26 February 1988), as quoted in Gitelman, 'Glasnost', p. 152.
71 *Moscow Magazine* (January 1991), p. 17.
72 *Keston News Service*, no. 314 (1 December 1988), p. 9.
73 *Ibid.*, no. 318 (2 February 1989), p. 16.
74 *Ibid.*, no. 325 (11 May 1989), p. 19.
75 *Ibid.*, p. 5.
76 TASS (17 November 1989), in FBIS, *Daily Report* (Soviet Union), 20 November 1989, p. 89.
77 *Frankfurter Allgemeine* (6 October 1988), p. 3.
78 *Keston News Service*, no. 326 (25 May 1989), p. 14.
79 *Ibid.*, no. 324 (27 April 1989), p. 3.
80 *Ibid.*, no. 334 (21 September 1989), p. 8.
81 *Ibid.*, no. 316 (5 January 1989), p. 7.
82 *Ibid.*, no. 321 (16 March 1989), p. 5.
83 *Ibid.*, no. 304 (7 July 1988), p. 15.
84 *Ibid.*, no. 327 (8 June 1989), p. 12.
85 *Ibid.*, no. 297 (31 March 1988), p. 9.
86 Quoted in Oxana Antic, 'Smaller Religious Denominations Flourish in New Conditions', in *Radio Liberty: Report on the USSR* (15 February 1991), p. 10.
87 *Keston News Service*, no. 330 (20 July 1989), p. 7.
88 Quoted in *New York Times* (1 December 1989), p. 1.
89 *Keston News Service*, no. 355 (26 July 1990), p. 8.
90 *Süddeutsche Zeitung* (25–6 August 1990), p. 2.
91 *Keston News Service*, no. 349 (3 May 1990), p. 6; and *Corriere della Sera* (Milan), 2 July 1990, p. 3.
92 *Moscow News* (10–17 June 1990), as cited in *Keston News Service*, no. 352 (14 June 1990), p. 7.

PART II

Policy apparatus

The Council for Religious Affairs

OTTO LUCHTERHANDT

The beginnings of the present-day authority for the state control and supervision of religious communities reach back to the October Revolution, namely to the commission formed in 1917 by the National Commissariat of Justice, which, under the direction of the well-known lawyer M.A. Rejssner, formulated the edict of 23 January 1918 on the separation of church from state and school from church which is formally still valid today.[1] After completion of that task in April 1918, this commission was continued in an interministerial special commission, also established by the commissary of justice, for the continuing development of cult-legislation. The commission was then integrated in May of 1918 into the Commissariat as the department for administration of the edict of separation. Led by the prominent Bolshevik P.A. Krasikov, its main task consisted in the practical accomplishment of the liquidation of the now secularised church property. Soon it was referred to as the 'liquidation department' or, alternatively, the '8th department'. In addition, the department had the characteristics of a consulting agency for the central governmental apparatus. In other words, it should provide binding answers to questions from the side of state institutions on the application of the cult-legislation, rule with final authority and precedent-setting influence in eventual disputes, and develop drafts for further cult laws. Furthermore, and this was most unusual for a department of the ministry of justice, it should also observe and co-operate in controlling the political activities of so-called 'clerical parties', in other words those powers in the religious communities which stood in opposition to the Soviet state. Thus the religious board of control's double function, valid until recently, emerged at a very early point in time. These functions were, primarily, fulfilment of administrative or judicial consultation duties, and, secondarily, the strategic battle against the churches and other religious communities.

55

At the beginning of the 'NEP' period (1922) when the Agencies for Internal Affairs were re-organised, control of religious associations allowed by the new rules was transferred to the National Commissariat of Internal Affairs (NKVD). The general administrative departments of the local Soviets subordinate to the NKVD were now responsible for the registration and confirmation of church organisational measures reserved for the state.[2] Because of this and the secularisation of church property in accordance with their conclusion, the cult department of the Justice Commissariat had lost considerably in importance. The department temporarily escaped its own liquidation by the personal intervention of Lenin. Transformed into the 5th department of the justice commissariat, it maintained its specific judicial control and consultative functions[3] in the state apparatus, in other words, it was to take care of the incontestable application of relevant legislation through the officials and courts. It did this not without success through brisk departmental correspondence[4]. One main fruit of their work was the exemplary edition of the Soviet religious legislation[5] provided by Professor P.V. Giduljanov, which in its quality has not nearly been equaled even today. Although the 5th department was decidedly anti-religious, under the respectively anti-clerical leadership of Krasikov, its mode of operation delineated itself still through a certain striving towards objectivity and juridical accuracy, in brief: through a level of professionality upon which one could only wistfully look back later.

The strategic political fight against the religious communities, the observations and oppression by the anti-communist powers within them, and also the partial co-operation with groups loyal to the regime as well as the manipulative demands of separatist activities in the churches was the work of the Cheka from the beginning[6], or later – from 1922 – of the 'State Political Administration' (OGPU), in which a sub-department for church questions existed under the direction of E.A. Tuckov.

In order to co-ordinate the various state institutions concerned with religious communities, a Ministry for Cult Matters was instituted, directed by P.G. Smidovich. This was set up in August 1924 with the Central Executive Committee (VCIK) of the Russian Federation. In 1931, after the dissolution of the NKVD, the ministry was elevated to a collegially composed 'Central Standing Commission with the Chairmanship of the VCIK', also led by Smidovich. Subordinate to it were placed regional and local commissions, which brought together within themselves the religious legislative competencies of the 5th department of the NKVD[7]. This organisation of religious control stayed in existence when the NKVD reorganised, and was united with the OGPU at the union level in 1934. In 1937/8 the cult commissions were dissolved anyway. The state control over religious communities went over to the NKVD, which had become in the meantime an all-powerful apparatus of terror. That was only appropriate, since the religious institutions still existing at that time, clergy and active laymen were being persecuted under the slander of 'clerical-fascism'. This function of strategic opposition to, infiltration, division and destruction of, religious communities, as well as anti-religious propaganda, which had been institutionalised in the Cheka (OGPU) since the revolution, had completely suppressed the administrative and legal methods of religious supervision.

The dissolution of the commission resulted in further centralisation in religious affairs, because the jurisdiction in question no longer lay with the republics, but rather with the union, and it has remained so up to the present.

The situation changed fundamentally in the course of the religious–political turn-around, which Stalin executed during the Second World War. In the Council of the National Commissariat under the direction of Georgi G. Karpov, a prominent functionary from the 'Church Department' of the NKVD, the 'Counsel for the Affairs of the Russian Orthodox Church' was created on 14 September 1943 and the Counsel for the Affairs of Religious Cults for the non-orthodox religious communities on 19 May 1944[8]. As before, the 'Commissions' had to control adherence to the cult legislation, to draft new religious laws from the government on command, and to decide on applications for the return of church buildings. But its main task now, as an institutional connection between the central state and party leadership and church administrations, consisted of providing smooth communication between the two sides, thereby securing the execution of the state's politics of religion.[9] In this, the stronger accent lay in co-operation.

Furthermore, the Councils were assigned the function of a neutral decision-making authority for the smoothing out of local disputes. 'The council takes measures for the elimination of abnormalities in the interrelation between congregations and clergymen on the one hand, and the local agencies of the Soviets on the other, when such abnormalities occur.[10] Analogous tasks were maintained by the 'authorised agents', who were under contract by the 'Councils' in the Cabinet Council of the Union and autonomous republics, as well as in the executive committee of the district and regional soviets.

The assignment of tasks of the two councils reflects the attempt, at that time predominant in religious politics, to keep the relationship of the regime, especially to the Russian Orthodox Church, as free of tension as possible. This course was basically to the benefit of the other, mainly national–religious communities[11]; yet there were exceptions in the phase of late Stalinism, namely, parallel to the Sovietising of the Baltic, the West Ukraine and East–Central Europe, the Catholic Church in the western regions of the USSR was exposed to administrative pressure, and, under the disguise of the fight against 'clerical–fascist' powers, to severe terror tactics and deportations[12]. The Jewish cultural community was also the victim of the strong repressive actions of a barely hidden anti-semitism.

When the party and state leadership announced its new ideological–political programme of the 'unfurled building up of communism' after the take-over in power of N.S. Khrushchev 1958–9, this step of massive re-ideologising of domestic politics brought with it a consequential change of course in religious politics as well – once again a period of intense anti-religious propaganda, administrative suppression and persecution of religious communities. This would also have an effect on the function and methods of the 'Councils' quite soon[13]. On 21 February 1960, the former NKVD functionary Karpov, who had done nothing to hinder a careful revolt by Patriarch Aleksii against the religio-political crackdown, was replaced by the party *apparatchik* Vladimir A. Kuroedov, who was supposed to have administered the state control of religion for the next quarter century from that time on[14]. Shortly thereafter the party and state leadership undertook significant changes in the main tasks of both 'councils':[15]

1 the consistent realization of the party line and of the Soviet state in terms of religion, the control over the correct application of the Soviet cult legislation through the central and local Soviet agencies as well as through the religious organizations;
2 the realization of the relationship between the government of the U.S.S.R. and the centers of religious organizations, the complete instruction and prompt informing of the Central Committee of the CPSU [!] and of the Soviet government about the activities of these organizations;
3 the enlistment of the religious organizations and their leading personalities in the fight for peace, in exposing anti-Soviet propaganda, which is being carried out in foreign states, as well as in the elucidation of Soviet cult legislation and the situation of religion in the U.S.S.R.

If the main function of the Religious Board of Control according to the statutes of 1943/4 had been to be an agency of assistance and mediation between the party leadership and the religious communities, the transformation of the once again decidedly anti-religious 'party line' and an administration of repressive religious legislation now stood in the foreground. Added to this was the instrumentalisation of foreign church relations for the propagandistic goals of Soviet foreign politics, particularly its misuse in covering up new religious persecution from the critical view of foreign countries, a dimension of Soviet religious politics, with origins reaching back to the Second World War.

The change of priorities in the function of the Councils was furthered by an increased centralisation in the state practice of religious control. Indeed, the instruction issued by the Councils on 16 March 1961 'on the application of the cult legislation', which deviated from the custom in legislative procedure, was handled and approved directly by the party and state leadership, and strengthened the jurisdiction rights of the Councils with respect to the executive committees of the local Soviets. The registration of the congregations, the withdrawal of registration, as well as the opening and closing of cult buildings was now bound to the specific agreement of the Councils. Apparently the Moscow headquarters wanted to have full control over the realisation of the new course of the lower levels on the bureaucracy.

In accordance with Khrushchev's favoured ideological concept of the mobilisation of social forces for the fulfilment of state tasks, in which one attempted not only to come closer to the elimination of religious attitudes, but especially to the 'dying away of the state', 'supervisory commissions for the enforcement of cult legislation' were set up within the framework of local Soviet executive committees[16]. They were supposed to research all evidence of religious life on location, to take statistical and cartographic surveys, as well as to submit suggestions to the political authorities as to how one could further limit the activities of the religious communities with the help of legal regulations. Because the commissions were mainly under the auspices of representatives of the (local) institutions of education, cultural and social organisations (*Komsomol*, trade unions, the *Znanie* society), and of the control and justice agencies, they were at the same time co-ordinating instruments of the city and district party leadership for the execution of their specific anti-religious operations.

Through the indiscriminately pursued persecution of all religious communities, the formal preferential treatment of the Russian Orthodox Church by the organisation of the Religious Board of Control became obsolete. Thus it followed that both Councils were combined to create the Council for Religious Affairs in the Cabinet Council of the USSR on 8 December 1965[17]. All important decision-

making functions were then transferred to this council at the expense of
the local administration; the authorisation of the local Soviets limited to
the control by observation of the congregations and the initial processing of applications, which had to be submitted particularly in the case
of the founding of religious societies. With this, the state special control
over religious communities reached a tentative high point of concentration and centralisation in terms of a development which ran almost
continuously from the time of the October Revolution.

The organisational structure of the Council for Religious Affairs

The execution of state jurisdiction in the area of religion and the church
through the authorities had no basis in the Stalin constitution of 1936.
It is legitimised today, however, by article 73 number 12 of the constitution of 10 July 1977, since it of course has to do with 'questions' which
'are of importance to the whole Union'.[18] The Council for Religious
Affairs does not have the status of a ministry, but is rather one of the
special councils at the level of a main administration with Union-wide
jurisdiction, which the cabinet council may institute according to
article 131 number 2 of the Union constitution. The chairman of the
Council, thus, does not belong to the cabinet council as a member, but
is subordinate, like a minister, to the chairmanship of the cabinet
council and ultimately to the Central Committee of the CPSU.

The organisational structure and work routine of the Council are
regulated by its (still) valid statute from 10 May 1966, so that one can
formulate a certain picture which, however, is not exact, owing to the
incomplete nature of those rules. As its title 'Soviet' already indicates,
the Council's members have equal say, in principle just as before, in the
Central Commission. The basic decisions are made and jointly accounted for in (plenary-) meetings.[19] The board (*kolegija*) consists of the
chairman of the Council, three vice-chairmen, as well as further members who are named upon recommendation of the chairman of the
cabinet council.[20] The chairman leads the selection procedure and the
internal course of business; he represents the Council to the outside, but
apparently he does not possess the authority to pass resolutions of
religious legal questions.

The administrative apparatus of the Council is divided into seven
departments:[21]

1 the department for the affairs of the Orthodox Churches;
2 the department for the affairs of the Islamic and Buddhist religions;

3 the department for the affairs of the Catholic, Protestant, and Armenian Churches, and of the Jewish Religion and Sects;
4 the department for international relations;
5 the legal department;
6 the accounting department;
7 the general department.

Thus, the apparatus is partly functionally determined; with this it follows the inherent rationality of the religious legal area of jurisdiction. The tasks of the 'general department' are not described in detail; yet one may assume on the basis of experience with the board structures and the organisational customs in the USSR, that it fills the function of a bureau of the chairman. Furthermore, it is responsible for the co-ordination of business, for personnel matters, and for the technical support of the board. And, finally, it may well be the most important crossing point between the Council and the Committee for State Security (KGB).

The department directors are to some extent simultaneously members of the Council.[22] In addition, by the authority of the office, the representatives of the Council in the Union republics belong to it as well.[23] It is not certain if all or only the representatives of the administrative councils of the (non-Russian) Union republics belong, which may be speculated in view of the federative structure of the country.

The Council maintains representatives not only in the administrative councils of the Union – and autonomous Republics, but also in the executive committees of the district and regional districts of the people's delegates. The representatives, thus, govern a quite extended geographic service area and find themselves therefore at a certain distance from the congregations. This has its reasons, because their main task is the control of the clergy (bishops, deacans, priests, pastors, mullahs etc.) as well as of the more important religious institutions (cloisters, enterprises, schools etc.), while the supervisory committees, which exist in the executive committees of the local Soviets, were devoted to the continuous control over the congregations. The council representatives take a certain double stance, because they are given the function of a liaison between the Moscow Central and the regional administrative officials as well. These have the exclusive right to suggest candidates for the occupation of related (*betreffenden*) positions, whose nomination follows then by the 'Council'.[24] The same is true for the release of representatives from service. They must therefore have the trust of the headquarters as well as of the region. The representatives are, of course, subject to the instructions of the 'Council' in their departmental tasks.[25] This means they are subordinate to its departmental control in terms of their personnel, service position. For their duties, however, they appear to be assigned to the various local administrative officials.

The tasks and methods of the religious agencies of control

a.   The ambivalence in the task assignment of the 'Council'

The legal description of the jurisdiction of the Council for Matters of Religion in the administrative council of the USSR showed a certain disagreement, even contradiction, which was almost typical for the control of religion in the Soviet state, and which gave it a deeply hypocritical tone. On one hand, the Statute of the 'Council' (Art. 2 and 3) conveyed the impression that state control of religion would serve only the 'lawfulness' within the country, in other words, the strict maintenance of the religious legislation by officials and citizens in the interest of a true freedom of conscience, and, furthermore, the juristic consultation of the Soviet government and other officials in religious questions, as well as the administrative support of the religious communities, namely in the sphere of international relations. On the other hand, the Council had the 'goal, to consistently [!] put the politics [!!] of the Soviet state into action in terms of the religions' according to Art. 1 of its statute. This means that the Council served, in the first place, as an administrative instrument of the repressive politics of church and religion of the communist party, a religious–political organ of the party and state leadership, and with this specifically partisan point of view, the Council had to look after each one of its individual jurisdictions. The main political goal was, until the collapse of the Soviet state in 1991, the suppression of and battle against the religions in the country. And the proper respectable and legitimate control of legality had to submit to this. Indeed, an opposition between the control of legality and the goal of suppression never really existed, because Soviet religious legislation so severely gagged the life of the religious communities, and conceded the state officials such unlimited decision-making authority in church affairs, that almost every arbitrary action could be justified and, as practice has shown, was justified.

However, after the well publicised meeting between the general secretary Gorbachev and the Holy Synod of the Russian Orthodox Church on 29 April 1988,[26] liberalisation gathered steam, leading ultimately to the passage in autumn 1990, of new religious legislation.[27] Early proof of this could be tentatively seen in the form of four drafts of the newly announced law on freedom of conscience and religion,[28] but also in the reality of numerous greater and lesser alleviations for the religious communities, as well as the altogether notably friendlier tone with which they have recently been publicly addressed. After 1986, the Council for Religious Affairs also changed its religious political practice under the leadership of Konstantin Kharchev, who had become the successor to Kuroedov at the end of 1984, a few months before Gorbachev's coming into power. This change came slowly at first, then with increasing openness and decisiveness, in step with the accelerated reform-politics. A tentative high point was seen in a published interview in the progressive magazine *Ogonëk* in November 1988, in which Kharchev settled accounts with the earlier religious policies with previously unknown and unprecedented severity on this subject, and supported radical changes.[29] His more liberal stance hit upon refusal and opposition, however, in the regional party and state apparatus, especially in the RSFSR and in the Ukraine. Apparently Kharchev had gone too far, because the ideological commission of the Central Committee of the CPSU opposed the legal model proposed by him in February. In May 1989 Kharchev was released from his post[30] and literally 'sent to the desert', namely placed as ambassador to Mauritania.[31] His successor was the former chairman of the national soviet in the Supreme Soviet of the USSR, Yuri N. Khristoradnov. It was not to be expected that the Council would steer an essentially different course under his direction, since the contents of religious policy apparently were steadily more strongly determined by the need for freedom of society which was increasingly and more pointedly being articulated.

In any case, it is clear in the meantime that the work of the Council for Religious Affairs since 1986 could not be judged in the same manner as before. The basis of the following characterisation is formed from previous practice which lasted decades, yet should be considered in contrast to the newer developments at the necessary points.

b. The tasks and methods of the 'Council' in Moscow

1. The relationship to the state security service (KGB)

The tasks to be fulfilled by the Council for Religious Affairs are usually summarised under the concept of control, which until now, however, could hardly be understood in the narrow sense of supervision of the religious communities, but rather in the sense of an active and intervening influence on their destinies with the goal of total control.

Here the task assignment of the Council differentiates itself from that of the state security service (KGB). The relationship of both institutions was extremely close from the very beginning, which is already shown in that the Council emerged in 1944/5 from the department of Churches of the NKVD.[32] When the KGB prepared operations in the realm of the churches, it might make use of the Council and the local authorities when it deemed it necessary. It is known that the KGB stood behind many religious operations of the agencies of control and the militia, through which religious events of citizens were more or less violently suppressed.

The state security service always occupied itself with two specific aspects with the religious communities: first it was responsible for the control and suppression of illegal, forbidden traditional sects which were actually, although secretly, in operation (for example, Jehovah's Witnesses), as well as schismatic separatists of the legal religious communities (for example, Reformed Baptists). Secondly, it tried to attract information from the clergy and other active members of the allowed churches in order to acquire its own picture of this sector of Soviet society, independent of the information of the Council and as true to reality as possible. This society has always been particularly problematic for the regime for ideological and political reasons. Thirdly, the KGB, as well as the Council, has defined its task in the intimidation of, and, when necessary, elimination of, successfully working clergy as well as dissidents appearing in the legal religious communities. Fourthly, the KGB tries to make useful the many sided foreign contacts of the religious communities for its operational tactics of disinformation, espionage, infiltration, counter-propaganda, etc.[33] Numerous departments within the fifth main administration occupy themselves with the mentioned tasks.[34]

2. *Continuing observation, inquiry, and inclusion of religious life*

Its statute created the misleading impression, that the Council for Religious Affairs only observed the religious communities to ascertain if they were following the cult legislation. In reality, however, its attention stretched to all religious happenings; it was comprehensive. This fact was proven most impressively in the report which the Council produced in 1975 on the condition of the Russian Orthodox Church for the attention of the Central Committee of the CPSU (Furov Report).[35] Several citations may illustrate this:

The synod stands under the control of the Council. Selection and placement of its permanent members remain as before in the hands of the council. Also the

candidacy of non-permanent members is previously agreed upon with the
leading collegues of the council. All questions which are up for discussion in
the Synod are discussed beforehand by Patriarch Pimen and the permanent
members of the Synod with the leadership of the council and its departments
... With steady, unrelenting attention the council and its local authorities
observe not only the members of the Synod and its activity, but also the wider
circle of the whole episcopate and its activity. No single ordination or transfer
of a bishop happens without a careful examination of the candidate by the
leading colleagues of the councils, whereby they stand in closest contact with
the authorities, the local state administration and other interested
organizations.[36]
With particular attention, the council observes the attitudes and the activities
of the bishops who actively appear in the country and look for opportunities to
secure the churches and their influence on the public.

These statements by the leadership of the 'Council' are also valid for
the other churches and religious communities which, like the Baptists,
were organisationally represented at the level of the Union. The
national religious communities in the non-Russian border republics
were also controlled by the authories of the Council.

In practice, the Council and its authorities developed various
methods of gaining information concerning the activities of the clergy
and religious institutions. The chairman and the leading colleagues of
the Council met regularly with the directors of the religious communities in order to be instructed on the current business agenda. Furthermore they set up, as they are so revealingly called in the Furov
Report, confidential contacts with individual church leaders. In addition, it became usual for the diocese bishops to look up the Council
during their yearly report with the Patriarchy. There they were questioned extensively about the atmosphere and situation in their official
region. Also, the authorities of the Council regularly summoned the
official leading clergy as well as the congregational clergy, a request
equal to an obligatory subpoena which a clergyman could hardly
refuse without punishment, considering the power-position of the
'Council'.

Since, of course, the authorities could only undertake a small part of
the control on their own, the observational activities carried out by the
'Commission for the Support of the Executive Commitee of the Soviets
of the People's Deputies in the Observation of the Legal Legislation on
Religious Cults' (as it has been called in its full description since 1966)
had notable value. Indeed, they were contracted to research: the forms
and methods of the activities of religious organisations, their influence
on the populace, especially on youth, the adaptation of the clergy to

the contemporary restrictions and their sermons; in other words every-thing which takes place in the realm of religion.[37] Here it once again becomes strikingly clear that the control of religious life by the state officials in the USSR was not a protection of rights, but rather a suppression of practised religion.

A further important source of information of the religious agencies of control flowed from the cult legislation which required that almost all religious activities which went beyond the usual services, namely personnel decisions, organisational actions, financial and economic intentions, and religious services outside of the cult building, obtain the agreement of the Council, its authorities. In order to do this, the requisite forms had to be submitted.[38] At once, these filed processes and materials formed the basis for the statistics of the Council, the tabulation of which was regulated with unusual detail by an order from 13 October 1968,[39] a fact in which one can see the weight the regime attributed to the quantitative aspects of religious life until its end in 1991. The religious organisations were statistically included, those legally allowed, as well as those just factually existing, as were their administrators and registered members, the super-regional church governing bodies and leadership ('clerical centres'), the clergy of all levels and degrees, the sacral buildings, the cloisters, pilgrimage locations, educational institutions, workshops and other religious establishments. Furthermore, in 1957 at the latest, the practice was begun *Extra legem* to count the most important religious official acts (baptisms/circumcisions, marriages, funerals) via state audit of church records, in order to ascertain the circle of faithful actually practising in the country.

Of course, the Council did not limit itself and its authorities to a purely numerical ascertainment of religious happenings, but rather they kept archives of this on file and kept especially a personal file on each clergyman corresponding to the cadre-file in the party–state realm.[40]

3. Active steering of the religious communities

At least beginning with the religious persecution under Khrushchev (1958–1964)[41] the religious board of control used the collected infor-mation only in order to influence and manipulate the fate of the religious communities much more effectively by active intervention in the interest of the communist system, as the state security service had also always done. The general goal stood unshakably solid through this gradual weakening and final destruction of the very organisation which alone removed itself from total, complete integration into the totalitarian ideological state. In this decisive point, a basic transformation of truly revolutionary quality could take place under the influence of Gorbachev's *perestroika*: namely, when the party and state recognised not only – agonisingly – the legality of the religious communities, but also their legitimacy. This means the unlimited right to existence of religion as an irrevocable dimension of human life. In the meantime there were a number of indications of such a change in attitude on an ideological level, among which the most important was probably the officially presented opinion that there was, for example, above all class-related political requisites, a level of general human values of universal validity, whose basis could be of a religious nature.[42] According to this tendency, religion would lose its political blemishes and gain recognition and a place on a common platform of philosophical–political co-existence of religious and nonreligious citizens. Now, with the collapse of the Soviet state, it is all the more conceivable that a new view of religion will be adopted with all the consequences entailed in such a change. A decisive measure for such a change is already contained in the contents of a law in writing on freedom of conscience and belief and, not lastly, the profile which the religious agencies of control will show in right and in practice in the future.

Because of their virtually unlimited position of power, the Council and its authorities have, in the course of the decades, developed and practised a number of forms and methods of steering and manipulating religious–church life. We are now relatively well informed about these, thanks to the religious samizdat. One can differentiate between two principal strategies: first, the immediate decision of religious questions by prohibitions, for example, in terms of certain religious services and other church events, or via orders as 'suggestions' with the practical effect of a command, as in personnel questions; second, the immediate steering of religious happenings through administrative pressure on the church leadership, in other words through the misuse of canonical power of jurisdiction and religious official authority for state purposes. Both procedures are characterised by a more or less far-reaching trespass, through a usurping extension of the legal authority of the religious board of control in the domain of religion.

This practice was facilitated and even encouraged by the aforementioned peculiarity of Soviet religious legislation, which allowed the state unusually far-reaching authority to help decide and intervene in the organisational, personnel, economic, financial, publishing, and other affairs of the religious communities from the start.

From the essence of control, however, it followed that the Council and its authorities might not become involved in every such case on their own initiative, but rather had to wait for the appropriate actions, applications, and forms from the side of the church. Especially they had to limit themselves in the denial or approval of church suggestions. Indeed, they also held to this procedure of belated investigation and sanction in innumerable cases. It does not take any special imagination to see that the Council could change to active directives quite easily. For example, when it could freely, and completely legally, refuse any candidate for a bishop's seat until a candidate more acceptable to itself was nominated, and it was only a question of economy of process when the Council immediately suggested its candidate itself, and this took place in practice in uncounted cases.[43] The border between a rather reactive, passive act of control and the active structuring of religious life was therefore vague. The two could not be separated because of the political assignment of the religious board of control. At the same time, it was part of the basics of Soviet propaganda, aimed at veiling reality especially in the realm of religion which was particularly critically observed from abroad, that the Council and its authorities usually justified their actions by citing 'violations of the cult legislation'. In practice it was therefore characteristic that the authorities and the local administrative officials only named the supposedly violated law, or factually substantiated the accusation concretely in exceptional cases. Normally they were satisfied with any all-inclusive allegation, which would forestall any unacceptable religious activity, because they were either not very familiar with the legal rules, or because they deemed it superfluous to justify their activities to religious citizens, owing to their superior position of power. The transition of legal control to active intervention in religious affairs was also made plain by the statute of the Council for the Affairs of the Religions, namely by the authorisation 'to give the religious organizations . . . binding direction in terms of the rectification of their violations'.[44]

The following overview concentrates on the second aspect of the active, operative manipulation, because it is particularly characteristic of the true manifestation of the religious agencies of control since the era of Khrushchev. Furthermore, relatively little attention has been devoted to this aspect in scholarly literature until now. Certainly, this was also the first sector from which the religious agencies of control were to retreat, as the contrasting liberalisation (since 1987/8) in the religious sphere unfolded.

The direct and indirect intervention in internal church affairs encompassed almost all areas of business, including so-called purely religious matters, which actually should be hermetically sealed off from the communist ideology. Especially the latter, however, emerges undisguised in cited passages of the Furov Report, that namely the Council 'strives for agreement on the final decisions of the Holy Synod' beforehand. Interventions in the realm of religious services often had the character of prohibition, or had to do with certain irritating hindrances in the execution of events. Experience sums itself up in the following overview:

1. The religious officials were bindingly instructed to register their official actions on certain forms, whereby the applicant – in the case of a baptism it had to be both parents – had to submit their identification cards. This registration practice was introduced in the second half of the 1950s via verbal direction, in order to keep non-conclusive material on the methods of the officials with their expected negative propagandistic results from the public eye.[45] The insights available to the state by way of church records formed a basis for a massive administrative and propagandistic atheist pressure on the citizens in question, especially at their place of work. In time this lever had a planned prohibitive effect on citizens participating in religious ceremonies and openly practising their beliefs. In the meantime the practice of registration is supposed to have been stopped, although whether everywhere or only in the jurisdictions of those where more liberal conditions had already been introduced, such as in the Baltic states, cannot yet be judged.

2. The restrictive regimentation of religious ceremonies was sharpened through internal church regulation in many aspects on the suggestion of the Council. A memo from the Patriarchate on 22 December 1964 ordered all church leaders in the Moscow diocese to undertake baptisms only in churches and only after the completion of documents by the parish congregational administration.[46] The authorities repeatedly affirmed the prohibition of baptism on weekdays.[47]

3. The sermon, as a part of the religious service, was in itself free from (pre-) censor; yet the religious board of control continually took steps to suppress, or at least to neutralise, this legal remainder of religious propaganda. In terms of the Orthodox churches, one had little trouble with this since the sermon traditionally plays a subordinate role in the religious service. Clergy who were especially beloved, such as Dmitri Dud'ko or Vsevolod Spiller, were soon the victims of official intrigues. Here the church leadership placed themselves in the service of the state political censorship by their repeated warnings to the clergy for self-censorship. In the memo of the Metropolitan Seraphim of Kruticy and Kolomna, which he sent to the clergy of the

Moscow diocese on 14 December 1974, it was stated: 'If priests hold sermons, these sermons must be strictly orthodox in their contents, may only include explanation of the gospel being preached or epistles of the Apostles in the essence of their meaning by the holy fathers and teachers of the church. The sermons may not include any political or social problems or examples.'[48]

4. A commonly used means of inhibiting the execution of church services was the closing of a church building because of supposedly necessary repair measures, without the provision of a suitable alternative meeting place for the congregation, and without the actual fulfilment of any repairs. Contrarily, in most cases, and here the arbitrariness and cynicism of the religious agencies of control becomes especially apparent, religious organisations were forbidden from renovating their church buildings, rented from the state, apparently to dissuade a greater attraction of the people to the church. It was made impossible for the congregations to fulfil their contractual duty to care for the state property for which they were responsible.[49]

5. Within the framework of the strategy followed by Council, and in order to reduce the number of clergy, the religious board of control adopted a whole bundle of restrictive measures, at the head a drastic limitation of the seats of study at the few still allowed religious teaching institutions. In part, the authorities obliged the bishops to report the names of applicants for theological studies. In order to prevent an unwanted enrolment on an individual basis, the applicant would then be summoned to military service or not dismissed from military conscription, retained at work or receive no permission to live at the site of his studies;[50] in part, as a prerequisite to a successful application (on the side of the church) a formal permission to study was also required from the 'Council's' representative in the jurisdiction in which the applicant lived. Since the graduates of religious educational establishments cannot by far fill the need for priests,[51] the bishops have ordained increasingly more interested laymen since the 70s. Directives from the Soviet authorities were specifically aimed at this practice, to ordain as few priests as possible and, if necessary, then candidates from the diocese. To some extent they even issued prohibitions to this effect.[52] Since most study applicants came from the western part of the Ukraine, the Council and the local authorities in Ukraine took particularly restrictive measures.[53] On the initiative of the Council, the Moscow Patriarchate made the entrance to monk-status more difficult in that it forbade the ordination of monks for persons under the age of 30.[54]

6. The suppression of the recruitment of clerical trainees continued

with strict supervision of, and influence on, the teaching practices in educational establishments. In the Furov Report it was stated in summary with a welcome openness:[55]

The council asserts its influence on the many areas of activity of the religious educational establishments, supported by the rectors. It tries to teach their students patriotism and love of the soviet homeland. The forms and methods of our influence are multifaceted: assistance with the selection and employment of leading administrative personnel and the academic staff of the religious educational establishments, supervision of the educational materials on the constitution of the U.S.S.R. at seminaries and academies, introduction of a course on the history of the U.S.S.R., completion of the cultural and educational measures, supervision of the educational materials for some church subjects according to the interest of the state. It is understood that all of this takes place at the hand of the men of the Church themselves.

The Soviet state maintained influence particularly in the subject of 'moral theory', in the curriculum of which the main topic of Soviet ideology was worked into ethics, by 'suggestion' of the Council.

7. Overall the Council and its authorities viewed the ominous education of the clergy toward patriotism as a major task, although they were in no way authorised to do so by law. The goal of these efforts was not exclusively loyalty towards the regime – that was not enough for the state – but rather the voluntary, unconditional, active support of the internal and external political objectives of the Soviet Union. Since the destruction of the religious communities until now was a partial goal of domestic politics, the result of this 'educational work' boiled down to the cynical attempt to make the clergy step by step into compliant 'atheists in vestments'. The language of the Furov Report was completely submerged in this nonsense: 'One could prove with many examples how the bishops are led to lessen their religious activities through continuous political work with them.'[56]

While the episcopate, in other words, the leading representatives of the religious communities, were being directly 'educated' by the Council, the education of the theological students and the congregational clergy was left in the hands of the authorities:[57]

With the help of local state officials, the authorities of the council carry out systematically political work on the teachers and students of the religious educational establishments in that they hold personal and confidential conversations with them, they help the directors of the schools with the selection of lecturers or films or organize other cultural and educational measures on a broader basis.

Lectures and instruction by the authorities themselves were included in this.[58] They especially used the yearly gathering of the current clergy for this, who were, for a while, completely under the influence of political indoctrination.[59]

8. The personnel–political goal of a resigned, compliant clergy resulted in many cases in the authorities holding their hands protectively over such religious functionaries who, through their personal lives or administration, had disqualified themselves. Meanwhile, they made sure that respected and spiritually successful priests and bishops were harassed, replaced, dealt disciplinary measures or even driven from their professions. Here, the methods of the Council regularly followed this pattern: first one submitted the duties of a new clergyman (bishop, priest, presbyter, mullah etc.) to an exhaustive observation, then the authorities invited him to a conference in which they would charge him with one or another 'violation of the law', seriously warn him and request that he curb his activities. The regional authorities of the KGB would also be informed of this. If the warned clergyman did not fulfil expectations, the council authorities would compose a report for the Moscow central office, in which it would disparage the clergyman as a disruptive 'man of the church', who was trying to get around the laws on religion and would refuse co-operation with the authories. Then the Council would summon the wrong-doer to a conference. If this was also unsuccessful, they would request that the church leadership take appropriate measures against the recalcitrant clergyman. In the Russian Orthodox churches this usually led to transfer to another diocese, where the game could perhaps repeat itself. If the religious office-bearer found himself in the files of the state security service because of some political incident, his out-of-court disciplining was directed by the KGB.[60]

9. The state's removal of the clergy from the parish councils in 1961, and their restriction to strictly sacerdotal functions seriously weakened the churches, undermining the effectiveness of the clergy. Parallel to the exclusion of the clergy from the financial administration, the authorities went further to force the local religious organisations to make supposedly voluntary monetary contributions to a continually increasing degree to the quasi-state peace fund and other funds.[61] The contribution levels rose in time to 30 or even 40 per cent of the yearly income of a congregation. This means, in a sentence, a rate which in many cases threatened the coverage of the running expenditures of the congregation, especially for adequate upkeep of the church.

The exclusion of the clergy from the parish council and from the general congregational administration was reversed in the summer of

1988, when the Russian Orthodox Church received permission from the Council for the Affairs of the Religions to lift the statute of 1961 and put a new church statute into power (comp. Church Statute, Section VIII, point 9ff(?).). This happened on 8 June 1988 through the regional council, which was allowed to take place in celebration of the christianisation of the Kiev Rus'.[62] With this, one of the main causes of the notable disintegration of the structures of the religious communities was eliminated.

10. The Council found itself in a particularly close relationship with the publication organ of the religious communities, because it played the role of a special censor in the religious realm next to the general central censor Glavit. The Furov Report explains:[63]

All materials intended for publication in this journal [meaning the *Journal of the Moscow Patriarchate* – O.L.] are edited carefully by the leading co-workers and some members of the council . . . Often one comes upon a manuscript among the texts to be printed which is not in the interest of the state and the religious followers and does not contribute to a high civic consciousness and patriotic characteristics in the reader or which finds itself in contradiction to the norms of Soviet cult-legislation. Therefore, whenever the printing of an edition of the 'JMP' or another publication of the patriarchy [e.g. Church calendar, message of the patriarch or similar texts] is impending, the Council edits the text and provides observations and corrections, which the editor or the responsible editorial secretary of the 'JMP' then properly adopts.

How strong this censorship of the Council was, and how it was carried out in detail, we know quite exactly from the deacon Vladimir Stepanov, who worked in the publications department of the Moscow Patriarchate until 1981.[64] According to his report, the Council would obtain the printing proof, for example of the September edition of the *Journal of the Moscow Patriarchate*, at the latest by the 20th of the previous month, and would screen it within a week. Objections were related to every theme and aspect. Above all stood the goal to allow only a minimum of substantial information about the inner-church situation to go through. Furthermore they attempted to weaken characterisations of church and Christian life which might serve as models by stylistic levelling and deletions, and in general to remove as much as possible all information and pictures which could improve the vitality and effectiveness of the religious communities in the Soviet state.

The Council also crossed over to operative, active production of publications in its censorship. Stepanov writes:[65] 'The Council for Religious Affairs do not just give this or that "editorial" suggestion. It determined eventually also the entire construction of the magazine, in which the actual church historical happenings were allowed only a third of the total space. Everything else is peace politics, oecumenical. The space of the article which the church uses has to be bought with the space that the state uses.'

4. On the discussion on the new organisation of the religious agencies of control

On the basis of the regional practice of the state in terms of the religious communities, which has become more liberal on the whole although to different degrees, and also on the basis of existing drafts of a law on the freedom of conscience, one could assume that the number of cases, in which the religious communities need the permission of the state ('registrations', 'confirmations' etc.) in order to act legally would become noticeably fewer. The result of this was that the religious agencies of control would lose a considerable part of their previous position of power. The loss of power would become even greater if – as it is demanded from various sides – the denial of a registration, for example as a religious organisation, could be challenged in court. As a result of this, the reform of the religious legislation was forcibly joined to the question of which duties the religious agencies of control would have in the future and how it should be organised. The fact that this question was being answered differently by the noted legislative drafts, indicates that this was one of the most debated problems of the reform. There were also indications that this point of disagreement played a role in the fall of Konstantin Kharchev.

The first legislative draft, which became known in the summer of 1988, assumed the continuing existence of the Council for Religious Affairs and its continuing association with the Council Ministries of the USSR. The legal scholar Rosenbaum had another new higher-ranking agency in mind, however:[66]

The specialized state control over attention to legislation on the freedom of conscience as well as the decision of other questions, which are tied to the realization of the right of citizens to freedom of conscience, are carried over to the All-union State Committee of the USSR for Questions of Religion, which is to be constructed from the presidium of the Supreme Soviet of the USSR in the proceedings of Article 122 of the constitution of the USSR, and which takes effect on the basis of a regulation to be validated by the Council of Ministers of the USSR.

The committee, as the author commented in his suggestion, should be in charge on site of locally independent responsible authorities who would be only subordinate to the central authorities and to raise the control 'to a qualitatively new level'. The promotion of the religious board of control to the level of a ministry, their resulting higher authority as well as the stronger independence, was supposed to lead to a better guarantee of freedom of conscience and religion than before, according to Rosenbaum.

Apparently Rosenbaum was able to achieve a certain effect with his ideas, since Kharchev moved in the same direction in his spectacular *Ogonëk* interview in November of 1988; indeed, he went even further:[67]

The Council for Religious Affairs will also probably change in the Council of Ministries. I see it in the role of a permanently active commission in the presidium of the Supreme Soviet of the USSR. Such commissions could also be formed in the Union Republics. From an administrative agency, which the Council for Religious Affairs now is, it changes into an agency of common power, whose decisions must be binding for all in a legal state.

Apparently Kharchev wanted to upgrade his board to a parliamentary control agency via the executive, in the area of religion and church, with which, of course, a certain change of function towards a more obvious accentuation of a legal guarantee of religious freedom was to be tied. Unmistakably, he tied his suggestion to the 'Central Permanent Commission in the Presidium of the VCIK', in other words, to the construction of religious control in the early 30s.[68]

The second more official legal draft published by Kharchev soon thereafter did not maintain the suggestion, but also does not further refer to the Council, but rather only generally to the 'Agency of the USSR for Religious Affairs'.[69] The question remained thus unanswered. In the third legal draft from the Council which became known in the West at the end of September there were also no changes.[70] It is therefore rather probable that decision on the organisational reconstruction of the religious agencies of control and the determination of its tasks will be made in a further special law.

Postscript

The law finally passed by the Supreme Soviet of the USSR on 10 October 1990 'on freedom of belief and religious organisations'[71] solved the controversy over the way in which state control of religious communities should be organised. In principle it held to the previously existing 'Council for Religious Affairs in the Ministerial Council of the USSR', but provided for its transformation into a representative, consultative, and communicative agency of the Union government. This change in function seemed logical, since the 'Council' largely lost its previous power of authority and voice over religious organisations through the new law. Even so, the new delineation of its jurisdiction was not unproblematic. Article 29 shows this. It reads:

The State Council of the USSR for Religious Affairs is a centre for information, consultation and experts. In this function it
– maintains contacts and co-ordinates relationships to the analogous institutions in the Union and autonomous republics;
– founds a council of experts made up of theologians, representatives of religious organisations and specialists on questions of human rights to carry out theological judgements and gives an official position on requests from agencies of the state administration and from the court when necessary;
– co-operates upon request of religious organisations in reaching agreements with state organs and provides the necessary help in questions which require the decision of a state agency;
– facilitates the securing of mutual understanding and tolerance between religious organisations of different persuasion within the country and abroad.
The state agency of the USSR for Religious Affairs is formed by the Ministerial Council of the USSR.

At first glance, and especially under the impression of the sorrowful experiences with the religious control in the Soviet state, the reader may be inclined to consider the cited description of tasks to be harmless and to greet them without reservation. Upon closer and more critical inspection, a number of questions and objections appear, in light of which the reorganisation of the state control seemed dubious.

The following aspects should be considered:
First, it is highly questionable if the necessity exists for 'co-ordination' of work, also for the provided state religious agencies. Since the religious communities are mostly nationally defined and distributed, their 'natural' partners are the state officials in the respective Union and autonomous Republics. Furthermore, it was unclear what is meant by 'co-ordination' and which rights this designation gave to the renewed 'Council'? To judge by language usage and government practice, co-ordination certainly includes a certain administrative power of direction over the co-ordinating agency.

Secondly, more than a doubt existed that the 'Council for Religious Affairs of the Ministerial Council of the USSR' could be the appropriate institution to function as an 'expert centre', whether for questions of rights or for theological judgements. The 'Council' had been, and was still, factually subordinate to the ideological functionaries of the Central Committee of the Communist Party; at the same time it had had the character, both in terms of function and personnel, of a branch of the state security apparatus, the KGB. Ruled by the directives, administrative and political handicaps, of that power apparatus, and without a recognisable identity itself, it had played a key role in the operative fight against religious citizens and their communities since its founding in 1943/4. As an institution, the 'Council' was thus fully compromised. It did not outwardly possess the authority required of a board of experts of the intended model and would not be able to obtain it for this and other reasons. The popular cry for 'human rights' and legal protection seemed truly shabby and sounded more like mockery in light of decades of arbitrary practice on the part of the 'Council'.

Thirdly, there was no apparent need for an additional, special transmission partner between the state, i.e. the Union, and the religious communities. Legal questions which arise in the practices of church life, for example in the context of building plans or educational measures, have to be decided by the authorised official according to their individual measures which are domain-specific. The maxim of equal treatment is valid here, although it is open to modification according to subject – in such cases sacral specifics, but not so that such difficult problems are brought out that a special board would have to be called in.

Fourthly, and contrarily, the transformation of the 'Council' into a state co-ordination agency carried the danger, in light of its past, that the other state agencies – form-building to financial agencies – as before were politically equal on the basis of a unified 'religious policy' and were consistently directed in terms of their administrative practice. This may take place today in favour of the religious communities, which is the defence of the official proponents of this solution, but it is in the nature of things and is also a real experience out of the history since 1917, that the course of 'religious politics' can alter itself. Representatives of the 'Council' basically verify this evaluation themselves when they prove the fundamental nature and irreversibility of the reorganisation of the relationship between state and church not with legal arguments, but rather in reference to the above mentioned top-level meeting between Gorbachev and the leadership of the Russian Orthodox Church. The future of Russia apparently holds no place for a state 'religious policy', should the state–church relationship be truly legally systematised, in other words, on the basis of a reformed constitutional system of government. A continuation of the 'Council' would rather endanger such a change in paradigm in established church law from politics to law.

Fifth, the institution of a state 'data bank' for information from the realm of religious communities arouses considerable doubts. A certain contradiction immediately appears here, because, in contrast to this, the law empowered a prohibition which originated personally from Lenin in underlining the maxim 'religion is a private affair', that in official documents no reference to religious affiliation is allowed (Art. 4 Sect. 1 USSR law). If one takes into consideration that, in the past, especially since the fifties, the early determination of religious 'data protection' in Soviet law was systematically violated or avoided, and that the state pursued the forced atheisation of the populace for decades under the slogan of 'individual work with believers', in other words with airing and violation of religious secrets, strong distrust was in order for a plan which would build up a data central of the Union with information from the realm of the religious communities.

In light of the battle of the Union 1989–90, represented by party and state leader Gorbachev and the cabinet president Ryzkov, and the battle of the federal organs for survival in general, and the Cabinet Council of the USSR for the smallest loss of control to the republics, one can understand the decision of religious law to allow the 'Council' to continue to exist in modified form as an attempt to 'save' as much control and political influence for the ruling centralised, conservative powers in the Central Committee and Cabinet Council bureaucracy, and also in the politically less important, but highly sensitive area of 'religious policy' and of state church law as is possible in consideration of the covetousness of the republics.

In contrast to such attempts, the former Soviet Republics are going their own way in the question of state control over religious communities. There, where the democratic powers have been able to advance themselves recently, the will to break with the unfortunate past of special board of control for religion rules. An especially impressive example in this respect was the law passed by the 'highest' Soviet of the Russian Federation on 25 October 1990 'on the freedom of religion',[72] because it forbids without hesitation special state control agencies over the religious communities. The pertinent Art. 8 Para. 1 Sect. 2 determines:

'On the territory of the Russian Federation, no sovereign agencies of the state power or government offices may be set up, which are specifically for deciding questions tied to the realisation of the rights of citizens to religious beliefs.' Art.11 Sect.1 transfered control of the adherence to religious legislation from the Soviets and justice agencies and also added in support (Sect. 2): 'The realisation of state control through other state agencies, political parties or official persons is forbidden.' This addition is potent in that it forbids, for example, the previously obligatory involvement and inclusion of the KGB, in other words, of the Communist Party, in the 'control' of religious communities with the inclusion of 'other state agencies' and 'political parties'!

The Russian Federation did not, however, completely refrain from a special agency in the governmental realm. Not yet provided for in the legal draft of the authorised parliamentary board of the Russian Federation, and probably developed in contrast to (and neutralising!) the transformation of the 'Council for Religious Affairs' of the Soviet Union, the Russian Federation law (Art. 12) provided for the establishment of a committee of experts which, however, would differ considerably from the 'Council' in terms of its constellation, as well as in its institutional connections and its tasks:

The consultative council of experts of the board of the 'highest' Soviet of the Russian Federation (!) for questions of freedom of conscience, of religious belief, of compassion and charity is formed from representatives of religious organisations, social organisations, state agencies, theologians, lawyers and other specialists in the realm of freedom of conscience and of religious belief. The composition of the council is verified by the presidium of the 'highest' Soviet of the Russian Federation on the recommendation of the 'highest' Soviet of the Russian Federation for questions of freedom of conscience, of religious belief, compassion and charity.
The consultative board of experts

> founds a data bank on religious organizations which are registered in the Russian Republic, as also in terms of the fulfilment of legislation on freedom of religious belief;
> advises the board of the 'highest' Soviet of the Russian Federation on questions pertaining to freedom of belief, of religious confession, of compassion and charity;
> administers legal and theological verdicts and takes official positions on inquiries from the side of agencies of state administration and the courts.

In that this council of experts is conceived as an agency assisting the parliament, pluralistically constructed and not provided with any administrative function, the above mentioned concerns, especially about the installation of a data bank, do not apply to it in the same measure as the future 'Council on Religious Affairs'. The Russian Federation law furthermore solves the problem of control over adherence to religious legislation by the religious communities in a manner typical of a constitutional state, namely through the judicial system.

The Latvian Republic has also gone its own way in its law 'on religious organisations' of 11 September 1990.[73] It provides for the foundation of a 'Consultative Council for Religious Affairs' in the 'highest' Soviet of Latvia, in which every legally recognised religion or faith in Latvia delegates a representative (Art. 2 Para. 3). Subordinate to the Consultative Council is the 'Department for Religious Affairs' formed by the government of the Republic (Art. 2 Para. 4). It has the task on one hand, to provide help upon request by the religious communities 'in organisational, legal, social, economic, and other questions', and on the other hand, to represent the government *vis-à-vis* the religious communities (Art. 2 Para. 2). The 'Department' is also responsible for the registration of religious organisations, but is subject thereby to judicial control (Art. 5 Para. 6). It cannot itself administer the dissolution of a religious organisation which has violated the law, but rather must bring it before the court (Art. 11 Para. 2).

Also this construction of the organisational relationship between state and church is harmless from the standpoint of human rights and the constitutional state.

The question remains open, however, if such decisions in the religious laws of the Republics which contradict the religious laws of the Soviet Union will hold up, and if Moscow will succeed in the power struggle with the Republics in reinstating the now practically destroyed administrative control over religious communities.

Translated from German by Margaret Brown

Notes

1 For the history of the religious agencies of control in the USSR see Otto Luchterhandt, *Der Sowjetstaat und die Russisch–Orthodoxe Kirche* (Cologne, Verlag Wissenschaft und Politik 1976), p. 32, 37–8, 56ff, 85ff, 100ff, 132, 212ff.

2 *Voprosy istorii religii i ateizma*, 5 (1958), p. 20.

3 Cf. P.V. Giduljanov, *Cerkov' i gosudarstvo po zakonoda–tel'stvu RSFSR*, (Moscow, Gosizdat, 1923), p. 3.

4 Cf. the Report of Activities of the 5th Department for 1923, Revojucija i Cerkov' 1924, No. 1–2, S. 111.

5 See note 2.

6 See especially Bohdan R. Bociuriw, 'Church–State Relations in the USSR', in M. Hayward and W.C. Fletcher (eds.), *Religion and the Soviet State: A Dilemma of Power*, (London, 1969), S. 80ff.

7 Details in Luchterhandt, *Der Sowjetstaat* (note 1), p. 85–8.

8 V.A. Kuroedov, 'Iz istorii vzaimootnosenij gosudarstva i cerkvi', in *Voprosy istorii* (1973) 9, p. 15–31.

9 V.D. Bonc-Bruevic, 'Svoboda sovesti v SSSR' (1957), in his *Izbrannye socinenija*, I, (Moscow: 1959), p. 73–89 (87).

10 Bonc-Bruevic, *ibid.*

11 Cf. G. Karpov's speech at the Council of Bishops on 24 November 1944, Text: Patriarch Sergij i ego duchovnoe nasledstvo, Moscow, 1947, p. 309.

12 See V. Stanley Vardys, *The Catholic Church, Dissent and Nationality in Soviet Lithuania*, (New York: Boulder, 1978), p. 62ff, 74ff.

13 In further detail, Otto Luchterhand, *Die Religionsgesetzgebung der Sowjetunion*, (Berlin (West): Berlin Publishing House, 1978), p. 24ff.

14 Kuroedov had background in history and pedogogy and was, furthermore, the party secretary in the Sverdlovsk region. See *Kommunist* (1954), Nr. 18, p. 53.

15 Joint resolution of the CC of the CPSU and the cabinet council of the USSR 'on the strengthening of control of the adherance to the cult legislation' of early 1961. The resolution was not published. Proof of, and excerpts from, it are found in the report of the chairman of the Council for the Affairs of the Religious Cults, A.A. Puzin, given on 5 February 1964, at a conference of Central Asian ideology functionaries on 'the Soviet cult legislation and the tasks towards strengthening of control on their realization'. The text is also not published, but came to the West as a type-copy and in an edition in the institute 'Glaube in der 2. Welt', available through Zollikon/Schweiz; Manuscript, p. 74.

16 Details in Luchterhandt, *Der Sowjetstaat* (note 1), p. 220.

17 This took place via a decree of the Council of Ministers. Cf. *Sobranie Postanovlenij SSSR*, 1965, No. 25, Art. 221.

18 The change of constitution on December 1, 1988 has not (yet) touched the division of jurisdiction between the Union and the Republics. This is reserved for the expected further revisions of the Union constitution in 1990. In light of the almost thoroughly national character of the religious communities in the Soviet state, the release of jurisdiction by the Union to the republics would be in order, since this situation already existed until 1936. The current work on a (unified) Union law on freedom of conscience, belief and religious organisations certainly stands in the way of the possibility of such a development. Even if the law in its final version should stay so brief and fragmentary, as is expected considering the already existing drafts, the Union republics will have notable latitude for individual, even more liberal religious legislation.

19 Cf. the formulation in Art. 7 of the Statute of 10 May 1966, Text: V.A. Kuroedov/A.S. Pankratov, *Zakonodatel' stvo o religioznych kul' tach Sbornik materialov i dokumentov*, 2nd edn, Moscow 1971, p. 78–83.

20 Art. 6 of the Statute.

21 Cf. the ordinance of the Council of Ministers of the USSR on the structure and the personnel positions of the central apparatus of the Council for Religious Affairs of 17 March 1966, Text: Kuroedov/Pankratov (note 19), p. 83.

22 For example, the leader of the Orthodox department, Michajlov; contrarily, the leader of the legal department, Tatjana Belokobylskaja.

23 Cf. Art. 6 of the Statute.

24 Cf. Art. 8 of the Statute.

25 Art. 8 Part 1 of the Statute.

26 *Pravda*, 30 April 1988.

27 See from the numerous materials just: Gosudarstvo i cerkov': God soglasija, in: *Izvestiia*, 29 April 1989, p. 3.

28 From the Council for Religious Affairs, three drafts have become known so far. The first was published in the summer of 1988 in *Samizdat* (see *Russkaia Mysl'* (22 July 1988) p. 5), the second was officially relinquished to the church leadership for comment in February 1989 and published (see *Russkaia Mysl'*, 7 April 1989); The third draft of the Council, which contains several meaningful improvements over the previous ones (division of the state and atheism; legal protection of rights in religious affairs), became known in the West at the end of September 1989 (see *Rukaia Mysl'*, 29 September 1989, p. 5). In addition, the leading Soviet specialist for religious legislation, the lawyer Yuri A. Rozenbaum, published a proposal worked out by himself on the request of the government parallel to the second draft of the Council (February 1989). See *Sovetskoe Gosudarstvo i Pravo* (1989), No. 2, p. 91–8.

29 *Ogonёk* (1988), 50, p. 2–4.

30 See Lutherische Welt-Information 1989, No. 25, p. 9, *Glaube in der 2 Welt* (Zollikon/Schweiz) 1989, 7/8, p. 9.

31 Konstantin Kharchev had held a position in diplomatic service before his transfer to the Council, namely as ambassador to Guyana.

32 See the text in note (4) as well as Astrid von Borcke, *KGB. Die Nacht im Untergrund*, (Neuhausen-Stuttgart: Hänssler-Verlag 1987), p. 116.

33 See Borcke, *KGB. Die Nacht* 110ff.

34 John Barron, *KGB. Arbeit und Organisation Des sowjetischen Geheimdienstes im Ost and West*, (Bern/Munich: Scherz 1974), p. 99; 114.

35 'Iz otceta Soveta po delam religii – cleman CK KPSS', Text: *Le Messager – Vestnik Russkogo Chrisianskogo Dvizenija* (Paris: 1979), 4:130, p. 275–344; *Der Stand der russischen orthodoxen Kirche*, Verlag Glaube in der 2. Welt, Zollikon 1980.

36 The KGB is meant here especially.

37 Cf. Art. 5. lit.c of the model regulations of the Commissions from 26 November 1966, Text: Kuroedov and Pankratov, *Zakonodatel' stvo* (note 19), p. 161–4.

38 In detail, Luchterhandt, *Die Religionsgesetzgebung* (note 13), p. 46ff.

39 Briefing on the statistical inclusion of the religious organisations, the churches and church buildings as well as the proceedings in the registration of the executive organ of the religious organizations and church servants, Text: Kuroedov and Pankratov, *Zakonodatel' stvo* (note 19), p. 133–49.

40 Cf. Art. 15 lit.d of the briefing of 1968.

41 Bishop Feodosii of Poltava and Kremenchuk points out in his complaint to Brezhnev on 26 October 1977 that the authorities of the Council had behaved correctly until then. Text: *Glaube in der 2. Welt* (Zollikon/Schweiz) 1982, No. 2, p. 57–75.

42 See the editorial article 'Socializm i Religiia', in: *Kommunist* (1988), no. 5; M.S. Gorbachev in his address in his meeting with the Holy Synod of the Russian Orthodox Church in: *Pravda*, April 30, 1988, p. 2; furthermore, Yu. Karlov, Nravstvennost' v mirovoj politike, in *Mezhdunarodnaia Zizn'* (1988), No. 4, p. 3ff.

43 See also the above mentioned citations from the Furov Report in note 35.

44 Art. 4 lit.b.

45 Petition of the priests N. Esliman and G. Yakunin to Patriarch Aleksii, Text: *Grani*, 61 (1966), p. 181; V. Spiller, in: *Istina* 1965/66, p. 494, Petition of the bishops Feodosii of Poltava and Kremenchuk to Brezhnev (1977), Text: *Glaube in der 2. Welt*, 1982, 2, p. 71f.

46 Text (proof) in A. Krasnov-Levitin, *Bol' naja Cerkov'*, p. 9/10.

47 Furov Report (note 35), p. 7.

48 Text: *Glaube in der 2. Welt*, 1976, 7/8, S. 58–60 (60).

49 Petition of Bishop Feodosii (note 41), p. 59ff.

50 Bishop Feodosii, p. 67f.

51 Cf. the numbers in the Furov Report (note 35), p. 14f; 25ff.

52 Bishop Feodosii, (note 41), p. 68f.

53 Bishop Feodosii; Furov Report, p. 26.

54 Furov Report, p. 45.

55 *Ibid.*, p. 27.

56 *Ibid.*, p. 4.

57 *Ibid.*, p. 28.

58 Bishop Feodosii (note 41), p. 68.

59 See the report on the conference in 1985 in Rostov on the Don, in: *Glaube in der 2. Welt* (1986), 5, p. 10.

60 The open letter of the monks deacon is revealing in this aspect, V. Chaj-bulin, to the Arch bishop of Vladimir and Suzdal' on 23 November 1975, Text: *Glaube in der 2. Welt* (1976), 7/8, p. 49ff.

61 To the application bishop Feodosii, petition (note 410), p. 65f.

62 Text of the statute: *Religion in der UdSSR*, Monatsbulletin der Presseagen-tur Nowosti (1988), No. 9.

63 Cf. note 35, p. 33.

64 V. Stepanov, 'Zur gegwärtigen Lage in der Russisch–Orthodoxen Kirche', in: Glaube in der 2. Welt 1983, 5, p. 20ff, 22ff.

65 *Ibid.*, p. 25.

66 Art. 11 part. 2.

67 *Ogonëk* 1988, No. 50, p. 3–5 (5).

68 Cf. above in note 7.

69 Art. 25.

70 *Russkaja Mysl'* 29 September 1989, p. 5.

71 Vedomosti S'ezda Narodnikh Deputatov i Verkhovnogo Soveta SSSR (1990), no. 41, Article 816.

72 *Sovetskaia Rossiia* (10 November 1990), p. 5.

73 *Ibid.* (3 October 1990), p. 2.

4

Some reflections about religious policy under Kharchev

JANE ELLIS

We learned more during 1989 about the processes governing the formulation of religious policy in the USSR than for decades previously. A number of frank statements in sections of the Soviet press, above all those by Konstantin Kharchev, the former chairman (until June 1989) of the Council for Religious Affairs under the Council of Ministers of the USSR (CRA) provided an insight into the numbers of party and government bodies involved with religious policy and the rivalries which beset them. In fact, so far as the available evidence suggests, this has always been the case throughout the Soviet period. Policy on religion (as on other matters) appears to have evolved through the intervention of bodies with different interests, through factional struggle and through personal conviction, rather than from any clear, consistent policy developed by the CPSU. Trotsky in the early 1920s and Khrushchev in the early 1960s are both examples of the latter factor, as Philip Walters suggests in his chapter (pp. 9–11, 19–20). The infighting and obstructiveness revealed by Kharchev simply means that, in the age of *glasnost*, such struggles can no longer take place entirely behind closed doors.

Kharchev's disclosures came chiefly in a series of three increasingly frank interviews in the weekly magazine *Ogonëk* with journalist Aleksandr Nezhny, who made no secret of his own sympathy for the rights of believers. It transpired that Kharchev gave the first of these interviews, in May 1988, when he already knew that his position at the CRA was in jeopardy because of the opposition he was encountering from other bodies. Having been appointed to his post in December 1984, i.e. several months before Mikhail Gorbachev came to power, Kharchev initially maintained the status quo where religious policy was concerned. He made no concessions to religious believers, and did not hinder attempts by state and party to curb their influence, just as his predecessors had done.

What caused Kharchev to change his stance and begin making increasingly positive statements about the valued role of believers, particularly the Russian Orthodox Church, in rebuilding Soviet society, is still not entirely clear. Since the chairmanship of the CRA has never been a particularly prestigious post, and does not have ministerial rank, it was at first assumed that he was carrying out the behest of some higher-placed, but unknown, functionary or functionaries. Kharchev's own version of events, however, which eventually emerged in his third *Ogonëk* interview, cast himself in the role of a crusader against entrenched bureaucratic interests. Moreover, in a conference speech in London in July 1989, he spoke of his change of heart in terms almost of a Damascus Road experience.[1] While allowance must be made for self-justification and for a rather bombastic personality, it still seems that there may be some truth in this view.

I propose to return later in this chapter to the workings of the bureaucratic machinery involved in religious policy at the present time, as revealed by Kharchev and others. While this cannot hope to be either a conclusive or comprehensive survey, given the extreme fluidity of the present situation in the USSR, it will at least indicate how these matters have been arranged, or have evolved, in the recent past. It is of interest that neither of the two chapters in this book which might perhaps have been expected to reveal the means by which Soviet religious policy is, or has been, developed has in fact been able to do so to any great extent. Both Philip Walters's chapter on 'A Survey of Soviet Religious Policy' and Sabrina Ramet's chapter on 'Religious Policy in the Era of Gorbachev' have turned out to be chronicles of events rather than detailed analyses of who was responsible for any given turn of events. This is not a criticism: Walters in particular attempts to supply reasons for the fluctuations in policy on religion and to link them to the overall political situation and the ascendancy of one or another individual or school of thought. The point I am making is that for most of the Soviet period, information about precisely which bodies were involved in decisions on religious policy is lacking, as is evidence of the mechanisms by which they operated and the precise reasons why one point of view prevailed over another.

An important consideration here is that policy on religion has never been in the forefront of policy-makers' minds. It has always been a matter of secondary concern – if that – dependent upon larger political, economic, and ideological decisions. This continues to be true even today, despite the much higher profile of religion generally in the

Soviet Union, when the adoption of a new law on religion was long postponed due, in part surely, to the overwhelming problems of the nationalities and the economy.

Ramet helpfully identifies four phases in religious policy under Gorbachev, (pp. 33–38), but without suggesting underlying causes or specific decisions which may have led from one phase to another. It is entirely possible that there were no such specific decisions, and that the opening up of religious freedom may be attributed to the fact that Gorbachev's policy of *glasnost* has gathered speed under its own momentum: the point is that we do not know for certain which is the case. Ramet, in fact, traces change in religious policy to *ad hoc* adjustments. She is undoubtedly right to conclude that the Russian Orthodox Church has benefited far more than any other religious body from the change in religious policy under Gorbachev – especially in the early phases – a point to which I shall return below. Her suggestion that Gorbachev's aim was to obtain 'a partial legitimation of Soviet rule' (pp. 32 and 47) is sound, although, as she herself suggests, even that aim must now be called into question.

Returning to the more immediate question of how religious policy is decided upon at the present time, we find that statements by Kharchev and others throw some light upon the matter. They also indicate how officials concerned with religion began to take a more realistic view of the matter from the first part of 1988 and how this impinged upon Gorbachev's meeting with Russian Orthodox leaders in April 1988. In the first of his three *Ogonëk* interviews,[2] Konstantin Kharchev gave an estimate of 70 million believers in the USSR as a whole. This amounted to virtually a quarter of the entire Soviet population and was a significant admission, since previous spokesmen had always (in the teeth of such evidence as was available) claimed that believers numbered little more than 10–20 per cent of the population and that they were mostly elderly. Kharchev's statement was the first sign that the Soviet authorities were now prepared to acknowledge that believers were a significant sector of the population and, consequently, influential.

This statement should be put in context: it came as preparations for the celebration of the Millennium of Christianity in Russia, Ukraine and Belorussia were imminent. Preparations for this momentous event had begun five years earlier among the Soviet ideological apparatus. A distinct two-pronged approach was adopted.[3] While government officials made it clear that the church was free to celebrate its anniversary without hindrance – since it enjoyed full freedom of religion – they also made it clear that it was a matter of no interest to the Soviet population at large. Simultaneously, ideological workers systematically attempted to undermine any claims the church might make to have had a significant influence in Kievan Rus' and its descendants in terms of either history, culture or morality. There were even strong attacks on the church's role from some quarters, suggesting that it had had a negative influence, and might even have had a detrimental effect on a healthy pre-Christian culture.[4]

As Ramet has already noted in her chapter, this line began to change as the millennium celebrations approached, and the notion became current that the Orthodox Church had played a healthy role that was beneficial to Russian history and culture.[5] Gorbachev's meeting with Orthodox leaders in April 1988 was the confirmation of this, a confirmation which it would have been difficult to go back on subsequently. The Millennium celebrations in June and July were covered extensively in the Soviet press and television, and from then on reference to the church's contribution to national life became routine in sections of the Soviet press, notably the government newspaper *Izvestiya*. By the latter part of 1989 it was not unusual to find statements by Orthodox leaders and events in the church's life featured even in the section of the paper headed 'Official Reports', normally devoted to governmental and inter-governmental meetings.[6]

There was an obvious pragmatic motive for the change in attitude to religion, particularly to Orthodoxy. That was that Gorbachev, desperately needing the support of the bulk of the Soviet population to force through his reforms, could not afford to ignore such a numerous population sector. He had already begun to win a little goodwill from some believers, for example by his strong anti-alcoholism campaign (even though this subsequently foundered). By making such public concessions, he was clearly hoping for their votes to follow.

Kharchev pursued this line in his first *Ogonëk* interview by suggesting that a new policy should be devised to stop the growing number of believers from becoming hostile to the state. He suggested a policy of toleration and co-operation, in line with Leninist principles. These principles, he said, included legal-representation (right of juridical personality) for the churches; the right to teach religion to children in a private capacity; the publication of more Bibles and scriptural texts; and a more active church role in charitable work.

At about the same time, however, Kharchev gave a private lecture to the Higher Party School in Moscow which put a very different gloss on these statements.[7] Though he proposed the same changes, the reasons he gave for them were very different. To take one example, he said that a reason for allowing churches a more active role in charitable work was that the state was simply not in a position to refuse such offers of help in hospitals and homes for the elderly – in Moscow alone the state had a shortfall of 20,000 ancillary hospital staff. 'If the believers want to carry bed-pans, let them.' Having admitted to *Ogonëk* that the CRA was receiving delegations from all over the USSR demanding the return of their churches, Kharchev told the Party School that the return of ancient monuments to the church had advantages for the state, which would no longer be responsible for their upkeep. He also claimed that the party had a duty to formulate a more coherent policy on the churches, and to play a role in the appointment of church personnel: 'The appointment and placing of Orthodox priests is a matter for the party.' Kharchev pointed to past success in state manipulation of church personnel: 'It is in the appointment of Orthodox bishops and clergy that the party has had the greatest success.'

During his tenure of office Kharchev made a number of trips abroad, including to the USA and UK, during which he energetically promoted the view that the USSR was moving towards religious freedom. This was a part of the larger campaign that the Soviet Union undertook after Gorbachev came to power to improve its image in the world at large and to demonstrate that it was moving towards greater freedom of speech and of belief. For example, on a visit to Coventry, England, in November 1988, Kharchev told his audience that: 'The present stage of *perestroika* in the relationship between church and state clearly shows practical measures to rectify the mistakes of the past ...'[8] However, he began to gain a reputation for making rather sweeping, poorly thought-out statements, and also for making promises that he did not, or could not, keep, as when he promised, during a visit to the USA, that all religious prisoners of conscience would be freed before the end of the year.[9] Whether this was part of the USSR's image-building policy which proved impossible to implement, or whether Kharchev himself was attempting to put pressure on bureaucrats back home to fall in with what may have been his own ideas, has not subsequently been clarified.

Kharchev's second interview with Aleksandr Nezhny was published in *Ogonëk* in December 1988.[10] He went much further than he – or indeed any other official Soviet spokesman – had ever gone before in terms of admitting past and current mistakes and proposing changes in religious policy for the future. A recurring theme in the interview was the obstructive behaviour of local officials, opponents of *perestroika*, who, Kharchev claimed, were acting against the law. Kharchev said he was in favour of greater freedom of activity for believers, for example, in opening churches, publishing of Bibles and other books and in other areas. He also said he envisaged a diminished role for the CRA in future.

Kharchev began by claiming that there had been a 'breakthrough' in the opening of new churches: in 1987, 16 new Orthodox churches had been registered, and in 1988, 'more than 500'. However, he conceded that there were still not sufficient churches, and worship buildings for all religions, everywhere. He gave, unprompted, an example of villagers in Podgaichiki, Terebovlya district, Ternopil region in Ukraine, who were refused permission to register a church by local officials, whom Kharchev named. The chairman of the Ukrainian CRA, N. Kolesnik, 'who ought to have explained to these comrades that they were violating Soviet legislation, authenticated their refusal with his signature'. The villagers then had to travel to Moscow to seek justice. Kharchev called this a 'most harmful and dangerous thing for our *perestroika*' when 'local leaders . . . provoke people to travel to Moscow'.

At this point the reader might have expected Kharchev to provide a 'happy ending' and relate that the believers' problems were over once they turned to his office in Moscow. In fact, he did not give the ending to this particular story but continued: 'And what if a person can't find support in Moscow either? What if here too he comes up against a bureaucrat, an indifferent executive, a cold functionary? All this happens! Then he'll return and say to the people at home: there is no justice, don't look for it.'

Kharchev claimed that in 1988 the CRA had reversed eighty-three refusals by local authorities to register religious societies. He went on: 'Regional and republican leaders telephoned me, asking: on what basis did you do this? I replied: on the basis of the law. But some responsible comrades still have fresh in their memories the times of "rule by telephone", the times when you could close a church and disband a religious society by one telephone call.'

The interviewer, Aleksandr Nezhny, then referred to a number of repressive acts against the Russian Orthodox Church that took place in the years immediately following the 1917 Revolution including the killing of Metropolitan Vladimir of Kiev in 1918, the execution of Metropolitan Veniamin of Petrograd in 1922, and the wrongful accusation that the church had refused to surrender its valuables to help victims of the 1921 famine. The dates were significant since they were all in the period when Lenin was in power. Discussion about rehabilitating victims of repression in the Soviet press at that stage had related only to the Stalin and post-Stalin period. Publication of

Nezhny's comments was a sign that rehabilitation of victims of repression during the period when Lenin was in power might be under consideration, though Lenin himself had not been named in that context.

Kharchev's response to this was that the chief thing was to reform the 1929 Law on Religious Associations 'as quickly as possible'. He noted that although the 1929 law had not been repealed, it was being disregarded in practice. He cited as an example charitable work being carried out by Seventh-Day Adventists, Baptist and Orthodox, which was still technically illegal. But he recognised that 'we must change at the root the norms defining the life and activity of the church and believers in our state'. Concerning the Law on Freedom of Conscience which was to replace the 1929 legislation, Kharchev said that a draft should be submitted 'for the judgement of the entire people'. The bodies involved in producing a draft had consulted representatives of religious organisations of 'practically all confessions'. Kharchev suggested impatience when he said that the examination of proposals 'had been rather drawn out'.

Nezhny quoted two biblical commandments which Soviet Christians could not fully obey within the law: 'Love your neighbour as yourself' and 'Go into all the world and preach the Gospel to the whole of creation.' Kharchev agreed with the implications of this as expounded by Nezhny. He accepted Nezhny's point that believers, through taxation, were in effect paying for anti-religious propaganda. Article 52 of the Constitution should be amended 'to offer equal rights to both atheists and believers'.

Kharchev then mentioned that education was a key question for believers and that while religion – specifically, Orthodox doctrine – would not be taught in schools, private religious education should be permitted. He said that churches should have full right to juridical personality. He also said the church should have its own printing press and print far more Bibles than at present. He agreed that Bibles and works of the Church Fathers and of theology could be published by the state publishing houses Nauka (Science) and Mysl (Thought).

Kharchev even questioned whether registration of churches in its then form would continue to be necessary at all. 'If you gather together with your comrades and sing songs, no-one will threaten you. But if you all pray together, without receiving special permission – expect trouble.' The principle of requiring permission for registration should be abandoned, Kharchev asserted, and if it were, there would be no further need for the local commissioners (*upolnomochennye*) of the CRA. Their role should be taken over by the local Soviets of Peoples'

Deputies, who would arbitrate in any conflicts. Kharchev envisaged that the CRA itself would then become a different kind of body.

What was striking about the comments and proposals Kharchev made in this interview was that if they came into force, believers would have gained most of what they had been campaigning for over the last twenty-five years or more. All of the points he and Nezhny raised had appeared time and time again in *samizdat* appeals and open letters, and many of their authors had been imprisoned as a consequence. (This should not however be taken to imply that church activists necessarily accepted all Kharchev's statements at face value. A group of Orthodox activists who met him in his office shortly after the interview was published, on 12 January 1989, said that while he made plenty of calls for co-operation and expressions of good will, typical of the Soviet leadership of that time, there was a dearth of concrete acts to back them up.)[11]

A notable feature of Kharchev's interview was that, although he was discussing matters of concern to all churches and religions, he referred predominantly to the Russian Orthodox Church. Nearly all his examples concerned Russian Orthodoxy, and other churches were mentioned only briefly in passing. The striking photographs accompanying the interview were all of Russian Orthodox believers. Other outstanding questions, such as the legalisation of outlawed religious groups, notably the Ukrainian Catholic Church, were not mentioned. This suggested that some special or leading role might be being envisaged for the Russian Orthodox Church, and subsequent developments bore this out.

During spring 1989 rumours circulated for several weeks that Kharchev had been, or was about to be, relieved of his post. Visitors to the CRA office or enquirers by telephone were told that he was 'ill' or 'recovering from an operation'. Finally it was confirmed that he had been dismissed in June.

In July 1989, Kharchev gave a paper at a conference in London, England, to which he had been invited while still in office.[12] He began by asserting that his transfer from the CRA was an entirely routine matter. He had not been given a reason for his transfer, but then he had not been given a reason when he was appointed to the CRA either. He had had talks at the highest level and the work of the CRA had been evaluated positively. Positive results had been achieved in one of the most complex areas of *perestroika*. His transfer in no way meant a change in policy, nor a reversal of *perestroika* in church–state relations. He had been assigned to the Ministry of Foreign Affairs where he had worked previously, as ambassador to Guyana and was awaiting an

ambassadorial posting (though not to the United Arab Emirates as
announced on the conference programme).

Kharchev noted that when he had been appointed to the CRA, a
western radio station had reported that 'Konstantin Kharchev, a
party bureaucrat with higher education credentials and experience as
an ambassador, had been appointed to this post in order to suppress
religion.' Four years later the comments were quite different:
'Kharchev achieved positive results during the democratic transformation in relations between church and state.' When he had arrived at
the CRA, church–state relations had been in a crisis situation. The
crisis was deep and dangerous and affected the party. Old thinking,
pre-*perestroika* thinking, prevailed: according to it, 'the church and
communism were irreconcilable enemies'. Kharchev admitted that at
that time he shared these ideas, but when he came up against reality in
a religious setting, he found that what he had thought was wrong. He
met many thousands of believers, lay-people and priests, not only in
the USSR, but also abroad. These meetings convinced him that the
distortion of Marxist–Leninist thinking on religion, which had
occurred after Lenin, was wrong. The distortions had been introduced
by the party bureaucratic machine, by Stalin and by stagnation, which
had lasted for decades. He experienced a crisis of consciousness and
did not know how to approach his work. Then *perestroika* began. It did
not begin at the same time everywhere; it began in the church at the
end of 1985 and beginning of 1986. Its architect was Gorbachev.
Kharchev said that it was not only his own ideas that had changed,
but also those of the party, especially Gorbachev. The chief architect
does not design every single room of a house, but his ideas are put into
practice by others.

Describing *perestroika* as a 'human struggle' in which he, like others,
had made mistakes, Kharchev said it was a mistake to think in terms
of supporters and opponents of *perestroika*. That was 'old thinking',
dividing people into friends and enemies. Only by co-operation could
religion and atheism both make progress. Kharchev had come to the
conclusion that if religious teaching helped to unite people, to help
them live in this hard world, then it was a teaching which communists
must peacefully accept. The leaders of *perestroika* were now able to put
humanitarian questions in first place, even above class questions,
which would have been heresy four years ago.

Summarising achievements to date, Kharchev first noted that they
had changed the moral climate in the Soviet Union where the church
was concerned. The attitude towards believers was now normal, non-
hostile. Accompanying Kharchev at the conference was Mikhail

Kulakov, leader of the Seventh-Day Adventist Church in the USSR, who said at this point that he was no longer ashamed to say anywhere in the USSR that he was a believer: moreover, people now respected him. This was a new experience for him, as previously he had been told that only communists have high ideals. Kharchev, resuming his speech, said that believers could have the highest human qualities.

Kharchev asked rhetorically what was best for the leader of a country – a citizen who believed in something or one who believed in nothing at all? He himself preferred someone who believed in some set of values. In its struggle against belief, the party had achieved *bezdukhovnost* (dearth of spirituality) and had brought about the person who believed in nothing. 'Which is better for the Soviet Union, the person who believes in Jesus Christ or the person who believes in nothing? My answer is, the believer.'

A second achievement to which Kharchev pointed was the strengthening of the material base of the church, without which no doctrine had the means to influence the masses. Churches, monasteries and seminaries had been opened, Bibles were no longer forbidden; though things were still far from perfect.

A third step forward was the concept of a law-based state. Having studied the 1929 law carefully on coming to the CRA, he had found it to be undemocratic. The secret instructions on religion had been abolished. The new law had been worked on for four years, and the most important points it would include were the right of a church to juridical personality; the freedom to teach religion; and the registration of churches no longer to require permission. Some proposals in the draft law were already being carried out in practice, notably charitable work.

In conclusion, Kharchev referred to Gorbachev's concept of the common European home: 'How can there be a home without icons?'

This address was given at an invitation-only conference and was not widely reported. One article which did appear in the British church press[13] was later to be picked up by a Soviet newspaper, but the English translation was not published in the US Seventh-Day Adventist magazine until the beginning of 1990.[14] The force with which Kharchev had expressed his change of heart was therefore limited to a relatively narrow audience.

All the more striking then, for most readers, were the lengths to which Kharchev went in his third *Ogonëk* interview in October 1989.[15] In it he explained how members of the Ideological Department of the Central Committee of the CPSU had thwarted his attempts to introduce new thinking into Soviet policy on religion, and how he was ousted from his post at the CRA. He claimed, however, that Mikhail Gorbachev showed some support for his proposals. He also claimed that leading hierarchs of the Russian Orthodox Church had complained about him to the Supreme Soviet behind his back (rumours to this effect had by then already been circulating for some months).

Kharchev agreed with his interviewer – again Aleksandr Nezhny – that at first he had followed the policy of his predecessors at the CRA, namely 'total subjugation of church to state'. But when he began to demand that the authorities should 'keep the law' in their dealings with believers, i.e. the 1929 Law on Religious Associations, there was a strong negative reaction from regional party chiefs, who began to put pressure on the party *apparat* in Moscow. He then clashed with the two or three people within the Ideology Department responsible for religious policy. He said that the personnel there had not changed as a result of *perestroika*.

This was the first time that the role of the Ideology Department in formulating religious policy had been made public so explicitly. Its involvement had, of course, been suspected beforehand – it was inconceivable that it would not have any involvement in the field of religious policy – but its key role was now being spelt out by Kharchev.

Kharchev went on to refer to KGB influence in church affairs. He said that initially he had good relations 'with "the neighbours" (as we call the KGB)' but now believed that the 'state surveillance of religion' was a part of the administrative system, which must be 'decisively dismantled' if the church was to be freed from 'every kind of interference from outside'. The widely suspected KGB interference in church affairs had not been commented on publicly so frankly before, apart from a somewhat ambiguous reference by Boris Yeltsin earlier in the year. Yeltsin has criticised KGB interference in religion during the Supreme Soviet's confirmation hearings for ministerial posts, including that of Chairman of the KGB. He said:

serious changes were needed in the attitude of the KGB toward the church. A very democratic process is underway in our country, and attitudes toward the church are changing among the political leadership and in society in general. State security services must seriously restructure their attitude, and perhaps cease completely busying themselves with the church as an independent organisation . . . In short, find another way to deal with it.[16]

Kharchev told Nezhny that his ideas for celebrating the Millennium of the church the previous year had met with strong resistance from *apparatchiks*. Also a Politburo member had opposed his idea of building a cathedral in Moscow to commemorate the occasion: 'A new church? What for? Let them build churches in Poland, but we won't.' However, Kharchev continued: 'In the end we succeeded in bringing our proposals to Mikhail Sergeyevich Gorbachev', who 'valued their political and moral significance'. Following this, Gorbachev met Patriarch Pimen and members of the Holy Synod at the patriarch's request, which 'went a long way towards defining policy on the church'. Gorbachev was the only person Kharchev mentioned as expressing any support for his ideas.

Kharchev was clearly trying to suggest that he had support at the top and was thwarted only by lower-level *apparatchiks*. He made a similar point later in the interview with regard to the long-delayed new law on religion, which he said had had to be referred to the Ideology Department before going to the Supreme Soviet as originally planned. While there was no doubt an element of self-justification here, the basic thesis was valid.

Kharchev described how he had had to tackle problems with his own deputies at the CRA. One of them, dissatisfied with Kharchev's 'principles and methods', informed the Propaganda Department of the Central Committee of his 'errors' – without telling Kharchev. This led the head of the department, Sklyarov, to recommend to the Secretariat of the CC that Kharchev be relieved of his post, but the Secretariat did not support the recommendation. Kharchev also proposed, in line with *perestroika*, that the CRA staff be reduced by 10 per cent, including the dismissal of two of his three deputies. A decision to this effect was signed by the Prime Minister, Nikolai Ryzhkov, at the end of 1988, Kharchev claimed, but it was never implemented.

Kharchev asserted that an attempt had been made to smear him by a rumour that he had furnished his flat at the expense of the church. He had, however, kept the documents which proved that his furniture was acquired legally.

By far the strangest revelation in this interview was the reason for his dismissal, which Kharchev said had been given to him by a member of the Politburo: he 'had not found a common language with the ideological *apparat*, the "neighbours" and the leadership of the Russian Orthodox Church'. The Politburo member's concern over good relations between the CRA and the Orthodox leaders would have been unheard-of not long before, and might be taken to imply genuine concern for the welfare of the church in the new era of *perestroika*, but linking them with the other two bodies mentioned tends to undermine this assumption. The inclusion of the third element in this unholy trinity, however, might have come as more of a surprise had it not

been for the persistent reports from a number of sources, referred to
above, that Orthodox hierarchs had complained at the highest level
about Kharchev's interference in church affairs. The linking by the
Politburo member of church leaders and the KGB suggests a proxim-
ity of attitudes that would bear-out longstanding allegations of close
contacts between the two.

Kharchev stated that some members of the Holy Synod visited the
Supreme Soviet to complain about his interference in church affairs.
(It must be remembered that while this would have been an unthink-
able initiative in the past, the new Supreme Soviet had been recently
elected by the newly elected Congress of Peoples' Deputies, which
included two members of the Holy Synod, Patriarch Pimen and
Metropolitan Aleksii of Leningrad, as well as another senior hierarch,
Metropolitan Pitirim of Volokolamsk.) Kharchev attributed this
action principally to 'the growing power struggle within the leadership
of the church'. Whereas in the past this might have been taken as a
smear on the church by a state spokesman, it now rang true. This was
partly because the elderly patriarch had been ill for some time and was
not expected to live long, so that there was a struggle over the question
of his successor, and partly because the allegation was supported by
other sources within the church.

Kharchev stated: 'I suspect that some members of the Synod, from
force of habit, have counted more on the support of the authorities
than on their own authority in the church.' Again, this could have
sounded like a slur, but in fact this view to a large extent coincided
with the comments of church activists, who have been publicly com-
plaining for the last three decades about the subservient attitude of
church leaders to the state.

Perhaps the most curious fact about this third interview is that it
was given at all. Kharchev had been reassigned to the diplomatic
service and was awaiting an ambassadorial posting and there would
seem to be no reason for him to comment on issues concerned with his
previous job. Here, as well as at the London conference, he was at
pains to point out that he had changed his viewpoint on religion, while
remaining 'a communist' and 'a convionced materialist'. He said that
he had begun to read the Bible for the first time while at the CRA, and
that it and the Koran had given him 'an exceptionally great deal'. The
most likely explanation for the interview is that, as a declared
supporter of *perestroika*, Kharchev was ready to ally himself with other
pro-*perestroika* forces – such as *Ogonëk* and Nezhny, not to mention
Gorbachev himself – against the *apparatchiks* who opposed it.

Kharchev had actually named the officials who opposed him during the course of his interview with Nezhny, but these were cut from the published version in *Ogonëk*. This was at the time when Gorbachev had just summoned the editors of a number of leading newspapers and journals and warned them that some of them were pushing the limits of *glasnost* too far. There followed an attempt by Ideology chief Vadim Medvedev to sack the editor of the hugely popular *Argumenty i fakty*. Nezhny, however, subsequently revealed the names, in an interview with Radio Liberty, as follows:

> The Politburo member who gave Kharchev the reason for his dismissal was Vadim Medvedev, chairman of the Ideology Commission. Kharchev said in the interview that he had had two conversations lasting up to one and a half hours with him.
> It was also Medvedev who ordered cuts to be made in the published interview. He reportedly said there would be 'great difficulties' for *Ogonëk* if the names were published.
> The Politburo member who opposed building a cathedral to commemorate the Millennium was Yegor Ligachev, widely regarded as the leader of the conservatives in the Politburo.

Observers in the west suggest that he was unable to carry many of them with him, despite his enthusiasm and his (latterly) positive attitude to church–state relations. His performance did not match up to his capacity to analyse problems, which he did in a way fully in accord with *perestroika*.

A particular irony is the role apparently played by the Russian Orthodox leadership in his downfall. Kharchev had been instrumental in helping to give their church a higher profile and a greater role in the country's life than at any time in the entire Soviet era. It is possible that their opposition to him came about because he was pushing them to take greater advantage of the church's new opportunities than their background, experience, and hardly learned caution had prepared them for. It is also likely that they may have resented his agreeing to meet independent church activists, who had long been a thorn in their flesh through their public criticisms of the inactivity of the church leadership. In a strongly hierarchical church, they would inevitably see this as a diminution of their authority. It is noteworthy that Kharchev's recommendations for specific changes coincided to a large extent with the reforms for which church dissidents had been calling for so long, as noted above, but there is no reason to suppose that church hierarchs would object to these particular changes. Some of them had been working behind the scenes for the same ends, and, once *glasnost* was well under way, began to refer to the desired changes publicly. And Kharchev's analysis of the church's problems did not need to be especially penetrating – the major areas of unfreedom the church suffered were glaringly obvious to any unprejudiced observer.

It came as no surprise that members of the conservative establishment whom Kharchev had attacked so strongly retaliated in similar terms. A swinging attack on his purported claim to be a 'champion of religious freedom' was published by a Professor A. Ipatov[17]. He maintained that Kharchev was cashing in on changes which were already underway in order to enhance his reputation. He also strongly defended the leadership of the Russian Orthodox Church.

The article began, unusually, with a quotation from an article in the *Church Times*, published in London, which described the conference the previous July, at which Kharchev had been presented with an award for his services to religious liberty. Ipatov's article was entitled 'Will He Go Down in History as "Saint Konstantin"?', a reference to a comment during the conference that Kharchev had opened so many churches in the USSR that he should be named 'Saint Konstantin'.

Ipatov disputes Kharchev's claim that he was responsible for having the Millennium of Christianity in 1988 celebrated at a national, as opposed to purely church, level – and cites a signed statement by Kharchev in October 1987 in support of his argument. He also supports the move by the Holy Synod of the Orthodox Church to go to the Supreme Soviet to complain about Kharchev's interference in church affairs. Ipatov said this was done with the blessing of the patriarch, whereas Kharchev had said it was done without his knowledge. Ipatov also strongly criticised Kharchev for talking about a leadership struggle at the top of the Orthodox Church in the lifetime of an existing patriarch, and for proposing methods to elect his successor.

Ipatov had a theory as to why Kharchev had divulged to *Ogonëk* his 'sensational revelations' which 'have attracted the attention of many readers'. Kharchev, as noted, had returned to the diplomatic service to await an ambassadorial assignment and Ipatov suggested that: 'The ex-chairman [of the CRA] probably feels that he is about to become an ex-ambassador and therefore [the *Ogonëk* interview] can provide a full explanation for this: he criticised the *apparat* so his appointment to a leading position is being dragged out.' Possibly Ipatov was more prescient than he realised: Kharchev was not given an ambassadorship until October 1990 (to the United Arab Emirates).

Ipatov appeared to be motivated chiefly by concern for the Russian Orthodox leadership: he mentioned no other denominations. However, some of his assertions were dubious. For example, he claimed that Kharchev insisted on the appointment of a layman as deputy chairman of the Economic Management of the Moscow Patriarchate when this post should be occupied by a bishop, but this claim by Ipatov cannot be substantiated. In claiming that Kharchev wished to reorganise the Holy Synod, Ipatov ignored assertions by Kharchev and others that there had been serious financial mismanagement – even though this issue was discussed in the Church Times article from which he quoted.[18] In defending the leadership, Ipatov was forced to ignore the critical voices within the church.

A more substantial attack followed in the pages of *Ogonëk* itself.[19] Its author was Aleksandr Degtaryev, first deputy director of the Ideological Department of the CPSU Central Committee – the body Kharchev had indicated to be his chief source of opposition. Degtaryev accused Kharchev of 'insufficient competence and lightweight irresponsibility decked out in the vocabulary of *perestroika*' and pointed out that he had had no interest in religion before taking up his post at the CRA. In particular, he criticised two speeches Kharchev had made. The first of these was the speech referred to above (page 4) to a closed gathering of the Higher Party School in Moscow in March 1988, which, as Degtaryev notes, was leaked to the West and published in a number of papers there. Degtaryev quoted a number of statements by Kharchev with which he strongly disagreed, notably that selecting and placing candidates for the priesthood was a matter for the party. He also noted the comment of a journalist in *Le Monde* that the Soviet authorities did not contradict Kharchev's assertion.

The second speech Degtaryev criticised was made to the Academy of Social Sciences in December 1988. Here, he claims, Kharchev defended his record regarding the failure of an 'economic experiment' in the form of a church bee-keeping co-operative in Siberia. Admitting that it had not gone according to plan, Kharchev allegedly said: 'So what? After all, it's the church's money.'

Referring to the 'unprecedented' appeal of the Holy Synod to the Supreme Soviet concerning Kharchev's interference in church affairs, Degtaryev claimed that any priest or believer would consider Kharchev's remarks in his *Ogonëk* interview 'blasphemous' and 'unpardonable interference in the internal afairs of the church'. Degtaryev said this had not been the first complaint by church leaders: Lithuanian Catholic bishops had complained about Kharchev's treatment of them in May 1988 and of two Muslim leaders in April 1988. The latter had objected to Kharchev's plan of setting up an information and analysis department within the CRA, financed by Muslim funds. Degtaryev also said that between 1985 and 1988 some employees of the CRA were paid out of 'several tens of thousands of roubles at the expense of the department of international contacts of one of the denominations'. Also, church funds had been used for generous gifts to foreign delegations and even subscriptions to periodicals for the CRA.

Degtaryev claimed that Kharchev changed members of church delegations meeting foreign religious organisations and even headed a Muslim delegation to Democratic Yemen. This behaviour had caused concern among religious leaders in several countries.

Degtaryev criticised Kharchev and Nezhny for suggesting that Kharchev's proposal to disband the CRA altogether was part of the struggle against bureaucracy. In fact, he said, Kharchev had proposed replacing it with a State Commission for the affairs of believers and religious associations – in effect, giving himself ministerial rank. He also dismissed Kharchev's attempts to reduce the number of CRA deputy chairmen from two to one, claiming that Kharchev was simply trying to get rid of two of his persistent critics.

In conclusion, Degtaryev said that Kharchev suffered from a 'lack of theoretical preparedness, of sufficiently deep understanding of processes taking place in the religious sphere, of know-how in organising the work of the CRA' and 'impulsiveness, inconsistency, ambition'. He said that both the Central Committee's Propaganda Department and then, in December 1988, its Ideological Department, recommended leadership changes in the CRA, but they were not upheld. It was only after the complaint by the Russian Orthodox leaders that he was removed, proving, Degtaryev claimed, that the bureaucracy did not win 'a victory', as Kharchev had claimed, but rather suffered a defeat, since church leaders had been successful where they had failed.

Sourly noting that Kharchev had made a 'soft landing' and was drawing an ambassador's salary while awaiting a posting, Degtaryev ended his article somewhat oddly: 'God is his judge!'

While there was no doubt some substance in many of Degtaryev's allegations, his main motive seemed to be to quash a continuing source of embarrassment to the party. It is impossible to establish the veracity of the various allegations and counter-allegations, and pointless even to try to do so when the parties concerned are more interested in defending their positions and reputations than in an objective search for the truth. But it is worth noting that the allegations of financial mismanagement, both by Kharchev against the Moscow Patriarchate and by Degtaryev against Kharchev, are a key matter in the whole affair. While the truth may never come out, we should note that the 'root of all evil' has been playing a significant role in the matter of church–state relations. However, for Degtaryev to have raised allegations of serious financial mismanagement by Kharchev at such a late stage was curious, since Kharchev had claimed in his third interview with Nezhny that the party had earlier been seeking ways to compromise him financially (over the matter of his furniture). Why should the party have tried that kind of smear tactic if there were financial irregularities within the CRA for which they could have censured Kharchev? Finally, Degtaryev's admission that the Orthodox leaders had succeeded in having Kharchev removed where two departments of the Central Committee had failed is an unprecedented statement by a party official, since it accords church leaders the power of influencing events. The implication of this seemed to be that Degtaryev was trying to underline that the party was still committed to the new, more open policy on church–state relations despite Kharchev's removal. Nonetheless, it is clear that a reforming chairman had failed to gain the independence and authority he was seeking for the CRA against the entrenched interests of the Central Committee and the KGB, who retain a controlling influence over religious policy.

The 'business as usual' line has been continued by Yuri Khristoradnov, Kharchev's successor, in the very few public statements he has made since taking office some time in June 1989. While reaffirming the attitude to *perestroika* in church–state relations, he has maintained a much lower profile than Kharchev had. His first known interview did not appear until October 1989, and then in the *Pravitelstvenny vestnik* (Government Herald, not in a large-circulation publication.[20] He concluded the interview with the statement: 'As for religion as such, the attitude to it has not essentially altered. However, the struggle of opinions, we now realise, must be conducted on the basis of equality, with the two sides respecting each other.' Khristoradnov here was clearly adhering to a more conservative line than Kharchev by reiterating the party's longstanding attitude to religion at the same time as recognising the need for an equal dialogue.

Earlier in the interview, Khristoradnov had made some points which showed he was prepared to perform his new role in the spirit of *glasnost*. For example, he said that there had been 12,000 Orthodox churches in 1956, reduced to 7,000 by 1965: no Soviet spokesman had previously been known to give a figure for the mid-1950s. Moreover, Khristoradnov's figure gave strong support to the already widely held suspicion that the Russian Orthodox Church's claim that it had 20,000 churches when it joined the World Council of Churches in 1961 had been greatly inflated.

Khristoradnov, in common with other spokesmen on church–state relations, was prepared to admit that mistakes had been made in the past: there could be 'no return to the primitive scheme under which religion was regarded as opium and believers as an insignificant part of the population'. He went on to say that: 'What has been going on until now cannot be called anything other than infringement of believers' rights.' Khristoradnov admitted that most of the mail the CRA received consisted of complaints: '[Believers] are not admitted to institutes of higher education, they are not taken on for work, they are given negative references, they are not allocated flats . . . Sometimes it becomes quite absurd.'

Khristoradnov was evidently brought into the CRA as a safe pair of hands after the ups and downs of Kharchev's tenure of office. Born in 1929, he has spent nearly all his career working his way up through the party ranks in the closed city of Gorky, a city with a reputation for conservativism. One of the longest-running, unsuccessful campaigns to open Orthodox churches was mounted by believers in Gorky, beginning in 1967 and revived again in 1977, and it seems almost certain that Khristoradnov would have had some involvement in the decisions to refuse their repeated requests. And Gorky was also regarded as a suitable place of exile for Academician Andrei Sakharov from 1981 to 1987, at which time Khristoradnov was First Secretary of the party Regional Committee. Latterly he held the post of chairman of the Council of the Union, one of the two chambers of the Supreme Soviet, an undemanding position since the Council met briefly and infrequently. He lost this post when a new Supreme Soviet was elected in June 1989. Evidently it has not been thought necessary for the CRA to have a young or innovative chairman at this time, and this suggests that the new policy on religion will be adhered to without further changes.

Khristoradnov made his first trip abroad, to Norway, only in April 1990, nearly a year after taking office. He was still giving an impression of continuity: he said the party had had a wrong attitude to religion; the church had been isolated from society which was wrong, but that measures were being taken to correct this; that the authorities wanted believers not just to have the opportunity to go to church, but to take part in the process of renewal. Despite separation of church and state, believers were a part of the population and had a right to play their part. However, a new and possibly unexpected development for him was to find himself sharing a platform with two leading Orthodox activists (Father Georgi Edelshtein and Viktor Popkov) and a member of the Keston College research staff (Michael Rowe): even Kharchev had never had a comparable experience.[21]

All this unedifying public mudslinging over religious policy strongly suggests that no-one is in overall charge of it. The fact that the adoption of the new Law on Freedom of Conscience continued to be delayed also indicated this: the various bodies concerned with it (identified by Kharchev as the CRA, the Ministry of Foreign Affairs, the Ministry of Justice, the Procuracy and the Academy of Sciences, plus also the Institute on State and Law, which produced one of the drafts of the new law) continued to fail to reach agreement. On 12 April 1990 Tass reported that the Supreme Soviet had considered a further draft and sent it back for further work. The Law on Freedom of Conscience was finally adopted in September 1990, after prolonged private and then public (in the Congress of Peoples' Deputies) disagreement over religious education of children. Despite the concessions given to believers following the new line made public early in 1988, no-one, it appears, had the power to define precisely how far these concessions are to go. Gorbachev, beleaguered as he was by the overwhelming problems of the nationalities and the economy, seemed unlikely to do anything further to back up the lead he gave by meeting Orthodox hierarchs in April 1988.

While all believers undoubtedly now have greater freedom than at any time in the past, the greatest beneficiaries of the change in policy have been the Orthodox leadership. The most senior hierarchs now have a high profile at national level, which is shared to a lesser extent by diocesan bishops. While this certainly allows the Orthodox faithful greater freedom than formerly, it leaves some key problems unresolved. The church is being called upon to play a greater and very demanding role in national life without any kind of internal review of its attitudes, resources, and personnel – without internal *perestroika*, in fact. True, problems can now be discussed more openly than in the past, but this has not yet led to changes bringing about the quality of leadership for which many church members have been calling. Lately there have even been reports of diocesan bishops quashing initiatives by young, energetic, and committed priests. Doubts about the church's capacity to meet huge new challenges are being openly voiced, in the Soviet press and elsewhere, by even some bishops, as well as priests and laymen.

Furthermore, the high profile of the Orthodox Church is an important component of the new image which the Soviet Union became eager to project. Image is not to be derided, as it requires at least some substance to back it up: the danger is that the image will be taken as a complete and faithful reflection of reality. Outside the USSR the impression was, by 1990, widespread that the question of religious freedom there had been virtually resolved, when church members knew – and could say so in sections of the Soviet press – that many obstacles to freedom remained to be overcome. In helping, willingly or unwillingly, to project a more favourable image abroad, Orthodox leaders were, ironically, performing the same function that they had performed under Brezhnev, albeit in greatly changed circumstances. They had fallen virtually into the role of a state church, and all the signs suggested that the CRA and other bodies were happy for them to fulfil that function.

Notes

1 'Crisis of Conscience', *Liberty*, January–February 1990.
2 *Ogonëk*, June 1990.
3 *Religion in Communist Lands* 16:4, 1988, pp. 293–4, 300–1.
4 *Ibid.*; also *RCL* 15:2, 1987, pp. 198–9.
5 *Moscow News* 14 June 1987; *Nedelya* 23–29 May 1988; *Meditsinskaya gazeta* 30 March 1988; *Izvestiya* 31 May–17 June 1988.
6 *Izvestiya* 3 September 1989.
7 *Russkaya mysl* 20 May 1988 p. 4.
8 Speech at St Mary's Guildhall, Coventry, England, 14 November 1988; typescript at Keston College.
9 *Keston News Service* (*KNS*) No. 283, 10 September 1987.
10 *Ogonëk*, 50, December 1988.
11 *KNS* No. 317, 19 January 1989.
12 The conference was organised by the Washington DC-based International Religious Liberty Association in the Queen Elizabeth II Conference Centre, London, England. Kharchev spoke on 24 July 1989.
13 'The Apotheosis of a Soviet Official', Jane Ellis, *Church Times*, London, 11 August 1989.
14 See note 1. For a reference to the Soviet paper, see note 17.
15 *Ogonëk*, 44, October 1989.
16 *KNS* No. 331, 3 August 1989.
17 '*Voidet li on v istoriyu kak "Svyatoi Konstantin"?*', *Sovetskaya Rossiya*, 22 November 1989.
18 See note 13.
19 '*Neobkhodimoye poyasneniye k "tretyemu razgovoru"*', Aleksandr Degtaryev, *Ogonëk*, 48, November 1989.
20 *Pravitelstvenny vestnik*, 20, 1989.
21 *KNS*, No. 347, 5 April 1990.

5

The state, the church, and the oikumene: the Russian Orthodox Church and the World Council of Churches, 1948–1985

J.A. HEBLY

One of the most interesting developments in the 1960s was the arrival of the Russian Orthodox Church on the world ecumenical scene. The Third Assembly of the World Council of Churches in New Delhi voted overwhelmingly, on 30 November 1961, to accept this church's application for membership. Until then, the Russian Orthodox Church had remained aloof from the world *oikumene*.

The entry of the Russian Orthodox Church into the World Council of Churches was only the overture to a suddenly more active participation in international church life. In Debrecen, Hungary, in November 1958, an international meeting of churchmen was held, on the initiative of J. Hromadka, the Czech Reformed theologian; this meeting brought together Christian groups and private individuals from churches in both Eastern Europe and the West, to further the cause of world peace. Soviet delegates were also present.

In 1959, the Conference of European Churches was founded in Nyborg, Denmark, and the Russians were among the founding members. This organisation was intended to serve as a forum and meeting place for European Christians from East and West, to bridge political antagonisms as well as the age-old confessional divisions between the churches of the Reformation and Orthodoxy.

In 1961, the Pan-Orthodox conferences started, with a meeting in Rhodos, to prepare for a Great and Holy Pan-Orthodox Synod. The aim of the conference was to study ways of reconciling and uniting the sundry churches of the Orthodox communion. The conferences have continued ever since, and the Russian Orthodox Church continues to play a predominant role in them.

Contacts with the Orthodox sister churches had already been established since the end of the Second World War. Patriarch Aleksii visited the Orthodox churches in the Middle East in May/June 1945 and a Church Conference of Heads and Representatives of the

Autocephalous Orthodox Churches was convened in Moscow 9–18 July 1948 on the occasion of the 500th anniversary celebrations of the autocephaly of the Russian Church. This conference, however, had not been convened to mark a new openness towards the ecumenical movement, but was rather an appeal 'to all Orthodox Churches to adopt the most effective measures for the purpose of preserving the principles of true Christianity in the world from the powerful seductive influence of the modern ecumenical movement. The Russian Church calls them to follow her example and to refuse to participate in it', as Archpriest G. Razumovsky, Vice Chairman of the Department for Foreign Church Relations of the Patriarchate (set up by the Holy Synod on 4 April 1946), said in his address to the conference.[1]

This Moscow conference was fully in line with the traditional Orthodox theory of Moscow as the 'Third Rome', and with the Stalinist policy of consolidation of Soviet hegemony. 'Obviously, for the Russian Church to win preeminence over the entire Orthodox world would be of significant interest for the foreign policy of the Soviet state.'[2]

Although the first Pan-Orthodox conference in Rhodos, which gave special attention to the relations of the Orthodox churches with the rest of the Christian world, had agreed that the Orthodox churches would not send observers to the Second Vatican Council, the Russian Orthodox Church decided unexpectedly, at the last moment, to send two representatives to Rome – another sign of the changing policy of the Russian Orthodox Church in the international field.

It is clear that the years around 1960, strangely enough one of the most difficult periods in the recent history of the Russian Orthodox Church, marked by internal persecution and restrictions, saw a blossoming of ecumenical activities and the opening of a new chapter in its external relations. The change seems to have been the result of a general shift in the foreign policy of the Soviet Union in the post-Stalin era. A reappraisal of the participation of the Soviet Union in international organisations also took place in those years, resulting in a series of Soviet applications for membership in bodies previously shunned by the Kremlin. The Soviets resumed membership in the International Labor Organisation in 1954, joined UNESCO for the first time that same year, and returned to the World Health Organisation in 1957, after an eight-year absence.

It might be assumed that the reasons for participation in the work of UNESCO and other specialised agencies of the United Nations might be very similar to those which the Soviet government might have had in giving the green light to the Russian Orthodox Church to join the World Council of Churches. Chris Osakwe[3] quotes the Soviet author K.P. Rubanik, who justified the Soviet entry into UNESCO in 1954 after a virtual boycott of almost nine years, by writing that 'the entry of the Soviet Union into UNESCO was dictated by its efforts to contribute to the attainment of international peace through the extension of the cooperation of all countries in the field of education, science, and culture'. The contribution to peace and the support of progressive peace-loving forces will also be one of the main motives for allowing the Russian Orthodox Church to take up contact with the ecumenical movement during a period when many churches from the newly independent countries were also joining the ecumenical movement. Gradually, those responsible for Soviet foreign policy discovered the useful role which the Russian Orthodox Church could play in international affairs. It is hardly imaginable that the regime which pursued a repressive policy in regard to the churches within the Soviet Union and allowed them only a very restricted liberty of worship, would grant them the possibility to build up independent relations with international church bodies. Foreign relations of churches are part of the general foreign policy of the Soviet Union and its principal aims and objectives are obligatory guidelines for the churches as well.

The first contacts with the World Council of Churches

The Russian Orthodox Church, which from the time of the October Revolution in 1917 until the Second World War was completely cut off from any form of contact with the rest of Christianity, did not take part in the process which led to the formation of the World Council of Churches at the first Assembly in Amsterdam in 1948. The first contacts after the Second World War with the Provisional Committee of the World Council of Churches in Process of Formation were quite understandably characterised by a large measure of caution on both sides. There was, however, in ecumenical circles, a renewed interest in the Soviet Union. The common struggle against National Socialism and the resurgence of the Russian Orthodox Church had fostered the hope that new developments lay ahead.

As early as April 1946, the World Council of Churches sent an official invitation to the Patriarch of Moscow for a meeting with a delegation of the Russian Orthodox Church later that year, for purposes of getting acquainted and of informing the Russian Church of the Council's proposed activities. The invitation was accepted, but the meeting had to be postponed, and participation of the Russian Church in the Amsterdam Assembly did not come about. The presidents of the World Council were informed that Russian Orthodox Church leaders had decided to refrain from taking part in the ecumenical movement 'with its present tendencies'.[4]

During this period, emphasis was being placed on consolidating the position of the Moscow Patriarchate in the Orthodox world, and contacts with the World Council were beyond the sphere of interest of the state authorities. Since the church had only recently been enlisted for the purpose of establishing foreign contacts, no clear policy had been outlined with regard to this western-oriented movement. It seems most probable, in the light of the initial acceptance of the invitation, that the government intervened and that the church conference in Moscow was especially intended to provide a clear motivation for a rejection of the invitation to join the universal fellowship of churches.

Archpriest G. Razumovsky read before the plenary session an immensely long paper, in which he did not show any understanding of the ecumenical movement, which had 'the ideal of an ecumenical Church, namely the effort to establish a Universal Protestant Collective Papacy'. The Russian Church should not waste its time and energy in participation in the ecumenical movement, the more so 'because our state has taken upon itself the heavy burden of letting social justice triumph on just the same basis as is proposed by Christian teachings'. The Amsterdam Assembly was disappointed by Moscow's reaction, but saw as one hopeful element the fact that the reasons given for the negative decision were 'based upon a complete misunderstanding of the true nature of our movement – a misunderstanding such as can easily arise in a Church whose leaders have no first-hand knowledge of ecumenical life . . . We should keep the door open for the Church of Russia and other Orthodox Churches.'[5]

However, for the time being, the Moscow Patriarchate remained aloof, although it expressed its interest in the confessional problems of church unity. The social side of the ecumenical activities, however, was regarded as pro-western, linked with imperialist forces and influenced by bourgeois ideology. Patriarch Pimen gave a lecture at the University of Loensu, Finland, in 1974, entitled 'An Orthodox View of Contemporary Ecumenism',[6] pointing to

the original, not only purely Western but entirely pro-Western, character of the structure, activity, and politico-social orientation of the World Council of Churches in the period of its establishment and during the Cold War. This forced the Moscow consultation of 1948, faced with such onesidedness, to take up an attitude of watchfulness and waiting.

But it would be another decade before the first official conversations between representatives of the Russian Orthodox Church and the World Council of Churches could take place in Utrecht (7–9 August 1958). In this period, an occasional exchange of letters took place and documents were forwarded, but contacts were scarce in those dark days of the Cold War.

The Russian Orthodox Church confined its international activities to an active participation after 1949 in the World Peace Council and a certain pressure was exerted on the World Council through different channels to take part in the meetings of this Council. The World Council took a very clear stance and it was of the opinion that the Orthodox Church was used as a means to win the confidence of western Christians.

The Commission of the Churches for International Affairs (CCIA) issued a short statement (6 August 1951) clarifying the stance of the World Council 'in view of misleading peace proposals which are currently being circulated'. The statement continues:

We condemn any extension of oppression carried on behind the facade of propaganda for peace. We believe that it is the duty of all governments and of the United Nations to recognize the dignity of man as a child of God, and to protect the rights of the individual. Every denial of fundamental rights should be made known and resisted. Christians can witness convincingly to peace only if they and their Churches, in their relations with one another across all frontiers, put loyalty to their common Lord above any other loyalty.[7]

This last sentence seems to be a reprimand to the Patriarchate whom they reproached for his docility to the views of the Kremlin.

When, after the Evanston Assembly of the World Council of Churches (1954), a statement on the international situation, which appealed to governments and peoples to help in the relief of present world tensions, together with the report of the section on international affairs of the Assembly was transmitted to the Patriarchate, Metropolitan Nikolai replied that, 'This declaration of the World Council of Churches meets the unanimous desire of the peaceloving forces.'[8] After Evanston, the peace activities of the Council began to evoke the attention of the Kremlin and bilateral contacts between the Russian Church and the western churches became more frequent. The resultant mutual visits did not only allow the Russian Church leaders to come into contact with the life of the Protestant churches in the West; they also familiarised the West with the hitherto unknown Russian Church.

The first ecumenical leader to visit the Soviet Union was Martin

Niemöller (in December 1951/January 1952), who played a prominent role in the debate on the rearmament of West Germany. He was personally invited by the patriarch and said afterwards, in his report to the Executive Committee of the World Council, of which he was a member:

The basic question with which I went to Moscow was: is there really a Church there or only a propaganda instrument? To put the matter another way: is the Russian Church a servant of Stalin first or of Christ first? This, as it appeared to me, is the crucial point for the Church and for its ecumenical relations.[9]

This question continued to haunt the minds of western Christians. The identification of Kremlin politics with the cause of peace and justice was a constant feature in the thinking of the leadership of the Russian Orthodox Church throughout the period under review. This so-called patriotic stance was often singled out for praise, as for instance at a meeting addressed by the Vice President of the Council for Religious Affairs in 1976. He observed, on that occasion, that the clergy supported ever more intensely the internal and external policies of the Soviet government – not only by preaching patriotism, but by preaching *Soviet* patriotism.[10] The intention of the Kremlin in giving the church the green light for joining the ecumenical movement is very clearly expressed in a report of the first official delegation which visited the Soviet Union in June 1962, after the admission of the Church of Russia into the World Council of Churches. The problem which the 'support' of the state authorities for the ecumenical activities of 'their' church might pose for the World Council was clearly formulated in a memorandum of 20 February 1962, by Paul B. Anderson, one of the few experts on the Soviet Union advising the World Council. He asked,

Will the possibility of Soviet 'penetration' face those in key positions in constituent bodies with the obligation to acquire more thorough knowledge of basic principles, policies and procedures of the Soviet government and, more particularly, of the Communist Party of the Soviet Union? In what ways may communist principles, policies, and procedures seek current application to the specific areas of activity of each WCC unit?[11]

In my opinion, the expertise here demanded from the World Council leaders was still not very impressive.

Very soon it became clear that a critical and open discussion of the consequences of the Russian Church's membership would become very difficult, and that the World Council of Churches as a source of information about the situation of the Russian Churches would dry up. An article by John Lawrence, another expert advising the World

Council, raised a protest from the Russian side.[12] There was, as the report of the delegation in 1962 said,

evidence, both in discussion with the representatives of the state and with representatives of the State Department for Orthodox Affairs with whom the group met, that pressure is being put upon the Church in this matter of peace.[13]

What many believers in the Russian Church thought about the new ecumenical activities of the leadership of their church is expressed by Fr. Gleb Yakunin and Lev Regelson, in their letter of 15 October 1975 to Philip Potter, General Secretary of the World Council. They wrote,

In 1961, the Russian Orthodox Church joined the World Council of Churches. For the Russian Church that year was marked by an increasing wave of anti-religious terror and by forcible closing of churches, monasteries, and theological schools everywhere . . . The believers of the Russian Church never harbored any special illusions about the membership of the Moscow Patriarchate in the World Council of Churches. That act was sanctioned by the government during the period of the extremely brutal persecution of religion, and obviously followed the government's own strategic aims, quite remote from any consolidation of Christian positions in the modern world.[14]

How did the Kremlin view the World Council of Churches?

It will have to be borne in mind that the leadership of the Orthodox Church had its own religious and spiritual motives for its wish to join the ecumenical movement, although it also has to be assumed that in the Russian Orthodox Church there exist, as in other churches, differing views on the desirability of ecumenism.

The church wished to partake in the dialogue on the unity and universality of the whole church, to represent the voice of Orthodoxy and not to remain on the sideline when other Orthodox churches developed relations with the Christian world, to strengthen its position in its own society, and to find spiritual support for building up its life.

For the ruling party, these motives were certainly not decisive. Some publications of Soviet ideologists give a clear picture of the views of the ruling party on the ecumenical movement. According to N.S. Gordienko, the World Council of Churches is fundamentally an instrument of western political interest groups and the entry of churches from socialist countries is seen as a possibility to align this council with the really progressive peace forces.[15] The participation of churches from socialist countries in an international church body could only be justified if these churches functioned in such a body as defenders and protagonists of socialism and tried to change it into an ally in the struggle for worldwide social revolution. For Gordienko, the World Council of Churches was, therefore, not a forum in which the churches might try to find, in common counsel, their own answers to social and political questions, where they might try to develop their own visions and their own values. On the contrary, it was the arena where western capitalist and eastern communist ideas confronted each other and collided. The duty of representatives from churches in socialist countries was, according to the party ideologist, to fight what he regarded as reactionary forces in the *oikumene,* to represent socialist positions, and to blunt anti-communist tendencies.

A more recent book by Y.V. Kryanev does not differ essentially from that of Gordienko. Kryanev also rejected the view that the World Council could take up an independent position on social and political matters. For a Marxist, this pretension was untenable. Kryanev maintained that a reorientation (within the World Council) was taking place, but warned that there were still

endeavors to create an atmosphere of anti-communism and anti-Sovietism. Reactionary Church leaders from Western countries, incited by imperialist circles are continuously trying to play up the question of human rights with tendentious and falsified material.[16]

The original intention of the World Council was fully misrepresented here.

The rise of the ecumenical movement was closely linked with the idea that the churches could free themselves from national and ideological links and could find new possibilities for a prophetic witness. The ecumenical movement was, from its very inception, a daring effort to lead the churches out of the slavery of national, political, and ideological captivity, a liberation movement in the churches, away from the old links between throne and altar, and from conformism to society. Visser 't Hooft, one of the main architects of the World Council, clearly expressed what he regarded as the central conviction of the ecumenical movement:

We believe in the Lordship of Christ and in the right of the Church to proclaim the implication of this belief for relationships in the social and political community. We cannot give up this conviction without giving up the very substance of the ecumenical movement. In this matter, we cannot compromise with the Moscow patriarchate or with any other Church or government which denies the right of the Church to exercise its prophetic ministry.[17]

This principle was in sharp contrast with the views of Marxist ideologues. They dismissed the idea that an international church body could take up an independent position between the two contrasting socio-political systems which dominate the world. The churches had to take the side of justice – they argued – that is, the side of socialism; they should become partisans of the oppressed in the international class struggle between oppressors and oppressed. By allying oneself with the progressive forces, one was acting objectively. The position of Soviet church representatives in the World Council was not an easy one. They were expected not only to represent their churches, but also their government. The pre-Gorbachev Soviet regime brooked no criticism from outsiders (Christian churches being in this category) and admitted no deviation or even critical distance from the official party line. These representatives were not only influenced by their political, national, and socio-economic backgrounds, as is the case for everyone, but were not allowed to voice their own opinions on social and political questions, only to echo the official positions of the ruling party. By being part of this Council, however, the Russian Church was drawn into a discussion on all sorts of problems on which its prelates had no expertise, which were not discussed in their own church meetings, and on which they could not pronounce themselves in the internal discussion in their own country.

In many respects, they were conservative not only in questions of faith and order, but also on issues which play an important role in progressive circles in the West, circles which, in many regards, have a dominant voice in the ecumenical discussion. On issues such as sexism, feminism, racism, militarism, science and faith, and the like, Russian Orthodox Church representatives showed over and over again that their church was not on the side of liberalism and progressive thinking.

The Soviet authorities, in allowing the Russian Church to enter into the ecumenical movement, apparently had a very restricted conception of what was going on in this movement. They regarded it purely as a sort of peace organisation and as a useful instrument in supporting Soviet proposals in the field of international politics. They wanted to use this possibility to oppose actions of churches in the field of religious liberty and human rights insofar as these were directed towards the socialist countries; to strengthen anti-'imperialist' tendencies; and to advance a positive image of socialism.

The impact of the Russian Church
on the World Council of Churches

It is very difficult to determine to what extent a particular church or group of churches can influence the policy of such a complicated and pluriform body as a world fellowship of churches. The influence of the Russians should not be exaggerated. The Russian Orthodox Church can certainly not be held responsible for any supposedly Marxist influence on the *oikumene*. For Russian Orthodox theology, there should be no confusion between theology and ideology, no structural integration of church teaching and Marxism. A dialogue between Christianity and Marxism was wanted neither by the church nor by the party. The Russian theologian N.A. Zabolotsky criticised a report of a World Council commission, noting,

It should be definitely stated that the liberation theology and its particular conclusion – the theology of revolution – have ideological implications. Social, economic, and political elements in this type of theology are in essence merely human reflections on world processes. But in such cases, there will inevitably be a clash both in ideas and in action between similar ideologised theologies and other ideological structures.[18]

The Russian Orthodox Church was wary of liberation theology. Metropolitan Filaret of Kiev and Galicia said, in an interview in 1985, that he appreciated the efforts of theologians in South America 'to bring their Christian faith into line with actually living, by this faith, since without a Christian life, the concept of faith itself becomes meaningless'. But he continued, 'Unfortunately, proponents of the theology of liberation do permit a separation of one from the other and even an underestimation of the importance of faith.'[19]

Repeatedly the Russian Orthodox Church has criticised certain programmes and trends in the World Council. In his message to the WCC Central Committee, after the Bangkok Conference of the Commission on World Mission and Evangelism (1973), Patriarch Pimen expressed 'perplexity and great regret' in the face of 'a deliberate trend toward a one-sided and detrimental understanding of salvation in the spirit of boundless "horizontalism" '.[20]

Russian criticism has its roots in Orthodox theology and in what Levitin-Krasnov has called the conservatism of 'a conservative Church in a conservative state'.[21] The Russians often complained about the numerical and intellectual preponderance of the Protestants in the Council, and, in the early 1980s, raised the issue of the representation of the Orthodox churches. Certain proposals were made, and in the Central Committee meeting of 1982, they even said, during the discussion of these proposals, that, if they were rejected, some Orthodox churches might reconsider their involvement in the Council. About western proposals on the representation of women, they remarked that these would create many difficulties in Orthodox churches and might endanger their continued presence.[22] When one views the large range of issues with which the World Council has occupied itself, it will be very difficult to prove that any of these has been brought into the ecumenical discussion by the Russian Orthodox Church. The western and Third World churches are responsible for the agenda of the Council, and whatever radical or other influences there might have been, issue from their representatives. 'The source of the protest against the West is the West', as Jacques Ellul has noted.[23] The influence of the delegates from churches in the Soviet Union has not been such, even according to Marxist observers, that they have been able to dictate the agenda of the World Council, but they certainly did exert their influence to prevent subjects displeasing to the authorities at home from becoming the object of study and action in the Council. The issue of human rights, and especially religious liberty in socialist countries, was long relegated to the background, as a result of Russian Church pressure; social, economic, political, and ideological problems of the socialist world were similarly hushed up. The World Council has long spoken critically about the western world and about western social and political problems, but throughout the period 1961–85, it was unable to speak in the same way about the socialist world. On the other hand, when, in a statement of the World Council, the invasion of Afghanistan was mentioned among the threats to peace, without any mention of any protest of the Russian Orthodox Church delegate, the Russian Church (as was admitted later) experienced difficulties at home, at the hands of Soviet authorities, 'because the statement had been misused by the Western media'.[24]

The Russian Orthodox Church has no tradition of a prophetic critical mission in society, and has not been able to develop a real involvement in the problems of society as western ecumenical churches have. The Russian Church delegates accepted the critical witness of the World Council as long as it was directed toward the non-socialist world, but refused to accept it when directed toward their own society. Moreover, they wanted the WCC member churches to 'recognise' that injustice had been overcome (allegedly) in socialist society, and to concede the putative legitimacy of the Russian Church's collaboration with leftist political forces in the world arena.

For example, in his report on the final document of the Nairobi Assembly, Bishop Mikhail wrote *inter alia*:

We must ascertain that, speaking about negative phenomena in the world – unjust distribution of material goods, exploitation, poverty, hunger, oppression, illiteracy – the document orients itself almost exclusively toward the capitalist countries and partly toward the Third World. It leaves aside the rich experiences of the socialist countries, experiences which, as is well known, were acquired in the struggle against these evils until their radical removal. Accordingly, the descriptive part of the report and the recommendations suffer from the usual onesidedness and shortcomings.[25]

The Bishop seems to understand by onesidedness and shortcomings the fact that the evils of the capitalist world are mentioned without at the same time mentioning the good, the abolition of these evils, in the socialist world.

N.A. Zabolotsky wrote an article in the same vein in 1982, arguing that all the evils of the world were concentrated in 'capitalist' societies, while about socialist systems he had only positive things to say.[26] For instance, exploitation and impoverishment, whether at home or in exploited countries of the Third World, were 'the West's social problem' and justified the class struggle in the developed 'capitalist' countries, the liberation movements in the Third World, and the programmatic statements in this direction on the part of the World Council of Churches. Nowhere was it indicated that the World Council of Churches had any task in respect to socialist societies other than that of co-operating with them. Its task was restricted to the system where 'injustice is causing suffering'. There it should have to promote concrete action for structural change, in order to promote freedom from oppression, exploitation, and racial discrimination.

In many respects, the representatives of the Russian Orthodox Church, when social and political questions were on the agenda, can be regarded to have been emissaries of a system which assumed that it was in possession of the truth and of the exclusive knowledge of the way to a future of justice and peace. The silence of the World Council on Eastern Europe, which may certainly be attributed to the influence of the church delegates from these countries, was clearly demonstrable by the special issue of the *Ecumenical Review* dedicated to the work of 'Church and Society'.[27] This symposium of essays gave the impression that Eastern Europe did not exist. It was totally passed over. In general, the active participation of the Russian churches was able to prevent critical pronouncements on the Soviet Union and its policies. When the pressure from western churches became too strong, as was for instance the case after the Soviet invasion of Czechoslovakia in

1968, and the Council did speak, the East European churches raised a protest.[28] The World Council repeatedly declared that it was aware of this onesidedness. 'There are situations', the Central Committee of the WCC conceded in 1973, 'which should have been mentioned'.[29] Later, after a rather heated debate on repression and human rights violations, the Melbourne Conference declared,

Some countries and people we dare not identify for the simple reason that such a specific public identification by the conference may endanger the position – even the lives – of many of our brothers and sisters, some of whom are participating in this conference. We therefore confess our inability to be as prophetic as we ought to be, as that may, in some instances, entail imposing martyrdom on our fellow believers in those countries, something we dare not do from a safe distance.[30]

This ecumenical conference considered some delegates as hostages of the ruling party of their homeland, in order to ensure that nothing was said or done that might be unacceptable to those who had them in their power. This is a very disturbing fact which affected the central tenet of the ecumenical movement: the right of the church to proclaim the implications of its belief in the Lordship of Christ for relationships in a social or political community.

The World Council was, in a certain sense, involved in the captivity of the Russian churches and the selectivity of the Council's prophetic witness is detrimental to its position and its authority. But we have to be very precise: the World Council did not yield to Soviet propaganda or to the political influence of the USSR's representatives in its main programmes. It has been the influence of western and Third World churches which have been responsible for the WCC's programmes over the years. The creative impact of the churches from the USSR has been very restricted.

One of the tasks which, according to Soviet ideologists, was entrusted to the church in its international relations was: to unmask bourgeois propaganda about the persecution of the church in socialism. It seems that this task was accomplished in a rather satisfactory way. Up to the 1960s, the issue of religious liberty had been a main concern of the World Council of Churches. One of the last declarations on religious liberty came from the New Delhi Assembly, the same assembly which approved the application for membership of the Russian Orthodox Church. It was meant as a guideline for further action and the Assembly also decided to set up a secretariat for the study of religious liberty issues. From 1959 to 1967, a bulletin was published: *Current Developments in the Eastern European Churches*. This bulletin provided information and documentation especially on the church in the

Soviet Union. The aggressive character of atheist propaganda and the closure of churches and chapels were elucidated, but *Current Developments* did not publish any samizdat material, which, in the 1960s, began to arrive from the Soviet Union.

The World Council has never given any attention to samizdat since the entry of the Russian Church and the Secretariat for Religious Liberty was terminated by the Uppsala Assembly in 1968. All responsibility for study and action was passed to the Commission of the Churches for International Affairs, a body in which the Russian Church is permanently represented. We can clearly see a shift of interest in the course of the 1960s, and, from the Uppsala Assembly onwards, the attention given to religious liberty gradually gave way to other concerns as ecumenical priorities. Declarations about religious liberty began to be seen as a product of western culture and the furthering of its implication as a tool of western politics.

The Third World became the focal point of ecumenical interest and the East European churches professed their solidarity with the aspirations and policies of the Third World churches, supporting the latter's criticism of the imperialist western world. This reflected not only a growing influence of churches from the Soviet Union in the ecumenical movement, but just as much the lack of interest among western church delegates in the issue of religious liberty and the religious situation in Marxist countries. Those who were committed to the cause of the churches in communist countries encountered an increasing denial of support in the World Council of Churches. A growing estrangement came about between them and the official ecumenical movement. This estrangement reached a tragic summit in a publication by a staff member of the Commission of the Churches on International Affairs which stated:

Many Christians in the West saw the possibility of propitiating for their sins of omission during fascist rule by turning to a fervent commitment to the religious liberty of their sister Churches in Eastern Europe. And in doing so, they played directly into the hands of a political maneuver which has succeeded in tearing the continent even further and irreparably asunder.[31]

A completely false and distorted view, but it is interesting to note that this aggressive statement comes from an American staff member. There was, in fact, a tendency in publications on religious liberty issuing from the desk of the Commission on International Affairs, to discourage those who were dealing with the situation in Marxist–Leninist countries, and even to denounce them as misusing the issue of religious liberty for political ends and as a propaganda weapon against the offending state. I cannot establish the extent to which delegates from the Soviet Union can be held responsible for that.

The Evanston Assembly (1954) spoke in a resolution about its concern and sorrow that a veil of silence had been forcibly drawn over the life and testimony of many churches. This veil of silence unfortunately existed until into the Gorbachev era, as far as the World Council was concerned. For example, when the situation of the churches in the USSR was put before the Nairobi Assembly (1975), the result was a long-term project which finally led to nothing. Study and action on the part of the WCC on the issue of religious liberty in the Soviet Union seems to have been blocked by the Russian Orthodox Church above all.

Closing remarks

A new religious policy has now been formulated in the USSR. It might be assumed that political control over the leaders and organisational structures of the officially recognized churches, 'a policy consistently pursued since 1945', as John Anderson remarks,[32] will not be continued. There are, however, some elements which have to be taken into account when viewing the future of Russian participation in the ecumenical movement.

First, participation in the World Council of Churches has mainly been a concern of the leadership of the Russian Orthodox Church, or more particularly of the Department for Foreign Relations, the most extensive office of the synod. Ecumenical activities have been reserved for the official leadership. In the life of local parishes, ecumenical influence is still very restricted. On the contrary, the Orthodox churches registered some strong objections, in the Central Committee meeting in Geneva in 1976, against direct contact between the World Council and local parishes. Nothing which does not proceed from the hierarchy of the church could be taken up in the life of the church. The absolute embargo on all information from the West, until recently, enabled the Russian Church leaders to allow only what they themselves judged useful to filter through into the life of the church.

Second, ecumenical work has in general been closely associated with the 'struggle for peace' in the *Journal of the Moscow Patriarchate*. For the ordinary believers, insofar as they have been able to get to know anything about the participation of their church in ecumenical activities, it must have been extremely difficult to distinguish between the ecumenical confessional activities and the political peace activities of their leaders. An existential involvement in the ecumenical fellowship has not been possible for Russian Christians. In the western churches, the *oikumene* is rooted in the life of many parishes and ecumenical programmes are discussed and supported. Nothing of this kind has been possible in the Russian Orthodox Church and the inner reservations about the *oikumene*, which exist in Orthodoxy, have never been the subject of an open and lively dialogue in church life after the Church Conference in Moscow in 1948.

Russian Church members have never observed any special relief of their situation through interventions of the World Council; on the contrary, they have often wondered about the positive evaluations given by naive ecumenical visitors about religious conditions in the USSR. Church members have little reason to accept the value and purpose of the ecumenical movement.

Third, it is not unlikely that, in the period before us, the Russian Church leaders will have to take into account not only the wishes of the government but also the voice of the church people. It has been observed that strong Russian nationalist feelings existed in the church, and that the traditional elements in the religious life of the believers are dominant. This is quite understandable after a long period of persecution and curtailment. The involvement of Orthodoxy in social and political issues and the collaboration with non-Orthodox believers is not a matter of course for traditional Orthodox believers. And the association of leading church circles with the official peace movement has never evoked the approval of the members, though we may regard the dissident samizdat literature as trustworthy. More inner freedom in the church, more open discussion about church policy, might lead to a change of ecumenical policy and to a reconsideration of the participation of the church in international life.

And fourth, after his visit to the Soviet Union in 1959, Visser 't Hooft wrote the following:

One of our companions quoted to me the remark of an Orthodox professor: 'The Russian Orthodox Church has passed the test.' This is an interesting remark because it would seem to be true in one sense and untrue in another. It would seem to be true in the sense that, when the great persecutions came, it was expected that the Church would collapse, but it did not do so. It remains a tremendous fact that the Russian Orthodox Church exists and that is not all, for it is also important that the Church has not become a syncretistic body as were the Deutsche Christen in the National Socialist period in Germany. One does not get the impression that any attempt is made to create a synthesis between Christianity and Marxist ideology.

But to say that the Orthodox Church has passed the test would seem to be wholly untrue if it means that this is the only test which it will be asked to pass during this period of history. It would seem that one of the biggest tests is yet to come, namely, whether the Orthodox Church has anything relevant to say to Marxist or post-Marxist humankind. The great issue would seem to be whether, in spite of its unmistakable spiritual life, the Church may not in fact become an anachronism. Its strength is in its faithful adherence to its tradition. But this strength may become a weakness if that adherence is not only to the spiritual content of that tradition, but also to its forms.[33]

These words seem to me to remain as relevant today as they were when they were first committed to paper.

Notes

1 Actes de la conférence des chefs et représentants des Eglises Orthodoxes autocephales réunies a Moscou 8–18 July 1948 (Moscow, 1950).
2 William C. Fletcher, *Religion and Soviet Foreign Policy 1945–1970* (London, Oxford University Press, 1973), p. 86.
3 Chris Osakwe, *The Participation of the Soviet Union in Universal International Organisations* (Leiden, 1972) p. 141.
4 J.A. Hebly, The Russians and the World Council of Churches: Documentary survey of the accession of the Russian Orthodox Church to the World Council of Churches, with commentary (Belfast, Christian Journals Ltd, 1978) p. 33. To be quoted as 'Doc. survey'.
5 Doc. survey p. 47.
6 Published in C.G. Patelos (ed.) *The Orthodox Church in the Ecumenical Movement: Documents and Statements 1902–1975*, (Geneva, WCC, 1978) p. 325.
7 Doc. survey p. 68.
8 Doc. survey p. 80.
9 Doc. survey p. 58.
10 Service Orthodox de Presse et d'Information, no. 12 (November 1976).
11 Doc. survey p. 119.
12 John Lawrence, 'East and West – The New Opportunity', in *Ecumenical Review* 14:3 (April 1962).
13 Doc. survey p. 79.
14 Doc. survey p. 118.
15 N.S. Gordienko, *Contemporary Ecumenism* (Moscow, Academy of Sciences of the USSR, 1972).
16 Y.V. Kryanev, *Khristianskii Ekumenizm* (Moscow, Publication Political Literature, 1980).
17 W.A. Visser 't Hooft, 'The World Council of Churches and the Struggle between East and West', in *Christianity and Crisis*, 9:13 (July 1949).
18 CCPD Documents (18 November 1980), p. 22.
19 Quoted in William van den Bercken, 'Holy Russia and Soviet Fatherland', in *Religion in Communist Lands*, 15: 3 (Winter 1987), p. 275.
20 Quoted in Patelos (ed.), *The Orthodox Church*, p. 51.
21 Anatolii Levitin-Krasnov, *Die Glut deiner Hände – Memoires eines Russischen Christen* (Luzern: Rex Verlog, 1980), p. 271.

22 Report of the Central Committee of the WCC (Geneva, 1982), pp. 27, 50.

23 Jacques Ellul, *Trahison de l'occident* (Paris, 1975), p. 29.

24 Report of the Central Committee of the WCC (Geneva, 1980), p. 64.

25 *Stimme der Orthodoxie* (1976), 10, p. 41.

26 N.A. Zabolotsky, 'The Society of the Future: Justice, Participation, and Sustainability', in *Journal of the Moscow Patriarchate* (1982), 1, pp. 69–74, and (1982), 2, pp. 67–72.

27 *Ecumenical Review*, 25:1 (January 1985).

28 Report of the Central Committee of the WCC (Geneva, 1969), p. 138.

29 Report of the Central Committee of the WCC (Geneva, 1973), p. 23.

30 Leon Hoewell, *Acting in Faith* (Geneva: World Council of Churches, 1982), p. 42.

31 Erich Weingartner, *Human Rights on the Ecumenical Agenda* (CCIA Background Information, 1983), no. 3.

32 John Anderson, 'Soviet Religious Policy under Brezhnev and After', in *Religion in Communist Lands*, 11:1 (Spring 1983), p. 28.

33 Report of Visser 't Hooft, quoted in Doc. survey p. 97.

PART III

Education, socialisation, and values

·6·

Fear no evil: schools and religion in Soviet Russia, 1917–1941*

LARRY E. HOLMES

'In practice, no less than in theory', the *ABC of Communism* declared in 1919, 'communism is incompatible with religious faith'.[1] In the ensuing struggle against religion, the Party assigned schools a critical role. They were to replace religious instruction with teaching designed to counter religious sentiment among children and parents.

It was much easier said than done. Rhetoric was cheap and plenty of it followed throughout the period under study. Designing an appropriate curriculum, creating a mechanism to transmit it to the school, and implementing it in the classroom proved difficult and fraught with controversy. At the top, the Commissariat of Enlightenment, the state agency responsible for schools, found itself embroiled in a rivalry with the League of Militant Atheists, an organisation loosely associated with the Communist Party. At the middle of the educational apparatus, regional and local departments of education, especially during the 1920s, exercised an independent voice, modifying instructions from above. Finally, below, teachers, parents, and pupils resisted orders from above. They had their own reasons, some unavoidable, others laudable, and still others hardly praiseworthy.

This study examines the extent to which authorities in the Russian Republic expected primary and secondary schools to attack religion and the degree to which those schools did so. It turns out that, notwithstanding loud talk to the contrary, schools in the 1920s and 1930s were not suitable instruments for the eradication of cardinal tenets of popular belief. Active and passive resistance by officials,

* Research for this article was supported in part by a grant from the International Research and Exchanges Board (IREX), with funds provided by the National Endowment for the Humanities and the United States Information Agency. I gratefully acknowledge separate grants from the National Endowment for the Humanities; the Kennan Institute for Advanced Russian Studies; the Russian and East European Center at the University of Illinois; and the University of South Alabama. None of these organisations is responsible for the views expressed.

125

teachers, parents, and pupils blocked efforts at change from above. Indeed, the shoe often was on the other foot. Resistance from below contributed to a reshaping of official policy.

Four sections follow. The first reviews Marxist and Leninist ideology regarding religion and schooling. The next three examine educational policy, popular attitudes, and classroom practice for separate chronological periods: 1917–1928, 1928–1931 and 1931–1941. This periodisation corresponds to major shifts in policy. Actual classroom practice and its impact on religious belief remained, as we shall see, remarkably consistent from 1917 to 1941.

1. The ideology

Marxism–Leninism

Marx, Engels, and Lenin displayed little interest in an assault on popular religious belief in schools or anywhere else. Their ideology alerted them to the pointlessness of doing so. As part of the superstructure, religion would disappear as a consequence of socio-economic transformation and the spread of knowledge. The 'religious humbugging of mankind', Lenin said in 1905, would cease with the end of economic slavery.[2] All three urged caution to avoid a religious backlash. Expressing satisfaction with the Paris Commune's attempt at removing religious instruction from the public schools, Marx did not proceed to demand anti-religious teaching.[3] In 1874, Engels scolded French *communards* in exile who would outlaw every religious manifestation and organisation: 'This much is sure: the only service that can be rendered to God today is to declare atheism a compulsory article of faith.'[4] When appealing in 1919 for 'widespread scientific education and antireligious propaganda', Lenin hastened to add: 'It is necessary to take care to avoid hurting the religious sentiments of believers, for this only serves to increase religious fanaticism.'[5]

Attitudes toward institutions, such as the church, and toward individuals or groups who allegedly used religion to exploit the faithful, were another matter. Then Marxists were quite prepared to throw caution to the wind. Nevertheless, the ideology of Marxism–Leninism implied a condescendingly tolerant attitude toward religious sentiment among common citizens. It certainly did not require strident anti-religious propaganda in the school. The Commissariat of Enlightenment (Narkompros) accepted this aspect of Marxist–Leninist ideology and acted accordingly.

Narkompros

The first Commissar of Enlightenment, Anatoly Vasil'evich Lunacharsky, made religion into a special object of concern. Since declaring himself a Marxist in 1890, he had insisted on emotional and ethical commitment as an essential prerequisite for the building of a new order. For him, Marxism was precisely the source of just such inspiration. His initial volume of *Religion and Socialism*, published in 1908, portrayed Marx as a moral philosopher who had formulated a 'scientific and human religion'. Driven by emotional fervour, the proletariat would become God, save itself and create a new world. Lenin objected strongly to such philosophical free-lancing and 'God-building'. On the narrower issue of religion and schools, however, Lunacharsky's position was simpler, matching that of Lenin. The Commissar opposed direct action, favouring instead aesthetic, academic, and labour education as the best remedy for religious belief.

Lunacharsky's assistant at Narkompros, Krupskaya, agreed and went to considerable lengths to make her point. She did so as head of the Pedagogical Section of the State Academic Council, the body responsible for devising school curricula throughout the 1920s. Then and well into the 1930s, she opposed ridicule, abuse, and legal compulsion. In her estimation, religion was best combated through instruction in natural science (especially in evolution), labour training, social studies, and history.[6]

One of Krupskaya's colleagues at the Pedagogical Section, Pavel Petrovich Blonsky, held a similar view, but one more reflective of his training in philosophy and psychology, subjects which he had taught before the revolution at Moscow University. Religion provided impressionable adolescents with an outlet for aesthetic yearnings, poetic moods, and sexual romanticism.[7] He urged drawing and music at school as a better and more creative release.

2. Nonreligious instruction, 1917–1928

State and Narkompros policies

The new Soviet regime moved immediately toward the creation of a fully secular school system. Within months of the October revolution, it had required religious organisations to surrender control of their educational institutions to the new Commissariat of Enlightenment, forbade religious instruction in any school offering a general curriculum, and banned 'religious images of any description' in all state institutions, schools included.[8] At the same time, Narkompros brought forth its prized creation, the United Labor School, as the only elementary and secondary school for the entire Russian Republic. The Commissariat recommended an end to homework, most standard textbooks, promotion examinations, and marks. It encouraged socially useful labour, modelling, shopwork, and a practicum in a factory. Beginning in 1921, its Pedagogical Section aggressively encouraged adoption of the complex method. As devised by the Section, this method focused attention not on subjects but on a series of themes arranged under the headings of nature, labour, and society. A topic under study on any particular day would relate to the theme of the week, which, in turn, would correspond to the broader themes of the month and year.

Yet this rush to change things had its limits. Narkompros showed no interest in anti-religious instruction. It allowed the observance of religious holidays of note. A recommendation in December 1922 that the winter vacation extend from 5 January through 20 January permitted the celebration of Christmas and Epiphany on their traditional dates (by the Gregorian calendar to fall on 7 and 19 January).[9] For Christmas, the same remained true the following year when the Narkompros Collegium suggested 1 through 15 January. Nor were holidays associated with Easter an object of concern. More important considerations were at stake. The spring break was to be set by local departments of education according to the dictates of climate.[10] Narkompros had in mind, of course, the need for children to work during spring planting. That this policy might allow the observance of many religious holidays was of no consequence. Religion would pass on, the victim of the spread of socialism and knowledge.

Na putiakh k novoi shkole (On the Paths to the New School), edited by Krupskaya for the Pedagogical Section, took the same approach. Religion was dying off of its own accord, one teacher confidently wrote for it in 1923. The school not the church was rapidly becoming the master of children. He praised teachers who tactfully ignored displays of belief such as children crossing themselves.[11] One year later the journal printed an item, 'The Experience of Antireligious Propaganda Among Children', critical of requisitioning of crosses and forbidding of church attendance.[12]

Narkompros did occasionally explain that its policies were not to be confused with indifference. It joined *Pravda* in 1923 in specifying 'a struggle against religion' as one of the criteria in a contest to find the best teacher in the Russian Republic.[13] The following year, a circular issued jointly by Narkompros and the Party's arm for adolescents, the

Young Communist League (*Komsomol*), called upon teachers to counter religious influence among the young.[14] Yet in both cases, religion was hardly a major consideration. *Pravda* presented an extensive list of criteria, which included the quality of academic instruction and a teacher's activity on behalf of the school library, adult education, and the collection of the harvest and agricultural tax. The circular was equally concerned with what *Komsomol* and Narkompros could do to curb smoking and cursing. Three years later, the Narkompros Collegium failed to mention anti-religious instruction when it set the rules for finding the best primary school in the land.[15] Nor did major educational conferences and congresses pay much attention to the subject. Officials and teachers assembled at the Conference on Contemporaneity and Social Studies (May 1923), the First All-Union Congress of Teachers (11–19 January 1925), and the All-Russian Conference of Secondary Schools (5–10 July 1925) discussed in detail the content, methods, and objectives of schooling, but showed little interest in shaping the curriculum to curb religious sentiment.[16]

When Narkompros did make religion the sole object of its attention, it signalled no change in policy. A letter, 'On Nonreligious Training in the Primary School', issued by the Pedagogical Section in mid 1925, repeated earlier claims that knowledge of science and technology would render superstition and belief in God obsolete. 'A special inculcation of antireligiosity in the soul of the child', the letter stated, 'is absolutely not necessary'.[17] Narkompros took this opportunity once again to remind departments of education and teachers to avoid open confrontation with religious sentiment. Krupskaya later recalled that the Pedagogical Section issued the letter to rein in a few teachers who proposed communism as a new religion.[18]

Narkompros virtually ignored religion in its curricula and syllabi. So did provincial departments of education. Like Narkompros they assumed that a scientific understanding of water would rid children of a belief in water spirits, of wood spirits, and of society of God.[19] Any reference to 'religious prejudice' in a section on social studies came in the same sweeping call for the study of electrification, the tractor, the Party, and the alliance (*smychka*) between rural and urban areas. In 1927, a Narkompros syllabus for social studies in rural schools went little further. Under the heading 'Other Questions of Rural Life' it mentioned a 'Struggle Against Superstition and Prejudice' among many issues meriting attention.[20]

More so than Narkompros, some provincial departments encouraged a systematic presentation of history. But they did so by providing more information on political developments and not on religion and the church.[21] When Narkompros itself began to show more interest in the subject during the mid and late 1920s, little if any more anti-religious instruction occurred. Although the Protestant Reformation now received more extensive treatment in a history of Western Europe, it was still regarded as only one factor among many in the struggle against feudalism. Economic and social developments remained far more deserving of study.[22] So it was with the popular textbook *The Brief History of Russia* by M.N. Pokrovsky, the dean of Soviet Marxist historians and Narkompros official partly responsible for these syllabi. In this volume, Pokrovsky did little more with religion than refer to Russian Orthodoxy as a continuation of native animism, mention the secularisation of the church by the Romanovs, and comment on the use of the church by the merchant bourgeoisie and serfowners.[23]

Syllabi for native language and literature likewise avoided anti-religion. Whether issued by Moscow or by local departments, they called for an acquaintance with the local dialect, folk tales, and literary classics. It was left up to the instructor to decide how this material might be used to disabuse the youth of religion. A reading list for a survey of Russian literature issued by the Viatka department of education in 1921 even recommended without commentary Orthodox legends and the Lives of Saints.[24]

Religion fared no worse in syllabi for natural and physical sciences. Viatka's 1918 curriculum emphasised nature as the source of all information and thereby dispensed with any need to battle against God.[25] Narkompros programmes emphasised the evolution of the universe, of the Earth, and of biological life.[26] Religion was irrelevant. So was any attack on it.

There remained one area of potential importance for anti-religion. From its inception, Narkompros had insisted on learning through doing, an approach that encouraged activity outside the classroom. Yet the leading advocates of the school's involvement in the community said surprisingly little about the local church and the religious as potential targets of such activity. Thus, V.N. Shul'gin, active member of the Pedagogical Section, Director of the School Methods Institute, and shrill champion of socially useful activity, urged teachers and pupils to get involved chiefly in promoting voter turnout in local elections, eradicating adult illiteracy, and raising industrial production.[27]

Conditions

Narkompros promised little in the way of countering religion. It delivered even less. Conditions militated against anything more. Neither their training nor experience predisposed teachers toward taking up the challenge of anti-religious propaganda, even if asked. Ben Eklof reminds us that when little more than instruction in the rudiments of reading, writing, and arithmetic was expected of teachers, advanced training was unnecessary and could even be a hindrance.[28] But effective incorporation of anti-religious propaganda into a curriculum, standard or progressive, required skills that generally would be lacking in a cadre with little higher and specialised pedagogical training.[29] Teachers with the most experience were, of course, precisely those who had grown accustomed to the pre-revolutionary curriculum. As late as 1926 about 40 per cent of the teachers in the Russian Republic claimed ten or more years of experience.[30] Recent additions to the teaching corps, even if they came from the ranks of the working class and peasantry, did not necessarily mean a new attitude, since opposition to anti-religious propaganda permeated all socio-occupational categories. Nor did affiliation of a growing number of teachers with the Party indicate a change. In the 1920s, teachers had a variety of reasons to associate with the Party that included its skeptical attitude toward anti-religious agitation.

Conditions were often so bad that regardless of their intentions many instructors could not cope with any curriculum, religious or anti-religious. The cessation in 1921 of pretence of central funding for primary and secondary schools turned a bad situation into a disaster. Many schools were forced to close. Those schools that survived were short of the most essential of items: glass for broken windows, nails for repair work, desks, benches, paper, and pencils. To make life more difficult, teachers were expected to perform a stunning array of chores outside the classroom. They were told to assist local soviets and co-operatives (often as bookkeepers), advise Pioneer and *Komsomol* groups, wage war against adult illiteracy, help with the collection of the harvest and the agricultural tax and, in some cases, carry out anti-religious agitation in the community. Little wonder many teachers quit.[31] Those who chose to stay to combat religion found themselves adrift without help from above or below. As one disappointed zealot reported in 1927, neither Narkompros nor anyone else had issued special texts or directives.[32] And what was one teacher in a village school to do when instruction transpired in a church amidst the 'noise of church singing'.[33] The 'noise' was symbolic of problems far more serious than inadequate physical facilities.

Popular opposition

During the first decade of Soviet power, the local community repeatedly frustrated initiatives to alter the traditional way of doing things. At first, parents insisted on preserving God's place in the school. A 1918 investigation discovered that some local soviets supported religious instruction.[34] A study of Tver province uncovered religious teaching in rural schools.[35] One mother pointed out that the capital itself was not immune. She had moved to Moscow expecting that her son would be the recipient of a new education. Her words betrayed her disappointment. She found instead the old boring rote learning and mechanical exercises. Worse yet, pupils were taught to read and recite prayers after lessons.[36]

Other parents were prepared to insist, by harsh means if necessary, that their child recite prayers at school. Teachers inclined to remove prayer and icons from the classroom feared physical reprisals. Early in 1918, teachers in Riazan gathered to brood about the possibility for 'conflict with the masses'. Others bombarded Moscow with reports of threats of bodily injury if religion were removed. Krupskaya reported on their plight in a 1918 article for the Narkompros periodical *Narodnoe prosveshchenie*.[37] The following year, while on a six-month trip through the Volga-Kama region, teachers told her that they left icons hanging in their classrooms to avoid irritating the populace.[38] They acted wisely. A tense moment, and disaster narrowly avoided, occurred near Nizhnii Novgorod in December 1918. At noon a crowd of mothers gathered at a school demanding their children and threatening teachers with murder to make their point. They had come in the belief that on this day Antichrist would visit the school to deprive children of their crosses and leave his mark on them. The school was left with few pupils, but with a full complement of teachers frightened though apparently unharmed.[39]

In the following decade, parents and the community found more subtle ways of resisting godlessness at school. The cessation of central funding in 1921 enhanced their chances by making schools dependent on parents who paid for their children's education. Unable to support schools, Narkompros reluctantly allowed the charging of fees. What it feared most soon transpired. A partial privatisation of the public school system resulted. Some schools charged 150 to 200 rubles a year accounting for 40 per cent of their total revenue. By 1928, 32.5 per cent of the income of secondary schools came from fees, a figure higher than the pre-revolutionary period's 28.2 per cent.[40]

Much the same resulted from the introduction of the contract system (*dogovornaia sistema*). In 1922, Narkompros permitted contracts between local departments of education and agencies prepared to finance the schools. The measure proved popular and indispensable. One year later at least one-third of the Republic's primary schools depended on such an arrangement.[41] Many of these contracts were deals struck between teachers and parents, creating, in effect, private establishments. Narkompros should not have been surprised. Its statute allowing contracts had, and not coincidentally, repeated the State's ban on private schools.[42]

These changes in financing militated against any substantive changes in the curriculum. The cause of anti-religion suffered as a result. Teachers, educational officials, inspectors, and parents alike testified to the effectiveness of popular resistance from below. Paying parents of pupils in the secondary grades insisted on a preparatory curriculum for higher education. Anything else was thought to be a waste of time and effort. Working class and peasant parents who did not pay or paid considerably less preferred a primary school featuring the three 'R's' (sometimes for religious reasons) and respect for their elders. An inspector of rural schools commented that anything else was regarded by the peasantry as 'so much mumbo-jumbo [and] Bolshevik nonsense'.[43]

Narodnoe prosveshchenie observed in 1923 that some parents used the contract system to force a reintroduction of icons and religious beliefs. A delegate to the First All-Union Congress of Teachers commented sadly that peasants regarded teachers primarily as purveyors of Bolshevism and atheism.[44] About a year later, at one of many regional educational conferences, a teacher from Perm', bored by endless speeches, turned to a colleague to ask how it was going in her village. A forlorn reply followed: 'People demand the teaching of religion.'[45] A survey of peasant opinions in a rural district in Moscow province in late 1928 registered complaints about the absence of religion in schools.[46] Another survey of 28 cantons (*volosts*) in Penza province was even more revealing. 'It is necessary to teach children in the fear of God', a peasant said, 'or they will grow up to be hooligans and thieves'. Others chimed in that religious instruction was necessary for developing a love for Mother Earth and elders.[47] One group of teetotaling religious sectarians, the Molokane (Milkdrinkers) forged an intriguing alliance to remove one teacher apparently too adept at anti-religious propaganda. They united with the executive committee of the local soviet to replace the accused with the wife of the soviet's secretary.[48]

When holy days conflicted with school days, the latter often came out second best. Narkompros had tried to avoid such confrontation, but it could not take into account all religious holidays especially those of local import. A partial survey of schools for the 1926/7 academic year found that absenteeism followed no particular pattern in urban schools, while conforming to the agricultural cycle in rural areas (high during fall harvest and spring planting). Narkompros maintained that only 5.6 per cent of the absenteeism in rural primary schools could be attributed to unofficial (presumably religious) holidays.[49] This low figure, however, was a poor indicator of conflict between school and religious celebration. First, an allowance in the academic calendar for the agricultural cycle permitted religious holidays associated with the fall and spring. Second, regardless of the season, many local departments of education found discretion the better part of valour and cancelled school on religious holidays. When they did not, trouble ensued. Narkompros acknowledged this harsh reality when it addressed its local departments at the beginning of the 1926/7 academic year. It ordered them to stop what it labelled 'massive absenteeism on religious holidays'.[50] It was the best Narkompros could do, and it did not help a bit. Schools that operated on the traditional date of Christmas, now 7 January, had very low attendance. That day in 1927 in a district in the city of Yaroslavl', over 30 per cent of first and second graders did not attend, nor did over 40 per cent of pupils enrolled in the fourth grade. One year later, 37 per cent of the enrolment in fifteen elementary schools in Voronezh skipped. Two of these schools experienced an absentee rate of 50 per cent, and one, School No. 14, of 60 per cent. Pupils in senior classes in Leningrad boycotted classes. The absentee rate in Yaroslavl' on Epiphany (now 19 January) dwarfed that which had occurred on Christmas. That day about 55 per cent of the first, as well as second, graders stayed home, as did almost 70 per cent of the fourth graders.[51]

Classroom practice and new policies

Like parents, teachers thought of the school as a conduit for useful information, and not as an agent of cultural transformation. They too wanted an emphasis on literacy in the primary grades, and on basic subjects at the secondary level. Difficult conditions reinforced among them a desire for the traditional. Absenteeism, a brief academic year, and a pronounced dropout rate made it imperative, in the eyes of many teachers, that they focus on the fundamentals when they had the opportunity. During the mid 1920s, a child who enrolled in school remained on the average for only 2.77 years.[52] In such circumstances, if teachers and parents were to achieve what both desired, then every possible moment had to be devoted to instruction in the three 'Rs'. Anti-religious instruction was a luxury no one could afford, even if a few thought it desirable for ideological or political reasons.

Positioned uncomfortably between teachers below and Narkompros above, many provincial departments of education agreed with the former by favouring a traditional approach. Even when rhetorically pledging fealty to Narkompros, these departments issued curricula and syllabi with a predetermined body of knowledge and skills arranged by subject.[53] None other than the Moscow Department of Education openly challenged its superior. In 1926 its curriculum for grades five through seven stated it bluntly. Schools should not lose sight of the 'eternal mission of the school at all times' to teach reading, writing, and arithmetic.[54]

By the mid 1920s even the Party found occasion to encourage the academic side of life with no concern for anti-religion. On 24 August 1924, the Orgburo of the Central Committee told Pioneer organisations to cut back on their extracurricular activities and devote more attention to schoolwork.[55] Almost exactly a year later, the Central Committee instructed Pioneers to achieve a 'normalization of their activity' in the school. In the meantime, it ordered rural *Komsomolites* not to interfere with teachers.[56] *Narodnoe prosveshchenie* followed with an article indicating that the responsibilities of membership in the Pioneers and Young Communist League might be contributing to failure at school.[57]

Prodded from many directions and by their own sense of duty, many teachers paid only lip service, if that, to the new education. Rabkrin confirmed all this and more in its brutally frank appraisal of educational practices in 41 cantons, presented to the Pedagogical Section on 10 December 1925. It repeated its harsh message about a year later in a report to the All-Russian Central Executive Committee.[58] Another critic found instruction in social studies despicably traditional. Writing in the journal of the Central Committee's Department for Agitation and Propaganda (Agitprop), *Kommunisticheskaia revoliutsiia*, he lodged his complaint in intriguing language. Social studies often amounted to something akin to 'theology' and an 'incomprehensible catechism'.[59]

By the mid 1920s, Narkompros admitted that it had proved more effective in mapping an uncertain future than in negotiating the present. Many schools had never taken up the challenge of the new curriculum, and those that did soon regretted it. Deluged by the preferences of parents, pupils, teachers, and provincial educational officials, Narkompros began to respond in a way that meant even less concern for countering religion. On 29 January and then on 29 May 1926, the Pedagogical Section discussed curricula for grades five through seven with a focus on content arranged by subject matter.[60] Published curricula that followed for these grades and for the initial two years of the primary school did precisely that, as did curricula issued the following year.[61] 'The new school', Narkompros now declared in its 1927 programme for the primary school, 'values academic skills in native language no less than the old'. Its secondary school curriculum forbade the use of hours designated for academic subjects to be spent in preparation for holidays or campaigns of any sort.[62]

Entrance examinations given by higher educational institutions in 1926 and 1927 reinforced this trend toward the traditional. A large number of pupils, the best the schools could offer, performed atrociously. Many students demonstrated little knowledge of science, mathematics, Party history, the 1917 revolution, Russian literary classics, punctuation, and spelling.[63] Investigations by Narkompros and its departments of education revealed that some secondary pupils could barely read.[64] About half of the children of elementary school age (eight to eleven) in the Russian Republic did not attend school at all in the 1927/8 academic year. Little over half of the children in this age group were classified as literate.[65]

Thus by 1927, all the main players in the educational system – parents, teachers, rectors, provincial departments of education, and now Narkompros itself – expressed little interest in countering religion. Never an important element in syllabi or in the classroom, it now seemed likely to be forgotten altogether, above and below. There was, however, an organisation in place prepared to disrupt this new-found harmony and to rush in where Narkompros dared to tread.

The League of Atheists

In 1922, Emelian Mikhailovich Iaroslavsky, Party historian, propagandist, and member of the Party's Central Committee, founded *Bezbozhnik* (The Godless), a newspaper dedicated to the eradication of religion through knowledge. In Moscow a rival group proposed a direct assault on religion. The dispute was settled, for the moment at least, in 1923. That year a special commission of the Central Committee and the Twelfth Party Congress condemned crude attacks. Two years later, the group around *Bezbozhnik*, still under Iaroslavsky's leadership, formed the League of Atheists.

The League and Narkompros initially coexisted peaceably. In 1923, the Ivanovo–Voznesensk department of education, which did not favour anti-religious instruction, placed Iaroslavsky's *Bibliia dlia veruiushchikh i neveruiushchikh* (Bible for Believers and Non-Believers) on its list of recommended literature for social studies.[66] The League's new journal, also named *Bezbozhnik*, featured innumerable short articles in large print on science and technology as the antidote to religion. It made no effort to tell Narkompros how to conduct its side of the business. In mid-1926, the journal featured a large portrait of Lunacharsky as part of its regular series 'Gallery of the Godless'.[67] In February of the following year, Narkompros's Collegium granted the League a subsidy of 6,000 rubles.[68]

These developments occurred, however, when the first strains in the relationship had already appeared. In theses for a 1926 conference on anti-religious propaganda, the League's central committee condemned as 'liquidationist' any effort to limit such propaganda to instruction in the natural sciences.[69] Iaroslavsky followed with an article for *Kommunisticheskaia revoliutsiia*, chastising Narkompros for ignoring the conference. He proceeded to demand greater efforts to rid all textbooks of religious vestiges.[70] It was mild criticism in comparison with what would come.

In May, 1927, the League failed in its desperate plea for an additional subsidy from Narkompros.[71] It responded aggressively. Its new journal, *Antireligioznik*, took the Commissariat to task for setting vacation periods that allowed for the celebration of Christmas and Easter.[72] That October, the League engaged in Narkompros bashing at a Conference of Anti-religious Educators. N. Amosov, busily distinguishing himself as one of the League's most acerbic critics, equated mere non-religious instruction with the 'liquidation of all elements of atheistic work in our schools'.[73] Recent curricula, he observed, had made the situation worse and thereby had contributed, if only indirectly, to a rise in the religiosity of youth.

The League continued its offensive on 25 November at a conference 'Antireligious or Nonreligious Training in the School'. Amosov and other spokespersons for the godless demanded the replacement of non-religion with anti-religion. Delegates told Narkompros yet again to redraw school vacations to confront Christmas and Easter. Teachers were told to end 'desertion from the antireligious front'.[74] This time, Narkompros responded. It sent the head of its State Academic Council, Moisei Mikhailovich Pistrak, to reaffirm the primacy of non-religious instruction. Narkompros opposed, he insisted, sloganeering and the replacement of religion with an 'antireligious belief' (*verovanie*).

Pistrak indicated a willingness to allow some modification of the school calendar but only with academic considerations in mind.[75] His effort was ridiculed.

3.   The cultural revolution, 1928–1931

Anti-religion

The cultural revolution and collectivisation of agriculture called forth concerted attacks on churches and the faithful. The League of Atheists basked in the glare of official support. In June 1929, Maksim Gorky, Nikolai Bukharin, and even Lunacharsky came to address its second congress. They found a new toughness manifested in a resolution adding the word 'militant' to the organisation's title.

A rechristening to 'League of Militant Atheists' corresponded well to a shrill campaign already under way against Narkompros. Beginning in 1928 the League's publications seized upon any and all surveys that purported to demonstrate a failure of the non-religious curriculum. With a flair for the supposedly scientific, *Antireligioznik* and *Kommunisticheskaia revoliutsiia* presented allegedly incontrovertible evidence. Absenteeism ran rampant on religious holidays.[76] Other studies argued equally precisely that in a district in Moscow, 40 per cent of the seventh graders still believed in God. In one school there, a model institution named after none other than Joseph Stalin, 92 per cent of the pupils were supposedly believers. More such reports poured forth, heralded for their apparent accuracy. An investigation in Vladivostok of senior pupils and one in Khabarovsk of secondary school graduates discovered that 44 per cent believed in God. Thirty per cent of the elementary pupils in Perm' and of seventh graders in a district of Moscow prayed and 27 per cent of the same went to church. In one Moscow school, 60 per cent of the pupils attended religious services. An inspector of rural schools in Moscow province delivered a less precise but devastating report. He claimed that a majority of the children frequented church and prayed before dinner and bedtime.[77]

The League sallied forth to save the day from this putative religious revival. *Antireligioznik* obliged with so many articles that it devoted an entire section of its annual index for 1928 to anti-religious training in the schools. More such material followed in 1929, and a flood of it the next year. It recommended what Lenin and others earlier had explicitly condemned – carnivals, farces, and games to intimidate and purge the youth of religious belief. It suggested that pupils campaign against customs associated with Christmas (including Christmas trees) and Easter.[78] Some schools, the League approvingly reported, staged an anti-religious day on the 31st of each month. Not teachers but the League's local set the programme for this special occasion.[79]

Never one to let any part of the curriculum slip by unattended, Amosov suggested ways to co-ordinate physical examinations and anti-religious propaganda.[80] Health or illness had nothing to do with mysterious forces. Nikolai Aleksandrovich Flerov, recipient of a medical degree from Moscow State University in 1911, took a different approach. He linked worship with disease. Children should be taught that processions, church services, and kissing the cross spread harmful germs.[81]

Pravda, Izvestiia and *Revoliutsiia i kul'tura* joined the League's criticism of Narkompros to make for a very loud chorus. The Communist Academy added its voice with a major publication demanding that instruction in history inspire hatred toward the religious and the church. Without active anti-religious propaganda, it declared, history was nothing more than an academic subject.[82]

Promises, promises

Narkompros promised to do better. Krupskaya admitted that anti-religious work had 'weakened somewhat' during the past few years, as curricula had emphasised factual knowledge.[83] Moisei Solomonovich Epshtein, Deputy Commissar who had been one of the chief architects of these curricula, confessed that non-religious training was no longer suitable.[84] At the League's second congress, Lunacharsky acknowledged that it was past time to launch an anti-religious offensive in the school. He claimed his Commissariat had already begun.[85]

Lunacharsky was correct, an offensive had already begun. A December 1928 conference of school inspectors sounded more like a gathering of officials from the League of Militant Atheists. Its resolution, 'On the Next Measures for Antireligious Work in the School', called upon Narkompros to devise curricula, syllabi, instructions, and textbooks to expose the 'obscurantist reactionary role of the church and religion'.[86] The Commissariat's *Narodnoe prosveshchenie* began to sound like the League's *Antireligioznik*. Beginning in 1929, it featured a regular section 'For Antireligious Training'. *Na putiakh k novoi shkole*, still edited by Krupskaya, followed suit with articles in praise of the cultural revolution and anti-religious instruction. So did *Vestnik prosveshcheniia*, the publication of the Moscow Department of Education, and its successor in 1930, *Za Kommunisticheskoe vospitanie*; the journal of the teachers union, *Narodnyi uchitel'*; and the provincial journals *Shkola i*

In the clutches of prejudice

A teacher points to the new Soviet Gregorian calendar designating 25 December as the proper date for Christmas. An old peasant, the parent of the pupil, holds up a calendar turned to 7 January, the date for Christmas according to the Julian calendar in use before the 1917 revolution. The teacher asserts: 'Celebrate, my dear, Christmas on the new date!' The parent shouts back: 'No, in the old way!' The pupil, the new Soviet person in miniature, declares: 'Why are you pestering me? Maybe I don't want Christmas at all.' The artist is S. Bersukov. Source: *Uchitel'skaia gazeta*, no. 51 (226) (14 December 1928), p. 4.

zhizn' (Nizhnii Novgorod), *Nash trud* (Yaroslavl') and *Nizhe-Volzhskii prosveshchenets* (Saratov). The most obvious change occurred at *Uchitel'skaia gazeta*, the teachers union newspaper (renamed *Za Kom-*

munisticheskoe prosveshchenie at the beginning of 1930). The spirit of campaignism now engulfed this source, once so informative of the shortcomings of Kremlin policy and the problems of classroom practice. Through articles and cartoons, often of a mean satirical sort, it enjoined teachers, parents, and pupils alike to attack a wide assortment of political and social evils including religion. In April and May 1929, Narkompros ordered all educational institutions to hold classes on Christmas, Epiphany, Easter, and Ascension Day. Narkompros recommended that regional departments appoint inspectors of anti-religious propaganda.[87]

It was all more show than substance. The publication of articles and cartoons and the holding of school on religious holidays could hardly make a difference. The suggestion for anti-religious inspectors was hardly practical. Narkompros knew as much. Neither it, nor any of its departments of education, had the funds or the personnel to inspect schools for any purpose. Narkompros had little intention of taking up the agenda of the League of Militant Atheists.

Apart from its rhetoric, Narkompros refused to make anti-religion a fundamental element in its programme. It opposed efforts to close schools to children of priests or anyone else on grounds of social origin.[88] At the League's second congress, while acknowledging the need for an anti-religious offensive, Lunacharsky defended non-religious instruction. For good measure, the Commissar reminded his audience that Lenin had warned against atheistic propaganda in the schools.[89] Lunacharsky was as good as his word. From Orenburg province a distraught father informed Narkompros by telegram that his daughter was being dragged before a court formed by the school council and *Komsomol* cell. The charge was church attendance. Lunacharsky immediately ordered the court's abolition.[90] His stubbornness on this, as well as on other issues, led to his removal from office. In September 1929, Andrei Sergeevich Bubnov, former head of Agitprop and most recently secretary of the Central Committee, replaced Lunacharsky. Bubnov brought with him the sharp rhetoric of the cultural revolution including vigorous calls for anti-religious education.

Yet Krupskaya remained at Narkompros to defend its traditional position. She denounced purging of children and grandchildren of priests. The nineteenth-century radical, Nikolai Gavrilovich Chernyshevsky, she acidly observed, had been a son of a priest.[91] While accepting more anti-religious propaganda even in kindergartens, she still defended non-religious training as proper in its own day and implicitly still of value. Her definition of permissible anti-religious instruction seemed suspiciously like what had heretofore been labelled

non-religious training – a materialist curriculum highlighting evolution, the arts, and labour. She did not think it advisable to require
anti-religious propaganda of every teacher. Even religious teachers
might remain in the schools as long as they kept their beliefs to
themselves.[92] And what of the League's claim that attitudes such as
hers had allowed a religious revival? Krupskaya abruptly dismissed
the argument. The League's surveys were, she said, not scientific.[93]

Blonsky also took issue with the League's 'science'. Its own figures
revealed a decline in religious sentiment as children progressed
through school. Blonsky dismissed the religious as either the mentally
obtuse or those who remained attracted to the aesthetics of worship.
Blonsky then provided some figures of his own. A study of Moscow
pupils found that only 5 per cent of the seventh graders were religious.
This low figure resulted not only from the influence of school and
society, but also from a dropping out of the least fit mentally. Taking
into account all children of ages eligible to attend secondary school,
Blonsky found that only 15 to 20 per cent could be considered
believers, and for many of them this belief was superficial.[94]

Narkompros curricula and syllabi still avoided anti-religion.
Appeals to combat religion seemed somewhat perfunctory when compared to intense calls for involvement in planting, harvesting, and
industrial production; for campaigns against moonshine and all
manner of vermin (bugs, beasts, and man); and for the celebration of
revolutionary holidays. New textual materials from Narkompros and
provincial departments of education took a similar approach.[95]

The Moscow Department of Education pursued such a course with
its 1929 programme for social studies in the fifth grade. The topic 'the
church's reactionary role' existed alongside a host of more important
items for study: 'the tractor as a factor in the agricultural revolution'
and the 'significance of machine–tractor stations'; films 'The Struggle
for the Harvest', and 'Old and New'; and the newspapers *Komsomol'skaia Pravda* and *Ekonomicheskaia zhizn'*.[96] Textbooks in the form of
monthly journals (*zhurnaly-uchebniki*) took the same approach. One such
publication, *Shkol'naia brigada* (The Shock Brigade), after bowing to the
gods of anti-religion, focused on the factory, harvest, Pioneers,
machines, and human 'wreckers'.[97]

Practice

During the cultural revolution, Narkompros could boast of significant
arithmetical successes. From 1928 through 1930, the number of
elementary and secondary schools in the Russian Republic grew from

85,000 to over 102,000 and enrolment from 7.9 to 11.3 million, increases of 20 and 43 per cent. The enrolment in the primary grades alone rose by 48 per cent to achieve near universal education for children aged eight to eleven in urban areas and a 90 per cent enrolment in rural regions. The number of all schoolteachers in the Republic increased by 50 per cent from 1928 through 1931.[98] Yet this expansion added to the burdens of an already underfunded system. Schools in rural and urban regions lacked everything from firewood to desks and notebooks. Teachers remained overworked, underpaid, and subject to abuse by local officials. Information gathered by Narkompros and by the League revealed frequent instances of a refusal to conduct anti-religious instruction.[99] A great many teachers continued to concentrate on the fundamentals. Parents too preferred it that way.

Neither teachers nor parents regarded anti-religious instruction as a suitable subject.[100] In one recorded instance, the latter disrupted a school's anti-religious evenings with provocative questions about shortages and queues at the marketplace.[101] In Samara, pupils, presumably led by their elders, protested against the closure of churches.[102] Very few schools organised anti-religious circles, held anti-religious evenings, subscribed to *Antireligioznik*, or sponsored a wall newspaper with anti-religious articles.[103]

Then in 1930 and 1931, Narkompros began to adjust its public rhetoric more toward its own academic agenda. Resistance to anti-religion from below, its own misgivings, and a renewed concern for academic performance pushed the Commissariat in this direction. Entrance examinations to technicums and higher educational institutions in 1929 and 1930 revealed serious deficiencies on the part of school graduates in every subject from Russian language to physics, mathematics, chemistry, and history. Testing of pupils still in school provided more disturbing results.[104] *Antireligioznik* showed more concern for the academic side of school life,[105] and Bubnov began to show more interest in it.[106] In late August and early September, articles and an editorial in *Uchitel'skaia gazeta* demanded improved instruction in the standard academic subjects.[107]

New educational policies to match were not long in coming. On the eve of the 1931/2 academic year, 25 August, the Party's Central Committee secretly decided the issue. Anti-religious instruction would fare badly in a rush toward a more traditional curriculum.

4. Non-religion revisited, 1931–1941

Academic performance, 1931–1935

On 5 September 1931, *Pravda* published the Central Committee's historic resolution, 'On the Primary and Secondary School'. It was but the first in a series of Party and State decrees which, by the mid 1930s, required standard textbooks, fixed lesson plans, homework, and annual promotion examinations. In an intriguing twist, several Narkompros officials, Krupskaya included, worried that the pendulum might swing too drastically away from a critical treatment of religion.[108] Their concerns were justified. Anti-religion lost much of its former importance; only traces of rhetoric remained to remind teachers, parents, and pupils of the immediately preceding period. There was much, however, to bring to mind the philosophy and policies dominant at Narkompros prior to the cultural revolution.

Vacations once again allowed for an observance of Christmas and occasionally of Easter.[109] In early 1932, the head of a primary school wrote to Krupskaya concerning the absence of anti-religious circles. Worse yet, some of the non-teaching staff who lived in his own school disrupted anti-religious work by observing religious holidays. He asked Krupskaya if they could be fired for the transgression. She recommended against dismissal.[110] The following year, Deputy Commissar Epshtein believed that one primary schoolteacher had misused natural science to launch an attack on Easter.[111] Syllabi for biology and chemistry mentioned religious belief only in passing, as something inconsistent with a scientific understanding of the world. Syllabi for other subjects had even less to say.[112] Samuel Northrup Harper, professor of Russian language and institutions at the University of Chicago and a frequent visitor of Soviet Russia, found, in 1934, much less propaganda in schools than previously.[113] Narkompros officials could even joke about the change. Speaking to a conference on textbooks in early 1933, Epshtein commented that the school year would end with a holiday free of any cultural bomb (*kul'tbomba*). His audience laughed.[114]

At the same time, Narkompros rebuked one of its own, Evgeny Iosifovich Perovsky, a former schoolteacher, now member of several of the Commissariat's research institutes. Perovsky had submitted a manuscript, 'Antireligious Work in the Elementary School', for publication, in which he suggested night excursions to cemeteries to demonstrate the baselessness of superstitious fears. Sergei Alekseevich Kamenev, deputy head of Narkompros' Department for the Primary and Secondary School, thought the work guilty of crude excesses. So did other educational officials.[115] Members of the Pedagogical Research Institute shunted Perovsky aside as one who would waste too much of the Institute's time on a largely unimportant topic.[116] The most famous school in the USSR, Model School No. 25 in Moscow, pointedly avoided anything like Perovsky's recommendations. Its academic director, Aleksandr Semenovich Tolstov, explained that an earlier attack by a teacher on Christmas had only aroused interest in the holiday among pupils. The school henceforth limited its effort to more modest fare such as an exhibit, 'Science in the Struggle Against Religion'.[117]

At first, the League of Militant Atheists defiantly responded to these changes. Following the Central Committee's resolution in 1931, *Bezbozhnik* disingenuously declared that the Party required systematic not episodic attacks on religion.[118] In the years that followed, however, the League had little choice but to scale its expectations downward. It did hope for 'anti-religious moments' in academic subjects and campaigns against Easter in a pupil's leisure time.[119] Yet even these modest objectives still remained beyond the grasp of a League whose own membership declined from 5.5 million in 1932 to 2 million five years later. In 1932, *Antireligioznik* dropped its separate section on anti-religious training in the school, and thereafter acknowledged a decided lack of interest among teachers, parents, and pupils.[120] One report grumpily complained of an unacceptable incidence of belief among schoolchildren in God, witches, and all manner of spirits.[121] Narkompros ignored for the most part these complaints. It busied itself rather with threats to improved academic achievement: continuing shortages of everything from textbooks to pencils and paper; frequent grade repetition; and the low professional qualifications of teachers.

Thus, by the mid 1930s, forces above and below had manoeuvered Narkompros' rhetoric and policy into harmony with what had always been classroom practice. Only the League of Militant Atheists lamented the woes of anti-religion. That would soon change.

Purges and the rhetoric of anti-religion, 1935–1938

No institution, Narkompros included, could remain aloof from the tragic events that dominated the Soviet scene from 1935 to 1937. At first, Narkompros seemed quite capable of emerging from the purges and the terror with its organisation and policies, including non-religious instruction, fairly intact. In 1935, critics accommodated Narkompros by using its own academic standards to point to its failures, real and imagined.[122] The following year things took a turn for the worse. Critics launched an orchestrated and abusive campaign.

Among those in the forefront of the assault was none other than B.M. Volin, its First Deputy Commissar since December 1935. 'We need to kick in the teeth', he declared upon assuming his new post, 'pseudo-scientists in Narkompros who as in other commissariats engage in plain wrecking'.[123] A failure to promote anti-religion became one excuse to commence the kicking. In May 1937, *Pravda* editorialised that both Narkompros and the League had curtailed their anti-religious activities. *Pravda* urged that 'the teaching of academic subjects ... be thoroughly steeped in antireligious propaganda'.[124] Narkompros had little choice. It confessed its errors and hoisted the anti-religious flag.

On 19 July 1937, Bubnov dragged out the Pedagogical Section's 1925 letter for one more beating. It was a prime example of the 'rotten theory of nonreligious training'.[125] Four days later, the governing council at Narkompros complained of inadequate political training and an almost total absence of anti-religious instruction in the schools.[126] After avoiding the issue for years, Narkompros' Pedagogical Laboratory now demanded the infusing of every subject with anti-religious content.[127] It did not save the Commissariat and Bubnov from very rough treatment. A purge that followed swept up the Commissar and many of his colleagues. Arrested in October, 1937, Bubnov was shot in August of the following year.[128]

Even as the purge took away some of Iaroslavsky's colleagues at the League of Militant Atheists, advocates of a vigorous prosecution of religious belief acted with a boldness not seen since the cultural revolution. The League, whose membership rose to 3 million by 1941, revitalised its campaign for anti-religion at school. Narkompros contributed its fair share of accompanying propaganda. The lead article in its new journal *Sovetskaia pedagogika* accompanied Bubnov's removal with the accusation that the Commissariat had ignored anti-religious training.[129] Articles in this and subsequent issues through the spring of 1938 suggested how this mistake might be made good. Sporting the title 'Antireligious Training in the School', these items instructed teachers to tell their pupils how the clergy exploited the peasantry and supported Fascism; how the church had retarded Russia's cultural development; how sectarians had formed special White Guard detachments during the Russian Civil War; and how priests perched in belltowers shot at the masses below during the 1905 and February 1917 revolts. They also encouraged schools to organise circles and cells affiliated with the League of Militant Atheists.[130]

Practice: more of the same

Once more rhetoric proved easier than substance. Anti-religion remained more show than reality. The Commissariat's leaders and *Sovetskaia pedagogika* never ceased stressing academic knowledge as the top priority. When addressing anti-religion, they regarded it as only one part of a larger effort to instil proper behaviour and attitudes. Speech after speech and article after article, tripping over each other in rapid succession, demanded instruction in discipline, honesty, bravery, diligence, tidiness, Soviet patriotism, and proper posture. Curricula provided little more than anti-religious moments.[131] As before, the nation's instructional cadre preferred it that way. A resurgence of Russian nationalism even lent respectability to Christianity and the Russian Orthodox Church in history instruction. Both were regarded as unifying forces among Slavs in Kiev-Rus' and as transmitters of classical culture.[132]

Curricula for teacher training institutions usually contained an item 'Training in Militant Atheism', demonstrating the class essence of religion and the 'harm of "nonreligious" training'.[133] Primary emphasis, however, was on traditional subjects and on proper comportment. One old Narkompros hand nevertheless felt that Narkompros might have given too much to anti-religion. Pavel Nikolaevich Shimbirev, a teacher in a pre-revolutionary zemstvo school, an instructor in a teacher training college in Moscow, member of the Moscow Department of Education during the 1920s, then head of the pedagogical faculty of the Moscow Region Teachers Institute, objected in late 1938 to a draft programme for a course in pedagogy. He called critical attention to its stated purpose to 'expose religious views'. Shimbirev preferred a less confrontational approach, a 'patient explanation of the harm of superstition and prejudices'.[134]

Shimbirev need not have worried much. The trumpeting of official anti-religion had limited resonance in Narkompros syllabi, and less in actual practice. The League of Militant Atheists understood this state of affairs all too well for its own comfort. In 1938, Perovsky repaid Narkompros for its earlier rebuke by listing the educational system's sins. The great majority of syllabi were written in the 'typical nonreligious spirit'. He complained that the newspaper *Uchitel'skaia gazeta* had refused to publish a statement submitted by the League's Central Council. The Department for the Elementary School at Narkompros had blocked the publication of a collection of anti-religious works and had failed to sponsor the preparation of any similar material. Actual classroom instruction contained little anti-religious propaganda and there was little extracurricular anti-religious activity at school.[135]

Additional reports in *Antireligioznik* and *Sovetskaia pedagogika* confirmed Perovsky's charges.[136] No doubt the League's spokespersons engaged in hyperbole. Any manifestation of superstition among the youth (or teachers) might therefore be equated with an expression of religious sentiment. By this logic, schools and Narkompros failed egregiously because pupils took a cat crossing the road as an evil omen.[137] *Antireligioznik* reported on 'wild (*dikarskie*) superstitious vestiges' in a row of pupils who in succession poked each other in the side until the last touched the wall. The children thought they were ridding themselves of potential bad fortune, an effort made necessary by their ignorance of the day's lessons.[138]

These exaggerated fears aside, the unadorned facts were sufficient reason for concern when the League's Central Council met in April 1940. It was as if nothing had changed in the prolonged effort to bring anti-religion to the school. Even the ritual remained the same. Representatives from Narkompros came to indict their own organisation. The League had heard this before, too many times. Its head, Iaroslavsky, understood the situation well. He should have after witnessing twenty years of dissimulation. The Commissariat of Enlightenment, he said, had provided much talk but little action, much advice but little real assistance. 'It's time', Iaroslavsky concluded, 'to stop being limited to formal resolutions. It's time to act'.[139]

Conclusion

For Narkompros, there had never been a time to act. Its curricula had always avoided anti-religion as a critical item. Teachers rejected attacks on religion, refusing to implement what little the Commissariat asked them to do. The League of Militant Atheists complained loudly. It had minimal effect other than to document the extent to which the educational apparatus from top to bottom avoided assaults on religious belief. All players in the educational system, parents included, equated schooling with the transmission of knowledge and skills (and obedience). Difficulties facing the school, from shortages to the high dropout rate, reinforced a desire to focus on the fundamentals as much as possible. Anti-religion was not fundamental.

The early advocates of non-religious training hoped a secular school would contribute to a decline of religious influence. It might be argued that this in fact happened after 1917. Yet both the cause and effect in such an interpretation are problematical. Religious belief, a complex and often private matter, was (and remains) beyond adequate measure. As Krupskaya observed, the attempt by the League of

Militant Atheists to gauge it was anything but scientific. Counting outward forms of worship obviously would not do. Nor could questions concerning the nature of belief when, for so many, religion was anything but a consciously chosen intellectual phenomenon. Moshe Lewin has suggested that in rural Russia the rich demonology, the many spirits, and the spiritual significance of the peasant hut (*izba*) made religion an unmeasurable yet integral part of life.[140] Everyday reality itself would have to change for traditional Christianity to falter. Despite significant structural change brought on by collectivisation and industrialisation, for many common Russians that reality remained much the same. Belief in God and all manner of spirits continued into the 1930s. Narkompros and teachers chose not to confront this phenomenon directly. Russia above and below proved more resistant to change than expected.

Like Narkompros, the Communist Party worked within seen and unseen constraints. As Lunacharsky and Krupskaya made abundantly clear, Marxist–Leninist ideology itself could be used to squelch a temptation to attack religion in the schools. When, beginning in 1928, the Party did sponsor policies conducive to just such an attack, meagre results followed. Narkompros promised much during the cultural revolution, but delivered considerably less in its curricula. Teachers and schools decisively rejected anti-religion. Thus when the Party's Central Committee reversed the course of official policy in 1931, it did not act apart from the society to which it dictated. It followed, perhaps consciously, desired and actual classroom practice. Another burst of official anti-religion during the mid 1930s had little effect on Narkompros curricula and even less on classroom instruction.

Certainly the demographic revolution, urbanisation, bureaucratisation, the development of modern communications, or what generally might be called secularisation and modernisation, affected religious belief, even strengthening it for some Russians.[141] Perhaps, godliness took on a new form, as Pistrak and Narkompros once feared, of official 'antireligious belief', now replete with shrines, processions, a catechism, and a quasi-Puritanical code.[142] Modernisation combined with persecution surely reinforced among some people a desire for traditional and non-traditional religious experience (just as Marx, Engels, and Lenin predicted might happen). On the other hand, Alex Inkeles and David Horton Smith argue that schooling has been a powerful factor in bringing about modern attitudes and behaviour. They do not ascribe this result to formal instruction or any school subject. Rather they find that it is the hidden curriculum that contributes to the development of a modern mentality.[143] Be that as it may, from 1917 to

1941 Soviet Russia's schools contributed almost nothing to a direct assault on religion. The educational system, like society itself, proved more tradition-bound and inert than expected. Amidst talk about the transformation of humans and society, the school curriculum did not become an effective instrument for obliterating key elements of popular culture.[144]

Schooling is properly part of social history and social history, especially in matters of popular belief, moves slowly. Soviet Russia's schools, their leaders, teachers, pupils, and local communities, have proved no exception.

Notes

1 N. Bukharin and E. Preobrazhensky, *The ABC of Communism* (Ann Arbor, University of Michigan Press, 1966), p. 148.
2 V.I. Lenin, *Polnoe sobranie sochinenii*, vol. 12, 5th edn (Moscow, Izdatel'stvo politicheskoi literatury, 1968), pp. 146–7.
3 Karl Marx and Friedrich Engels, *On Religion* (New York, Schocken Books, 1964), p. 145.
4 *Ibid.*, p. 143.
5 Lenin, *Polnoe sobranie sochinenii*, vol. 38 (Moscow, 1969), p. 118.
6 N.K. Krupskaya, *Iz ateisticheskogo nasledia* (Moscow, Nauka, 1964), pp. 110–11, 152, 155, 176, 183, 192–3, 195, 204, 259, 263. Also *Na putiakh k novoi shkole* (henceforth *Na putiakh*), 7–8, (July–August 1928), p. 7.
7 *Na putiakh*, 2 (February, 1925), pp. 138–9 and *Na putiakh*, 4–5 (April–May 1929), pp. 68, 70; P.P. Blonsky, *Izbrannye pedagogicheskie proizvedeniia* (Moscow: Izdatel'stvo Akademii Pedagogicheskikh nauk, 1961), p. 551. Another member of the Pedagogical Section, S.T. Shatsky, emphasised the importance of aesthetic training, but did not link it so intensely to the eradication of religion's appeal.
8 *Narodnoe obrazovanie v SSSR. Sbornik dokumentov, 1917–1973 gg.* (henceforth *NO*) (Moscow, Pedagogika, 1974), p. 13.
9 *Biulleten' ofitsial'nykh rasporiazhenii i sochinenii* (henceforth *BORS*), 4 (23 December 1922), p. 2.
10 *BORS*, 23 (28 April 1923), p. 13.
11 A. Ganson, 'Religiia, moral', i polovoi vopros u detei i u iunoshestva', *Na putiakh*, 1 (January 1923), pp. 77–82.
12 P. Alampiev, 'Opyt antireligioznoi propagandy sredi detei', *Na putiakh*, 1 (January 1924), pp. 68–80 and 4 (April–May 1924), pp. 138–49.
13 *BORS*, 17 (24 March 1923), pp. 9–10; from *Pravda*, 20 March 1923.
14 *Ezhenedel'nik Narkomprosa RSFSR* (henceforth *Ezhenedel'nik NK)*), 26:46, (4 December 1924), pp. 8–11.
15 *Narodnyi uchitel'*, 3 (March 1927), p. 13.
16 For the conference on social studies, see *Narodnoe prosveshchenie*, 4–5 (April–May 1923), pp. 209–10; for the Congress of Teachers, *Narodnoe prosveshchenie*, 2 (February 1925), pp. 177–8 and I.G. Avtukhov and I.D.

Martynenko (eds.), *Programmy GUS' a i massovaia shkola*, 2nd edn (Moscow: Rabotnik prosveshcheniia, 1925), pp. 80–1; and for the Conference of Secondary Schools *Voprosy shkoly II stupeni; Trudy Pervoi Vserossiiskoi konferentsii shkol II siupeni 5–10 iiulia 1925 g.*, (Moscow, Narkompros, 1926).

17 *Voinstvuiushchee bezbozhie v SSSR za 15 let; 1917–1932. Sbornik* (Moscow, Gosudarstvennoe antireligioznoe izdatel'stvo, 1932), p. 289.
18 N. Krupskaya, 'Ob antireligioznom vospitanii v shkole', *Na putiakh*, 7–8 (July–August 1928), pp. 7–8.
19 *Primernye programmy po istorii dlia shkol II-i stupeni* (Moscow, Narkompros, 1920), pp. 37–44; *Programmy semiletnei edinoi trudovoi shkoly* (Moscow, Narkompros, 1921); *Novye programmy dlia edinoi trudovoi shkoly, NKP* (Moscow–Petrograd, Narkompros, 1923), especially pp. 8–9; *Novye programmy edinoi trudovoi shkoly pervoi stupeni* (Moscow, Narkompros, 1924); *Programmy dlia pervogo kontsentra shkol vtoroi stupeni* (Moscow–Leningrad, Narkompros 1925); *Programmy i metodicheskie zapiski edinoi trudovoi shkoly. Gorodskie i sel'skie shkoly I stupeni. Metodicheskie zapiski k programmam* (Moscow–Leningrad, Narkompros, 1927). See also the proposals presented by Krupskaya to the Presidium of the Pedagogical Section, February 1923 in Tsentral'nyi Gosudarstvennyi arkhiv (henceforth TsGA RSFSR), f. 298, op. 1, ed. khr. 45, l. 13.
20 *Obshchestvovedenie v trudovoi shkole*, 1 (1927), p. 55.
21 See *Semiletnaia shkola* (Kursk, 1921), pp. 90 ff; the syllabi of the Petrograd department of education, *Programmy dlia sel'skoi shkoly* (Moscow–Petrograd, 1922), pp. 42 ff; *Programmy dlia shkol l-i stupeni Vladimirskoi gubernii* (Vladimir, 1922), pp. 64–8; *Programmy I-i stupeni Edinoi Trudovoi shkoly* (Saratov, 1922), pp. 14–16.
22 'Programma po obshchestvovedeniiu dlia 2-go kontsentra shkol II stupeni (8-i i 9-i gody)', *Obshchestvovedenie v trudovoi shkole*, 2–3 (1927), pp. 109–19, especially p. 111.
23 M.N. Pokrovsky, *Brief History of Russia*, trans. by D.S. Mirsky, reprint of 1933 edition (University Reprints, 1968), I, pp. 49, 91–2, 95.
24 *Primernyi plan rabot v shkole I-i stupeni*, (Viatka, 1921), pp. 27–8; *Semiletnaia shkola* (Kursk, 1921), pp. 90 ff; *Primernye programmy shkoly I stupeni*, vypusk l-i (Perm', 1922), p. 66; *Programmy-minimum dlia Edinoi Trudovoi shkoly l-i i 2-i stupeni* (2nd rev. edn) (Petrograd, 1922), pp. 50 ff.
25 *Edinaia trudovaia shkola i primernye plany zaniatii v nei* (Viatka, 1918).
26 *Novye programmy dlia edinoi trudovoi shkoly*, 1 (Moscow–Petrograd, Narkompros, 1923), pp. 8–9.
27 See his presentation, 'Socially Useful Schoolwork', to the Pedagogical Section, 11 March 1926, in TsGA RSFSR, f. 298, op. 1, ed. khr. 41, 11. 60, 65–84.
28 Ben Eklof, 'The Adequacy of Basic Schooling in Rural Russia: Teachers and Their Craft, 1880–1914', in *History of Education Quarterly*, 26:2 (Summer 1986), p. 206.
29 In the mid 1920s, only about one-third of the elementary and secondary teachers in the Russian Republic had any kind of specialised pedagogical

training. Only slightly more than 10 per cent had any higher education. About the same percentage possessed no more than an elementary education. See the detailed table in *Statisticheskii ezhegodnik; sostoianie narodnogo obrazovaniia v SSSR (bez avtonomnykh respublik) za 1924/25 uch. god* (Moscow, Narkompros, 1926), p. 97 and *Na poroge vtorogo desiatiletia; praktika sotsial'nogo vospitaniia* (Moscow–Leningrad. Gosudarstvennoe izdatel'stvo, 1927), p. 78; *Narodnoe prosveshchenie*, 11 (November 1926), p. 30.

30 *Statistichekii sbornik po narodnomu prosveshcheniiu RSFSR 1926 g.* (Moscow: Gosudarstvennoe izdatel'stvo, 1927), pp. 82–3, 93–5, 108–9, 120–1, 124–5 and *Narodnoe prosveshchenie v SSSR 1926–1927 uchebnyi god* (Moscow, Gosudarstvennoe izdatel'stvo, 1929), p. 242.

31 *Na putiakh*, 3 (March 1929), p. 46.

32 *Antireligioznik*, 11 (November 1927), pp. 48, 55.

33 *Vestnik prosveshcheniia*, 5 (1929), p. 119.

34 S.I. Shtamm, *Upravlenie narodnym obrazovaniem v SSSR (1917–1936 gg.)* (Moscow, Nauka, 1985), p. 138.

35 *Narodnoe obrazovanie* (Tver), 2 (1–20 February 1919), p. 98.

36 *Biulleten' Otdela Narodnogo obrazovaniia* (Moscow), 3 (March 1919), p. 58.

37 TsGA RSFSR, f. 2306, op. 1, ed. khr. 3277, l. 143; M.I. Voronkov, 'U kolybeli sovetskogo ONO', *Narodnoe prosveshchenie*, 10 (October 1927), p. 163; Krupskaya, *Iz ateisticheskogo naslediia*, p. 51.

38 Krupskaya, *Pedagogicheskie sochineniia*, 11 (Moscow, Izdatel'stvo Akademii Pedagogicheskikh nauk, 1963), p. 143.

39 A. Ivanov, 'Ocherki po istorii sovetskoi srednei obshcheobrazovatel'noi shkoly (1917–1925 gg.)', in *Uchenye zapiski. Iaroslavskii gosudarstvennyi pedagogicheskii institut*, 48 (Iaroslavl', 1961), p. 13.

40 *Ezhenedel'nik NK)*, 9:30 (24 April 1924), p. 2, and 24:74 (12 June 1925), pp. 2–3; *BORS*, 4 (23 December 1922), p. 7; Abraham Epshtein, 'The School in Soviet Russia', *School and Society*, 16:406 (7 October 1922), pp. 400–1; *Pedagogicheskaia entsiklopediia*, II (Moscow, Rabotnik prosveshcheniia, 1928), col. 283.

41 *BORS*, 26 (19 May 1923), p. 1; *Spravochnaia kniga po narodnomu prosveshcheniiu* (Moscow, Krasnaia nov', 1923), p. 31.

42 *Uchitel'skaia gazeta* (henceforth *UG*), 56:69 (10 December 1925), p. 2; M. Epshtein, 'Voprosy massovoi obshcheobrazovatel'noi shkoly', *Narodnyi uchitel'*, 1 (January 1927), p. 23; and the judgement rendered in *Vestnik prosveshcheniia*, 5–6 (May–June 1928), p. 125.

43 *UG*, 12 (18 December 1924), p. 3.

44 *Narodnoe prosveshchenie*, 2 (1923), p. 63; *Narodnyi uchitel'*, 1 (January 1925), p. 41.

45 K. Konovalova, 'S uchitel'skoi konferentsii,' *Narodnyi uchitel'*, 4 (April 1926), p. 58.

46 See the survey of peasant opinions in Volokolamsk district (*uezd*) in *Vestnik prosveshcheniia*, 3 (March 1929), p. 25.

47 N. Rosnitsky, *Litso derevni* (Moscow–Leningrad, 1926), p. 95.

48 *UG*, 35:158 (26 August 1927), p. 3.

49 *Narodnoe prosveshchenie v SSSR 1926–1927 uchebnyi god*, pp. 25–8. Absenteeism amounted to 25 days in rural locales and 16 in urban.
50 *Ezhenedel'nik NK)*, 35 (3 September 1926), p. 11.
51 For Yaroslavl', *Nash trud*, 12 (December 1927), p. 11; for Voronezh, N. Amosov, 'Slovo za Narkomprosam', *Antireligioznik*, 3 (March 1928), p. 51; for Leningrad, I. Chernia, 'Klassovaia bor'ba za shkol'noi stenoi', *Kommunisticheskaia revoliutsiia*, 17–18 (September 1928), p. 82.
52 *Narodnoe prosveshchenie v RSFSR; statisticheskii sbornik* (Moscow–Leningrad, Gosudarstvennoe izdatel'stvo, 1928), p. 177.
53 Larry E. Holmes, 'Soviet Schools: Policy Pursues Practice, 1921–1928', *Slavic Review*, 48:2 (Summer 1989), pp. 234–53.
54 *Programmy dlia vtorogo kontsentra shkoly semiletki (V, VI i VII gody obucheniia)* (Moscow: Izdatel'stvo MONO, 1926), p. 12.
55 *NO*, pp. 265–7.
56 *Direktivy VKP po voprosam prosveshcheniia* (Moscow–Leningrad, Narkompros, 1930), pp. 132, 136.
57 The failure rate for Pioneer boys and *Komsomol* girls was higher than the average. See V. Krylov, 'Uchashchiesia v shkolakh II stupeni', *Narodnoe prosveshchenie*, 9 (1925), p. 68.
58 TsGA RSFSR, f. 298, op. 1, ed. khr. 41, ll. 18–19 ob.; *Narodnoe prosveshchenie*, 11 (November 1926), pp. 3–8, 27–34 ff.
59 V. Postnikov, 'Neskol'ko zamechanii o praktike prepodavaniia obshchestvovedeniia', *Kommunisticheskaia revoliutsiia*, 24 (December 1926), p. 36.
60 TsGA RSFSR, f. 298, op. 1, ed. khr. 41, ll. 36–8, 124–7 ob.
61 *Programmy GUS'a dlia pervogo i vtorogo godov sel'skoi shkoly I stupeni (s izmeniiami, sdelannymi na osnovanii ucheta opyta)* (Moscow, Narkompros, 1926); *Programmy i metodicheskie zapiski edinoi trudovoi shkoly. Vypusk l. Gorodskie i sel'skie shkoly I stupeni. Programmy* (Moscow–Leningrad, Narkompros, 1927) and *Programmy i metodicheskie zapiski edinoi trudovoi shkoly. Vypusk 2: Gorodksie i sel'skie shkoly I stupeni. Metodicheskie zapiski k programmam* (Moscow– Leningrad, Narkompros, 1927). For grades five through seven, *Programmy i metodicheskie zapiski edinoi trudovoi shkoly. Vypusk 3. l-i kontsentr gorodskoi shkoly II stupeni* (Moscow– Leningrad, Narkompros, 1927).
62 *Programmy i metodicheskie zapiski. Vypusk 2*, p. 155; *Programmy i metodicheskie zapiski edinoi trudovoi shkoly. Vypusk 3*, p. 31.
63 A. Kancheev, 'O podgotovke k vysshei shkole', *Izvestiia* (3 November 1926), p. 7; *Ezhenedel'nik NK)*, 13 (30 March 1928), pp. 23–4; A.I. Abinder, 'Itogi vstupitel'nykh ispytanii v vysshie uchebnye zavedeniia RSFSR v 1927 g.', *Nauchnyi rabotnik*, 10 (October 1927), pp. 41–54; I.I. Loboda, 'Zametki ob ekzamenakh po obhschestvovedeniiu', *Nauchnyi rabotnik*, 10 (October 1927), pp. 55–8.
64 B. Gur'ianov, 'Po stantsam Dona', *Narodnyi uchitel'*, 7 (July 1926), p. 74; *Russkii iazyk i literatura v trudovoi shkole*, 2 (1928), p. 143; *Vestnik prosveshcheniia*, 10 (October 1927), p. 106; I. Veksler, 'Po shkolam Leningrada', *Narodnoe prosveshchenie*, 1 (January 1927), pp. 28–37; *Na putiakh*, 7–8 (July–August 1927), pp. 78–9.

65 I. Zakolodkin, 'Kul'turnye nozhnitsy', *Narodnoe prosveshchenie*, 11 (November 1928), p. 110; *Narodnoe prosveshchenie v RSFSR; statisticheskii sbornik*, p. 170; *Pedagogicheskaia entsiklopediia*, 3, columns 787–8, 803–4; *Narodnoe prosveshchenie v SSSR. I. Predvaritel'nye itogi shkol'noi perepisi* (Moscow, Gosudarstvennoe izdatel'stvo, 1929), p. 12; *Kul'turnoe stroitel'stvo Soiuza sovetskikh sotsialisticheskikh respublik; sbornik diagramm* (2nd edn, Moscow–Leningrad, Gosudarstvennoe izdatel'stvo, 1932), p. 27; *Massovoe prosveshchenie v SSSR k 15-letiiu oktiabria*, Part 1 (Moscow, Gosudarstvennoe izdatel'stvo, 1932), p. 29.

66 *Programmy dlia shkol pervoi i vtoroi stupeni* (Ivanovo-Voznesensk, 1923), p. 54.

67 *Bezbozhnik*, 12 (June 1926), p. 6.

68 TsGA RSFSR, f. 2306, op. 69, ed. khr. 814, l. 120.

69 Joan Delaney, 'Origins of Antireligious Organizations', in Richard H. Marshall, Jr (ed.), *Aspects of Religion in the Soviet Union, 1917–1967* (Chicago, University of Chicago Press, 1971), p. 121.

70 Em. Iaroslavsky, 'Itogi soveshchaniia antireligioznikov pri Agitprope TsK VKP(b)', *Kommunisticheskaia revoliutsiia*, 10 (May 1926), pp. 10–11.

71 TsGA RSFSR, f. 2306, op. 69, ed. khr. 823, l. 3.

72 V. Trunov, 'Antireligioznaia propaganda i shkol'nye kanikuly', *Antireligioznik*, 6 (1 June 1927), p. 24.

73 *Antireligioznik*, 11 (November 1927), p. 9.

74 *Antireligioznik*, 1 (January 1928), pp. 113, 118–25.

75 *Antireligioznik*, 1 (January 1928), pp. 115–18.

76 S.P. Egorov, *Antireligioznoe vospitanie v nachal'noi shkole* (Moscow–Leningrad, 1929), p. 10.

77 Egorov, *Antireligioznoe vospitanie*, p. 11 and *Antireligioznik*, 3 (March, 1928), p. 60; I. Chernia, 'Klassovaia bor'ba', p. 82; *Vestnik prosveshcheniia*, 3 (March 1929), p. 144.

78 *Antireligioznik*, 12 (1929), pp. 81–91 and 3 (March 1931), p. 70; articles by Amosov in *Antireligioznik*, 7 (1928), pp. 75–88 and 3 (1929), pp. 75–9.

79 *Antireligioznik*, 5 (May 1931), pp. 83–5.

80 *Antireligioznik*, 12 (1928), p. 59.

81 *Antireligioznik*, 6 (1928), pp. 71–81.

82 N.K. Kusik'ian, "Internatsional'naia i antireligioznaia propaganda pri prokhozhdenii kursa istorii v 8-i i 9-i gruppakh", in *Osnovnye voprosy prepodavaniia istorii* (Moscow: Izdatel'stvo Kommunisticheskoi akademii, 1930), p. 184.

83 *Na putiakh*, 7–8 (July–August 1928), p. 12; Krupskaya, *Iz ateisticheskogo naslediia*, p. 176.

84 *Narodnoe prosveshchenie*, 8–9 (August–September 1929), pp. 61–2.

85 The speech was reported in *Bezbozhnik*, 1 (January 1934), p. 18.

86 F.F. Korolev, T.D. Korneichik and Z.I. Ravkin, *Ocherki po istorii sovetskoi shkoly i pedagogiki, 1921–1931* (Moscow, Izdatel'stvo Akademii Pedagogicheskikh nauk, 1961), p. 289.

87 *Pravda* (14 April 1929) and issues of *Ezhenedel'nik NK)*, 18 (26 April 1929), p. 64; no. 20–1 (17–24 May 1929), p. 19; and 26 (28 June 1929), p. 23.

88 For example, the statement from the Narkompros Collegium, 18 April 1929, in *Ezhenedel'nik NK)*, 20–1 (17–24 May 1929), p. 22.
89 Lunacharsky's speech was published years later, in *Bezbozhnik*, 1 (January 1934), p. 18.
90 Korolev, *Ocherki*, p. 296.
91 N. Krupskaya, 'O chistke shkol ot ryzhogo elementa', *UG*, 36:263 (27 March 1929), p. 2; Krupskaya, *Pedagogicheskie sochineniia*, II (Moscow, 1958), pp. 380, 382, 386.
92 See Krupskaya, 'Ob antireligioznom vospitanii v shkole', *Na putiakh*, 7–8 (July–August 1928), pp. 8, 12; *Na putiakh*, 1 (January 1929), pp. 12–13; Krupskaya, *Iz ateisticheskogo naslediia*, pp. 175–6, 180, 184, 189, 192–3, 259.
93 Krupskaya, *Iz ateisticheskogo naslediia*, p. 183.
94 P.P. Blonsky, 'Religioznost' i nereligioznost' nashikh shkol'nikov', *Na putiakh*, 4–5 (April–May 1929), pp. 67–70, 73, 75; Blonsky, *Izbrannye pedagogicheskie proizvedeniia*, p. 551.
95 See the many curricula and syllabi from 1929 and 1930 available at the Library of the Academy of Pedagogical Sciences in Moscow.
96 *Vestnik prosveshcheniia*, 11 (November 1929), pp. 88–9.
97 *Shkol'naia brigada, zhurnal-uchebnik dlia 1-i i 2-i grupp shkol I stupeni Moskovskoi oblasti*, 2–3 (1931) and *Shkol'naia brigada; zhurnal-uchebnik dlia tret'ei i chetvertoi grupp shkol pervoi stupeni Moskovskoi oblasti*, 2 (November–December 1930).
98 *Kul'turnoe stroitel'stvo SSSR; statisticheskii sbornik* (Moscow–Leningrad, Gosplanizdat, 1940), p. 40.
99 *Vestnik prosveshcheniia*, 2 (February 1929), p. 134; *Ezhendel'nik NK)*, 10–11 (1 March 1929), p. 10; *Antireligioznik*, 9 (1929), pp. 85–6.
100 *Vestnik prosveshcheniia*, 3 (March 1929), p. 20; *Biulleten' Narkomprosa RSFSR* (henceforth *NKP*) 17 (10 June 1930), p. 19.
101 *Antireligioznik*, 3 (1929), p. 80.
102 *UG*, 207:767 (26 August 1931), p. 1.
103 M. Kuznetsov, 'Itogi antireligioznogo vospitaniia v shkolakh', *Antireligioznik*, 9 (1929), pp. 85–91.
104 F.F. Korolev, *Sovetskaia shkola v period sotsialisticheskoi industrializatsii* (Moscow, Gosudarstvennoe uchebno-pedagogicheskoe izdatel'stvo, 1959), pp. 134–5; *Biulleten' NK)*, 5 (10 February 1930), p. 14. See the 1931 survey of pupils in the fifth, sixth and seventh grades in 27 schools in eleven districts of Leningrad: *Narodnoe obrazovanie v Leningradskoi oblasti za 15 let sovetskoi vlasti* (Moscow–Leningrad: Gosudarstvennoe uchebno-pedagogicheskoe izdatel'stvo, 1932), p. 65, and an analysis of Moscow students in M. Sokolov, 'Chego dostigla shkola v bor'be za likvidatsiiu svoego 'korennogo nedostatka'', *Za kommunisticheskoe vospitanie*, 4 (April 1932), pp. 10–21.
105 M. Burtseva, 'Politekhnicheskaia shkola i rabota iacheek SVB', *Antireligioznik*, 6 (June 1931), pp. 77–81.
106 A.S. Bubnov, *Stat'i i rechi o narodnom obrazovanii* (Moscow, Izdatel'stvo Akademii Pedagogicheskikh nauk, 1959), p. 189; *Kommunisticheskoe prosveshchenie*, 17 (5 September 1931), pp. 11–17; *Za kommunisticheskoe prosvesh-*

chenie, 201:767 (26 August 1931), p. 2; *Fizika, khimiia, matematika, tekhnika v sovetskoi shkole*, 6–7 (1931), pp. 4–6.

107 *UG*, 201:767 (26 August 1931), p. 1; 203:769 (28 August 1931), p. 1; 206:772 (1 September 1931), p. 1.

108 *Na putiakh*, 11–12 (November–December 1931), p. 69; Krupskaya, *Pedagogicheskie sochineniia*, 10, p. 391.

109 *Biulleten' NK*), 65 (25 November 1932), p. 2; *NO*, p. 170; *Uchebnye plany nachal'noi, nepolnoi srednei i srednei shkoly* (Moscow, Narkompros, 1936), p. 2. Spring vacation was set in 1932 for 20–31 March in urban areas and in rural areas two seven-day periods from 20 March through 20 April to be determined by local authorities. In 1935, roughly the same provisions prevailed, although the break was shortened in urban and rural schools to six days.

110 Tsentral'nyi Partiinyi arkhiv Instituta Marksizma-Leninizma, f. 12, op. 1, ed. khr. 758, 11. 334, 232.

111 M. Epshtein, 'K zadacham nachal'noi i srednei shkoly', *Kommunisticheskaia revoliutsiia*, 12 (August 1933), p. 58.

112 *Programmy srednei shkoly. Biologiia, khimiia* (Moscow, Narkompros, 1935); *Programmy srednei shkoly. Matematika, fizika, cherchenie* (Moscow, Narkompros, 1935); *Uchebnye plany nachal'noi, nepolnoi srednei i srednei shkoly* (Moscow, Narkompros, 1936); *Programmy nachal'nmoi shkoly* (Moscow, Narkompros, 1935).

113 Samuel N. Harper Papers, University of Chicago, Box 33, Folder 13, pp. 25, 33–4. Harper had visited the USSR previously in 1926, 1930 and 1932.

114 M.S. Epshtein, 'O proverochnykh ispytaniiakh i podgotovke k novomu uchebnomu godu', *Kommunisticheskoe prosveshchenie*, 3 (1933), p. 49.

115 TsGA RSFSR, f. 2306, op. 70, ed. khr. 2064, 11. 145–6.

116 Nauchnyi Arkhiv Akademii Pedagogicheskikh nauk (henceforth NA APN), f. 13, op. 1, ed. khr. 4, 1. 16.

117 Tsentral'nyi Gosudarstvennyi arkhiv Oktiabr'skoi Revoliutsii i sotsialisticheskogo stroitel'stva goroda Moskvy, f. R-528, op. 1, ed. khr. 267, 11. 23, 61–2.

118 *Bezbozhnik*, 21 (November 1931), p. 5.

119 F. Oleshchuk, 'Zadachi antireligioznoi raboty sredi molodezhi', *Antireligioznik*, 3 (May–June 1936), p. 21; *Antireligioznik*, 2 (March–April 1935), p. 26.

120 Issues of *Antireligioznik*: 4 (July–August 1933), p. 28; 3 (May–June 1936), p. 21; 5 (September–October 1934), p. 36; 1 (January–February 1935), p. 26.

121 E. Perovsky, 'O sostoianii antireligioznogo vospitaniia v shkole', *Kommunisticheskoe proveshchenie*, 5 (1934), pp. 59, 62, 67.

122 See Bubnov's evaluation of the criticism of *Pravda* and the Central Committee: Bubnov, *Stati'i i rechi*, pp. 312, and *Kommunisticheskoe prosveshchenie*, 5 (1935), pp. 8–9.

123 B.M. Volin, 'Bor'ba za gramotnost' – osnovnaia zadacha shkoly', *Kommunisticheskoe prosveshchenie*, 1 (1936), p. 29.

124 *Pravda* (7 May 1937), p. 1.
125 *Biulleten' NK*), 16 (15 August 1937), p. 2.
126 *Biulleten' NK*), 17 (1 September 1937), pp. 4, 10.
127 NA APN, f. 17, op. 1, ed. khr. 63, 11. 197–207.
128 Interview with Bubnov's daughter, Elena Andreevna Bubnova, Moscow, 8 April 1990.
129 *Sovetskaia pedagogika* (henceforth *S*)), 4 (October 1937), pp. 2–3. This issue was not submitted for printing until November 11.
130 Ia.P. Demeshchenko, 'Antireligioznoe vospitanie v shkole', *S*), 4 (October 1937), pp. 90–1; *S.N. Belousov, 'Antireligioznaia propaganda i antireligioznoe vospitanie v shkole', S)*, 1 (January 1938), pp. 40–59; A.S. Sheinberg, 'Antireligioznoe vospitanie v srednei shkole', S), 3 (March 1938), pp. 20–35.
131 *Programmy nachal'noi shkoly* (Moscow, Narkompros, 1937) and *Programmy nachal'noi shkoly* (Moscow, Narkompros, 1938).
132 A.V. Shestakov (ed.), *A Short History of the U.S.S.R.* (Moscow, Co-operative Publishing Society of Foreign Workers in the USSR, 1938), pp. 22–4.
133 *S)*, 5 (May 1939), p. 39; 6 (June 1938), p. 24, 28, 32; 10 (October 1938), p. 80; 9 (September 1940), pp. 55, 59.
134 *S)*, 12 (December 1938), p. 52.
135 E. Perovsky, 'Narkompros ne rukovodit antireligioznym vospitaniem uchashchikhsia', *Antireligioznik*, 8–9 (August–September 1938), pp. 40–1.
136 A.I. Markova, 'Ob antireligioznom vospitanii detei v nachal'noi shkole', *S)*, 10 (October 1939), pp. 80–2; *Antireligioznik*, 8 (August 1938), p. 2.
137 *S)*, 10 (October 1939), p. 81.
138 *Antireligioznik*, 3 (March 1941), p. 24.
139 *S)*, 6 (1940), pp. 142–3.
140 Moshe Lewin, 'Popular Religion in Twentieth-Century Russia', *The Making of the Soviet System* (New York, Pantheon Books, 1985), pp. 57–71.
141 See the memoir by Wolfgang Leonhard, *Child of the Revolution*, trans. by C.M. Woodhouse (London, Collins, 1957), p. 99. Leonhard, the son of a German Communist, attended a Soviet secondary school during the late 1930s.
142 Nina Tumarkin, *Lenin Lives! The Lenin Cult in Soviet Russia* (Cambridge: Harvard University Press, 1983) and Vera S. Dunham, *In Stalin's Time; Middleclass Values in Soviet Fiction* (New York, Cambridge University Press, 1976).
143 Alex Inkeles and David Horton Smith, *Becoming Modern; Individual Change in Six Developing Countries* (Cambridge: Harvard University Press, 1974), pp. 133–43.
144 For a later period, see the conclusions in David E. Powell, *Antireligious Propaganda in the Soviet Union: A Study of Mass Mobilization* (Cambridge, MIT Press, 1975), pp. 52–5.

Soviet schools, atheism and religion

JOHN DUNSTAN

What has been the rationale of traditional atheistic education in the USSR? First, atheism being part and parcel of the Marxist–Leninist worldview on which communist education was based, atheistic education was an indispensable underpinning component of communist education. Second, the very fact of religion's survival meant the existence of an alternative ideology or ideologies representing a dangerous challenge to CPSU hegemony. The identification of nationalism with religious affiliation was a striking case in point. The challenge was essentially intolerable and had to be fought. Third, religion was not merely a system of ideas or a manner of thinking, any more than Marxism–Leninism was; both were systems of belief which were supposed to lead to the formation of attitudes and result in patterns of behaviour involving the ability to distinguish between right and wrong and to choose the better action. Although in certain instances the outcomes were similar, in other respects they were fundamentally different, and so religious morality was regarded as an insidious alternative to communist morality. It was an important task of atheistic education to expose this.

Such was the position up to 1988, when within two months there could be detected the earliest shaking of the foundations of policy structures in both education and religion. They had already been jogged. Even before the historic CPSU plenum of January 1987 had set the pace of political *perestroika*, a group of innovatory educators had launched their 'pedagogy of cooperation' based on new, trustful relationships between teachers, children, and parents. Later in 1987 Soviet newspapers started to publish appeals for the reopening of churches. The February 1988 plenum, despite the conventionality of its statements on atheistic education and indeed on upbringing generally, in fact damned the 1984 school reform either with faint praise or with outright repudiation, and gave its blessing to various new directions including radical curricular innovation, diversification, and the pedagogy of co-operation. This had implications for upbringing nonetheless. Then on 29 April 1988 in the run-up to the Millennium celebrations M.S. Gorbachev met Patriarch Pimen, spoke of the contribution of believers to *glasnost* and *perestroika*, promised a new law on freedom of conscience, and referred to 'our common cause' in the realm of ethics and morals.[1] With this conjuncture of developments on the educational and religious fronts, it became natural enough for some to link the two by voicing their dreams of religious education.

We shall explore these matters further in the course of this chapter. First we shall examine the aims of the traditional atheistic education of school students. Then, as we proceed to look at atheistic education in the classroom, we shall consider some of its major themes as linked to curricular content and exemplified in literature for teachers. Extracurricular activities provided further contexts for pursuing the stated goals, though the paracurriculum or 'hidden' curriculum might bring unintended outcomes. A scrutiny of approaches to teaching in and out of class provides a necessary complement to our survey of curricular matters and leads to further reflections on teachers and teacher education. Next, we shall review the major trends and continuing problems of the atheistic upbringing of young Soviet citizens in the mid-1980s. A final section will discuss the beginnings of religious education in the USSR.[2]

The aims of atheistic education

The chief aim of Soviet atheistic education was to instil a materialist world outlook. According to this the world can be completely known – whereas religion is conventionally held to stress the mystery of creation – and natural and social phenomena can be correctly explained. On such a basis, there are unlimited possibilities for the world's transformation by man.[3] These principles were to be conveyed by giving the pupils a knowledge not only of science and social life, but also of atheism itself, and by involving them in relevant social activity. For the second major aim of atheistic education, which sprang from the first, was to convince students of the unique validity of the materialist world outlook and the alleged worthlessness of the religious world view. Religious ideas were to be resolutely opposed, and children under their influence were to be set free from them. This meant that a critique of religion and an explanation of its social functions must form part of atheistic knowledge. It also meant, since one learns in the process of doing and especially in collective action, that children should put their knowledge into practice, marshalling their material and arguing their case, and develop a positive attitude to such activity.[4]

I have already alluded to the existence of rival moral codes as a justification for atheistic education. At a time of growing anxiety about unofficial youth culture, juvenile delinquency, and slackening of family ties – the darker side of the coin of material progress – there was good reason to put forward, as a third cardinal goal of atheistic education, the assertion of communist morality, even though it might be subsumed under the second aim just mentioned. Certainly it was emphasised in the Soviet literature of the mid-1980s, for both atheism and religion were said to be increasingly concerned with social and ethical problems.[5] Communist morality felt itself undermined by two contrasting religious approaches. The traditional one is that atheism and morality are incompatible, that only faith in God can be a firm basis for morality, and that an atheistic society is therefore intrinsically immoral.[6] A more modern and subtle line taken by some churchmen was that communist morality is good and pleasing to God, and in effect derives from religious origins. Some young believers saw parallels between the dedication of working-class heroes and that of Jesus. In either event, educators would need to point out the allegedly egoistic and passivity inducing tendencies of religious morality, which led to an illusory happiness[7] (in Marx's famous phrase).

Atheism and the formal curriculum

Although the Soviet teacher's primary duty is to teach the subject effectively, he or she – and we shall use the latter pronoun as being statistically more probable – is officially bidden to be an upbringer as well. In the mid-1980s atheistic education was therefore one of many subsidiary concerns which had to be made to fit the overarching didactic goal. How far this happened in practice depended on the teacher's own interests and enthusiasms. The only exception, a minor one, to this general pattern was the social studies course taken by final-year pupils, where there was teaching directly on atheism itself. It contained two lessons on the materialist view of history and the scientific world outlook respectively, though these seem to have accounted for less than 3 per cent of the course. It was evidently through the other subjects that the bulk of formal atheistic teaching was meant to take place. We proceed to survey this, in accordance with our framework of the threefold aims. Much of the content may be regarded in the West as highly controversial, but our purpose now is to present it, not to offer a systematic critique of it.

The materialist world outlook

The essence of this position is that the world is cognisable, explicable, and transformable. The main subjects for instilling these ideas are the natural sciences, and the appeal is to the intellect. Key themes are the primacy and indestructibility of matter, its material unity, evolution, the causality of natural phenomena, and man's potential to change the natural world. Ideas about the uncreated character of the material world are formed through lessons on the circulation of water (in nature study, at age 9-plus); electrical phenomena in the atmosphere, and the process of destruction of hard rocks and formation of gravel, sand and clay (10-plus); photosynthesis and the accumulation of energy in plants (biology, 11-plus); laws of conservation (physics, from 12-plus, and chemistry, from 13-plus, to 17); metabolism and the conversion of energy (biology, in the top form, with 16-plus entry); and the destruction and formation of cosmic objects (astronomy, ditto).[8] (This reflects the programmes of the early to mid-1980s, citing the age-group rather than the number of the grade or form because the numbering system was to be changed.) In particular, the law of the conservation of energy has convincingly proved that energy in nature does not come into existence and disappear; it merely changes from one form into another. This was considered to refute theological notions of creation and the last things,[9] for the aims of atheistic education overlapped.

Similarly, teaching about the material unity of the world had the incidental function of giving the lie to dogmas about the dualism of earth and heaven and of body and soul. The discoveries of Copernicus, Galileo, Kepler, and Newton prove that terrestrial and celestial mechanics express the same laws of motion. Mendeleev's law of the periodicity of the elements, studied in the 14-plus chemistry course, applies both to earth and the observable universe; this is proved by chemical analysis of specimens of lunar soil and meteorites, and by spectral analysis of objects located in the distant cosmos. In the biology course, starting at 11-plus, the pupil studies the interaction of animate and inanimate nature.[10] The section on the cell and the individual development of organisms, at 16-plus, deals with the discovery of the universality of cellular structure, which gives substantial support to the idea of the unity of origin of all life in the natural process of evolution.[11]

Nature study and biology display the causal conditionality of the phenomena and processes of organic nature. The new curriculum for six- and seven-year-olds under the 1984 reform contained a new subject, the name of which is literally translated as 'Acquaintance with the Surrounding World', or more catchily 'The World Around Us'. In 1990 it was still in place. The syllabus included material of the kind pioneered at the experimental School No. 18 at Pavlovsky Posad. The children there carried out daily observations outside the school and then talked about them in class, as the following example shows. A child said, 'Yesterday I saw some puddles with ice on them. Today the ice has gone . . . I saw some green grass and some butterflies.' Asked how these changes had come about, the children attributed them at first to the arrival of spring. Then the teacher asked, 'But when spring comes, what does that depend on?' 'The sun starting to get warmer.' 'So what do all those changes in nature depend on?' 'The sun.'[12] It is of general importance for children to see links and dependences between phenomena, and to be able to explain their patterns of development. But the teacher had also to point out that because all phenomena had causes there did not have to be a supreme cause.

The cognisability of the natural world has important implications for man's place in it. Here history, mathematics, and geography lend support to the natural sciences. In history too the students learn about great scientists and their discoveries and inventions. Fourteen-year-olds hear from their maths teacher that for 2,000 years mathematicians tried unsuccessfully to prove the fifth postulate of Euclid, but Lobachevsky was able to show on a materialist basis that it was undemonstrable, and in so doing discovered a new geometry.[13] In geography lessons, the pupils are taught about man's success in reforming the environment, the rational use of natural resources, and the planned development of the socialist economic structure.[14] This syllabus seems ripe for revision!

The reason given why authorities on atheistic education considered that its main thrust must be the positive presentation of a materialist world outlook was that increasingly the churches were modernising their attitude to science and theologians were ready to admit the unscientific nature of the Bible. There were exceptions to this, and teachers had to take account of them, as we shall see. Atheistic education in general, however, should move away from the traditional narrow approach of sporadically juxtaposing religious and scientific explanations of phenomena and debunking the religious ones. This requirement did not apply to the teaching of younger children up to the age of about fourteen, since they did not yet have a developed world view.[15] Thus there was still a place for the anti-religious approach, and indeed the more traditionally minded educators still attached great importance to it. In any event, the ability effectively to argue the atheist case entails a knowledge of the beliefs of the opposition.

Unique validity of the materialist world outlook contrasted with religious views

It was thought necessary not only to form a materialist world outlook in the pupils, but also to convince them that it was the only truly progressive and authentic stance. To expose the sham and dangerousness of religious ideologies, one had to consider the functions of religious beliefs and the roles of religious organisations past and present. The main subjects here were history and social studies, assisted by the natural sciences. The appeal was both to the intellect and the emotions, which ought to have given history a particularly useful part to play in the atheistic programme.

The school history course dealt, among much else, with the class roots of religion, the social role of religion and the church, the struggle of science with religion, and the crisis in religion.[16] In the sections on the history of Russia and the USSR, for example, it showed that with the christianisation of Rus' the church became the biggest feudal lord. The people turned to religion from ignorance, boredom with work, and social oppression. It then encouraged them to be submissive. When they rebelled, the clergy invariably supported the rulers. After the October Revolution, the clergy of all faiths resisted Soviet power, but after the 1920s they became loyal mainly because the workers were backing it (what about Stalin?). Before and during the Great Patriotic War, the Pope led his own anti-Soviet campaign. With the disappearance of the exploiting classes, religion in the USSR no longer had its traditional role of supporting them, but it remained the 'opium of the people'.[17] The history teaching should be reinforced by the literature course. Radishchev wrote in his ode *Vol'nost'* (Freedom), 'The power of the tsar protects the faith, the faith protects the power of the tsar.' Many other examples could be cited, but it should not be just a matter of presenting them to the students, but of stressing the atheistic orientation of Russian literature as social comment.[18] Socialist realism did it more drastically.

Less obvious subjects could also be pressed into the service of atheism, given teachers with sufficient enthusiasm. G.B. Romanova, a teacher of Russian language in the Uzbek capital of Tashkent, described what she did. She used proverbs and folktales firstly to illustrate and practice a linguistic point, and secondly to convey an anti-religious message. When teaching the Russian pronoun to fifteen-year-old Uzbek youngsters, she would use examples such as these: 'Who hopes in heaven will be left without bread.' 'What has been given to God has already been lost.' In Russian, these are rhyming couplets. 'In the discussion', she said, 'I help the pupils to see how faith in God originated. I ask them to explain the meaning of each proverb, stressing that these express the people's lack of faith in God and negative attitude to churchmen.'[19]

The struggle between science and religion was an obvious theme for what are called inter-subject links, which are historically of major importance in Soviet curriculum theory. Based on the Marxist dictum 'Being determines consciousness', the theory asserted that the totality of knowledge was a cosmos reflecting the external world, and the school curriculum was a restricted but (potentially) sufficient second reflection of the world. Since Marxism–Leninism was supposed to offer a complete way of looking at the world, the curriculum should likewise provide a holistic worldview, through completeness and integration. Here history came together with social studies, the natural sciences and mathematics. Perhaps the most typical theme was the Roman Catholic opposition to the Copernican view of the solar system, closely followed by the persecution of Giordano Bruno and Galileo. Sayings of religious notables were harnessed to the cause. Tomaso Caccini, the first priest publicly to denounce Galileo, apparently asserted that 'Mathematics is the creation of the devil.' Kierkegaard said, 'Faith relates to proof as to its enemy.' So, it was claimed, religion forbids discussion of the truth of Christian dogmas, while mathematics teaches that nothing be taken on trust. Men of science were also quoted. Russian writers were fond of the story of Napoleon's encounter with the astronomer and mathematician Pierre Simon Laplace. When Napoleon commented that Laplace's book *Exposition du Système du Monde* (1796) did not refer to God, Laplace allegedly replied, 'Sire, I had no need of that hypothesis.'[20]

Modern Christian apologists would probably argue that Laplace was a practising Catholic, and that even if the story were true its point surely was that physical theories must stand on their own merits. Soviet writers would most likely have seized on this explanation as an example of the insidiousness of modern theologians. For by the 1970s it was generally held that the conflict between science and religion had entered a new and different phase: that many leading churchmen had recognised the folly of continuing to decry scientific achievements and had moved to a policy of trying to reconcile science and religion. They claimed that religion and science are complementary, that religion strives to find God while science strives to find order in God's creation; and this intrigued many young people. They acknowledged that the world and everything in it are in a process of constant change and development, but still claimed the existence of the unchanging Prime Mover behind it all.[21] To give a more specific example, a theological interpretation of modern biological thinking about the origin of life stresses the enormous importance of enzymes for metabolism and maintains that they emerged before the various vital processes began; thus their presence in the cell indicates a transcendental prime cause.[22] Students were told to be on their guard against religious chameleons attempting to apply scientific discoveries to self-preservation for their own subversive ends.

Religion's adaptation to science was seen as one reaction to the so-called crisis of religion, caused partly by the scientific and technical revolution, and partly by the retreat from religion in many countries. Religion might also try to adapt its theology to socio-political reality. Typical examples of this approach have been that Jesus Christ was a working man and the first communist; that work is no longer to be considered a curse but a blessing and all should take part; that prayer is the 'highest form of work'; and that religion provides the ethical foundation for communist construction.[23] On a less abstract level, the crisis in religion was said to be exemplified by the churches' increasing tendency to concentrate their efforts on the younger generation and to adapt their methods accordingly.[24] Some of them organise music groups and rock festivals. Some Baptist communities have special preachers in charge of youth affairs.[25] Orthodoxy likes to appoint young priests who serve as mentors and models for young people, and also to involve teenagers as godparents at christenings. The line taken with youngsters by atheistic educators in response to these trends was, in effect, 'Don't let yourselves be fooled.'

It should not be assumed, however, that such phenomena were everywhere in evidence. In the backwoods, and particularly among some of the sects, the presentation of religion might be very traditional and fundamentalist still. Thus, there was still a role for old-fashioned ridicule of certain parts of Holy Writ, even though modern education-ists felt somewhat uneasy about it as a kind of facile lowest common denominator. It was in order, then, to point out to the pupils that as early as 200 BC a Greek mathematician proved, by calculating the length of the terrestrial meridian, that the earth is not flat. For a column of 3 million people to cross the Red Sea complete with cattle and baggage train would take not a day but a month; and this, the teacher must stress, was not the mistake of some half-literate priest, 'but of the omniscient "holy spirit" from whose dictation the Bible was allegedly written'.[26] With younger children, as mentioned earlier, this approach continued to enjoy full legitimacy, and the same applied where religion and folk-belief overlap. Yury Gagarin's famous athe-istic pronouncement was alive and well in 1986, and even living at the

Academy of Pedagogical Sciences model school at Pavlovsky Posad, where a nine-year-old girl declared, 'I've been told that when it rains it's God crying in the cosmos. I'd say that Gagarin was the first to fly into the cosmos and didn't see God. It rains because water from the earth evaporates and then turns into water again.'[27]

Finally, it was said, more conservative theologians were trying to find new ways of discrediting science. This was apparently characteristic of Protestant circles, influenced by pessimism among bourgeois scientists. They claimed that the scientific and technical revolution had lacked the moral basis which only faith in God could supply. Consequently, new technologies had led to the standardisation of work and the disappearance of the creative impulse. Ecological problems had arisen, characterised by the dying-out of life. In short, the natural sciences were confronted with ultimate problems which of themselves they could not solve. Such messages might be reaching young people. Educators had to address the situation by making it clear that these negative phenomena in the West sprang from capitalist abuses and were not inherent in science itself, whereas in the USSR man's relationship to nature was duly regulated by law.[28] Teachers in the area of the Volga delta must have been having some difficult questions to answer; though any of their students who are fans of the science-fiction writers Arkady and Boris Strugatsky may well have posed similar ones already.

Communist morality versus religious morality

The question of a moral basis for the scientific and technical revolution brings us again to the salient issue of the rival moralities. Atheistic education had to deal with moral questions because these were of concern to young people as they sought their path in life. Communist morality, it was contended, was based on universal human norms and embodied the best elements of what was common to mankind; but it took them from life itself, not from religious commandments. Indeed, 'only in atheistic society is it possible to create an atmosphere of high morality'.[29] The main subjects for instilling receptiveness to the communist moral code and repugnance for religious morality were those appealing to the emotions: literature, art, and music. These subjects, it was maintained, contained great possibilities for the formation of an active stance for living, the assertion of communist values, and soundly based criticism of religious moral precepts.[30] The last entailed a convincing repudiation of religious treatment of the meaning of life, and also of preachers' attempts to depict atheistic society as immoral.[31]

It can easily be envisaged how these subjects might be turned to atheistic ends. A copy of the 1978/9 literature syllabus lies before us.[32] Fifteen-year-olds studied, among much else, *What Is To Be Done?* by N.G. Chernyshevsky with his strong opinions about religious preaching, which 'consists in inuring the wretched and naked to the thought that they must be naked forever and must rejoice in their fate'.[33] M.E. Saltykov-Shchedrin's novel *The Golovlev Family* shows the hypocrisy of religious morality, while Tolstoy's *Resurrection*, set as optional out-of-class reading, speaks of the falseness and deception of Orthodox worship and ritual. It was nevertheless felt to be more important to accentuate the positive. Thus sixteen-year-olds studied Gorky's novel *The Mother* and saw how the revolutionaries open Nilovna's eyes to the causes of the workers' wretched situation, how she takes part in the struggle, and how this demolishes her faith in God.[34] Similarly, one can readily imagine the emotional effect of dramatic paintings and stirring songs. Occasionally the latter took on a surrogate quality, offering the daily support and companionship that Christians associate with Jesus. Consider the chorus of the well-known song 'Lenin is always with you', which appears in the 1978 music syllabus for twelve-year-olds:[35] 'Lenin is always alive. Lenin is always with you, in sorrow, hope and joy. Lenin is in your spring, in every happy day. Lenin is in you and in me!'

In view of the obvious potential of these subjects for effective atheistic education through appeal to the emotions, therefore, it is surprising to find repeated complaints that they were under-utilised for this purpose.[36] One writer stated that over the fifteen years to 1986 there had only been nine publications on the problem of atheistic education in Russian literature lessons.[37] The lack of interest in this area appears to be indirectly confirmed in James Muckle's authoritative study *A Guide to the Soviet Curriculum*. His chapter on arts education, which scrutinises and discusses the syllabuses for literature, music, and art in some detail, contains not a single reference either to atheistic education or to religion. In contrast to this, one of the five aims of the astronomy course was expressly 'to facilitate the development of dialectical–materialist attitudes and describe the evolution both of concepts of the structure of the universe and of the conflict of science with religion'.[38] The three subjects seemed to be more serviceable for extracurricular atheistic activities, to which we now turn.

Extracurricular activities and the paracurriculum

There existed, outside lesson time, a large number of possible facilities for atheistic education along with other upbringing goals. These were normally provided within the young people's organisations, but led by

the homeroom teachers (form teachers).[39] One wonders whether this
was because atheistic work was deemed too taxing for ordinary youth
leaders. Since there were many claims on homeroom teachers' time,
and many other upbringing concerns, all of which appear with
monotonous regularity in the literature as in need of increased attention and effort, the actual extent of extracurricular atheistic education
depended very much on teachers' interests. It was suggested that
subject teachers should become more involved, since they could usually deal much more effectively with atheistic aspects of their own
disciplines,[40] but again it was individual attitudes that were likely to
call the tune.

The potential channels were legion. With the younger Octobrists,
aged seven and eight, it was recommended that atheistic upbringing
took the form of telling them the natural explanation of things that
frightened them and teaching them not to be afraid of the dark. The
older Octobrists, in the eight to ten age-group, heard about stupid and
harmful superstitions and also 'the reactionary significance of religious
festivals and customs'.[41] The Pavlovsky Posad school, which was
experimenting with systematic atheistic education, asked its nine-
year-olds: 'What would you do if you heard that a goblin (domovoi) had
turned up in the shed?' It was pleased when 26 out of 30 said they
would go and check, compared with 12 in a control school. The most
mature reply was: 'I'd check whether there was a goblin in the shed.
Of course, there wouldn't be. But to prove it to people who believe in
goblins anyway, I'd have to take them with me.'[42] From there they and
the youngest Pioneers were given things to read on atheistic topics,
and jobs to do such as preparing displays.

From about the age of twelve, the aim was gradually to progress to a
more abstract level of atheistic understanding, but also to move to a
much wider range of activities so that the Pioneers' knowledge could
be put into practice. This is why the extracurricular side of atheistic
upbringing was normally regarded as more important than what happened in the classroom, although that opinion was not much
trumpeted abroad because of the need to encourage subject teachers.
The themes of extracurricular atheistic education were more or less
the same as those addressed in lesson time and already described, and
for maximum effect should be linked to them; but there was obviously
a lot more scope for diversified application: preparing and giving talks,
organising and participating in special meetings and concerts, issuing
magazines, and eventually engaging in collective atheistic propaganda
or individual atheistic evangelism (not a Soviet term!) with believers.

Let us have some examples. Pupils' talks might be on such subjects as 'What is religion?', 'The social roots of religion', 'Why do people need religion?', or on primitive forms of religion and specific faiths of the present day. Teachers were advised to listen to the talks in advance so as to make any necessary corrections.[43] Special afternoon or evening meetings were organised and presented by the teachers and children themselves, preferably in year-groups and related to individual disciplines in the middle school years, but becoming interdisciplinary at the senior stage. The fifteen-year-olds might combine geography and chemistry studies at a meeting entitled 'Chemistry, god and harvest'. Subject clubs or circles, which were apparently not much utilised for atheistic education purposes, were, however, recommended to put on joint presentations at an earlier age. Such a meeting for twelve-year-olds was suggested on the theme 'The Flood: Legends and Reality': geography, biology, mathematics, and history were combined to prove the impossibility of a world flood, to expose the naivety of singling out Mt Ararat as the highest peak, to refute the notion that the plant world could be preserved under deep water for a long period, to demonstrate the inadequacy of the Ark for accommodating its cargo of animals and fodder, and to place the story in the context of other ancient myths about floods.[44] Meetings and debates might be held on subjects like 'The meaning of life' or 'Where is man's happiness?' These were felt to be particularly valuable because of the holistic approach to upbringing – not just atheistic – that they required.

There were special clubs for activists called Young Atheists' Clubs. Like other special-interest circles they were of mixed ages, usually from eleven to seventeen. They started off as informal study groups, but the aim was to develop them into power houses of atheistic activity in the schools. They were subsequently organised into sections, for example, for arranging talks and panels, issuing a monthly wall newspaper, assembling information packs, and circulating literature.[45] This helped other Pioneers to compose their own atheistic talks, and also to produce magazines, highly regarded as a teamwork activity. At some schools, atheistic activism was centred on the Atheists' Room or Museum. At Demidovka Secondary School in the Ukraine, exhibits included a model of the firmament, a diorama of Giordano Bruno being burnt at the stake, a 'Cosmonauts Corner', with a working model of a sputnik moving round the globe, and stands and information files devoted to a variety of topics on science, religion, and atheism: 'Science and religion on the origin of life on earth', 'New secular rituals', 'Popular wisdom on religion', and so forth. The students were divided into three sections: acquisitions and maintenance, excursion guides, and mass cultural work.[46]

The culmination of extracurricular atheistic work was reckoned as having been achieved when the young people went out and spread the secular gospel themselves. This was thought to strengthen them in their own convictions. They might begin by gentle persuasion of their classmates from religious homes, though, as we shall see, this sort of activity came to be viewed with much more circumspection than had been the case twenty years earlier, and zealous teenagers were not necessarily the best people to tackle what might be a very delicate job. Outside the school the youngsters were encouraged to exert atheistic influence at home, where grandmothers in particular were regarded as fair game (but frequently tough old birds), distribute popular scientific and anti-religious literature, locate lapsed believers and recruit them for atheistic work, and organise cultural events with an atheistic message for people in the neighbourhood.[47]

The 'hidden' curriculum is by now a familiar concept, referring to those aspects of the teaching and learning process that result unofficially or inadvertently from it. They are unofficial in that they are not laid down in formal documents. Since so many of these in the Soviet school of the mid-1980s were not in fact hidden, Muckle also uses the term 'paracurriculum'.[48] The Greek prefix has the sense of 'alongside'. We certainly think this term preferable, where it can be used at all, but must confine ourselves to its applicability to atheistic education.

Some typical examples of the paracurriculum in western countries might be ceremonies and symbols. The Soviet school of the mid-1980s – as well as the world outside – had both, and slogans too. Ritual was meant to reinforce official values, and these were secular ones. Furthermore, enjoyable ceremonies helped to unite religious children with the collective. In the RSFSR, the school youth organisations prepared sixteen-year-olds for the conferment of the internal passport, the initiation ceremony into citizenship of the secular state, whose flags and emblems were to be seen also in the schools. Slogans extolling the materialist and atheistic worldview might also be found there. But there was nothing unofficial or undeclared about them. Indeed, the 1984 Guidelines said specifically, 'Educational work must make wider use of the symbols of the Soviet state.'[49] It is not at all appropriate to attribute these features of Soviet schooling to the 'hidden' curriculum or paracurriculum, for they were overt facets of the curriculum itself.

When we turn to inadvertent outcomes, however, it is a different story. Two recent incidents will serve to highlight these. The millennium of the adoption of the Christianity by Kievan Rus' received much coverage on British television. One of the programmes contained scenes of atheistic education in a Soviet school. The Pioneers sat in their desks and one by one expressed opinions which it was obvious – and in one case excruciatingly so – they had learned by heart. There was no discussion and the atmosphere was grim. To be sure, we must allow for the stress caused by the intrusive cameras. But we must also remember that authority nowhere encourages the mass media to pry into bad schools; this school must have been regarded as a good one. It is also fair to say that many Soviet writers on atheistic education would have been highly critical of such a performance. If it was at all typical, they would have had every right to be alarmed. The secular catechism seemed to have been learned to satisfy the teacher's expectations. Presumably it was thought better to oppose 'incorrect' views with other views and arguments learned parrot-fashion than to remain silent. But there was no evidence that the 'correct' arguments had been internalised and exercised in such a way that these young people could have held their own against persistent adversaries.

The other incident recalls a basic and intrinsic problem of atheistic education. If you have forbidden fruit in the house, it is dangerous to leave it in a bowl on the table. Soviet educationists took the line that the fruit was much more attractive if it was a forbidden topic; it was far better to talk openly about its insipidity and its rottenness, so that nobody could possibly want to taste it. Now such an approach may work with young and conventionally minded older children, or when the teacher is much respected. But its pedagogical weakness is that it precludes personal experiment. More thoughtful and independently disposed youngsters may well want to find out for themselves. At a meeting in Birmingham in June 1988, the well-known dissident Irina Ratushinskaya said in reply to a question that it was hearing about atheism in school that led ultimately to her commitment to the Christian faith. Although few will go to the barricades for what they believe, intelligent young Soviet citizens were attending church services – it was claimed that they just wanted to hear something different, but the significant point is that they were there at all – and the average age of members of certain sects is said to be decreasing.[50] For some of them at least, a causal connection with their school experience seems probable, and this cannot have been an intended consequence of it.

Approaches to atheistic teaching and influence

In examining the content of atheistic education in the Soviet school, in and out of class, we have incidentally looked at many forms in which that content was expressed, and some of the methods whereby it was intended to be taught and learned. The purpose of the present section is to consider some broader methodological aspects of atheistic teaching and upbringing. One such has already been touched upon: the basic pedagogical truth that material and techniques must be related to the degree of maturation of the pupils. Although the Soviet approach to the psychology of teaching and learning is somewhat different from what normally pertains in the West, being traditionally geared to what the child can achieve by hard work with the additional help of teacher and classmates, rather than to a prescribed developmental level, other general principles have universal applicability. Sensible teachers proceed from the known to the unknown, from the pupil's environment and experience to the wider world, from the concrete to the abstract. While the first two of these begin early, children cannot start to cope with abstractions much before their teens. Younger children are more responsive to approaches directed at the emotions, and atheistic concepts are difficult in any case. This is another reason why the rote-learning of atheistic arguments by children of 11–12 was regarded by the experts as futile, and almost certainly the main reason why the very tough meat of formal atheistic instruction was left until the final school year and later. It was both easier and more effective to hook atheistic education on to disciplines whose content was more specific and concrete.

Teachers were also exhorted to be attentive to their pupils as individuals. This meant that they should develop varying approaches which should rest on three major considerations. These were the degree of existing atheistic or religious conviction in the pupil, the nature of his or her religious affiliation, if any, and the necessity of a sensitive attitude towards him or her *vis-à-vis* the other children. Whereas subject teachers had to put the demands of the syllabus first, class teachers and Pioneers leaders had to proceed on the basis of whether there were young believers in the class at all. To establish this, they asked them questions such as 'Why have we had a good harvest?' or 'What sort of things are you afraid of?', or got them to write essays or do drawings on free-choice subjects or at home.[51] The results were analysed also for information on family background. Pupils' behaviour, such as non-participation in extracurricular activities, should also put teachers on their guard.[52]

Students of the incidence of religious belief in the USSR are familiar with the five-to-seven-cell typologies used by Soviet sociologists of religion and atheism. On one wing there were convinced atheists who took part in agitation and propaganda, then passive atheists who did not translate firm beliefs into action. The teacher's job was to involve them in atheistic work. Next came primitive (*stikhiinye*) atheists whose

attitude to religion had developed spontaneously through their growing up in a non-religious environment. The teacher had first to form in
them a proper materialistic basis for their attitude and turn it into
conviction. In the middle were the indifferent, vaguely disbelieving
perhaps, but unwilling to adopt any kind of stance against religious
belief. As well as taking pro-atheistic action, the teacher had to protect
them against possible religious influences. Those believers whose faith
was least firm were commonly designated 'waverers'. They believed in
the existence of some sort of omnipotent supernatural force; this was
usually because of family influence which had been mitigated by the
school. They were subject to doubts and inner conflict, and teachers
were to begin by encouraging such doubts, in collaboration with youth
leaders and librarians, and also confer with parents. 'Work with
parents' was still more necessary in the case of 'believers by tradition',
youngsters who followed religious rituals out of habit, but did not
normally study the faith. Ideally, parents should be persuaded to
allow their children the option of the atheist path, thus avoiding strife;
but this was difficult, and in the event of outright, lasting contention
the child was to be actively supported. Finally, convinced believers
were the most problematic of all, as they were not susceptible to
rational argument. It was here that the character of the religious
affiliation came most prominently into play.[53]

Let us consider the former atheistic line on four major religious
denominations: Orthodoxy, Catholicism, Islam and Reform Baptism.
Orthodox believers were considered to be affected much more by
ritual and tradition than by preaching and Bible study, and to have a
somewhat passive attitude to transmitting the faith. Youngsters might
be susceptible to the atmosphere in church, the influence of icons, and
exciting religious holidays and ceremonies such as christenings. A kind
of residual Orthodoxy, part of the traditional culture, might still be
present in families evincing little religious belief. The church was
thought to cash in on the people's innate patriotic impulse and sense of
justice, and had latterly been supporting foreign national liberation
movements as divinely inspired.[54] The school was bidden to provide its
own attractive rituals and leisure activities, to develop in the children
– unfamiliar with argument in this area – an informed attitude to the
harmfulness of religion, and to alert them to the falseness of the
church's self-presentation as a progressive force in modern Soviet life.

Ritual, tradition, and sometimes attempts to modernise the message
were also deemed characteristic of Roman Catholicism, but there were
certain additional features. The traditional faith might be linked to
indigenous nationalism, as in Lithuania. The clergy, it was said, cast

themselves in the role of champions of the stable family as the context of religious education, and also took an active and illegal line themselves as religious educators. While not usually opposing membership of the secular youth organisations, they sometimes held catechism classes, or young people's services with special music and singing.[55] In addition to their obligation of providing counter-attraction and enlightenment for the youngsters themselves, teachers had increased responsibilities in the field of parent education.

Islam presented atheistic educators with frequently intractable problems. Religious practice was, and is, inextricable from traditional culture. It was not only a question of unacceptable attitudes to the place of women in Soviet society and the education of girls. In the words of a Soviet scholar, family and tribal interests were put above Party and state ones. Young people were said to acquire a narrowly egoistical understanding of friendship as against socialist internationalism. Collectivism was replaced by forms of mutual responsibility justifying any arbitrary action to the advantage of one's group interests.[56] Conservative ways, rooted in the extended family, helped religion to persist. Much scope was provided for clerical influence over youth. The only way to overcome this was to transform the microenvironment. Teachers had their familiar part to play, but it was also a matter of extending secular institutions such as crèches, nursery schools, and women's councils, and involving young people, especially girls, more systematically in working life.[57] In rural areas they stood in great need of leisure facilities. In contrast to this broad canvas of activity, it appears, atheistic endeavour was all too often reduced to the narrow confines of criticising the mullahs.

The atheistic education of Reform Baptists' children was also perceived as problematic, for reasons partly similar and partly different. Baptism was an all-encompassing way of life for these people too, but they had been steeled in adversity, a minority standing out from those around them, with their own alternative community. While for both Muslims and Reform Baptists doubt in God's existence is a sin, the former usually refused to discuss the question altogether while the latter might be quite articulate and unshakeable in arguing their case, passing on this skill to their young people. Thus, teachers were told, there was little point in reasoning with such children. Rather the priority should be to provide a class collective that was warm and welcoming, with interesting activities. The key period for exerting atheistic influence was adolescence, when the youngsters' naturally heightened desire for autonomy and peer-group identification might make them readier to break out of the hold of family and religious community. It was a challenge to the school, however, because it was equally in late childhood and adolescence that youngsters were integrated more systematically into church life following the ceremony of baptism, with purpose-built clandestine organisations such as youth clubs.[58]

The need for a sensitive attitude to young believers applied across the denominational board. In atheistic education generally, but particularly in this area, there had been a marked move away from the stridency of the Khrushchev era and the immediately succeeding years. This is exemplified in a comparison of two editions of the *Pioneer Leader's Handbook (Kniga vozhatogo)* for 1968 and 1982.[59] In the latter a 'softly-softly approach' was advocated. Browbeating was likely to strengthen the parents' influence and undermine the moral authority of the school. Tactlessness and mockery caused withdrawal and alienation, entrenching religious dispositions yet further.[60] If the believing youngster's peers joined in the ridicule, matters would go from bad to worse.

The teacher's individual approach should not be critical, because that would put the pupil on the defensive. She should be always gentle and at first patient, biding her time; then enquiring, seeking to know why the pupil went to church or was a believer; and only later, when the youngster began to feel the need to discuss, expressing cautious doubt in his or her arguments.[61] By showing respect the teacher was more apt to gain the child's trust, and then the child would be more receptive to other ideas and preferred modes of behaviour, carefully presented. A relationship based on confidence was more likely to bring to light home circumstances, such as poverty or illness, which might be conducive to religiousness. The teacher, and indeed the pupil collective, might then be able to intervene in a supportive way. And not only in the case of believers – it was precisely when this did not happen that the churches sometimes stepped in and made converts.

Reference has been made more than once to parent education, or 'work with parents' as it has usually been known in the USSR. This too was part of the school's and the teacher's responsibilities (although not limited to them: colleagues at work or the 'production collective' were also regarded as a potentially strong social and moral force). The atheistic education of parents had both collective and individual forms. Parents' evenings gave opportunities for talks to the assembled mothers and fathers and to some extent for individual chats. Suggested lecture topics were: 'Modernisation of religion in present conditions;' 'The harm of religious festivals and customs'; 'The atheistic education of children in the family'.[62] If there happened to be many religious families in the area, it was recommended to adopt a more oblique approach by selecting topics with an atheistic element, such as 'Inculcating the ability to live in a collective'; here the speaker might allude to the stress caused to children by fear of mockery from their fellow pupils for their religious allegiance.[63] Lecture courses might form part of campaigns of atheistic education such as that held in Novoaleksandrovsk District, Stavropol' Territory, under the banner of 'Atheistic knowledge for every family'. This one-week series of events involved Party meetings, parents' meetings, seminars and conferences for local Party and *Komsomol* secretaries and adult educators, library exhibitions and the setting-up of 'Atheists' Corners'. It was claimed that practically the whole population was reached, and that reliable feedback was secured on local religiosity and the effectiveness of atheistic education.[64]

On the individual level, home visits might be more fruitful and were certainly necessary. The teacher could then see something of the pupil's family background for herself, try to identify any religious affiliation, and appraise the basic reason for religiosity, whether tradition, attractiveness of the ritual, loneliness, personal difficulties, or some other cause. This would, to some extent, determine the initial approach: if the cause could be removed by sorting out the problem, the teacher should start there, while if it was rooted in ethnicity she should at first leave it alone and 'demonstrate the falsity of religion in other questions less significant to the believer's religious ego'.[65] In Islamic areas, male teachers from the local nationalities should also be involved; there, Russian teachers speaking only Russian had additional hurdles to overcome when trying to deal with the identification of religion with nationality, yet lacking inside knowledge,[66] and possibly being perceived as representatives of an alien ideology and culture. The same could be said of strongly Catholic areas.

Patience and discretion had become hallmarks of the favoured approach to parents as well as to their children. Believers were usually very willing to discuss their children's work, health, and behaviour; but if the teacher expeditiously brought the subject round to their religious influence, the barrier of the 'amoral atheist' stereotype came crashing down.[67] So the wise teacher concentrated on praising them for their children's qualities. She got through to them by way of their parental feelings: they should feel that their children were good and treated with respect in school, but to be even better they should be brought up without religious prejudices.[68] And children deserved the joy of their classmates' companionship in leisure activities in and out of school.

It was not only believing parents who needed to be reached. Although 'grandmas' liberation' has become a more noticeable feature of the Soviet scene during the past fifteen or twenty years, grandmothers are still quite conspicuous in upbringing roles, given the very high level of female employment. The negative influence of believing grandmothers was frequently addressed in anti-religious literature, but the old ladies themselves were usually regarded as beyond atheistic redemption. Some did not think this good enough. Thus a school in the Chuvash ASSR arranged atheistic meetings, concerts, and films specifically for grandparents, assisted by pupils and parents. More active use should be made of the senior citizens themselves; retired teachers could be particularly effective.[69]

With so much concentration on the atheistic enlightenment of believers, accompanied by the prevalence of non-belief at a rather rudimentary and uninformed level, some atheistic educators came to feel that such non-believing families were being neglected. There was still a worldview to develop, and the sects might be on the watch for easy prey. The fact that parents did not hold any religious beliefs by no means signified that their children received atheistic education at home. A survey of 1981 among non-believing women workers at three factories in Glazov, Udmurt ASSR, revealed that fewer than 10 per cent gave their children atheistic education, while 35.7 per cent thought it necessary but did not do it themselves. This was partly because parents felt helpless. There was said to be an increasing need for the atheistic education of parents to be differentiated according to whether they were believers or non-believers. They had expressed the wish for teaching materials related to the age of their children. This area of atheistic work amounted to a new field for research.[70]

The need for atheistic teacher education

There were two major problems concerning teachers as the agents of atheistic education: one was that they were often indifferent to it, the other was that they frequently had a superficial understanding of it. In these respects they reflected the adult population as a whole, whereas their responsibilities were greater than the average citizen's. When they made no effort to widen their own knowledge, sometimes apparently because they found the whole matter too difficult, this lack of interest was communicated to the children. Their work was unsystematic, neglecting the potential of the teaching materials, failing to make due connections between the various sectors of upbringing, i.e. not linking the atheistic component with the aesthetic, moral and ideological–political elements, and taking a formalistic attitude to the pupils' own atheistic activity.[71] This called into question the effectiveness of the atheistic education they had themselves received, and the remedy was seen in greatly improved initial and in-service training.

At pedagogical institutes (higher educational institutions training teachers) and universities, up to 1989, 'scientific atheism' was a compulsory subject. That it was also a by-word for boredom is well-known; but what is a little surprising is that, if one may generalise from the situation at the Lenin State Pedagogical Institute in Moscow in the late 1970s, it comprised a mere 24 hours or 0.5 per cent of the students' total workload.[72] The present writer has described elsewhere the content of the textbook.[73] Of the 274 pages of text, 11 were devoted to 'The system of scientific–atheistic education', while less than one of these referred specifically to children and young people.[74] It is clear that this was of next to no use for teaching the student teachers how to go about their immediate atheistic tasks. The situation was somewhat better only in places like the Chuvash State University with its 470-hour specialisation (for historians) in the history of religion and atheism, including 34 hours on the theory and practice of atheistic education, though this too seems to have been targeted at adults.[75]

In response to this unsatisfactory state of affairs, the USSR Ministry of Education ordered that the scientific atheism course at pedagogical institutes be extended by about 50 per cent. All students were to write papers for public defence. The course should include teaching practice in extracurricular atheistic activities, in options in atheism at the senior stage, and in giving subject teaching an atheistic slant. The Herzen Pedagogical Institute in Leningrad drew up a new syllabus which was introduced in all such institutes from 1983/4. It included such topics as 'Role of the Soviet school in forming and developing mass atheism in the USSR', 'Different religions' forms and methods of influencing the younger generation', and 'The teacher's role in the atheistic education of young people'. Various special courses were also set up.[76]

As for the serving teacher, in-service training would seem from various accounts to have been provided in a somewhat haphazard manner. The Institutes of In-Service Teacher Education (*instituty usovershenstvovaniya uchitelei* or *IUUs*) had major responsibilities here but were criticised for failing to discharge them adequately.[77] Some, however, provided courses with the help of the local pedagogical institute. Otherwise in-service training was obtained through the system of Party education or the adult education facilities of the *Znanie* Society. These, however, were not intended specifically for teachers, so in recent years Party bodies organised purpose-built theoretical and methodological seminars for them. An important aim here was to get away from the traditional narrow anti-religious approach and to concentrate on forming a scientific worldview.[78] Training for the atheistic education of parents was not forgotten, for regional IUUs might mount short courses of six to eight hours on 'Current problems of atheistic education in the family'.[79]

Problems of atheistic education in the later 1980s

Up to 1987–8, before *perestroika* had begun to have a recognisable effect on the subject of our study, it seemed that the atheistic show must go on, for religion continued to survive in popular consciousness. But, as we have seen, there were considerable problems. Why was it that teachers so often displayed the indifference which we have mentioned? The fact that atheism is a complicated matter to inculcate offers a pedagogical reason. Good teachers are usually inspiring teachers. It must be intrinsically difficult to wax enthusiastic about a non-concept. An entity which is said not to exist is markedly more elusive than one for which the reverse is claimed. One can scarcely deal with the former without referring to the latter. And it will not always do to dangle the forbidden fruit before the pupils' eyes and tell them it is all an illusion. A few may want to stretch out their hand to find out if it is really there. Reflections of this kind may well have prompted teachers to feel that discretion was the better part of valour.

Other reasons were not peculiar to the teaching profession. People had heard so long that religion was dying out anyway that it was not surprising if they thought intervention unnecessary. The school curriculum was materialist, the whole social system was materialist, and the pupils were assumed to be atheists. Religion was considered to be so much an anachronism that it had lost whatever harm it once had. People were supposed to be mature enough under socialism to make the right decision for themselves, thus any pushing in the desired direction was superfluous.

These perceptions were very difficult to shift, and they gave cause for concern among atheistic educators. As we discussed at the start, a rival ideology could not be tolerated. It would provide the stimulus for rival patterns of behaviour, such as when, inside the Soviet frontier, the religious is identified with the national in people's consciousness. Fulfilling religious ceremonies and customs itself becomes a behavioural norm. Moreover, religion may well present itself as more humane than atheism. An optimistic collective-oriented secular creed may be perfectly acceptable to most people when things are going well, but it has little to offer in the crises of life when individuals are thrust upon their own resources and find them wanting. In 1988, the Soviet mass media began to concede this. To be sure, love and support can be offered by family, friends, and workmates whatever they believe, and comradeliness is a demand of the secular ideology. At the institutional level, however, caring is in the forefront of the responsibilities of the religious community; it cannot normally be said to constitute that order of priority at the workplace (though sometimes it does), and the social services have their limitations. And even if the church should fall short or friends be lacking, the person with a firm religious faith will still draw strength and comfort from it. Neither can such a faith be shaken by rational argument.

And young people? Over and over again one had heard that young people were turning to the churches. It was certainly not a mass movement, but it was noticeable enough among the more thoughtful and better-educated. 'We can see the development of an active, even though relatively small, stratum of convinced young believers, from whom to a significant extent the body of the clergy is formed', a leading Party atheist wrote in 1986.[80] There was concern because it was partly from this group that the creative intelligentsia would in future replenish their ranks. What sort of messages would they bring to their audiences and their readers?

The beginnings of religious education

All these problems, considerable though they were, must have seemed slight to atheistic educators compared to the *rapprochement* with the church signalled by Gorbachev's remarks to the Patriarch in April 1988. The modern churchmen's line which they so deprecated, on the religious essence of communist morality and the common nature of spiritual and temporal ethical goals, was outdone by the CPSU General Secretary himself with his acknowledgment of past short-comings in church–state relations and his talk of 'our common cause'. The new law on freedom of conscience which he promised was finally enacted on October 1, 1990. It not only affirmed the right of parents to bring up their children according to their own attitude towards religion, the right to education irrespective of religious stance, and the right of registered religious organisations to set up educational establishments and groups for the religious education of children and adults, to engage in other teaching, and to maintain charitable boarding schools. It also declared that the state funded neither religious bodies nor 'activity associated with the propaganda of atheism'.[81] For some, this seemed to call into question the very legality of atheistic education, confounding the confusion of social studies teachers in particular.[82]

Our earliest reference to religious education in a state school dates from October 1988, when the late Father Aleksandr Men', parish priest of Novaya Derevnya near Moscow, was reported in the government newspaper *Izvestiia* to be visiting School No. 67 in the capital for talks on Christianity and cultural, ethical, and philosophical matters.[83] This practice seems to have been slow to spread beyond Moscow, Leningrad, and one or two other cities, but in the meantime optional courses on the history of religion for senior school students were being introduced in Tbilisi, under the direction of the leading Soviet educational innovator Professor Shalva Amonashvili – various 'great faiths' were to be studied, but they began with Bible texts[84] – and elsewhere. This included School No. 470 in Leningrad, where an Orthodox cleric took part and parents and ex-pupils were also invited to attend.[85] In 1989 optional 'History of Religion' replaced compulsory 'Scientific Atheism' in Russia's higher education. From January 1990, religious instruction (*Zakon Bozhii*) – called by that name and not some euphemism – has been an elective on the timetable of Lithuanian schools.[86] In Russia, however, any kind of religious teaching in state schools remained rather rare, and atheism sometimes lingered on.

I shall conclude with a look at the problems of religious education. All its sectors are faced with a shortage of teaching materials and, as they expand, of skilled and dedicated personnel. Sunday schools often lack a suitable place to meet. Religious education in ordinary state schools has additional difficulties. When the draft law on freedom of conscience and religious organisations was going through the Soviet parliament, there was serious controversy over a provision which would have specifically permitted educational institutions to make their premises available outside school hours for the religious instruction of pupils. On a vote of 303 to 46, the clause was eventually deleted. That did not formally prevent it, for 'anything that is not prohibited is permitted, as deputies agreed', and in any case another clause allowed religious bodies to use unspecified premises made available to them for this purpose.[87] Indeed, an earlier proposal to ban religious instruction from schools giving general education[88] had also been thrown out. Yet still the law did not give the advocates of religious education the implicit, let alone explicit, right to extend their activities into the state sector which they had sought. Neither did it relieve the accommodation problems of the Sunday schools.

The press discussion prompts two thoughts: that in the matter of religious education churchmen will still have to reckon with the opposition of convinced atheists, and that there are those who have no wish to replace one orthodoxy in the school system by another (the pun is inevitable rather than intentional). It is likely that the latter include not only people holding the middle ground, but also some atheists and some believers. If, however, the church is unable to occupy the ideological house as it is gradually vacated, for lack of opportunity, experience or presence, all sorts of devils may come in and appropriate it, whether from occult movements or the seamier side of capitalism. But even if the church does take possession, how effective can it be?

There are also representatives of all three camps who, for different reasons, hold grave doubts as to the fashionable view of religious education as the panacea for the country's moral ills. Atheists and agnostics may hark back to the ethical condition of Holy Russia, or look westward and see nothing there for their comfort. While some Christians gaze starry-eyed at the West's religious freedom and derive idealised conclusions about the level of faith and morality in Western society, others look more perceptively homeward and inward. 'Our common cause', in the state's view, was about morality alone, and certainly up to mid-1990 churchmen speaking in schools and on the media were supposed to confine themselves to this. Some toed the line more than others; some were swifter than others to feel the constraints on their new acceptability. They agreed that the exposition and discussion of Christian moral precepts was unlikely to have much effect on young people's attitudes and behaviour without a change of heart based on repentance and faith.

Notes

1 M. Bourdeaux, *Gorbachev, Glasnost and the Gospel* (London, Hodder and Stoughton, 1990), pp. 43–5.
2 Because of other contributions to this volume, and because of the wish to avoid replication of earlier work, the present article will focus particularly on curriculum and method. For a broader treatment of atheistic education, e.g. in relation to questions of religiosity, see J. Dunstan, 'Atheistic education in the USSR', in G. Avis, (ed.), *The Making of the Soviet Citizen* (London, Croom Helm, 1987), pp. 50–79. For an up-to-date study of Soviet atheism in general, see D.V. Pospielovsky, *A History of Soviet Atheism in Theory and Practice, and the Believer*, 3 vols. (Basingstoke and London, Macmillan Press, 1987–8).
3 Examples of a vast literature presenting these principles in a pedagogical

context are: E.P. Bel'chikova, 'Metody i metodicheskie priemy form-irovaniya nauchno-ateisticheskikh vzglyadov uchashchikhsya', in *Nauchno-ateisticheskoe vospitanie uchashchikhsya* (Moscow, Izd. APN SSSR, 1986), pp. 67–77, at p. 68; O.G. Budnaya, 'Obogashchenie ateisticheskogo opyta mladshikh shkol'nikov', in *ibid.*, pp. 78–89, at p. 78; and O.S. Prokhorova, 'Opyt obobshcheniya raboty shkol po ateisticheskomu vospitaniyu uchashchikhsya', in *ibid.*, pp 125–32.

 4 Yu.S. Gurov and B.N. Konovalov, 'Kharakter proyavleniya i prichiny indifferentnosti uchashchikhsya k ateizmu i religii', in *Ateisticheskoe vospitanie uchashchikhsya: opyt i problemy* (Moscow, Pedagogika, 1981), pp. 33–40, at p. 37; I. Galitskaya, 'Ateisticheskoe vospitanie shkol'nikov', *Politicheskoe samoobrazovanie*, 1984, 1, pp. 91–7, at pp. 91–2; and Budnaya, 'Obogashchenie', pp. 78–9.

 5 V.I. Gal'perin, 'Vzaimosvyaz' i posledovatel'nost' ateisticheskogo vospitaniya pri izuchenii predmetov estestvennonauchnogo i guman-itarnogo tsiklov', in *Ateisticheskoe vospitanie*, pp. 48–59, at p. 58. For a frank and authoritative discussion of the need for atheistic *perestroika* in these areas, see V. Pravotorov, ' "Samaya bol'shaya oshibka" ', *Nauka i religiya*, 1987, 11, pp. 19–20.

 6 E.K. Arnaut, 'Osobennosti ateisticheskoi raboty s det'mi iz semei veruyushchikh', in *Ateisticheskoe vospitanie*, pp. 75–87, at p. 86; G.P. Ulyukin, 'Ateisticheskoe vospitanie mladshikh shkol'nikov v pionerskoi organizatsii', in *ibid.*, pp. 102–8, at p. 106; V.I. Garadzha, 'Nauchnyi ateizm v svete zadach sovershenstvovaniya sotsializma', *Voprosy nauchnogo ateizma*, 34 (Moscow: Mysl', 1986), pp. 6–25, at p. 16.

 7 I.I. Akinchits, 'Osobennosti nravstvennogo soznaniya molodogo veruyushchego', *Voprosy nauchnogo ateizma*, 35 (Moscow: Mysl', 1986), pp. 213–34, at pp. 219–21.

 8 Gal'perin, 'Vzaimosvyaz'', p. 54.

 9 *Ibid.*, N.A. Naumov, 'Mirovozzrencheskii (ateisticheskii) potentsial shkol'nykh kursov fiziki i biologii', in *Nauchno-ateisticheskoe vospitanie*, pp. 33–44, at p. 35.

10 Gal'perin, 'Vzaimosvyaz'', p. 55.

11 Naumov, 'Mirovozzrencheskii (ateisticheskii) potentsial', p. 41.

12 Budnaya, 'Obogashchenie', pp. 79–80.

13 Bel'chikova, 'Metody', p. 69.

14 Gal'perin, 'Vzaimosvyaz'', p. 49.

15 Yu.B. Pishchik, 'Kritika bogoslovskoi interpretatsii nauki i ee rol' v form-irovanii ateisticheskogo mirovozzreniya uchashchikhsya', in *Ateisticheskoe vospitanie*, pp. 59–68, at pp. 60–1.

16 For a full account, see R.M. Rogova (ed.), 'Atheistic education in the school, theoretical and practical issues', *Soviet Education*, 24, 1981–2, 8/9, especially pp. 115–23. (Translation of *Ateisticheskoe vospitanie v shkole: voprosy teorii i praktiki* (Moscow, Pedagogika, 1979).)

17 D.P. Plotkina, 'Rol' gumanitarnykh predmetov v ateisticheskom vospitanii shkol'nikov', in *Nauchno-ateisticheskoe vospitanie*, pp. 52–62, at pp. 55–7.

18 *Ibid.*, pp. 60–1.
19 G.B. Romanova, 'Ateisticheskoe vospitanie na urokakh russkogo yazyka', *Russkii yazyk i literatura v uzbekskoi shkole*, 1987, 3, pp. 30–3, at p. 31.
20 Yu.F. Fominykh, 'Ateisticheskii aspekt obucheniya matematike', in *Nauchno-ateisticheskoe vospitanie*, pp. 44–52, at pp. 45–7.
21 *Izuchenie obshchestvovedeniya v srednei shkole* (Moscow, Prosveshchenie, 1975), p. 99.
22 Naumov, 'Mirovozzrencheskii (ateisticheskii) potentsial', p. 43.
23 J.B. Cullen, 'On the methods, rationale and unanticipated consequences of Soviet atheistic "upbringing" ', *Religious Education*, 69, 1974, 1, pp. 72–87, at p. 80.
24 I.A. Galitskaya, 'Formirovanie nauchno-materialisticheskogo mirovozzreniya shkol'nikov: problemy i napravleniya issledovanii', *Voprosy nauchnogo ateizma*, 34 (Moscow, Mysl', 1986), pp. 194–202, at p. 200.
25 Yu. Plotnikov, 'Poka khot' odin . . .', *Uchitel'skaya gazeta*, 11 September 1980.
26 Fominykh, 'Ateisticheskii aspekt', pp. 45–6.
27 Budnaya, 'Obogashchenie', p. 82.
28 Pishchik, 'Kritika', pp. 62–3, 66; Akinchits, 'Osobennosti', pp. 226–7.
29 *Ibid.*, pp. 220–1.
30 Gal'perin, 'Vzaimosvyaz'', p. 49.
31 Arnaut, 'Osobennosti', pp. 85–6.
32 *Programmy vos'miletnei i srednei shkoly na 1978/79 uchebnyi god. Literatura* (Moscow, Prosveshchenie, 1978).
33 Quoted in Plotkina, 'Rol' gumanitarnykh predmetov', p. 61.
34 *Ibid.*, pp. 59, 61–2; *Programmy*, pp. 36–9, 42–3.
35 *Programmy vos'miletnei shkoly. Muzyka, 4–7 klassy* (Moscow, Prosveshchenie, 1978), p. 17.
36 With regard to literature: Gal'perin, 'Vzaimosvyaz'', p. 58; Galitskaya, 'Formirovanie', p. 197.
37 *Ibid.*
38 J. Muckle, *A Guide to the Soviet Curriculum* (London, Croom Helm, 1988), pp. 95, 105–28.
39 V.I. Gal'perin, 'Vneuchebnaya nauchno-ateisticheskaya rabota', in *Ateisticheskoe vospitanie*, pp. 87–95, at p. 88.
40 *Ibid.*, p. 89.
41 Ulyukin, 'Ateisticheskoe vospitanie', p. 105.
42 Budnaya, 'Obogashchenie', pp. 81–2.
43 T.A. Avdeeva, 'Iz opyta organizatsii sistemy raboty pedagogicheskogo kollektiva shkoly po ateisticheskomu vospitaniyu uchashchikhsya', in *Nauchno-ateisticheskoe vospitanie*, pp. 89–95, at p. 93.
44 Gal'perin, 'Vneuchebnaya nauchno-ateisticheskaya rabota', pp. 88, 92.
45 Rogova (ed.), 'Atheistic education', pp. 141–5 (for full details); *Kniga vozhatogo* (Moscow, Molodaya gvardiya, 1982), p. 122.
46 Prokhorova, 'Opyt obobshcheniya', pp. 129–30.
47 Gal'perin, 'Vneuchebnaya nauchno-ateisticheskaya rabota', pp. 90–1.

48 Muckle, *A Guide*, p. 175.
49 *USSR: New Frontiers of Social Progress* (Moscow, Novosti, 1984), p. 61.
50 Garadzha, 'Nauchnyi ateizm', p. 20.
51 Rogova (ed.), 'Atheistic education', pp. 69–70.
52 Arnaut, 'Osobennosti', pp. 76–7, 79.
53 The typologies vary in detail and the above is an attempt at a composite picture of their essentials. It is based on Rogova (ed.), 'Atheistic education', pp. 135–40; I.A. Galitskaya, 'Ateisticheskaya ubezhdennost' shkol'nikov', in *Ateisticheskoe vospitanie*, pp. 24–33, at pp. 31–2; *id.*, 'Ateisticheskoe vospitanie', p. 94; and Yu. S. Gurov, 'Sotsialisticheskii obraz zhizni i problemy ateisticheskogo vospitaniya molodezhi', in *Problemy istorii religii i ateizma*, (Cheboksary, Chuvashskii gosudarstvennyi universitet, 1981), p. 90, cited in Dunstan, 'Atheistic education', p. 70.
54 Rogova (ed.), 'Atheistic education', pp. 170–8, 181.
55 *Ibid.*, pp. 185–90.
56 M.K. Dzhabarova, 'Nekotorye rezul'taty issledovaniya otnosheniya molodezhi k ateizmu i religii (po materialam Tadzhikskoi SSR)', *Voprosy nauchnogo ateizma*, 34 (Moscow, Mysl', 1986), pp. 167–74, at p. 172.
57 *Ibid.*, pp. 171, 173–4.
58 Rogova (ed.), 'Atheistic education', pp. 200–8.
59 For details, see Dunstan, 'Atheistic education', pp. 51, 54–5, 62–4, 67–8.
60 *Kniga vozhatogo* (1982), p. 121.
61 Arnaut, 'Osobennosti', pp. 79–81, 83; S.P. Zhukauskene, 'Psikhologicheskie aspekty individual'noi raboty s veruyushchimi uchashchimisya i ikh roditelyami', in *Nauchno-ateisticheskoe vospitanie*, pp. 108–15, at pp. 112, 114. See also I.A. Galitskaya and N.T. Abramova, 'Ateisticheskoe vospitanie shkol'nikov', *Sovetskaya pedagogika*, 1984, 1, pp. 92–9, at p. 99.
62 Avdeeva, 'Iz opyta organizatsii', p. 94.
63 Rogova (ed.), 'Atheistic education', pp. 149–50.
64 A.V. Avksent'ev and B.N. Konovalov, 'Vzaimodeistvie shkoly i sem'i v ateisticheskom vospitanii', in *Ateisticheskoe vospitanie*, pp. 134–44, at pp. 136–7.
65 Rogova (ed.), 'Atheistic education', p. 155.
66 Avksent'ev and Konovalov, 'Vzaimodeistvie', pp. 140–1.
67 Arnaut, 'Osobennosti', p. 79.
68 *Ibid.*, p. 86; Zhukauskene, 'Psikhologicheskie aspekty', p. 112.
69 Avksent'ev and Konovalov, 'Vzaimodeistvie', pp. 139–40.
70 G.I. Tropina, 'Ateisticheskoe vospitanie shkol'nikov v sem'yakh neveruyushchikh', in *Nauchno-ateisticheskoe vospitanie*, pp. 120–5, at pp. 121, 124–5.
71 Prokhorova, 'Opyt obobshcheniya', pp. 131–2; Gurov and Konovalov, 'Kharakter proyavleniya', p. 40.
72 M. Matthews, *Education in the Soviet Union* (London, Allen and Unwin, 1982), p. 120.
73 Dunstan, 'Atheistic education', p. 66.
74 *Nauchnyi ateizm*, 2nd edn (Moscow, Politizdat, 1974).

75 G.E. Kudryashov, 'Nauchnye osnovy spetsializatsii studentov vuza po istorii religii i ateizma', in *Problemy istorii religii i ateizma*, pp. 54–67, at pp. 58, 62.

76 R.V. Pandre, 'Osnovnye napravleniya podgotovki propagandistov nauch-nogo ateizma i organizatorov nauchno-ateisticheskogo vospitaniya iz chisla studentov pedagogicheskikh vuzov', *Voprosy nauchnogo ateizma*, 34 (Moscow, Mysl', 1986), pp. 175–93, at pp. 183–4.

77 Gal'perin, 'Vzaimosvyaz'', p. 52.

78 A.S. Bainov and B.N. Konovalov, 'Partiinoe rukovodstvo nauchno-ateisticheskoi rabotoi v shkole', in *Ateisticheskoe vospitanie*, pp. 125–34, at pp. 126–8.

79 Avksent'ev and Konovalov, 'Vzaimodeistvie', pp. 137–8.

80 Garadzha, 'Nauchnyi ateizm', p. 9.

81 *Summary of World Broadcasts*, SU/0902 C1/1–5, 23 October 1990 (from *Pravda*, 9 October 1990).

82 See, for example, the correspondence and editorial comment in *Uchitel'skaya gazeta*, 1990, 40, p. 4, and F. Gorelik, 'Poteryali pokolenie?', *Uchitel'skaya gazeta*, 1990, 43, p. 3. For a much fuller examination of the development of religious education than is possible in the present article, see the writer's contribution to his edited volume *Soviet Education under Perestroika* (London and New York, Routledge, forthcoming).

83 E. Isakova, 'Svyashchennik Men' beseduet so shkol'nikami', *Izvestiya*, 22 October 1988. See also his obituary by M. Bourdeaux in *The Independent*, 14 September 1990, p. 28.

84 'News Roundup', *Keston News Service*, no. 319, 16 February 1989, p. 19.

85 S. Krayukhin, 'Svyashchennik v shkol'nom klasse', *Izvestiya*, 29 October 1989.

86 'V raspisanii – novyi urok', *Sovetskaya Litva*, 28 February 1990.

87 *Summary of World Broadcasts*, SU/0881 C1/2, 28 September 1990, and SU/0886 C1/1, 4 October 1990.

88 'O svobode sovesti i religioznykh organizatsiyakh', *Izvestiya*, 5 June 1990.

· 8 ·

The Ten Commandments as values in Soviet people's consciousness

SAMUEL A. KLIGER AND PAUL H. DE VRIES

1. The uniqueness of the situation

In the last few years, since the beginning of the epoch of *perestroika* in the former USSR, the problems of human values have been coming to the foreground of discussion and concern. They are also becoming more and more the actual challenges of personal decision and social debate.

The changes people are facing in the former USSR are truly historical. In fact, the post Second World War epoch has never seen such a global collapse of totalitarianism and a genuine 'geological' shift in systems of values. The value crisis led to a values' vacuum, and like nature that does not 'love' any vacuum, so the social nature does not like an 'emptiness' in values systems. The issue of what values will fill the present values vacuum has a momentous impact on the economic and political future in the transforming Russian society, as well as on twenty-first century western civilisation.

There is evidence that the decades of totalitarian control in the Soviet Union perverted basic human values. The savage struggle against religion and any religious ideas, ideals, and spirituality has led to an almost complete elimination in people's consciousness of any frame of moral reference. A type of relativist approach to values has been the substitute: only what benefits political aims is prized. Absolute values have been systematically criticised and profaned – rejected as mere 'abstract humanism' in political speeches, in official papers, and in everyday practice.

Numerous and brutal wars in which millions of people were forced to fight and which created tens of millions of victims, and the terror under Stalin that destroyed additional millions of people – these vicious events have depreciated human life, freedom, dignity, and rights. Economic disorders and low living standards have converted

187

wage-levelling, jealousy, and self-interest into 'virtues'. The universal downfall of morals is quite evident, and its ripple effects include the collapse of family values, growth of criminality, and the widespread bitterness of people. All these tragic processes have been examined in numerous Russian scientific and popular works in the last two years.[1]

When Gorbachev came to power and proclaimed the primacy of general human values, the former Soviet Union was already in a moral crisis, in a state of ethical instability. This condition of the nation was observed by A. Amalrik – the well-known researcher of the Soviet system in the 1970s, historian and dissident, who wrote:[2]

It is difficult to understand whether a majority of our people have . . . any moral criteria – notions such as 'honestly' and 'dishonestly', 'good' and 'bad', 'virtue' and 'evil' . . . which become a restraining and guiding factor in periods when the mechanism of public coercion falls away and each person is left to his own resources. I have an impression, wrong perhaps, that the [Soviet] people have none or practically none of such moral criteria.

The questions we are seeking to answer in our present research are: How do people cope with the collapse of official values? What enduring ethical standards are especially appealing within the present crisis? What role do spiritual values play after decades of doctrinaire atheism?

2.   The Ten Commandments as a framework of study

For the following reasons the Biblical Ten Commandments have been chosen as the framework for this study of Russian spiritual values:

(a) According to deeply rooted tradition in Russia, they are broadly recognised as a whole cultural–symbolic system. Although most people cannot even name all of them, when the Commandments are mentioned they are usually perceived as ancient, serious and important, tested by our ancestors' experience, deserving attention, and emotionally positively coloured.

(b) The Ten Commandments are directly related to the contemporary issues which worry a lot of people in Russia: economic instability, fear of new political idols, pollution, drugs, violent crimes, private property, family challenges (divorces, abortions, parent–child relations), corruption, and such like.

(c) They reflect what we call the 'eternal' and 'absolute' values – ones not dependent upon politics or consensus. In the present crisis of the whole Soviet empire, people instinctively are searching for something more reliable and firm. They psychologically conceive the Ten

Commandments as 'universal' values, which could replace the ones that go-out-of-fashion.

(d) The Ten Commandments provide a cross-cultural instrument, and they may be easily applicable in a very different social, economical, ethnical, and cultural groups within the Russia, as well as in other countries.

(e) The Ten Commandments appeal to the individual's liberty and responsibility. They are addressed first to individuals, not to the state or church for enforcement.

Although the Ten Commandments are the basic values of the study, we also utilise other value systems, such as the 'Business Ten Commandments', the 'Moral Code of the Builders of Communism', and some other popular ethical and cultural values.

3.   Empirical data resources

During the first half of the 1990s we obtained the following empirical (sociological) data:

516 telephone interviews, 20–30 minutes long, conducted in Moscow by means of random sampling procedure (represents population of the Moscow region – about 9 million people);

958 face-to-face interviews, each of one hour's duration, on the basis of the random selection in the Moscow region;

three Russian focus-group interview–discussions, conducted with:
  (a) Russian teenagers from one of the Moscow high schools;
  (b) Group of professional atheist–propagandists from Moscow;
  (c) Group of Moscow State University graduate humanities students;

four USA focus-group interview–discussions, conducted with:
  (a) American teenagers from a New York suburb public school;
  (b) American atheists from the New York area;
  (c) American Baptists from the New York area;
  (d) American Eastern Orthodox Christians in New York.

In this paper we will report and interpret the data from the telephone and face-to-face interviews, as well as from focus-group discussions with Russian and American teenagers.

4. Religious attitudes

Although organized religion does not play an important role in most people's lives, attitudes towards religion are quite diverse. Only 6.8% of the respondents in the telephone interview stated that the role of religion is very important in their own lives, and another 15.1% that it is important. Although women (8.1%) are almost twice as apt to consider religion 'very important' as men (4.4%), men (62%) are just as likely as women (66.4%) to consider the first commandment – 'There is one God' – to be absolute.

These responses reveal a huge gap between those who are practicing believers (22%) and those who are absolutely confident that the central content of belief is true (65%). Does this data show a deep religious interest that has not yet found opportunity for expression? Is there a widespread spirituality that atheistic propaganda suppressed but could not kill?

On a related question, the issue of God's existence divides people about equally. In our 1990 survey, 21.7% are sure that God exists, and 17.2% are sure that such a being does not exist. On this issue of belief in God's existence, men and women are almost mirror images. Women are far more likely to be sure that God exists (25.5%) than to be atheists (13.5%), while men are more likely to be atheists (24.2%) than to be sure God exists (14.8%).

Although only 20 to 25% of Moscow population support the belief in God, subconscious religious attitudes are substantially more significant. Answering the question 'What do you think the Biblical commandment "There is one God" means?' more than 54% stated 'it means that every person should have something sacred in his soul, should have God'. If only 14.8% confirm they always try to observe the commandment strictly, an additional 50.4% are trying to observe it occasionally.

The table below illustrates the significance of the idea of God in contemporary Russian society:

Table 1. *What do you think would change in the world if all people stopped believing in God?*

	men %	women %	all %
The world would change for the better.	6.0	2.3	4.4
Nothing would change in the world.	22.3	16.3	19.4
The world would change for the worse.	57.5	61.4	59.0
Other answers, e.g. it's hard to say.	14.2	20.0	17.2
Total	100	100	100

A convincing majority of about 60% of both men and women agreed the world would become worse if the belief in God became extinct. Even among those who proclaim themselves as atheists (sure that God does not exist), 45% now say that the world would change for the worse if no one would believe in God. Half of the atheists want God in society! The paradox could be explained in terms of the vacuum of values. If one personally does not believe in God, he or she understands nevertheless that society needs something sacred. The fear of a values vacuum in the society is stronger than atheists' personal claim of God's absence: let me be personally confident that God does not exist, but in the whole society belief in God should be present, because otherwise the vacuum of values may destroy humanity.

As a fact, among the fears in Soviet society the extinction of humanity is one of the more important in people's consciousness. Almost 25% of the whole Soviet population mentioned this fear, according to a national survey in 1989–90. It is more important than, for example, the fear of poverty (16.7%), physical pain (19%), return of mass repression (13.7%), criminals (14.6%), tyranny and lawlessness (22.5%), national conflicts (12.3%), and even the fear of death (14.7%). Only fears concerning possible sickness of one's children, war, natural disaster, and personal sickness – loom larger than the fear of the extinction of humanity.[3]

5. Human life and dignity

Far stronger than any of the others was Russian support for the commandments opposing murder and theft. Their support was virtually equal: 96.1% surveyed by means of telephone interview said that the prohibition of stealing always or usually applied, and 95.9% professed the same support for the commandment against murder.

However, this generic support turns out to be delusive. In the face-to-face interview, in which we were able to discuss the issue of murder and killing in detail, the picture becomes more clear, and even shocking. With the complex statement 'a human life is sacred, and a murder can never be justified', a mere 32.5% completely agreed, and 22.7% mostly agreed. Only about 10% disagreed. Thus, while the abstract attitude against killing in terms of the commandment is very strong, the resistance to murder or killing explicitly in terms of the spiritual value of human life is weaker. Moreover, when we engage people with concrete situations we can observe an unbelievable picture of the near nullification of human life's value. Table 2 makes the picture report the startling news.

We can see that in the list of 17 concrete situations there is not a

Table 2. *Statements about killing*

	Completely or mostly agreed[a]		
	all %	men %	women %
It is admissible to kill armed enemies during a war.	69.9	75.6	64.7
Killing is admissible only for the purpose of self-defence.	51.5	58.3	43.7
It is admissible to kill a criminal if he or she is sentenced to capital punishment.	48.1	54.1	42.8
Killing is admissible because of revenge or grievous offence.	5.5	8.2	1.9
Killing provoked by jealousy is admissible	3.5	5.2	1.9
A person's life can be taken if he or she is incurable and his/her decease makes him/her and the family suffer.	10.7	10.7	10.3
Killing is admissible upon religious motives.	2.0	2.6	0.0
It is admissible to kill representatives of those nations or peoples that have a harmful affect on others.	8.6	8.1	7.4
Sometimes it is admissible to kill an insane person.	9.2	10.3	8.4
A life of a new-born child can be taken if he/she is physically or mentally deformed.	18.6	13.7	24.2
It is admissible to kill those people who by their behaviour or mode of life mar the life of others (alcoholics, drug addicts, gays, prostitutes, etc.).	11.0	9.5	11.6
Killing of prisoners-of-war is admissible.	1.8	2.2	1.4
During a war deserters can be killed by sentences of military tribunals.	21.6	24.5	18.6
Spies, terrorists, and saboteurs can be killed.	30.5	36.4	24.7
It is admissible to kill hostages.	4.1	2.5	4.6
A prisoner who escaped from a prison can be killed.	8.3	7.7	8.9
A human nature is genetically inclined to killing.	4.8	5.2	4.2

[a]Since 3% of the respondents were not identified as either men or women, the figures for 'all' include some respondents that were not identified by gender, and so it is not an average of 'men' and 'women'.

single one where all respondents consider the killing to be absolutely forbidden. The most 'fortunate' are the prisoners-of-war, according to which the respondents manifested maximum charity. Clearly, for some Russian people, killing is possible in many imaginable situations. Moreover, in some cases when it seems homicide could not be admissible at all from the humanitarian point of view, the dominant Russian consciousness not only considers it permissible, but the proportion of people tolerating them is extremely high. For example, almost one out of ten allows killing an insane person, or one who is hopelessly ill, or somebody whose 'behaviour or mode of life mars the lives of others'. It is also shocking to think that almost a quarter of Moscow women agreed that 'a new-born child can be killed if he/she is physically or mentally deformed'.

Such attitudes towards human life are spread not only among the Moscow population. In the national survey mentioned earlier, 22.7% of all the population said those born with birth defects should be 'eliminated'. According to the data from this national poll, the people who should also be 'eliminated' include the 'members of religious sects' – 4.9%; 'mentally ill' – 2.8%; 'murderers' – 71.9%; 'AIDS infected' people – 16.8%; and prostitutes, homosexuals, drug addicts – between 28% and 34%.[4]

As one can see from Table 2, the value of human life among women is almost the same as among men. However, men are more aggressive in terms of revenge, jealousy, self-defence, and the treatment of spies, women are more cruel concerning deformed new-born infants, people with deviant behaviour, hostages, and even those who have escaped from a prison.

It is natural to assume that believers are more likely to oppose any kind of homicide in comparison with those who consider themselves non-believers or atheists. They believe more strongly in the biblical commandments and in the sacredness of life. From Table 3 one can see this tendency demonstrated: the stronger the religious attitudes of the respondents, the smaller the proportion of them are ready to kill a new-born infant, or a hopelessly ill human, or an insane person.

The value of human life and dignity also can be illustrated with some statistics of recent serious crimes against personality. This data reflects a disturbing tendency.[5]

Some specific aspects of homicides are also reported in the same *Izvestiia* issue: less than 20% of all homicides are committed because of profit; 20% of the victims are the murderer's relatives; almost half of all those murdered had a drink with their future murderers at the very time of homicide. If you think about such a tragic setting, so frequently

Table 3. *Row percentage of completely or mostly agreed that . . .*

	a newly born can be killed if he/she is physically or mentally deformed	a hopelessly ill person might be killed	it is admissible to kill an insane person
Consider themselves as believers	8.5	1.7	3.4
Rather believers than not	21.3	11.2	6.7
Do not consider themselves as believers	19.4	14.2	12.7
Consider themselves as atheists	20.6	17.7	17.7

Table 4.

	1988	1989	first half 1990 in comparison to first half 1989
Serious bodily injuries	37,191	51,458	+15.9%
Rapes	17,658	21,873	+14.1%
Homicides	16,702	21,467	+21.3%

repeated, these statistics alone say volumes about the erosion of human dignity in contemporary Russian society. It is hard to imagine the scale of values of a person who would first have a drink with his relative and then murder him.

The issue of abortion which is the focus of considerable public discussion in the US, is not so important for Russians. Whatever one's attitude towards abortion might be – whether to regard it as murder or as an admissible means of interrupting pregnancy – the consistent immense quantity is symptomatic of diminished human dignity and hope: a lack of parental planning, an absence of positive vision for family and future humanity.

The quantity of abortions in the former Soviet Union is grotesque. 90% of women who become pregnant abort their first child. Official statistics indicate 6.5 million abortions annually, while only 5.6 million children are actually born.[6] The figures are even more disturbing when we take into account a fair estimate of illegal abortions – for then the annual rate will reach between 8 and 10 million, which are nearly two abortions for every birth.

The moral estimation of abortion in our survey reflects this well-established behaviour. On the table below we can see different attitudes towards abortion among all the sample, among men and women, and among the believers and non-believers.

Table 5.

	all	men	women	believers	non-believers
Abortion is like a murder; it is inadmissible.	14.8	16.3	13.5	49.2	9.7
Abortion resembles a murder, and it is admissible only if there is any danger for the mother.	23.8	26.6	20.0	15.3	29.9
One cannot consider an abortion as a murder; in many cases this is the only choice for a woman.	42.4	34.8	50.7	13.6	39.6
An abortion has nothing to do with murder	13.1	16.7	9.3	10.3	16.4
Other answers, such as 'It is hard to say.'	5.9	5.6	6.5	11.6	4.4
Total	100.0	100.0	100.0	100.0	100.0

The data shows a high degree of tolerance towards abortion. The majority of 50–60% either do not want to consider abortion as murder, or they say that an abortion has nothing to do with a murder. The believers formed the only group with strong opposition to abortion.

6. Private property

After years of a 'command economy' when all the decisions on even the prices of individual items were decided within the secluded walls of the Kremlin and imposed on the rest of the society, why has the leadership been so slow to move on property reform? After years of his promises of real economic reform requiring the right of property ownership, why is Gorbachev now seeming to hedge on the key-stone of this economic reform? Does he think there can be sub-

stantial economic incentives if people cannot own a piece of the pie –
or a piece of the country?

Perhaps most importantly, we should ask why Gorbachev wants to
delay reform for a referendum on this issue, when popular sentiment in
favour of the ownership of property is strong. Could President Gorbachev be out of touch with the beliefs and values of his constituents?

We asked 516 people in telephone interviews about the importance
of the right to own property. To our surprise, 82% of the respondents
said that this is an absolute right, a right that 'always applies, irrespective of circumstances'. In fact, among the 19% remnant who still
support the 'cause of communism', the support of an absolute right to
property is even stronger. A substantial 83.7% of these modern Marxists affirm that we should always maintain the right to own property.

In an unexpected historical and philosophical reversal, among the
18% most opposed to communism the support for an absolute right to
property was actually slightly weaker – only 76.6%. Nevertheless,
while we could not ask our respondents about the details of Gorbachev's proposed property policy, the support for property ownership
is clearly deep and widespread.

We were surprised to notice that after years of *glasnost* a full 9.5% of
the respondents – although assured that their comments were confidential – found the question about devotion to communism too 'difficult to answer'. Nevertheless, these careful citizens were not at all
hesitant about the present pressing issue. Virtually all of these (98%)
endorsed the right to own property as an absolute, and everyone of
them called the command 'Don't Steal' an absolute moral standard.
This is the largest support for property rights from any single group.
Interestingly, this group represents an average cross-section of the
Moscow population in terms of party membership, religion, work, and
nationality, and it is only slightly less educated and slightly more
female and older than the average.

In addition to the right to property, we asked about a large number
of other values as well. Respondents were asked to evaluate 'commands' in the code of the Builders of Communism, statements from
the biblical Ten Commandments, and selections from other moral
standards. The sources of these values were not identified, so that the
respondents did not know that they were evaluating a statement from
the communist code or the Ten Commandments unless they had
independent knowledge of these.[7]

The commitment to an absolute right of property ownership actually ranked above six of the biblical Ten Commandments. It was
higher than even the commandments against adultery and envy.

While the commandments against stealing (93%) and murder (93%) ranked well above, those supporting the honour of parents (85%) and against false testimony (86.6%) were in the same general range as property rights. Since all four of those biblical commandments – no murder, no stealing, no false testimony, and the honouring of parents – are essential to the basic fabric of society, the inclusion of the right to property in the same stratosphere is a substantial endorsement by the Moscow population!

A comparison with the communist code is also instructive. None of the 'commands' of communism even approach the level of popular support that our survey showed for the right to property.

Moreover, the landslide support of property rights is actually stronger than the 82%. An additional 9.9% stated that the right to own property should usually be applied. Another 5.5% considered the issue a matter of indifference – the right to property may be supported, but it is not necessary. A few found the question to be either too difficult to answer or they refused to answer. Out of the 516 people interviewed on this question, only 4 actually opposed the right to own property.

Although 19% are still devoted to the cause of communism, not even 1% of the population will go so far as to support a basic foundation of communism:[8] the rejection of the right to property, the very first point of Marx's programme in the *Manifesto*. And only half of the tiny 1% in our survey who oppose property rights support communism! These numbers are so small as to be insignificant.

Our research was pursued in the Moscow region only, an area where free-market ideas have some currency, but our data is comparable to that produced by the All-Union Centre for the Study of Public Opinion – an agency of the Soviet government itself. These national polls were conducted more broadly and earlier than ours; people throughout the former Soviet Union were surveyed between the fall of 1989 and the spring of 1990. Nevertheless, 86.8% of the population supported – as either necessary or advisable – 'private citizens owning plots of land for independent agriculture'. In answer to another question, 76.7% said that enterprises for processing agricultural products should be owned by private citizens – either because this was necessary or advisable.[9] Thus a strong support for property rights exists in the country at large, not just in the Moscow region.

Curiously, in spite of this strong support, the government's national survey also indicated that only 46.7% of Soviet citizens were positive about 'having private property in our country' – and another 29.2% were 'neutral'. This seeming internal inconsistency is unexplained.[10]

Perhaps there has been a change over the long time duration of the government survey, or some of the respondents may be 'neutral' not knowing the kinds of property rights that might be implied, or the Moscow population is more 'progressive' on this point. Nevertheless, even the government's survey figures imply that only 24.1% oppose property rights.

As we could see in the section discussing the issue of homicide, the general opposition against killing is as strong as it is against theft: 96.1% respondents in telephone interview said that the prohibition of stealing always or usually applied. But when we turn to more concrete situations concerning theft, we can observe tolerance and relativity in people's consciousness and morality. Only 45.4% of the Moscow population say that they in fact 'always try to observe the commandment "do not steal" '. This answer is probably more honest than the former one.

In a list of nine unambiguous situations about which we asked people to estimate the morality of specific behaviour, the respondents were very tolerant with theft. Only 51.5% said that a person should be considered immoral if he/she 'borrows money from his/her neighbours and does not return it'. Only 48.5% consider a person immoral if he/she 'had a dinner at a restaurant and left without paying the bill'.

Moral estimations in some other simple situations are even more amazing: only 12–13% consider one's behaviour immoral if he/she 'did not pay rent for the apartment for three months', or 'does not pay the fare in a bus'. Thus, while the majority of Russian people support the general idea of private property, the respect towards other people's property and towards the owners is quite restricted. A contradiction is still present in people's systems of values: the value of private property is very strong as an idea of 'my' property, but the concept of respecting somebody else's property is rather weak.

The resistance to theft remains stronger than support for the right to property, since others can steal many things besides our property – time, freedom, dignity, children, opportunity, other rights, and such like. To our respondents in the Moscow region, the protection of their property against theft is as serious as life itself. Without property we cannot live with dignity, and without our lives we cannot utilise property. As Solzhenitsyn recently observed,[11]

It is impossible to create a righteous state without first having an independent citizen, and independent citizens cannot exist without private property. To own a moderate amount of property makes a person stable.

Should we be surprised, then, when 82% of the citizens of the Marxist Mecca consider the social right to property to be an absolute, and a total of 91.9% give noteworthy support to that right? The desire for property rights seems to be both substantial and natural.

7. Who is truly devoted?

During the 1950s and 1960s a frequently described exemplary case of devotion was a communist youth seeking to convert others. In America, stories of great sacrifice for the cause of communism were frequent in daily newspapers and in Sunday sermons. The visual image is still quite clear. A typical story went like this: a young man with great academic or corporate potential recoils from injustice in society and chooses to forego fame and fortune for the sake of a 'workers' paradise'. Such stories were used to spur American youth into greater patriotism or religious commitment. Otherwise the deep devotion of their communist counterparts might become successful, and the God-fearing stake in church and society would be lost. Similar stories of intensely devoted young communist men were told in the former Soviet Union in order to enhance and increase the lively level of communist devotion.

Now the image of the devoted communist has undergone a gestalt shift; however, by 1990 she is an illiterate grandmother with nothing to do.

First, and most dramatically, the typical devotee of communism today is a senior citizen. Almost half (46%) of the population between 57 and 76 years of age still profess to be absolutely devoted communists. This is more than twice the average level of devotion in the population. Curiously, all these people were twenty years old or older at Stalin's death, so their most formative years occurred before the earliest revelations of his 'excesses'. This elevated level of absolute devotion is spread fairly evenly throughout this senior-citizen population.

In sharp contrast, only 6.7% of young adults between the ages of 18 and 41 are so completely devoted. In fact, of the 60 people that we interviewed in the 18 to 26-year-old range, only 2 of them (3.3%) are absolutely devoted communists, and both of those are teenagers! This dramatic lack of support for communism among the youth bodes well for change in Moscow!

Second, such devotion to communism is notably strong only among the uneducated. If you are an adult absolutely devoted to communism, you are more than two and a half times as likely to have completed merely an elementary school education or less. Among these minimally educated people, the devotion to communism is nearly as strong (45.8%) as it is for the senior citizens (46.0%). Moreover, absolute devotion to communism is stronger than average only among groups with less than a high school education. Among the college-educated, such loyalty to communism is especially low (13.2%). Even though indoctrination occurred at every level of the educational system in the former Soviet Union, devotion is not automatic, and it cannot be taught.

The third distinctive feature of the absolute devotee of communism is that she is female. The difference between men and women is extraordinary. Nearly one quarter (23.7%) of the Moscow women are loyal followers, but only one in ten (10.4%) of the men are devoted. The women are more than twice as likely to be devoted to the cause as their male counterparts!

Why are women so much more devoted than men? One may speculate that – on the basis of a well-worn stereotype – women are more expressive. They just tend to be more firm in their loyalties and communicate this devotion more openly. Fortunately, this stereotype does not explain the present dramatic difference. For example, when it comes to strong opposition to communism, the roles are nearly reversed. One quarter (24.2%) of the men are strongly opposed to communism, and one out of seven (15%) of the women express such strong opposition. The men simply have a different perspective on communism, and they express their rejection of it as strongly as the women reveal their loyalty.

Our survey uncovered other characteristics of those who are absolutely devoted to the cause of communism, but these traits are all associated in some way with their senior citizen status or low education. For example, 34% of those who are presently not employed are absolutely loyal to the cause, but their lack of employment is primarily a result of their senior-citizen status.

It is curious, however, to look at it from inside the loyalist camp: more than 50% (53.1%) of all the devotees of communism are presently not employed. Among the ranks of the employed, however, communism is much less attractive. Only 17% of white-collar employees, 13.2% of blue-collar workers, and 8.5% of intellectuals are absolutely devoted to the cause of communism.

Other correlates with communist devotion are closely related to the communist line itself. For example, the one out of five Moscow citizens who consider the love of socialist countries to be an absolute guideline are twice as likely (39.1%) to be absolutely devoted to communism as the average Moscow citizen. This however, is to be expected.

There were, however, some surprises in the congregation of communist devotees. Communist party members are only slightly more likely to be loyal communists (26.8%) than are others. Even more surprisingly, devotion to the cause among people with religious convictions is at least as strong as the average population. For example, among those who consider themselves to be 'very religious', 25.7% are absolutely devoted to communism! The popularity of complete devotion to communism was much smaller among those who said that religion played no role in their lives (18.7%). Similarly, among those who believed that trust in God is an absolute, 23.6% are devout communists, and among those who are sure that God exists, 20.5% considered devotion to communism absolute. Perhaps 'atheistic communism' is not so monolithic as we had thought!

Of all the populations that we isolated, can you guess where devotion to communism is the weakest? It is among the members of the communist youth organisation, *Komsomol*. In this organisation of future communist leaders, only 3.2% express complete loyalty to the cause.

Just like absolute devotion to communism, intense opposition to this ideology enlists the support of about one out of five Moscow citizens (18.2%). However, this loyal opposition is more broadly spread out and evenly distributed among various population groups than is devotion. Young adults, ages 18 to 41, constitute perhaps the strongest in opposition (27.4%). People who believe God exists (23.2%), college-educated people (23%), blue-collar workers (21.7%), and men (24.2%) are only slightly more likely than the average citizen to be absolutely opposed to communism. Nevertheless, a noticeable chunk of *Komsomol* members (22.6%) are part of this group as well.

The very weakest opposition to communism comes from what are by now predictable sources: only 15% of the women, only 9% of senior citizens over 57 years of age, and only 3.5% of the least educated people are absolutely opposed to the ideology. Unexpected, however, is the weak opposition among those who consider themselves very religious: Only 14.3% are absolutely opposed to communism. Considering a history of persecution of religious people, that is surprising. Perhaps, though, many of these have given up their opposition out of frustration or exhaustion, or have withdrawn to a merely detached religiosity.

So, what is your image of a devoted Marxist now? She is perhaps a semi-literate, hobbling grandmother who has nothing to occupy her time – except holding together a less than perfectly consistent set of beliefs.

8.   Do we live in the 'best' world?

Generations of philosophers, politicians, and scholars held our world to be quite a sad and anxious place, if not a terrible one. Attempts to better human nature are almost as ancient as the world itself. Karl

Marx was hardly original when he insisted that the task of philosophers is to improve the world. Even ancient Pythagoras was probably not the first to try.

The striking changes in Eastern Europe at the end of 1989 showed very clearly where Marxist efforts to improve the world had brought it. Although most attempts to make a person better have failed, people have never stopped trying to improve others.

'To a certain extent we live in the best of all possible worlds' – according to groups of teenagers in New York and in Moscow who have participated in focus-group discussions. Four biblical commandments were discussed by these teams of teenagers (15–16 years old): 'don't steal', 'honour your parents', 'don't commit adultery', and 'don't create an idol'. One of the key questions of the discussion was: 'How would the world look if everybody (or almost everybody) observed these commandments?' A similar question was stated negatively: 'How would the world be if everybody stopped observing these commandments?'

The results of the discussions with both American and Russian teens were surprisingly similar. The commandment 'don't steal', for example, caused a vigorous debate. Youth in both countries consider the commandment to be related far more to the idea of the integrity of human personality than to the actual stealing of someone's physical property. The Russian young people argued that it is better to steal something material than to deprive a person of his/her time and psychological comfort.

One Russian student perceives at least three types of theft: material, intellectual, and psychological. She stated: 'If you have something expensive, you may expect that someone would want it, and therefore you will try to preserve your property. With psychological theft it is different; you can't be ready for it . . . And it is very difficult to restore an immaterial damage.' She is fully aware of the marked increase in material theft in Russia. Nevertheless, psychological theft remained a far greater concern.

However, neither the American nor the Russian teenagers reacted enthusiastically to the idea of a world without theft. Students from Moscow made several interesting observations: 'If the flowers never got sick before, any small illness would have killed them;' 'If there were too much light without darkness the world would be arid;' 'The less theft there is the more it hurts. One thief out of a thousand is worse than a hundred out of a thousand, because a strike you don't expect is more dangerous . . .'

The teenagers from New York mostly agreed, adding: 'A world

without theft would be a world without competition.' They argued that society should endure some degree of theft, for strong acquisitiveness is necessary for a vital economy. But should theft be tolerated in the realm of economic opportunity?

The discussion on the commandment 'Do not commit adultery' caused much controversy as well. In both countries, on both sides of the East/West gap, this value is related more closely to the concept of love rather than to marriage. If a person loves someone, he or she has, it seems, a *carte blanche* to do anything. Divorces, infidelity, promiscuity – all these are the results of a lack of love in the world. It is not infidelity itself that is blame-worthy, but sexual contacts with someone you don't love.

Although the number of divorces is tremendous and infidelity is widespread in both countries, the world would become a 'dull' and 'insipid' place, if everyone (or almost everyone) observed the commandment. On the other hand, if adultery were to become habitual, the world would be quite a disgusting place to live.

The young Americans seemed more stringent, devoted to obligations, and conservative than their colleagues from the East, who are inclined to regard the commandment merely through a psychological prism: it is better to expect someone to betray you than to be taken by surprise. The youth from both countries, however, tend to have a common paradoxical belief: although the level of adultery is not ideal, the present patterns of sexual fidelity could hardly be improved.

Neither American nor Russian students were very rigorous on the question of giving respect to one's parents. Their attitude on that issue could be considered Greek, rather than biblical – everything has to have measure, has to be within rational and emotional limits. It is a positive and even necessary thing to respect 'good' parents. With 'bad' parents it is up to each individual. Also, both groups of teens affirmed the right to marry without parents' permission.

If married, in a conflict between a parent and a spouse, the preference should be given to the spouse – feel most of the teenagers from both countries. This could be a problem especially in Russia, where the majority of young families are forced to reside with parents. Americans tend more to look for a compromise in parent–child disagreements.

For both groups a world where everybody strictly honours and respects parents is as unattractive as is one where parents are completely ignored. The former one is described as unhappy, because excessive honouring hinders people's lives and strengthens the power of the older generation over youngsters. The second one appears immoral – a cold but easy world without any obligations. It resembles society as described in Alduous Huxley's *Brave New World*: a complex of rational minds and amusement, without love or soul.

Concerning idolatry both groups acknowledged that they live in a world filled with idols. However, Russian teenagers associated idolatry especially with political leaders and propaganda, while the Americans mentioned money, enjoyment, success, and the idols of mass-media. In the eyes of the teenagers from Moscow, a world without idols is not only impossible, but unnecessary and not quite attractive: 'nobody would be trusted, everything could be estimated by the individual's rational mind'. But a society where the commandment 'don't worship idols' is totally rejected is believed to be a terrible place: 'it would look like a totalitarian state, like Stalinism, like a wolf pack where all fall upon the ex-leader to tear him to pieces'.

From markedly dissimilar places, nevertheless, these youth share a similar estimation of the present world's values. The two societies to which they belong are both quite removed from the ideals of the biblical commandments. While distinguishing between good and evil and recognising the importance of internal moral norms, both sets of teenagers see these commandments as measures, or means to their own ends, rather than as goals.

The philosophical ideas of moral relativity, deeply rooted in the minds of our present youth, may seem pretty attractive, except for one circumstance: the moral space occupied by good and evil is asymmetrical. Evil is more active, aggressive; tends to multiply faster, and is usually first to fill a moral vacuum. It is quite possible to agree with these youth that the world we are living in is not so terrible as some extreme rhetoric suggests. Nevertheless, the real question is: in which direction is the world drifting?

Some new data provide a startling warning. In the former USSR, as mentioned earlier, during the first half of 1990 in comparison with the same period of 1989, the number of homicides increased by 21.3%, rapes increased by 14.1%, serious bodily injuries increased by 15.9%. During the same period the homicide rates also increased dramatically in many major American cities: Boston (56%), Chicago (14%), Los Angeles (8%), New York (45%).[12]

This is the price we are forced to pay for living in the 'best' of worlds – one which is hardly balancing on the elusive border between good and evil, even inclining into an abyss of trouble. If these youths' complacency represents the next generation's attitudes, the values' vacuum we are now studying may become an increasing challenge in the former Soviet Union – and in the United States as well.

Notes

1 See, for example, numerous articles in *Sociological Studies*, volumes 1, 2, and 4, 1989.
2 Andrei Amalrik, 'Will the Soviet Union exist up to 1984?', *Ogonëk*, 9, 1990, p. 21.
3 *New Outlook*, a quarterly publication of the American Committee on US Soviet Relations, 1:3, Summer 1990, p. 32.
4 *New Outlook*, 1:3, Summer 1990, p. 34.
5 *Izvestiia*, No. 58, 26 February 1990, p. 6; and *Novoye Russkoye Slovo*, 1 August 1990.
6 See the youth weekly *Sobesednik*, No. 10, March 1990, p. 10.
7 The statement about maintaining the 'right of ownership of property' was taken from Nimrod McNair's *Absolute Ethics*, Atlanta, Executive Leadership Foundation, p. 39.
8 It should not be surprising, then, that only 26.8% of the 82 Communist Party members we surveyed are 'devoted to the cause of communism'. Notice also the data and analysis on communist 'devotion' in section 7 of this paper.
9 Reported in *New Outlook*, Summer 1990, pp. 17–21.
10 *Ibid.*, pp. 19, 20.
11 Aleksandr Solzhenitsyn, 'How We Can Rebuild Russia', *Novoye Russkoye Sloyo*, 22 and 23 September 1990.
12 *New York Times*, 18 July 1990, pp. A1 and D20. The New York statistic applies to the first three months only.

Out of the kitchen, out of the temple: religion, atheism and women in the Soviet Union*

JOHN ANDERSON

For many years it was a commonplace of atheist writings in the USSR that women made up the majority of religious believers. Indeed, it was not simply women, but 'backward' women of 'low political conscious-ness' – the elderly, the single, the poorly educated, and those somehow isolated from the 'production process'. While this was a phenomenon said to be common throughout the industrialised world, its character was in some ways more pronounced in the Soviet Union which, despite being a socialist country – and thus by definition more pro-gressive in its treatment of women than the capitalist world – had only recently taken the path of modern development. Moreover, Soviet women had been severely traumatised by their experience of war, revolution, and – unstated – terror, and were thus particularly suscep-tible to the consolation offered by religion.

In those parts of the old Russian Empire which had traditionally confessed Islam, the 'problem' of female religiosity was even more acute. Though women in Central Asia and other parts of the USSR were rarely allowed into the mosque or to play a prominent part in religious ceremonies, it was nonetheless religion that appeared to keep them in a subordinate position within society. Moreover, because they generally accepted this role and because they often took an important, and indeed primary, role in the education of very young children, women served as the main channel for the reproduction of 'religious prejudices'.

Central to this analysis was the suggestion that female religiosity was part of a wider problem, rooted in unjust social structures which used religion to keep the people obedient and submissive. The corol-lary of this was that with revolutionary social change and education the total number of believers, and the predominance of women among them, would decrease. Yet as the years passed the ranks of the *babushki* continued to be replenished, and not simply by the single or the illiterate. By the 1960s the average age of many congregations was

206

steadily declining, and the vast majority of women churchgoers had been educated in the Soviet period. A decade later a number of female intellectuals were coming into the Russian Orthodox Church, and, when feminist movements took their first tentative steps at the end of the decade, they were to have a significant religious component.

This chapter explores some of the issues raised above. As we proceed it will become clear that there remain considerable problems in examining the question of religiosity in the Soviet Union, problems that stem from the nature of religious belief itself and from the peculiar position that religion has occupied within that country. As will also become apparent, the materials available for such a study remain unsatisfactory and frequently the foreign observer has to rely on very incomplete sociological surveys or on tedious lists of what propagandists have done to combat female religiosity in their area.

This chapter is primarily concerned with the last twenty to thirty years, reflecting the changing policies of 'assault' (Khrushchev), 'attrition' (Brezhnev) and 'liberalisation' (Gorbachev).[1] Most of the data relating to female religiosity, however, necessarily predates the accession of Gorbachev, and it may well be some time before studies carried out in the more relaxed atmosphere of recent times become available in published form. Hopefully the proclaimed commitment of the Kremlin to honesty and openness in the social sciences, and its apparently benign attitude towards religion, will combine to produce adequate documentary evidence for a more thorough study of female religiosity in the USSR.

The first part of this chapter looks at the 'problem' in more general terms, using data and analysis based on studies of various parts of the USSR, but with special reference to Transcarpathia. The second part examines the situation in Central Asia, where very different social, religious and cultural factors give the question a rather distinctive colouring and where efforts to overcome 'survivals' have met with very mixed results. Finally, the chapter discusses some broader aspects of the question, noting in particular the changing nature of female religiosity in the USSR, and asking to what extent this is a 'problem' peculiar to the Soviet Union.

(a) The religious woman

The 'problem'

Are women in the USSR more religious than men? What proportion of practising believers are women? To what extent has the picture changed, if at all, in recent years? And, if women are more religious than men, why is this so? These are some of the questions addressed in this first section, and they in turn raise further problems.

What is meant by 'more religious'? Analysing religious adherence is problematic in any society, but especially so in the Soviet Union where a truly adequate sociology of religion has yet to be developed.[2] Here, where the overt expression of religious belief has often cost the citizen dear, certain categories of the population have for many years concealed their devotion to religious values or institutions. In this context the suggestion that the majority of believers are elderly, semi-literate women might appear to be something of a self-fulfilling prophecy, for they are the very group which has little to lose by open involvement in religious bodies.

Another difficulty, as already suggested, stems from the nature of the sources available. There are few systematic studies of the question of female religiosity, and those that do exist utilise no single framework of analysis and make no consistent use of data. Thus, some look at church attendance while others rely on the self-revelation of those polled: some deal simply with the categories of 'believer' and 'unbeliever', while others develop a relatively sophisticated typology.[3] These difficulties, which cannot be explored in depth here, mean that many of the figures given below provide a limited basis for generalisations about the nature and extent of female religiosity in the Soviet Union.

There can be little doubt that the majority of those to be found in Christian churches in the USSR are women. Studies carried out in the early 1960s, at the height of Khrushchev's anti-religious campaign, provided a fairly uniform picture of female preponderance amongst both church attenders and those prepared to admit to holding religious beliefs. Yet these same studies revealed a considerably wide range (from 65% to 95%) with regard to the percentage of believers who were female. As a rule the highest figures were to be found amongst the Orthodox, and the lowest amongst the Baptists.

At the top end of the scale were a series of spot checks carried out in Perm during 1963. On 28 March investigators visited the cemetery church and discovered that 93% of those attending services were women.[4] Teplyakov's well-known study of religiosity in the Voronezh *oblast* (1961–4) reported that around 85% of Orthodox believers were female.[5] As noted above, the figures for Baptist communities tended to be lower, with a 1963 survey of two Alma-Ata congregations revealing that 77% and 67% respectively were women.[6]

This numerical predominance was reflected in the administrative life of the churches where women played a key role in every area except for liturgical leadership. The groups of twenty (*dvadsatkas*), which formed the legal basis of religious associations, were – at least amongst the Christian churches – made up largely of women.

During the 1970s the proportion of women in many religious congregations began to decrease, and by 1983 one commentator could write that:

Certain religious organisations have been successful in halting the trend of the 1950s and 1960s to a process of ageing and feminisation.[7]

Nevertheless, the tendency for the Orthodox to attract more women continued and a study of the Ukraine published in 1987 stated that around three-quarters of Orthodox believers were women, though of believers as a whole only 60% were female.[8]

These figures, added to the observations of many visitors to the Soviet Union, give some indication of general trends. Clearly women have always made up more than half of most religious communities, but it is equally apparent that this trend became less pronounced during the 1970s and 1980s. The reasons for this will become evident when we look at how official sources have accounted for the high level of female religiosity.

Why are women more religious?

Leaving aside the issue of the objective reality of religious claims, and psychoanaytical explanations of female religiosity, the simplest and most straightforward view might be that once provided by an Intourist guide, who explained that there were greater numbers of women in church 'because women suffer more'. In the period 1914–45 the population of what is now the Soviet Union experienced war, civil war, famine, terror and yet more war. During these decades the population was decimated, but with male losses far outstripping female losses, women lost fathers, brothers, husbands and sons. With the loss of an entire generation of men, millions of women lost potential husbands and thus the opportunity of bearing children.[9] In such circumstances it was not surprising that many turned to religion for consolation – as they did in other parts of the world – especially in the immediate post-war years when some churches were re-opened. These women were uncovered by surveys which demonstrated that up to 50 per cent of many congregations were single women.[10] In more recent years it was the very absence of these circumstances which had contributed to the declining proportion of such women in many congregations.

Some explanations of female religiosity pointed to educational and social factors. Studies carried out in the 1960s revealed that the majority of female believers had been brought up before the revolution and thus had received little or no education – one writer found that 73.1% of female believers over 50 years of age had no education.[11] The problem was compounded when those areas became part of the USSR after 1945, for here even those with some education were likely to have been taught in a religious spirit.[12]

This latter factor was clearly of central importance in Transcarpathia, which had only been brought into the Soviet Union as a result of the Great Patriotic War. Prior to incorporation such educational establishments as existed had been dominated by religious organisations, including the Reformed Church, the Roman Catholics, and the Greek Catholics or Uniates. According to Timchenko all of these had been active in propagating anti-communism during the inter-war years. Moreover, as a predominantly agricultural region, economic backwardness combined with large-scale illiteracy to produce a population particularly vulnerable to religious propaganda.[13]

The problem was made worse by the fact that, despite the economic advances under socialism, many women remained isolated from the production process. As housewives, homeworkers, pensioners or invalids they tended to suffer from loneliness, and consequently sought relief in religion. Away from a collective working situation they found it harder to envisage the possibility of societal solutions to their problems and were less susceptible to the atheist influences of a normal working environment. That religious influence was less amongst working women was shown by a 1982 survey of 1,316 women workers in a Belorussian factory which revealed that only 3.2 per cent were convinced believers – though the number of convinced atheists was equally low.[14]

Other authors stressed that women frequently sought comfort in religion because of difficulties in their personal lives, problems which were often rooted in what are termed 'survivals of the past' in family relations. Though women now enjoyed unprecedented job opportunities, many men still failed to take account of this, say, by helping in the home. Hence many women were forced to work a 'double shift'. On top of this large numbers suffered ill-treatment from partners who beat them, usually when drunk, or simply deserted them. One author pointed out that in such circumstances the clergy were quick to condemn male sin and to offer the women an illusory safety in the church. In return the church gained the opportunity to influence the younger generation whose values were often determined by the women who brought them up.[15] Yet this does not explain why some sought consolation in religion and others did not.

This emphasis on the churches' socialisation of the women who in turn socialise the next generation is made much of in Timchenko's study of Transcarpathia. In part this process was said to stem from the fact that once drawn into the religious milieu women found it very hard to escape. As in any community the social pressure on women to remain became stronger the more they were drawn into the daily life of the religious community which gave meaning and structure to their existence. This in turn was reinforced by preaching which gave these structures a theoretical justification and encouraged women to bring up their families within the confines of the church. Moreover, in the agricultural regions of Transcarpathia the low educational level of many women meant that they were more easily taken in when priests used fabricated miracles or alleged appearances of the Virgin to reinforce their influence.[16] Another set of studies based on research in Ukraine as a whole also noted how, amongst the unregistered Baptist communities in particular, preachers and missionaries were especially active in teaching the importance of women being at home as much as possible so that children could be brought up in the faith.[17]

Overcoming female religiosity

If female religiosity was a consequence of the violent nature of much of Soviet history, of socio-economic backwardness, and of inadequate education, it seemed to follow that peace, economic development, and educational measures would lead to the decline of religious influences in Soviet society. In practical terms this had two policy implications in the post-Stalinist political context: further work aimed at drawing women into social production, and carrying out anti-religious and atheist work amongst women.

For Timchenko the 'decisive factor' in the emancipation of the women of Transcarpathia was their involvement in the production process which would provide them with new knowledge and experience which in turn would change their consciousness. Studies carried out in this region during the 1970s demonstrated that:

Amongst women separated from social production work the process of breaking from religion becomes significantly more difficult . . . For example, among 475 homeworkers polled in the Khusta *raion*, the quantity of believers was 2.5 times higher than among women employed in the Khusta feltworking factory and 3.4 times higher than among women working in the Khusta furniture factory.[18]

The same survey revealed that the levels of literacy varied according
to the type of work performed, with 46.7 per cent of those not working
in collective situations being semi-literate, as opposed to 1.1 per cent
in the feltworking plant. In these conditions there could be no doubt
how important it was to encourage women into the production process
and to provide the necessary child-care facilities that would enable
them to leave the home.[19]

Once drawn into the collective, women were said to be more susceptible to the various forms of atheist propaganda and other forms of
political enlightenment which all too often failed to reach women in
the home. We cannot explore these here in any depth, but they
included lectures, evenings of questions and answers, films, special
exhibitions exposing religion's falsity, etc.[20] The problem with many of
these measures was that they simply failed to reach women, whether
because so many were isolated from the production process or as a
result of the 'double shift' which meant that most women had no time
to attend those very lectures and evenings aimed at 'freeing' them from
'religious prejudices'.

Needless to say, none of these measures relate exclusively to women,
and the question that really needs to be tackled is whether female
religiosity differs significantly from that of men and to what extent
such differences might require different measures of socialisation.
With regard to the first question Soviet authors usually isolate two
possible distinctions between female and male religiosity: the allegedly
more emotional nature of women, and the fact that their religious
beliefs are more family-home oriented.

On the first Timchenko adopts a slightly ambiguous stance, arguing
that:

female religiosity does not have any principle distinction from male religiosity.
In this connection it is impossible to agree with bourgeois philosophers who
assert that by virtue of the 'low' level of consciousness, and by the
predominance of the emotional over the rational, 'women in all epochs were
more inclined to enthusiasm over religious matters', as feeling played a larger
role in religion than reason and thus 'religiosity was more extensive amongst
women than men'. The emotional nature of women is undebatable and this
circumstance plays an important role in the form of religious feelings and
moods. However, the fundamental causes of female religiosity have a social
character.[21]

So female psychology is said to play a role in distinguishing the religiosity of the two sexes, in particular in making women less resistant to
the emotional appeal of church rituals, which contrast with the drab-

ness of everyday life in many Soviet cities and villages and thus attracted many women who had no explicit religious beliefs.

Though new rites were only developed on a mass scale during
Khrushchev's anti-religious campaign, in more recent years numerous
writers have stressed their wider function within Soviet society.[22] As it
became increasingly accepted that socialism could not solve all
human-emotional problems by economic change alone, some authors
began to argue that rituals met a basic human need for a framework of
meaning and could be a useful tool of socialisation. Hence there soon
developed a wide range of socialist 'rites of passage' to supplement
more public rituals such as May Day and to compete with the rituals
provided by the major churches.

Recognising that church rituals were one of the major means by
which religious organisations attracted women, a number of sources
focus on the role of new, non-religious rituals in overcoming female
religiosity. What made ritual so important was the fact that it was
closely connected with lifestyle (*byt'*), and it was the way of life of women
that provided a further distinction between male and female religiosity.
Rites marked all the major events of a person's life, from birth to death,
and it was women who preserved the old customs and passed them onto
the next generation. If they could be persuaded to participate in the new
rituals it would be these that were transmitted to future citizens.[23]

Though the new rituals were inseparably linked with the everyday
life of women, they remained events that took place outside the home
and had to rely on people choosing to participate. If women were to be
reached more effectively, whether those with young children or those
housebound for other reasons, it was essential to find ways of penetrating the family situation. One way into the home stressed in Timchenko's study of Transcarpathia was via television and radio which
were capable of reaching women unlikely to attend more conventional
atheist events.[24]

A further method was to rely on the work of individual propagandists who could 'adopt' particular believing families. A short article
dealing with atheist work in a Transcarpathian collective farm isolated
various stages in individual work with believing families:

- getting to know the believers you are responsible for, in particular
    studying their type and level of religiosity, their general inter-
    ests and their social situation. At this stage it is essential to gain
    their trust;
- talking with them about various subjects, though not initially
    raising anti-religious issues;

— discussing 'world-view' questions, including the role of religion in
history, society and their own personal lives.

Alongside conversation it was important that atheist propagandists
showed the same concern for the practical needs of believers as members of religious communities showed for each other.[25]

The problem with this approach was twofold: it required propagandists of singular dedication and assumed that believers would
freely welcome into their homes those sent to 'enlighten' them. Here
the women's councils (*zhensovety*) had the potential to play a key role
because they often gained entrance to the home through their provision of advise and help on family matters. And, as Genia Browning's
study of the *zhensovety* makes clear, the women's councils tended to
predominate in rural areas where religious influence remained
strong.[26] Yet she also points out that there is a contradiction inherent
in their work, for in concentrating on matters relating to the bringing
up of the family the *zhensovety* tended to adopt a traditional understanding of family life which in other contexts was said to help the
preservation of religious influences.[27]

Most of the anti-religious measures outlined above were not
exclusive to women in their application, though aspects of each of
them were capable of being applied especially to women. Browning
notes the debates over whether women should be treated as a separate
category at the time of the establishment of the *zhensovety*,[28] and some
atheist writers would share doubts about the soundness of splitting
men from women in carrying out atheist work. Yet all recognise that,
at the very least, the social factors underlying female religiosity do
serve to differentiate it from that of men, and some would share the
view of Timchenko that every atheist organisation should have a special section for work with women.[29]

(b)   Women, Islam and atheism in Soviet Central Asia

The 'problem'

The position of women under Islam has always been a favourite subject for atheist propagandists in the Soviet Union, in many cases
providing a 'softer' target than religious ideas themselves. The basic
Soviet textbook on Islam puts it thus:

Many religions to varying degrees consider women as imperfect. But in
none of them is this expressed more clearly than in Islam. The Muslim
religion frankly declares that women are people of the second sort ... In the

Koran are to be found *adats* about the necessity of excluding women and the wearing of the veil . . . And in such cases the Koran preserved and strengthened the customs of the epoch, in which were reflected the humiliating and unequal position of women in feudal society.[30]

Another source goes further in arguing that 'nowhere in the world are there laws more cruel and inhumane' than the Koranic prescriptions relating to women.[31]

Not all authors take quite such a simplistic view. N. Ashirov, one of the more perceptive Soviet writers on Islam, takes issue with those who suggest that women have no rights under Islam, pointing out that the Koran actually allowed more to women than was customary in the Prophet's time.[32] In similar vein, officially appointed Islamic leaders in the Soviet Union frequently condemn customs which lead to the ill-treatment of women as having their origins in pre-Islamic traditions.[33]

Regardless of the 'theological' arguments it remains the case that, according to many Soviet sources, female religiosity in Central Asia must be combated above all because it encourages the humiliation of women. Until very recently the region's press carried numerous reports of women being kept secluded in the home, refused access to education, forced into marriages they have not chosen, and resorting to suicide to escape unhappy domestic situations. The situation was rendered even more complex by the fact that all too often many women still accepted these customs as 'normal'.[34]

If the attack on female religiosity aimed primarily at restoring – or, more exactly, establishing for the first time – the rights of women, it also had a further goal:

In struggling with female religiosity we not only deprive the church [read mosque. JA] of the basic contingent of believers, but also dam up one of the chief channels of religious influence on children and young people.[35]

It is for this very reason that:

every Muslim preacher pays special attention to 'working' with women, realising that if a mother will not educate her child in a religious spirit, and that if she does not teach them to observe religious rites, then the reproduction of religion will cease.[36]

In Central Asia the expression of female religious sentiment differs from that in the Christian churches insofar as women do not predominate in the mosques as they do in the churches. Some Soviet mosques still ban women from attending services, and so religious influence is exerted primarily through the home and strengthened by public opinion in the local *mahallah*. Passed on from generation to generation, often with the help of unofficial religious activists, Islamic ideas are extremely hard to combat in the domestic context. This difficulty is made worse by the fact that many of the traditions officially deemed unacceptable are defended as expressions of national identity by a large number of Central Asians.

Combating female religiosity: social change and education

Since the time of the revolution the Soviet authorities in Central Asia utilised various methods in their attempt to liberate women from religious influences. Social reconstruction was initially accorded the chief role, for it was felt that drawing women into the process of building a new life would help to destroy the helplessness before fate which religion was said to engender. This was to be accompanied by legislative changes to protect women from abuse, and by educational measures that would liberate both men and women from old ways of thinking. Over the last seven decades this approach waxed and waned, with periods of frenetic campaigning alternating with times of apparent 'drift'.

When Soviet authority was first tenuously established in Turkestan some of the more zealous party workers launched what were later seen as rather tactless assaults against traditional customs. Little wonder, then, that activists who quite literally tore the veils from women's faces were beaten up or even murdered by 'reactionary forces'. In the early 1920s, however, more flexible and realistic policies were favoured, aimed at combatting the subjugation of women. Special emphasis was laid upon:

the successful implementation of the land and water reform . . . the sovietisation of the villages, purging the soviets of class enemies that had managed to penetrate them . . . and enlisting a sufficient number of women into the party.[37]

From 1920 onwards women's sections were set up in a number of party organisations though initially, especially in the Fergana valley region where the war with the *basmachi* raged on, their work was limited primarily to the larger towns. One objective of these groups was educational – to raise literacy amongst Central Asian women. Those trained by the groups were sent out into the Muslim community to preach the new way of life.

Simultaneously the young Soviet state used the courts to tackle the 'woman question'. Various decrees of the Turkestan Executive Committee criminalised a number of traditional practices, and in October

1924 the Turkestan ASSR adopted the RSFSR Criminal Code which made *kalym* (bride price), polygamy, and under-age marriage illegal. In theory, such practices were further limited by the gradual destruction of the *qadi* courts during the mid-1920s though, as later writers were to indicate, such administrative measures often had the effect of driving old customs underground rather than eradicating them. It should, of course, be stressed that the liberation of women was aimed more broadly at breaking down traditional authority patterns and kinship solidarities capable of hindering the modernisation process favoured by the Bolsheviks.[38]

Most Soviet discussions of this period stress the central role of the *khudzhum* ('advance'), a symbolic propagandist campaign launched with great fanfare by the Central Asian bureau of the Central Committee in March 1927.[39] On 8 March, during demonstrations held in many Uzbek towns, hundreds of women came forward and burnt their veils. Over the next two months some 90,000 are said to have followed their example.[40] Although the repudiation of the veil was the key symbolic gesture associated with the *khudzhum*, the campaign was aimed at the whole array of customs thought to be oppressive of women. In Turkmenistan, for example, the campaign tackled *kalym*, polygamy, *kaitarma* (the withholding of the bride until the full price is paid), the abduction of brides, and enforced divorce. The campaign also aimed at drawing women more fully into the socio-political life of the region.[41]

Needless to say the *khudzhum* was opposed by 'class enemies in the forms of landlords and the more reactionary parts of the Muslim clergy'. According to one source, some 300 female activists were murdered by these groups in the Samarkand *oblast* alone between 1926 and 1928, and the figure reached 2,500 for the whole Uzbek republic.[42] Despite these problems the campaign was officially recognised as a success, as thousands of women were subsequently drawn into education and social production. Statistics from the period demonstrate that women were being brought into areas of life historically alien to their experience. For example, whereas in 1926 only 8 per cent of Central Asian women participated in election to the soviets, by 1934 the figure had reached 72 per cent. Such trends have continued to the present time in various fields. Thus in the early 1980s Nancy Lubin could write that 99 per cent of Central Asian women were officially said to be literate and that women made up some 47 per cent of the region's workforce,[43] though there is some evidence to suggest that the latter figure may have declined in the 1980s.[44]

Atheist assumptions

One of the basic assumptions of atheist writing in the USSR has been that 'objective factors' (i.e. the processes of social transformation) would play the decisive role in overcoming religion because by 'destroying its earthly base they isolated it from the sphere of social life'.[45] Such factors were initially seen as of particular importance in Central Asia, generally depicted as culturally and economically backward compared with Russia proper. For this reason it might have been expected that by the 1980s, when the region was at a level of development not too far behind that of European Russia, the 'problem' of female religiosity would have become less acute. In practice, however, problems persisted in this area. Numerous studies revealed that many women still did not work in collectives – partly because so many had large families and partly as a result of social pressure to keep them in the home – and that few actually visited the cultural enlightenment institutions where most educational work was carried out.[46]

The solution to the problem of female isolation from the collective – and, in Marxist thought, of the woman question in general – was to draw women into the production process, a solution usually asserted rather than explored in any depth. In general it was taken as read that with the 'perfection' of the socialist economy women would become less isolated from the production process and more integrated into collective work situations. This in turn would weaken their need for religion, especially as they could now turn to fellow workers for assistance and guidance, instead of to religious activists. The problem with this as a 'solution' was that by the 1980s, when labour surpluses were increasing in the region, a sufficient number of jobs in collective situations seemed unlikely to materialise – a 1988 article reported that in the Turkmen SSR alone some 600,000 new working places would have to be created for women by the end of the century.[47]

The official emphasis on 'objective factors' does not mean that more 'subjective' approaches were ignored. Since the late 1950s a wide range of educational measures have been adopted – at least, on paper – in an effort to combat the effects of religious ideas on the Central Asian population. Numerous sources describe the work of *zhensovety* (women's councils), clubs, lecturers, individual propagandists, medical workers, teachers, new rite specialists and other social activists. Yet, as the same sources often make clear, such activities are often poorly carried out – if they happen at all – especially in the rural areas where religious influences remain strong. Among the more common complaints are to be found: the failure of believers to attend atheist lectures; poorly prepared presentations; inappropriate subject matter – lectures on Russian Orthodoxy in an Uzbek village!; the tactless use of individual propagandists – for example, sending men to influence women.[48]

In addition to the educational measures routinely listed in Soviet sources, in recent years much emphasis has been placed on two other approaches: the introduction of new non-religious rites and the work of the *zhensovety*. The former are seen as going beyond the typical negation of religion in that they attempt, with varying degrees of success, to provide a positive counterweight to one of the most important manifestations of religious belief.[49]

Linked to Khrushchev's 'differentiated approach' to politics, the importance of the *zhensovety* is said to lie in the fact that they are more aware of women's real needs than is the case with the traditional propaganda apparatus, though many discussions of their work in terms of fulfilling the vanguard role in overcoming female religiosity 'under the leadership of party organisations' indicate that they differ little from the latter.[50] In 1981, for example, *Nauka i religiya* interviewed G.B. Bobosadykova, author of the above quoted article, Tadzhik Central Committee Secretary and Chairperson of the republican women's council. For her the essential role of the *zhensovety* was to draw women into the social production process and to assist in 'the emotional and psychological education' of women, particularly the overcoming of their own acceptance of so many patriarchal customs in family life. To this end members of the councils appeared on television, wrote in the press, gave lectures, initiated clubs and other places where women could go with their problems and sought concurrently to help women in coping with some of the difficulties they faced as mothers, especially by providing medical advice on caring for their generally large families. Yet repeatedly Bobosadykova falls back on lists of measures already taken and formalistic calls for women to become more involved in collective work situations, and like other commentators provides no real analysis of the successes and/or failures of the *zhensovety*. The overall impression given is that many of these institutions function rarely and poorly in many parts of Central Asia.[51] Since Gorbachev's accession there has been a renewed emphasis on the role of the *zhensovety*, though according to Mary Buckley they 'have yet to champion radical proposals'.[52]

'Campaignovshchina'

While anti-religious work in Central Asia has often been criticised for its formalistic nature, there were also frequent complaints about the tendency to rely on sporadic and poorly thought out campaigns –

'*campaignovshchina*'. The republic of Turkmenistan was the scene of one such campaign in the mid-1970s though, ironically, it was preceded by a warning from the republican Agitprop head about the need for atheist work to extend beyond 'brief and temporary campaigns'.[53]

As noted earlier, atheist work in Central Asia has often concentrated on the matter of the ill treatment of women said to be intrinsic to Islam, in part because female subjugation was seen as more obviously damaging to human personality, but also because overcoming traditional customs seemed easier than conquering their underlying ideology. Of particular concern were those traditions relating to marriage – *kalym* and *kaitarma*. Though many works written in the 1950s and 1960s suggested that such customs were dying out, official concern at their survival re-emerged in the central press during the latter decade. On at least four occasions *Pravda* noted that the seclusion of women and arranged marriages could be found even among communists in Turkemistan.[54] Elsewhere it was revealed that 8 to 10 per cent of crimes committed in the republic stemmed from 'survivals of the past', many of them relating to traditional marriage practices.[55]

From the early 1970s the matter seems to have been taken up with more vigour by the republican authorities, though it is not clear whether this stemmed from the centre exerting pressure on local leadership or was related to a greater personal commitment to antireligion on the part of the new Turkmen First Secretary M. Gapurov (appointed in 1969). Addressing a Turkmen Central Committee plenum in April 1973 Gapurov devoted considerable attention to atheist education as a composite part of internationalist upbringing, and more specifically stressed the need for a continued struggle with 'incorrect relations to women' and the ending of *kalym* in the immediate future.[56]

At first it seemed as though this call was no more than a routine attack on a particular social evil. Then in May 1974 *Literaturnaia gazeta* published an article by Turkmen writer Toushan Esenova under the title *Nenavistnyi kalym* (Hateful *kalym*). Reporting on a congress of women recently held in Ashkhabad Esenova noted the great advances made by Turkmen women under Soviet rule, but spoke regretfully of the survival of a number of dubious practices such as *kalym* and *kaitarma*. The former she saw as particularly objectionable in that by allowing the husband to effectively buy his wife it gave him unlimited property rights over her. Not only was this custom morally wrong in that it returned women to a kind of oppression characteristic of the past, but the price demanded was often very expensive. Esenova cited one, admittedly extreme, case where the sum required totalled 10,000 roubles, 100 robes and 20 head of cattle. Though, the article continues, the Turkmen Criminal Code provided a five-year term for parents receiving *kalym*, cases were very rarely brought to court. Public opinion in many areas viewed the custom as sacrosanct because handed down by previous generations, and even among the intelligentsia one could find women who boast of how much they fetched.

For Esenova the first step in combating this vice was the re-activisation of lethargic organisations:

I am not saying little is done in the republic to eliminate such survivals of the past, in relation to women . . . But isolated administrative measures will not put things right. It is necessary that each family, school, institute, newspaper, media institution and all social organisations take a more active part in the education of girls and women.

Such educational measures would have to be accompanied by the rigorous application of the Criminal Code. At one time this code had included an article rendering the seclusion of women resulting from *kaitarma* illegal, but this had been removed from the code issued in 1962 on the grounds that the custom had died out. Yet young girls continued to be kept at home after their marriage, sometimes for years, which in Esenova's view could not be tolerated.[57]

One month later the issues raised in Esenova's article were discussed at a Turkmen Central Committee plenum which adopted a resolution recommending that party committees:

draw up concrete plans for organisational and ideological–political measures in order to strengthen the struggle against survivals of the past; draw women more widely into participation in public life and to promote them to senior posts; recommend administrative organs to intensify the struggle against feudal attitudes towards women and to strictly observe the demands of the law in relation to persons committing crimes on the basis of such survivals . . . and to intensify preventative work in these matters.[58]

A subsequent editorial in *Turkmenskaya iskra* criticised a number of local party organisations for not taking the problem seriously, and emphasised that the struggle with such customs was 'the duty and responsibility' of all party members.[59]

Over the next two years the contents of the republican press suggested that a considerable propaganda campaign was being waged against these patriarchal customs. Numerous articles described the way councils of elders, *zhensovety*, or clubs for young girls were being activated to deal with the issue; others described the work of 'commissions for struggle with survivals' or summarised the plots of plays, films, and books about the old customs and the evil consequences of following them.[60]

Less clear were the results of all this activity. In April 1975 Esenova returned to the fray with an article summing up the initial results of the campaign. Though delighted that her proposal for the reintroduction of the Criminal Code article on *kaitarma* had been taken up, she was concerned that the custom remained strongly entrenched. Many Turkmen continued to see it as sanctioned by tradition, and parents were unwilling to incur public scorn by taking to court those who demanded the payment of *kalym*.[61] Early in 1976 the extensive discussion of Esenova's article was mentioned by First Secretary Gapurov. Though at that time he made no comment on the success or otherwise of the campaign,[62] when speaking in 1978 he admitted that 'optimal results' had not been achieved.[63] In 1979 republican Agitprop head N. Bairamsakhatov noted that in fact a modernised form of *kalym* had begun to appear, as witnessed in cases where the groom's parents might buy a car or build a house with no contractual arrangement apparently involved.[64]

Since Gorbachev came to power discussion of the continued survival of unacceptable customs relating to women has resurfaced, this time with a much franker analysis of the depth of the problem. A spate of newspaper articles published in all the Central Asian republics since 1986 have raised the question of the self-immolation of women resulting from, among other things, their being forced into marriages they did not want. An article in *Turkmenskaia iskra* in October 1988 reported that in the Mari *oblast* alone some 40 women had committed suicide during the course of the year.[65] Frequently communists were said to be setting a bad example in this field by not allowing their daughters to go on to higher education or by using their position to get higher bride price.[66] Though the press articles on the subject suggested that propaganda and collective work were the only way to combat such vices, published case studies would appear to indicate that at least some attempt was being made to apply criminal law against those involved. For example, in Geok-Tepe (Turkmenistan) a family forbade their daughter to marry at all when she refused to marry the man of their choice, and instead kept her closely guarded and frequently beat her. When the case came to court the mother was sentenced to four years and the girl's brother to five.[67]

What is less clear is whether this renewed assault, if such it be, will meet with any more success than its predecessors. Indeed, in the late 1980s the whole strategy has been contested in the Central Asian press, with one writer arguing that the public attention given to the subject has in fact worsened the problem by driving customs such as the payment of *kalym* underground.[68] Given the strength of traditional opinion in these regions, particularly in rural areas, it is hard to believe that those young girls willing to give evidence against their relatives would be able to remain in their home towns or villages. One author pointed out that, although he was unwilling to accept that customs such as *kalym* were impossible to eradicate, they would always be hard to combat whilst party workers turned a blind eye to such customs. Moreover, at a time when the Central Asian intelligentsia was beginning to explore more openly their national roots, there was a tendency to idealise all old customs whatever their provenance or nature.[69]

Towards a conclusion

This chapter has touched on various aspects of the relationship of Soviet women to religion and atheism, in particular: the predominance of women amongst Soviet believers, the reasons for this phenomenon, and the efforts of the state to overcome it. Yet as has also been made clear, the nature of female religiosity in the USSR has undergone changes in recent years, as those women attending places of worship have become younger and – along with the rest of Soviet society – better educated and have become a smaller proportion of religious believers as a whole.

Perhaps the most interesting, if untypical, example of this development was the short-lived appearance of a feminist movement in the Soviet Union during the late 1970s. What struck western observers on first reading the 1979 almanac *Women and Russia* was the strongly religious flavour of many of the contributions. In contrast to the majority of their western sisters the Russian activists were pointing to the church as a source of support for women and picturing Mary as an example to be followed rather than shunned.

A major premise of many of the contributors to this collection was that the true liberation of women presupposed spiritual change. The philosopher Tatyana Goricheva put it thus:

Undoubtedly it is necessary to struggle for the political and economic rights of women, and to demand equal rights, yet it is impossible to forget that this equality might turn out to be the equality of equally right-less slaves, and that no social revolution that is not simultaneously a spiritual revolution will free women.[70]

For Goricheva and some of her colleagues one of the chief roles of women was to reintroduce the values of the heart and the spirit into any process of change in the Soviet Union.

Not all the feminists shared this religious orientation and two groups soon emerged, the one grouped around the journal *Mariya* propagating a more explicitly religious understanding of the feminist task. This emphasis on the spiritual did not, however, preclude discussion of more concrete issues. The second issue of *Mariya* carried an interesting discussion on 'Women and the Family' in which contributors took differing views on how women should correspond to the chores of everyday life.[71] In this and other issues women tackled the questions of alcoholism, health care, sexuality, the upbringing of children, and abortion. On the latter they faced a dilemma, accepting the traditional Orthodox view of abortion as infanticide, yet unwilling to condemn women who took this road as a means of avoiding misery and unhappiness in Soviet conditions.[72]

Amongst the secular feminists, Tatyana Mamanova perhaps best expressed the reservations that some felt about the religious activists:

> One of my main differences with the *Mariya* group is that they think religion elevates women. Maybe after a period of trying to work inside the churches they'll become more feminist and leave.[73]

She also rejected the religious approach on the more practical grounds that it excluded all those who could not accept Christianity and thus potentially reduced the impact of the incipient women's movement.[74] These criticisms were taken up by some western feminists who occasionally adopted a rather patronising 'they'll grow out of it' stance, but they were strongly rejected by Goricheva who expressed concern that her western friends 'had no inkling of mysticism' and tended all too easily to dismiss Christianity as a set of repressive regulations and prohibitions. For her, faith in God was what made her truly human and gave her real personal freedom.[75]

The position taken by Goricheva and other Christian feminists was in stark contrast to the official analysis of female religiosity. For the former religion was a liberating force; for the latter a 'false ideology' which needed to be overcome. And it is this view of religion which in one sense serves to differentiate female adherence to religion in the USSR from that in the wider world. On the surface, as noted earlier, there appear to be few differences. Most churches have more women than men, and most churches tend to experience an influx of women during times of war or national disturbance. Yet in few countries does the state view this as a 'problem'. Of course, it is religion as a whole that has been viewed as problematic by the Soviet state, but the question of female religiosity has been rendered particularly acute because of its ideological implications. If the declared official aim is to create a 'new person' free from 'religious prejudices' it is essential to tackle the propagation of religious values at their source. And ultimately this is the home rather than the place of worship. Hence combatting female religiosity becomes a major task of anti-religious work.

Isolating the 'problem' was one matter, doing anything about it quite another. A reading of the available literature suggests an ambiguity about the need to utilise special means for tackling female religiosity. Some authors seem happy to rely on the gradual impact of social change and education; some suggest that anti-religious work does not require different approaches according to sex; and yet others favour more direct methods that tackled particular customs which humiliated women and initiated home-oriented propaganda aimed specifically at women. Most agree, however, that existing methods are often poorly implemented or even that they exist only on paper. In the case of atheist work among women, this has usually meant that most of the educational instruments used are not distinctive in their application to women. And this in turn points to a general contradiction in Soviet ideological work amongst women, for while much is said about the need to elevate women and provide them with a better life, when it comes to the division of power and resources they usually appear at the bottom of the list. This may be advantageous to the woman who has no desire to be 'liberated' from religion, but it would appear to seriously undermine official campaigns against female religiosity.

Though the current leadership has publicly committed itself to improving the position of women, it seems to have neither the time nor inclination effectively to combat religious beliefs amongst men or women. A positive result of this relatively more benevolent attitude towards religion, alongside the Kremlin's support for a less ideologically hampered social science, may be that Soviet scholars are able to carry out more substantial and reliable investigations of female religiosity. In the immediate future, however, it seems likely to be some time before women are induced out of the temple in the Soviet Union. Indeed, as the communist party ceases to exercise a leading role in the USSR during the 1990s, it seems unlikely that the apparatus of the state will continue to devote time or resources to overcoming 'religious prejudices'.

Notes

*My thanks go to Mary Buckley and Patricia Carley for their comments on an earlier draft.

1 These terms are useful in characterising the nature of religious policy

during the period under consideration, rather than terms formulated by those responsible for that policy.

2 On Soviet sociology of religion see Christel Lane, *Christian Religion in the Soviet Union – A Sociological Study* (London, George Allen and Unwin, 1978); William C. Fletcher, *Soviet Believers – The Religious Section of the Population* (Lawrence, The Regents Press of Kansas, 1981); and Jerry Pankhurst, 'Soviet Sociology of Religion', *Religion in Communist Lands* 10:3, Winter 1982, pp. 292–7.

3 D. Ugrinovich, *Vvedeniye v religiovedeniye* (Moscow, Mysl', 1985), pp. 143–4.

4 M.S. Pismanik, 'O sostoyanii religioznosti i nekotorykh osobennostiyakh nauchno-ateisticheskogo vospitaniya sredi zhenshchini', in I.D. Pantskhava (ed.), *Konkretno-sotsiologicheskoye izucheniya sostoyaniya i opyta ateisticheskogo vospitaniya* (Moscow, Moskovskogo universiteta, 1969), p. 213.

5 M.K. Teplyakov, 'Sostoyaniye religoznosti naseleniye i otkhod veruyushchikh ot religii v Voronezhskoi oblasti (1961–4)', in N.P. Krasnikov (ed.), *Voprosy preodoleniya religioznykh perezhitkov v SSSR* (Moscow, Nauka, 1966), p. 34.

6 V.A. Chernyak, 'O demograficheskikh osobennostiyakh obshchin EKhB g. Alma-Aty i Alma-Atinskoi oblasti', in A.I. Klibanov (ed.), *Konkretny issledovaniya sovremennykh religioznykh verovanii* (Moscow, Mysl', 1967), p. 214.

7 V.A. Saprykin: *Sotsialisticheskii kollektiv i ateisticheskoye vospitaniye* (Moscow, Politizdat, 1983), p. 67.

8 A.S. Onishchenko and N.T. Litvinenko (ed.), *Sovremennaya religioznost' – sostoyaniye, tendentsii, puti preodoleniya* (Kiev, Politizdat Ukrainy, 1987), pp. 43, 69.

9 Mary Buckley pointed out to me that in fact the state encouraged single women to have children during this period, and that the law on alimony was changed to give responsibility to the state.

10 Pismanik, 'O sostoyanii religioznosti', pp. 214–15; for an analysis of the reasons underlying the continued survival of religion in the post-war years see A. Zalesski (ed.), *Prichiny sushchestvovaniya i puti preodoleniya religioznykh perezhitkov* (Moscow, 1965).

11 Pismanik, 'O sostoyanii religioznosti', p. 216.

12 P.M. Mishutis, 'Opyt sozdaniya sistemy ateisticheskogo vospitaniya v Litovskoi SSR', in *Voprosy nauchnogo ateizma, Vyp. 1* (Moscow, Mysl', 1966), pp. 200–20.

13 I.P. Timchenko: *Zhenshchina, religiya, ateizm* (Kiev, Politizdat Ukrainy, 1981), pp. 9–39.

14 V.P. Makarenko, 'Voprosy ateisticheskogo vospitaniya zhenshchin-rabotits', in *Nauchny ateizm i ateisticheskoye vospitaniye – sbornik statei* (Minsk, 1989), pp. 103–11.

15 Pismanik, 'O sostoyanii religioznosti', pp. 220–1.

16 Timchenko *Zhenshchina, religiya, ateizm*, pp. 124–6.

17 A.S. Onishchenko (ed.), *Ateisticheskoye vospitaniye v sem'e* (Kiev, Politizdat Ukrainy, 1984).

18 Timchenko, *Zhenshchina, religiya, ateizm*, p. 59.
19 *Ibid.*, p. 61.
20 On atheist propaganda see David Powell, *Anti-religious Propaganda in the Soviet Union* (Cambridge, Mass.: MIT Press, 1975).
21 Timchenko, *Zhenshchina, religiya, ateizm*, p. 100.
22 See P.P. Kampars and N.M. Zakovich, *Sovetskaya grazhdanskaya obryadnost'* (Moscow, 1967), or V.A. Rudnev *Sovetskiye prazdniki, obryady, ritualy* (Leningrad, 1979).
23 Yu.V. Kilimnik, 'Sotsialisticheskaya obryadnost' – vazhnyi faktor preodoleniya religioznykh perezhitkov v semeino-bytovoi sfere', in Onishchenko (ed.), *Ateisticheskoye*, pp. 165–71.
24 Timchenko, *Zhenshchina, religiya, ateizm*, pp. 90–1.
25 M.V. Voron, 'Ispol'zuya vse faktory ideinogo vliyaniya', in Onishchenko (ed.), *Ateisticheskoye*, pp. 134–41.
26 G. Browning, *Women and Politics in the USSR – Consciousness Raising and Soviet Women's Groups* (Brighton, Wheatsheaf Books, 1987), p. 55.
27 *Ibid.*, pp. 96–111.
28 *Ibid.*, pp. 53–4.
29 Timchenko, *Zhenshchina*, p. 143; on women's clubs see Mary Buckley, *Women and Ideology in the Soviet Union* (London, 1989).
30 R.R. Mavlyutov: *Islam* (Moscow, Politizdat, 2nd. edition, 1974), pp. 91–2.
31 A.V. Belov (ed.), *O nauchnom ateizme i ateisticheskom vospitanii* (Moscow, Politizdat, 1974), p. 110.
32 N. Ashirov, *Evolyutsiya islama v SSSR* (Moscow, Politizdat, 1972), p. 96.
33 Eg. *Muslims of the Soviet East* 1976/4, pp. 6–9 and 1982/2, pp. 18–19.
34 *Nauka i religiya*, 1981/3, p. 5.
35 N.D. Gorokhova, 'Osobennosti individual'noi raboty s veruyushchimi zhenshchinami', in V.G. Pivovarov (ed.), *Individual'naya rabota s veruyushchimi* (Moscow, Mysl', 2nd. edition, 1974), p. 163.
36 *Nauka i religiya* 1981/3, p. 67.
37 R. Aminova, *The October Revolution and Women's Liberation in Uzbekistan* (Moscow, Nauka, 1982), p. 6.
38 On the broader implications of the emancipation programme see G. Massell, *The Surrogate Proletariat – Muslim Women and Revolutionary Strategies in Soviet Central Asia, 1919–29* (Princeton, 1974); on the decrees dealing with these matters see P.V. Gidulyanov (ed.), *Otdeleniye tserkvi ot gosudarstvo v SSSR* (Moscow, 1926), pp. 492–3.
39 On the *khudzhum* see B.P. Pal'vanova: *Emansipatsiya musul'manki* (Moscow, Nauka, 1982), pp. 163–201.
40 *Islam v SSSR* (Moscow, Mysl', 1983), pp. 62–3.
41 Pal'vanova, *Emansipatsiya*, p. 183.
42 *Ibid.*, p. 196.
43 Nancy Lubin, 'Women in Soviet Central Asia: Progress and Contradictions', *Soviet Studies*, 33:2, April 1981, p. 183.
44 *Pravda Vostoka* 23 May 1986 reported that women made up 43% of the workforce in Central Asia.

45 G.N. Plechkov, 'Ob'ektivnye usloviya religioznosti', in *K obshchestve svobodnomu ot religii* (Moscow, Mysl', 1970), p. 66.
46 *Kommunist Tadzhikistana*, 13 October 1976.
47 *Turkmenskaia iskra*, 22 March 1988.
48 Cf. *Individual'naya rabota s veruyushchimi* (2nd. edition, Moscow, Mysl', 1974), p. 135; L.N. Kotyreva, *Partiinaya organizatsiya i ateisticheskoye vospitaniye* (Moscow, Politizdat, 1975), pp. 147–8.
49 See Christel Lane, *The Rites of Rulers: Ritual in Industrial Society, The Soviet Case* (Cambridge, CUP, 1981).
50 G.B. Bobosadykova, 'O sovershenstvovanii form it metodov ateicheskoi raboty', in *Voprosy nauchnogo ateizma, Vyp. 31* (Moscow, Mysl', 1983), p. 199.
51 *Nauka i religiya* 1981/3, pp. 4–8.
52 Mary Buckley, *Women and Ideology in the Soviet Union* (Brighton, Wheatsheaf Books 1989), pp. 209–17.
53 *Turkmenskaia iskra* 22 February 1973.
54 Cf. *Pravda* 14 March 1965; 12 November 1965; 27 February 1966; 14 May 1968.
55 A. Mogilevsky, 'Prestuplenie na pochve perezhitkov mestnykh obychaev', in *Sotsialisticheskaia zakonnost'*, 1969/70, pp. 58–9.
56 *Turkmenskaia iskra* 3 April 1973.
57 *Literaturnaia gazeta* 22 May 1974.
58 *Turkmenskaia iskra* 5 July 1974.
59 *Ibid.*, 3 August 1974.
60 See for example, *ibid.*, 14 August 1974; 24 December 1974; 23 July 1975; 12 June 1976; 15 January 1977.
61 *Ibid.*, 8 April 1975.
62 *Ibid.*, 24 January 1976.
63 *Ibid.*, 23 March 1978.
64 N. Bairamsakhatov, *Novyi byt i islam* (Moscow, Politizdat, 1979), p. 36.
65 *Turkmenskaia iskra* 14 October 1988.
66 Cf. *Tajikistan-i soveti* 10 June 1987, printed in the BBC's *Summary of World Broadcasts* SU/6820/B/9, 15 July 1987; *Turkmenskaya iskra* 22 March 1988.
67 *Turkmenskaia iskra* 9 January 1987; cf. *ibid.* 9 August 1988.
68 *Ibid.*, 22 November 1989.
69 *Ibid.*, 9 January 1987; in private conversation with the author a Central Asian academic recently suggested that as seventy years of assaults on such customs had brought little change the time had come to accept them.
70 *Mariya 1*, Leningrad and Frankfurt (Frankfurt, 1981), p. 12.
71 *Mariya 2*, (Frankfurt, 1982), pp. 35–46.
72 See the comments cited in R.F. Morgan's interviews with 'The First Feminist Exiles from the USSR', in *MS*. November 1981, pp. 50–6, 80–3 and 102–8.
73 *Ibid.*, p. 108.
74 Reported by A. Holt in 'The First Soviet Feminists', in B. Holland (ed.), *Soviet Sisterhood* (London: Fourth Estate, 1985), p. 243.
75 Tatyana Goricheva, *Talking about God is Dangerous* (London, SCM, 1986), p. 90.

PART IV

Cults and sects

· 10 ·

Dilemmas of the spirit: religion and atheism in the Yakut-Sakha Republic

MARJORIE MANDELSTAM BALZER

In a magnificent pine grove on cliffs above the Lena River of Siberia, near where archeologists have found ancient pictographs of shamans (traditional medical and religious practitioners), it is still possible to join the poetic improvisational chanting accompanying *ohuokhai*, a Yakut-Sakha line dance. The beauty of the site brings out the spiritual in native hikers, who sometimes feel like expressing themselves in traditional ways. At the base of the cliffs stands a new *serge*, a sculptural pole that has become a symbol of Yakut-Sakha identity, marking connections to traditions, ancestors, and each other. Deeper in the taiga, are large imposing trees called *al lukh mas*, known as the hosts of 'real spirit keepers of nature', *ichchi*. They are presented with token offerings of coins and scarves by locals and visitors, who wish to preserve their personal sense of harmony and equilibrium with nature in the wake of modern ecological strife.[1]

Many of those who dance and chant poetry in sacred groves, commemorate rituals with new versions of traditional sculptures, and make offerings to spirits of nature are literate, bilingual, and reflective people. Their participation in various Yakut-Sakha rituals and their belief in certain ancient religious ideas does not prevent them from functioning in today's rapidly changing post-Soviet political climate. Rather, expressions of religious feeling have themselves changed with the times. Each generation remakes traditions, consciously and unconsciously, with and without outside coercion.

During the ferment of the late 1980s throughout the Soviet republics, attitudes toward religion, faith, and spirituality changed as part of more general attempts to recover lost sovereignty. The depth and extent of religious change can be probed by examining the situation of smaller nationalities far from Russian centres of political power. By 1990, two policy events were part of an improved climate for religion, indirectly affecting its practice in Yakutia. The first of

231

these, the long-awaited all-union Law on Freedom of Conscience, endorsed processes that were already underway. The second, the 'Declaration of governmental sovereignty of the Yakut-Sakha soviet socialist republic', presumed the validity of religion in the proclamation that the republic had the sole right to decide legal questions concerning 'the growth of language, culture and education'. Rights of cultural 'rebirth' (*vozrozhdeniia*) were claimed for the Yakut-Sakha and other native minorities (especially the Even, Evenk, and Yukagir) of Yakutia.[2]

The group featured here, traditionally called 'Yakut' in Russian and western literature, call themselves 'Sakha'. Insistence on this ethnonym or the compromise hyphenated form has become strong since the 1990 sovereignty declaration. The Sakha are the farthest north Turkic-speaking people and the second largest Siberian nationality (after the Mongolic Buryat).[3] Though Turkic, they are non-Islamic. Their religion has historically been a syncretic mix of spirit beliefs, shamanism and Russian Orthodoxy. Their ideologies stem from various religious and spiritual concepts, and from influences of Marxism–Leninism.

Many post-Soviet peoples, including the Sakha, are in the process of recovering, constructing, and reconstructing their identities by drawing on the well-springs of their cultural history, religion, and values without recapitulating these sources exactly. This is at once exciting and frustrating for the participants, particularly those educated intelligentsia most aware of comparable trends in other republics and countries. Such people are vulnerable to accusations of chauvinist nationalism. Yet they are taking advantage of relatively more flexible official approaches to spirituality, after decades of anti-religious campaigns.

Focus here is on a few of the ways some Sakha have traditionally expressed their spirituality, and have coped with Soviet policies promoting atheism. Religious and cultural revivals are discussed, with special attention to Sakha rituals, and some comparisons with religious practices among the Even, Evenk and Yukagir of the Yakut-Sakha Republic.

Traditional religion, Russian Orthodoxy and the issue of cults

In 1920, in Ust-Yansk, one of the farthest north regions of Yakutia, an elder told the Sakha ethnographer, A.E. Kulakovsky, a tale about a powerful shaman named Goose who had long ago foretold the coming of Russians. Goose foresaw:

(1) People crying in houses that had walls as smooth as human palms, all placed next to each other. (This described Russian log cabins.)
(2) On Yakut tables white things on which were drawn images of bullfinches. (This described tea cups.)
(3) Reindeer multiplied like mosquitoes.
(4) Cattle with hooves and half-circle horns (about cattle that arrived . . . [later] in the North).
(5) Narrow-figured people moving near the ocean with . . . white eyes and tall caps (about Russians).
(6) At the Yan River, a terrifying construction ten times bigger than a conical tent (a church).[4]

Goose warned of intensifying relations with incoming strangers. He was prophetic, especially regarding Russian attempts to change traditional religion, first with Russian Orthodoxy and then Soviet atheist campaigns. For the Russians, the most visible aspects of traditional religion involved shamans. Thus the whole complex Sakha religious and ritual system was collapsed into the term 'shamanism' (or sometimes 'black faith') with occasional mention of totemic beliefs stemming from ancient hunting and clan cults. Even Kulakovsky wrote of his ancestral religion as a cult, perhaps influenced by some Russian views that any ritual and belief system not part of a major world religion was a cult.[5]

Well before concerted Soviet anti-religious campaigns had begun, many aspects of Sakha beliefs were already changing. Cosmological ideas of nine heavens, layered above a middle world (earth) and an underworld, had been merged with Orthodox concepts of heaven and hell. One of the major sky-gods, *Aiyy Toyon*, was associated with the Christian god. A few Sakha community leaders sponsored church building, and some of their followers attended services at least on holidays. Priests competed with shamans for the attention of believers, although some priests were rumoured to apply to shamans for cures when they became sick.[6]

Pre-revolutionary repression of shamans was mitigated by a popular folk conception (among Russians and Siberian natives alike) that shamanism and Orthodoxy were not mutually exclusive, but rather compatible strategies for dealing with the supernatural. Repression was concentrated, in any case, in and near the capital, Yakutsk, the centre of the Eastern Siberian Russian Orthodox eparchy, where shamans cut their hair and hid their profession from Russians. One shaman named 'The-man-who-fell-from-heaven' told the Polish exile Sieroshewskii 'We do not carry on this calling without paying for it. Our masters (the spirits) keep a zealous watch over us, and woe betide us afterwards if we do not satisfy them! But we cannot quit it: we cannot cease to practice shaman rites. Yet we do no evil.' This shaman had 'several times been condemned to punishment; his professional dress and drum had been burned; his hair had been cut off, and he had been compelled to make a number of obeisances and to fast'.[7]

As in other areas of Siberia, when natives in Yakutia learned that Russian Orthodox priests and believers were themselves officially condemned by Bolshevik leaders, they temporarily returned to more open practice of their traditional religion. In the turmoil of the civil war, and the confusion of post-war revolutionary construction, shamanism was also more in demand. Curing the ills of the body politic, as well as the body–mind, had always been part of traditional shamanism, with at least some shamans considered to be moral authorities.

The means through which individual and community catharsis occurred were seances, an enactment of beliefs in shamanic ability to be intermediaries between the natural and supernatural worlds. The seances were intense emotional dramas, usually involving trance (of the shaman and sometimes others) with drumming, dancing, and audience involvement. In accord with Sakha beliefs, shamans in such seances regained lost souls of the sick, found lost objects, predicted the future, and suggested lucrative hunting routes. They coached people guilty of Sakha concepts of sin (taboo-breaking) into confessions. In the process, they used astonishing sleight-of-hand, ventriloquism, and possibly hypnotism to impress (often believing these tricks would not work if the spirits were not helping them). Eyewitnesses claimed to have seen shamans, while in trance, withstand cold, walk on hot coals, stab themselves without leaving scars, disappear and reappear, escape the bounds of ropes, and even induce or control floods, winds, and storms.[8]

A major native revolutionary hero, P.A. Sleptsov, tapping into the reputed power of shamans, took the revolutionary penname Oiunsky from one of the Sakha words (*oíuun*) meaning shaman. His influential poem, 'The Red Shaman', pitted the benevolent forces of the revolution against the dark forces of superstition and exploitation. Yet it also drew on Sakha spiritual and aesthetic traditions. Oiunsky became famous for collecting (and singing) the major Sakha epic (*olonkho*) Niurgun Bootur, and he founded what is now the Institute of Languages, Literature, and History. He died in jail in 1939, at the peak of Stalinist repression, but was rehabilitated under Khrushchev.[9]

The demise of religion

By the 1930s, in implementation of the 1929 law on religion and atheism, both Russians and native Communist party activists accused shamans of being the most notorious of all exploiters.[10] They were placed in the category of rich 'kulaks', even when they had taken only minimal fees for their services. (Actual pay varied by individual and community.) Traditional religion in all its manifestations was condemned as primitive superstition. Aspects of shamanic reputations that most pertained to the ability of shamans to do harm (steal souls) rather than cure (recover souls) were stressed by Communist Party propagandists, who feared and resented shamanic opposition to collectives, and to education campaigns.

A story still circulates in the Viliuisk area of northern Yakutia about a female shaman (*udagan*) named Alykhardaakh, who tried in the 1930s to combat local Soviet officials. It is worth recounting, not to shock (for it is somewhat racy), but to communicate the perceived power of shamanism and the complex nature of Soviet approaches to shamanism.

Before Alykhardaakh died there was a lot of pressure on her to stop shamanizing and to confess that she was a charlatan. But she was not, and she insisted that she would prove her strength to the Yakut men who were running the village Soviet. She invited them all to her hut and they sat on benches. First she stood by the fire and started dancing and calling to spirit helpers. She began her seance, in front of these men, dancing and drumming herself into trance. She called forth water, so that the men's ankles were covered with water, before she commanded that the water flooding her hut should stop. Then she called forth a pike and caught it for the men, to show them her strength. Finally she told the men to take their pants off, and all of them did. She asked them to hold their male organs and then she came out of her seance and commanded them to notice what had happened, that they were all still sitting there with their pants off. They begged her forgiveness for doubting her power, and bowed low to her, vowing never to bother her again.[11]

Most shamans by the 1930s were not so powerful or so lucky as to be spared public denunciation, confiscation of property, and persecution. They were branded as practitioners of fraudulent medicine and perpetuators of outdated religious beliefs in a dawning age of science and logic. As conservative leaders of anti-Soviet activity, they were sometimes jailed. A Sakha woman from the Suntar region, who had been a 'cultural revolution activist' and president of the village Soviet in a newly founded collective during the 1930s, remembered the campaign to eliminate shamans and kulaks:

In 1930, all the shaman drums were taken to museums. If shamans still had seances or hid their drums, their voting rights were taken away. This meant they were without any rights to land use or collective membership. They were class enemies, kulaks . . . Some did try to continue their work and to prove they could still cure.[12]

One Viliuisk area shaman, Spiridon, managed to maintain a secret practice and become president of his regional council. During the Second World War, covert shamanism revived somewhat in remote villages. Shamans were hired by families worried about loved ones at the front or starvation at home. But after the war, policies of increased education and medical attention meant decreased appeals to shamans by younger generations. Whereas in 1915, only a few Sakha attended the 64 Russian Orthodox church schools, by 1950 there were 592 Soviet schools, many with boarding accommodations for rural native children.[13] The focus of these schools was basic literacy and Soviet revolutionary history, with locally specific programmes stressing the failure of shamans to cure serious diseases like tuberculosis, and the moral bankruptcy of shamans who demanded payment (even of meat) for their deceptive seances. Political education, including programmes for adults, was oriented toward creating native teachers and Party cadres. Symbolic of the change in attitudes toward shamans was Sergei Zverev, a former shaman's helper (*kuturukhsut*) who renounced shamanism as fraudulent, and became a star of the Sakha theatre, even travelling to Moscow to win a cultural award.[14]

By the mid-1980s, most shamans were indeed discredited with their people by Soviet officials and doctors. One former shaman in the Suntar region was known for encouraging his daughter to perform well in medical school. Some local museums presented shamans in the form of wild-eyed, life-sized manikins capable of frightening both adults and children. Some parents even avoided telling their children about sha-manic ancestors. Many of the most powerful shamans died without passing on their esoteric knowledge or the details of their rituals. Yet, in the 1990s, stories of their strength abound, and fear of their graves is common among rural and urban Sakha. A few shamans practise, no longer in secret, for believers whose numbers are increasing for the first time in decades. Trend-setting democratic leaders are revealing shamanic ancestry with pride.

While the full force of Soviet anti-religious propaganda was targeted at shamanism, other less visible aspects of Sakha spiritual life were also discouraged both before and after the Second World War. Rituals of birth, tied to ancient beliefs about the fertility godess *Aiyysyt*, were condemned as unsanitary and dangerous for mothers and children. By the 1980s, many older Sakha village women recalled details about these rituals with some hilarity, mocking their stress on purification with oil rather than disinfectants. Some remembered cases of infant deaths during traditional rituals. One confessed that, during much of the Soviet period, women were 'just not up to' celebrating births with the traditional feasts and 'rituals of laughter' that previously marked the third day after birth. Yet a resurgence of respect for the meaning of *Aiyysyt* as life-giving had occurred by 1990, and prayers are still said to her.[15]

Rituals of death were transformed less dramatically, despite introduction of new Soviet secular rituals by the 1950s, designed to compensate for spiritual losses at significant life-crisis moments. Aspects of 'traditional' Sakha burials, in both villages and towns, continue to be syncretised with Russian Orthodox services, and symbols of Russian Orthodox crosses remain on many graves that face east in accord with older concepts. Soul beliefs, involving three souls or life forces (*sur*, *kut*, and *ichchi*, with three further aspects to *kut*) remain tied to concepts of reincarnation, proper burial, and respect for dead ancestors. In the late 1980s, one elder caused a sensation by insisting that at death he be placed on a platform, *arangas*, in the forest, as was traditional before Russian influence.[16]

Secular rituals, whether for birth, marriage or death, have not replaced, but merely been added to, sequences involving traditional and/or Orthodox rituals. A few Sakha also attend church services in Yakutsk, something that became possible in the early 1980s, when an exquisite multi-cupola wooden church was brought board by board from a nearby village and reconstructed by believers (mostly Russians) on the edge of town. Since the 1930s, this church had been used as a store. The badly destroyed main cathedral in Yakutsk, named for the Christian curer Sviatoi Nikolai, was used as a book repository until 1989, when it was promised to Russian believers.[17] Sakha who profess Russian Orthodoxy as a focus of religious orientation are rare, but occasionally an elder will disapprove of working on the major Orthodox holidays of Christmas and Easter.

Cultural revival and changes in spiritual life

The very success of Soviet anti-religious campaigns has led to fear that important aspects of traditional aesthetic and spiritual life have been lost. A renewed search for 'roots', revival of interest in the Sakha language, and research into Sakha 'folk wisdom' have become part of a resurgence of Sakha ethnic consciousness. Cultural revitalisation has been enhanced by policies of *glasnost*, and stimulated by 1990s activist groups such as *Sakha Omuk* (The Sakha People), *Kut-Sur* (Soul-Reason), and The Association of Folk Medicine, but it pre-dates Gorbachev.

Aspects of cultural resurgence began as long ago as the 1940s. Following the Second World War, the annual summer festival, *yhyak*, celebrating the making of mare's milk, *kumiss*, and the renewal of life after winter, was reincarnated as a victory celebration marking the return of Sakha soldiers. While *yhyak* had continued in a few regions (such as Suntar) on a modest scale in the 1920s and 1930s, in most areas of Yakutia it had been officially curtailed. Its popularity since the war has spread, to the extent that most village collectives sponsor *yhyak* annually at the end of June. The ceremonies vary, with some of the traditional religious meaning removed from the festival. Nonetheless, *yhyak* continues to open with prayers and libations of *Kumys* from a ritual cup, *choron*, to the earth. Fresh spring birch branches lining a ritual corridor have symbolic multi-vocal meanings of fertility and renewal. Dances, *ohuokhai*, are done to improvisational poetry that has deep resonance for its participants, who dance around a sculptured pole, *serge*, through the night and into the two to three days that the festival lasts. Wrestling, horse racing, and foot racing are still part of the festival, testing the strength of young people and creating an atmosphere (as was traditional) conducive to competition and courtship. Individuals interpret the festival in their own ways: some see religious significance, while others see only the chance to drink and have fun.[18]

Enough was perceived as healthy and celebratory in *yhyak* for Soviet officials, many of whom are Sakha, to risk sponsoring it. With the demise of the Stalinist slogan 'national in form, socialist in content', a more flexible approach to traditions developed. Since the late 1960s and '70s, some members of the Sakha intelligentsia also evolved new versions of certain selected rituals related to birth, marriage, and death. Whether consciously or not (depending on the individual), they have led a fascinating cultural revival. They have even added new rites of passage celebrations for graduation from high school or the university, using the traditional *serge* sculptures.

The case of changing wedding ceremonies is particularly illuminating, because many have increasingly syncretised traditional marital symbolism with modern social, political, and economic values. Put bluntly, people do not have fancy weddings unless they can afford them. After the revolution, during collectivisation, the war, and its harsh aftermath, marriages were modest – Soviet ideology de-emphasised the personal, and large celebrations were indecent, if not economically impossible. In the 1950s and '60s, small student or worker weddings were the norm, held in cafeterias or restaurants with close friends and family. They were drab and simple, as many of their participants now explain with a dismissive shrug. By the early 1970s, people who could afford bigger weddings, and whose social networks were expanding while their kin networks remained large, began escalating the size and elaborateness of their weddings. They participated in token, secular Soviet rituals at their local vital statistics office (ZAGS), while also arranging for more traditional rituals to be part of wedding carousing. By the 1980s, many marriages in both villages and towns, involving 100 or more guests, had become openly filled with Sakha symbolism and with alcohol.[19]

Since the 1970s, some Sakha weddings have revolved around the placement of traditional memorial poles, *serge*, back in fashion after decades of neglect. The poles (once used not only in rituals, but as horse hitching posts) are crowned with symbols such as a horse head or a *Kumys* cup, and are carved with curved designs signifying long life, as well as with the names of the couple, in modern Sakha script, plus the date of the wedding. During the weddings, line dances, *ohuokhai*, arc around the post. These are danced to improvisational chanting begun by a leader and repeated by the assembled dancers. Chanting is based on traditional poetic forms within which descriptions of nature and fertility are blended with new and joking observations about the couple. Sacred prayers or blessings, *algys*, are also sung by male or female family elders, for fertile, stable, multi-generation families, many guests, and, if appropriate, many cows and horses. At one wedding in 1985, the bride and her attendants arrived on horseback. At another in 1986, the bride arrived in a boat and was led to the groom's family hearth where she made a small food offering honouring the fire spirit, *Yot ichchite*. The bride who made this important symbolic offering was a sincere and sophisticated university graduate, who typifies a yearning for cultural meaning through which people can define themselves as Sakha.[20]

Weddings reveal only some of the interrelated ways ritual continues to be a conduit for communication of ideas about identity and cultural revival. The key symbol of the *serge* links the Sakha to their past, and yet has emerged in modern forms and contexts. Sculptural *serge* adorn the Yakutsk university campus, put up by grateful graduates. Members of scientific institutes put up *serge* together, to commemorate their institute's founding, and solidify their non-kinship commitment to each other. A fat white obelisk *serge* of 'friendship', complete with a

Soviet seal, resides in a main square in Suntar. On the grounds of annual festival sites, separate stately *serge* memorialise such diverse events as the end of the Second World War, anniversaries of Soviet rule, and the 300th year of Yakutia's incorporation into the Russian state. Thankful couples who have reached their 50th wedding anniversaries place *serge* in their front yards (especially in the dacha-land near Yakutsk). And urbanites visiting their rural homelands sometimes put up *serge* in private ceremonies of respect for their ancestors. One member of the Sakha intelligentsia who did this explained:

Serge are important monuments that will last longer than you. They tell much about a person – tall, straight, beautiful, elaborate . . . People will praise how long a *serge* has stayed upright. It is a very bad sign for a *serge* to tilt . . . It's leaving a trace of oneself in the outback. It gives a powerful feeling of calm and connection to Sakha ancestors and to Sakha culture. It's a living thing. I'm glad I did it.[21]

The significance of emotional attachments to a birthplace, homeland, and ancestors is illustrated through small, but special, ritual moments throughout individuals' lifetimes. When leaving a home valley, a Sakha may stop at an overlook, seek out a special grove and leave a token offering on a particularly large or unusual tree. The earth of someone's birthplace may be brought to them if they are living far away. Unusual places, such as a bank near where a river never thaws, even at the height of summer, can also be the sites of ritual offerings on trees. And at campfires in such sites, before anyone eats, the spirit of the fire, *Yot ichchite*, is given a small offering of food.[22]

Such personal moments, far from the eyes of Russian or native skeptics, are still part of the inner life of individuals from both villages and towns, despite their Soviet atheist upbringing. They are at the core of a personalised spiritual life that Sakha participants themselves explain as neither a cult, nor a religion.

Changes in Yukagir, Even and Evenk religion and politics

When asked about shamans and spirit beliefs in 1986, some Sakha replied that they no longer knew much about this, but that the Evenk (formerly called Tungus) minority of Yakutia knew much more. Indeed a popular Sakha conception attributed greater spiritual powers and knowledge to the Even and Evenk, who were less urbanised and less influenced by Soviet atheist propaganda. This idea relates to the concept of a more 'natural' (*aiylkha*) existence for Evenk and Even hunters, fishers, and reindeer breeders, even today. By extension, the

Yukagir, who numbered only 1,142 in 1989, live still more remotely, away from both the benefits and harms of civilisation.

These conceptions, equating remoteness, primitiveness, and spirituality, like all generalisations, are problematic. It is the tiny but articulate Even, Evenk, and Yukagir intelligentsias that have recently been paying attention to recovering native traditions and raising ethnic consciousness. The religious traditions they can draw upon (and transform) are still alive in the hearts, minds, and rituals of some native elders, although devastations of their material and spiritual life have been great in the Soviet period. The Evens (earlier Lamut) succeeded in 1989 in establishing a separate 'autonomous Eveno-Bytantaiskii raion' within Yakutia, which they hope will give them more control over their waning spiritual and material resources.[23]

Those Even, Evenk, and Yukagir who live in the remote taiga and tundra zones of Siberia have had at least a few years of Soviet education, and have access to television and radio. They too went through collectivisation, and sent soldiers to the front in the Second World War. Yet some have also maintained a connection to their natural surroundings, passed on through the centuries, that does mean spirit beliefs involving respect for the living essence of rivers, trees, rocks, and animals have been preserved. Rituals revering bear spirits were traditionally the most elaborate, and have lingering meaning today in beliefs about the sacred wisdom of the bear.[24] Spirit beliefs need not be romanticised or fetishised to be admired for their ecological approach to the environment.

One way in which this ecological approach traditionally was actualised by the Yukagir (whose culture has roots in the oldest 'paleo-Asiatic' Siberian traditions) was through sacred groves that were sites of shamanic rituals, and were also game preserves where certain animals were protected. The modern idea, taken up by some Yukagir and other Siberians, that large zones of the Siberian north be reserved for native peoples to pursue traditional, ecologically sound ways of life (including worship), is thus an extension of past interrupted practices.[25]

Siberian writers have pointed out bitterly that the only way to preserve the cultures of the smallest nationalities of the North is to save the people themselves. Some, including the articulate Yukagir ethnographer–linguist G.N. Kurilov, consider 'rebirth' especially difficult for the Yukagir, whose history of population devastation began before the revolution with smallpox epidemics, Evenkisation, and Yakutisation. It has continued in the Soviet period with low life expectancies, suicides, Russification, Yakutisation, and programmes of development that have been created, until recently, without consultation with the Yukagir.[26]

The decline of the Yukagir probably did more to discredit local shamans (sometimes called *i'rkeye* from the verb tremble) than Russian Orthodoxy, Soviet education, or anti-religious propaganda combined. Yet some Yukagir shamans, well into the Soviet period, were respected leaders among the small community of families for whom they shamanised. Their souls after death were worshipped as ancestor spirits, and each Yukagir clan considered its founder a shaman. The ancient Yukagir belief in reincarnation, thought to enable souls of specific deceased relatives to be passed onto worthy infants, clearly stemmed from a time when both the population and their religious beliefs were more flourishing. Yet in the 1980s, three years after a death, Yukagir families still practised divination, worshipped, and made food offerings at the grave of a deceased relative, crowned not with a cross, not with a star, but with reindeer antlers.[27]

Evenk shamanism has, in many ways, become the prototype for Russian and western conceptions of Siberian shamanism. This is owing to the Evenk shaman's strong reputation throughout Eastern Siberia, as well as to accidents of historiography and to the widely accepted theory that sources of many Siberian shamanic practices lie with the Evenk. Indeed the Evenk word for their traditional medical and spiritual practitioners is *shaman*.[28]

S. Shirokogoroff, the eminent Russian *émigré* scholar of shamanism, theorised that Evenk shamans were part of a highly adaptable 'psychomental complex', helping small communities cope with sickness, change and stress.[29] That adaptability has been tested to the limit in the Soviet period, as Evenk shamans, like Yukagir and Yakut ones, were discredited by Soviet school teachers, officials and propagandists. The peak of collectivisation in the 1930s marked the height of campaigns against shamanism, when many Evenk shamans were jailed. Nonetheless, Shirokogoroff's theory seems hauntingly valid in the context of a story circulating in the 1980s about an elderly grandmother shaman who was still practicing in a remote Evenk nomadic reindeer-breeding camp. The grandmother planned an elaborate seance to welcome her grandson home after his release from the Soviet army. He needed purification from the evil spirits of the military, and from having been away from his home amidst strangers. On his way home, he met a folklorist group making a film, and brought them to the camp. With some trepidation, they asked the grandmother for permission to film the seance, and she agreed to show them aspects of her shamanising. But when she actually got into trance, at the hearth of her traditional Evenk 'shaking tent' using a drum and other ancient accoutrements, her family became alarmed and stopped the filming. They were worried that their shamanising would become known in the local collective, and that spirits the grandmother conjured would turn on her and make her sick. All were enormously relieved when she came out of her trance, having been in it for an unusually long time.[30]

As with the Sakha, spirituality for many Evenk has shifted away from shamanic seances to less visible or dramatic manifestations of spirit and soul beliefs inherent in offerings to a fire spirit and in unofficial life-crisis rituals. Educated Evenk young people are delving for 'roots' into their own folklore, epic, song, and dance traditions. An Evenk musician explained in 1990, while gazing at a lily, 'Evenks are not Russian Orthodox – we are spiritual, animists, pagan. This flower, and all of nature, is my religion, and this is what is threatened with ecological destruction.'[31]

One of the most politically active and emotionally rousing of all Siberian native writers is the Evenk poet Alitet Nemtushkin, who said, as a delegate to the Party Conference in 1988:

I am an Evenk. My grief, of course, concerns my own people and other small populations and ethnic groups – their situation in today's complex and all-encompassing world. Long years before today were years of harsh struggles with national customs, ways of life. The struggles were against vaguely defined 'darkness' and 'backwardness'. I want not only to protest, but, if necessary, to revolt against such earlier stereotypical methods in nationality politics.[32]

Nemtushkin also proclaimed, in another forum:

I wish to thank all the Soviet peoples for their fraternal help in boosting the economy and culture of my region . . . I would also like to say that we have outgrown the children's trousers and no longer need to be under guardianship. Give us the right to take charge of our own destiny.[33]

This plea, to be allowed responsibility for their own decisions, extends from economics to issues of religion and spirituality, indeed to culture in the broadest sense. The current political atmosphere makes Alitet Nemtushkin's plea possible to make, but nearly impossible to fulfil. An Association of the Peoples of the North, established in 1989, has few funds and little clout, but may be a first step in fighting for demographic, ecological, and cultural survival.

Conclusion: the politics of culture

The Yakut-Sakha, with their 'autonomous republic' within the Russian Republic, have been in a better position to formulate at least some aspects of their own cultural life than the Even, Evenk, and Yukagir minorities within Yakutia. However, public manifestations of the Sakha cultural revival have also begun to stimulate ethnic consciousness among the other minorities.[34]

Comparisons of the politics of culture among the indigenous groups of Yakutia reveal that Soviet policies on religion have provoked interactive, not easily predictable responses. Both policies and practices have changed greatly since the 1920s, involving processes not always fully understood by the Russians who were trying to direct them. While revivals of ethnic consciousness and spirituality are not synonymous, they are related phenomena tied very much to the development of an educated urban elite.

In contrast, traditional religion in nomadic camps and remote villages continued, albeit persecuted and thus underground, throughout the Soviet period. This hidden, secret aspect of religion in Yakutia perhaps led the atheist Soviet public into rumours about the few remaining traditional religious practitioners as backward superstitious cultists. Yet shamanic seances are rare, and there is little evidence of organised cults in any conspiratorial political–religious sense. Instead, people today openly make pilgrimages to the few remaining shamans, some of whom are quite young. In 1990 an extrovert middle-aged shaman, Vladimir Kondakov, founded the Association of Folk Medicine, trying to unite traditionally competitive and secretive shamans in a new attempt to legitimise tradition. He explained, 'We need better conditions, social and material ... We also need contact with the earth, and a hearth, not a second story office. We need access to upper and lower worlds.'[35]

A native official stated proudly in 1986 that Yakutia was one of the least religious republics in all of the Soviet Union. He claimed, 'We have wiped out shamanism and Russian Orthodox influence was never very strong.' While he was correct to de-emphasise the organised aspects of religion, he was ignoring the spiritual and ritual dimensions of life that some people have rediscovered and others never lost. His statement confirmed that, until recently, organised practice of religion, and the passing on of religious concepts and rituals to children, was difficult under Soviet laws, particularly with zealous implementation of those laws by Yakutia officials.

In place of religion, some Siberian and Russian intellectuals have together tried to invent, since the 1950s, Soviet secular rituals of birth, marriage, wedding anniversaries, and death. Committees were formed and reformed, a few including indigenous ethnographers with patriotic intentions to merge native and Russian rituals, and imbue them with non-religious Soviet meaning. Yet official rites did not become substitutes for other ritual celebrations. Rituals introduced from above by committee, rather than organically evolving through gradual adaptation to new conditions, are mocked as superficial and artificial.

Since the 1930s, spiritual life has become personal and private. Some Marxist, Russified members of the Sakha intelligentsia are oblivious to the *serge* in their neighbour's front yards. But such symbols are compelling for many, whether urban elite or rural herder. The poetry of prayers has not died. In 1990 the emerging popular front, *Sakha Omuk*, was founded. Among other goals, it strives to enable spiritual life to be more communal. The group *Kut-Sur* is even more focused on stimulating religious revival through ritual and group prayer.[36]

With *glasnost*, a renewed sharing of values, including religious ones, has become possible among widening circles of Siberian natives. This is reflected first in cultural revivals, not only within the largest Siberian groups, but also in some of the smaller groups. It is reflected in increased communication among Siberians on the importance of preserving their ecological, cultural and spiritual legacies. They are not paralysed by nostalgia. Few wish to return to the practice of shamanism as it was at the beginning of the Soviet period, but many endorse re-evaluations of shamanism as having contributed much to the aesthetic, psychological, and moral substance of Siberian cultures. Some openly call themselves 'shamanists', and dream of founding schools for shamanic training.

Are the cultural revivals too little, too late? Are new versions of festivals such as the *yhyak* so de-sacralised as to become mere shells of their former selves? The Sakha themselves debate this, with folklorists and elders mourning the demise of ritual as it used to be practiced. Others argue that traditions, like people and ethnic groups, are never pure or bounded.

In a regional museum in the village of Cherkekh, the dynamics of some of these issues were played out informally during a 1986 festival honouring the once-jailed Sakha revolutionary hero-folklorist Oiunsky. The museum (a converted Orthodox church) has a room devoted to describing, and denigrating, aspects of traditional religion. In one corner is a rootless, but life-sized, tree representing the sacred *al-lukh-mas* still found with offerings in Sakha forests. With great humour, irony, and style, numerous festival participants placed coins and bits of cloth on the tree as 'spirit offerings'. As I added my coin, I realised they were both providing tokens for supernatural spirits, and lifting each other's spirits, in ethnic solidarity.[37]

Notes

1 These examples are from my fieldwork in Yakutia, February–July 1986 and June–July 1991. I am indebted to the International Research and Exchanges Board (IREX), Leningrad University, Yakutsk University, the Academy of Sciences Institute of Languages, Literature and History in Yakutsk (AN IIaLI), the Yakut-Sakha Ministry of Culture, and to the Kennan Institute of the Smithsonian's Wilson Centre for fieldwork and/or research support. I am deeply thankful to my Sakha language teacher, Klara Belkin, with whom I began studying in 1983; to 1988–91 Siberian visitors I. Alekseev, V. Shadrin, A. Borisova, A. Reshetnikova and A. Tomtosov; to Soviet ethnographers who made my fieldwork possible and enjoyable, especially A.I. Gogolev, P.A. Sleptsov, and the late R.F. Its; and to colleagues I. Krupnik, L. Black, and S. Kan for comments on this chapter.

2 The declaration was published in *Sotsialisticheskaia Yakutia* 28 September 1990, p. 1, the day after its passage. Its chances for viability have increased since August 1991, and it has already been relevant as a morale booster.

3 The Yakut-Sakha numbered 381,922 in the 1989 census, up from 328,018 in 1979. They live in a territory within the Russian Republic roughly four times the size of Texas, and have become a minority in their own republic, with Russians and others accounting for about 65 per cent. In contrast, they were 82 per cent of their republic, according to the 1926 census. Their population is predominantly rural, with traditional occupations of cattle, horse, and reindeer breeding still important, although they have many other diverse occupations. In comparison, the largest Siberian group, the Mongolic Buryat numbered 421,380 in 1989, but are divided, by a remarkable feat of gerrymandering, into several territories within the RSFSR.

4 A.E. Kulakovsky, *Nauchnyi trudy* (Yakutsk, Yakutsk. kn. izdat, 1979), p. 284. Kulakovsky was later repressed as a nationalist, with much of his writing published only posthumously.

5 Kulakovsky, *Nauchnyi trudy* p. 8. Kulakovsky explained that in his youth 'he himself believed' in the religious rituals and ideas described in his writings. I differentiate (1) general ideas of and yearnings toward spirituality in many, often syncretic, forms; (2) a traditional and elaborate system of cosmology, ritual, and beliefs that characterised Sakha religion; and (3) cults associated with specific aspects of traditional religion (e.g. bear hunting) or related to secret religious activity that therefore becomes politically significant. My approach to religion and its relation to ethnic consciousness is selectively influenced by Benedict Anderson, *Imagined*

Communities (London, Verso, 1985); Lola Romanucci-Ross and George De Vos (eds.), *Ethnic Identity* (Chicago, University of Chicago, 1982); Pedro Ramet (ed.), *Religion and Nationalism in Soviet and East European Politics* (Durham, Duke, 1984); and L.M. Drobizheva, *Dukhovnaia obshchnost' narodov SSSR* (Moscow, Mysl', 1981).

6 On Russian Orthodox influences in Sakha religion, see A.E. Kulakovsky, *Nauchnyi trudy*, e.g. pp. 17, 71; G.V. Ksenofontov, *Khrestes, shamanizm i khristianstvo* (Irkutsk, Russ. Geograf. Obshch, 1929). On priests applying to shamans for cures, see the 1880s memoirs of V.G. Korolenko, *Istoriia moego sovremennika* (Moscow, Khudozhestvennaia literatura, 1965, p. 751); and see p. 797 on Orthodox influences. Stories of priest–shaman interrelations were common into the early Soviet period through-out the North. Yakutisation of Russians also occurred.

7 W. Sieroshewskii (V.L. Seroshevsky), translated by W.G. Sumner, 'The Yakuts', *Journal of the Royal Anthropological Institute*, 31, 1901, p. 102. See also the original ethnography from Sieroshewskii's 1880–92 exile published as *Iakuty. Opyt etnograficheskogo issledovaniia* (T. I, St Petersburg, Imper. Russ. Geograf. Obshch., 1896), and reviewed by 'B' in *Russkii vestnik* November 1896, pp. 354–7.

8 These examples come from fieldwork, and from W. Jochelson, *The Yakut* (New York, Anthropological Papers of the American Museum of Natural History, vol. 33, 1933), pp. 103–23; and A.A. Popov, 'Materialy po istorii religii Iakutov Viliuiskogo okruga', *Sbornik muzeia antropologii i etnografii* T. 11, 1949), pp. 255–323. For a standard interpretation of shamanism as often harmful hypnotism see N.A. Alekseev, *Shamanizm Tiorkoiazychnykh narodov Sibiri* (Novosibirsk, Nauka, 1984), p. 188. Cf. M.M. Balzer (ed.), *Shamanism: Soviet Studies of Traditional Religion in Siberia and Central Asia* (Armonk, M.E. Sharpe, 1990).

9 See P.A. Oiunsky, *Stikhovoreniia* (Leningrad, Sovetskii pisatel', 1978); *Auymn'ylar* T. 7 (Yakutsk, Sakha sirineekhi kn. izdat., 1962. Collected works). On Oiunsky's life, see V.A. Semenov, *Tvorchestvo P.A. Oiunskogo* (Novosibirsk, Nauka, 1980).

10 On the 1929 law and Soviet anti-religious history, see George Kline, *Religious and Anti-religious Thought in Russia* (Chicago, University of Chicago Press, 1968), pp. 146–71. On the campaign in Siberia, see the journal *Sovetskii sever* for 1930–2; and K.S. Sergeeva, N. Ankudinov and A. Dobriev (eds.), *Shamany obmanshchiki* (Leningrad, Glavsemorput, 1939).

11 I heard several stories about this famed shaman and others who showed extraordinary supernatural strength to avoid or postpone arrest. This Viliuisk shaman predicted her successor would appear in a future generation, and indeed a young woman recently claimed to be her incarnation.

12 I am grateful to this former village Soviet president, T.I. Alekseeva, interviewed in Suntar in 1986. She also described the shaman, Luchunka, and his failure in the 1930s to cure an elderly woman who was 'sick all winter' after his shamanic seance.

13 On Russian Orthodox schools, see 'Svedeniia o Tserkovnykh skholakh

Iakutskoi eparkhii za 1915 god', TsGA IaASSR, f. 226-i, op. 2, d. 8373, 11. 38–9. Compare V.A. Protod'iakonov 'Iakutskaia ASSR v poslevoennyi period' in *Ocherki po istorii Iakutii sovetskogo perioda* (Yakutsk: Yakutsk. kn. izdat., 1957), p. 384, and V.A. Protod'iakonov, 'Iakutiia posle pobedonosnogo zchersheniia velikoi otechestvennoi voiny', in *Sbornik statei po istorii Iakutii sovetskogo perioda* (Yakutsk, Yakutsk. kn. izdat, 1955), p. 148. See also G.P. Basharin, V.N. Gemezov and L.M. Ivanova (eds.), *Kul'turnaia revoliutsiia v Iakutii (1917–1937)* (Yakutsk, Yakutsk. kn. izdat, 1968); V.F. Afanas'ev, *Shkola i razvitie pedagogicheskoi mysli v Iakutii* (Yakutsk, Yakutsk. universitet, 1966); G.G. Makarov, *Obrazovanie Iakutskoi Avtonomnoi Sovetskoi Sotsialisticheskoi Respubliki* (Yakutsk, Yakutsk. kn. izdat., 1957); Frances Cooley, 'National Schools in the Yakutskaya ASSR' in J. Tomiak (ed.), *Soviet Education in the 1980s* (London: Croom Helm, 1983).

14 I discussed Sergei Zverev with several people, including family members. A record was made of his shamanic singing by Melodyia (33 D 030639) 1978, produced and annotated by E. Alekseev, to whom I am indebted for the record and information.

15 I am grateful to the late I.M. Maksimova of Yakutsk, and to D.N. Anisimova, M.D. Efrimova, A.M. Fedorova, E.I. Fillipova, V.I., T.N., and T.R. Isakovy, M.I. Kiprianova, E.V. Nikiforeva, V.K. Pavlova, S.S. Petrova, F.E. Protodyakonova, A.P. Savina, M. Spiridonova, M.N. Timofeeva, of Katchakatse village, for data on family rituals. See Sakha scholar P.A. Sleptsov's, *Traditsionnaia Semia i obriadnost' u Iakutov* (Yakutsk, Yakutsk. kn. izd., 1989); and his 'Genesis kul'ta bogini Aiyysyt u Iakutov' in H.K. Antonov *et al.* (eds.), *Iazyk, mif, kul'tura narodov Sibiri* (Yakutsk, Yakutsk. universitet, 1988), pp. 112–17. Cf. M.M. Balzer, 'Rituals of Gender Identity', *American Anthropologist*, 1981, 83:4, pp. 850–67.

16 The 1991 burial of a close friend, I.M. Maksimova, included direct address to her departing soul, discussion of reincarnation, and Russian Orthodox timing for remembrance. Cf. pre-revolutionary exiles V.F. Troshchansky, *Evoliutsiia chernoi very (shamanstvo) u Yakutov* (Kazan, Uchen. zapiski Kazanskogo universitet, T. 70,kn. 4, 1903); and I.A. Khudiakov, *Kratkoe opisanie Verkhoianskogo okruga* (Leningrad, Nauka, 1969), pp. 291–300. See Sakha ethnographers Kulakovsky, *Nauchnyi trudy* 1979, pp. 59–61, 100–1; N.A. Alekseev, *Traditsionnye religioznye verovaniia Iakutov v XIX-nachale XX v* (Novosibirsk, Nauka, 1975), pp. 119–23; and A.I. Gogolev, *Istoricheskaia etnografiia Iakutov (Voprosy proiskhozhdenia Iakutov)* (Yakutsk, Yakutsk. universitet, 1986), pp. 61–74. See also I.S. Gurvich, *Kul'tura severnykh Iakutov-olenevodov* (Moscow, Nauka, 1977), pp. 139–46.

17 Cf. Christel Lane *The Rites of Rulers* (Cambridge, Cambridge University Press, 1981), pp. 67–88; Christopher Binns, 'The Changing Face of Power: Revolution and Accommodation in the Development of the Soviet Ceremonial System', parts I and II, *Man*, 1979, 14, pp. 585–606, 15, pp. 170–87.

18 I participated in 4 exuberant *yhyak* festivals in 1986 and 1991, and am thankful especially to colleagues and friends V.F. Iakovlev, I. and

L. Alekseev, V. and Z. Ivanov, A. and K. Romanov for guidance on complex multivocal *yhyak* meanings. Cf. I.A. Khudiakov, *Kratkoe opisanie Verkhoianskgo okruga* (Leningrad, Nauka, 1969), pp. 253–69; G.V. Ksenofontov, 'Prazdnichnyi algys na ysyakhe' in S.I. Nikolaev, *et al.*, (eds.), *Sbornik statei i materialov po etnografii narodov Iakutii* (Yakutsk: IIaLI, 1961), pp. 77–82; and A.S. Poriadin, 'Prazdnik yhyakh vtoroi poloviny XIXv', in S.I. Nikolaev, *et al.* (eds.), *Sbornik statei i materialov po etnografii narodov Iakutii* (Yakutsk, IIaLI, 1961), pp. 67–76.

19 Wedding feasts include delicacies such as horse meat kabobs and the slightly alcoholic *Kumys*. As before the revolution, some recent weddings have multiple stages, with rituals at both the bride's and groom's family homes. But parents rarely insist that the major feast be at the groom's home, as was customary when Sakha families were patriarchal and sometimes polygamous. See P.A. Sleptsov, 'Traditsionnye formy braka u Iakutov (XIX-nachalo XXv)' M.K. Pankratova, *et al.* (eds.), *Sem'ia u narodov Severo-vostoka SSSR* (Yakutsk: IIaLI, 1988), pp. 98–105.

20 In 1986, I delved for where the revival of interest in ritual had begun. My speculation centered on two regions (Alekseevsk, now Tatta, and Suntarsk) where pride in traditional culture is renowned, with focus on Suntarsk given its reputation for the best annual *yhyak* festival. But I learned the initial weddings with new *serge* began in the early 1970s among the dachas just outside the republic capital of Yakutsk. Thus the trend was born among Sakha intellectuals, with money to spend, social and kin ties to maintain, and motivation to express their identity in creative ways to each other. In the process, as ramifying numbers of Sakha from various areas attended and enjoyed 'traditional' weddings, the fashion spread back to the regions, where it caught on to varying, still evolving, degrees.

21 The quote is from A. Borisov, a prominent Sakha theatre director, and founder in 1990 of the group *Sakha Omuk* (The Sakha People). Foremost scholar of the *serge* V.F. Iakovlev theorises its roots are in ancient beliefs about sacred trees through which one could communicate with the supernatural. See his 'Yhyakh sergeler', *Eder kommunist*, 12 December 1979; 'Serge', *Eder kommunist*, 23 December 1979; and 'Yakutskie konoviazi', in N.K. Antonov, *et al.* (eds.), *Iazyk, mif, kul'tura narodov Sibiri* (Yakutsk, Yakutsk. universitet, 1988), pp. 161–8.

22 Each of these are examples I have witnessed. The head of the republic writers' union, Safron Danilov, in 1986 mentioned an incident in which a hunting party of Sakha writers fed food to the fire, to the relief of their elderly guide, who did not expect 'city folks' to do this.

23 A participant explained the Eveno-Bytantaiskii region was established by a committee composed of Evens, Russians, and Sakha, 'to resurrect the disappearing language, culture and way of life' of this Verkhoiansk area where Evens live relatively compactly. See D. Bubiakin, 'Mechta Evenov', *Sovetskaia Rossiia* (19 August 1989), p. 1; and V. Shcherban', 'Doshli do ruchki', *Sovetskaia kul'tura* (16 June 1990), p. 2. See also Mikhail Kolesov, 'Ia Even,' *Iakutskii universitet*, (26 November 1987), p. 3; and a publication

representing revival of Even folklore A. Prelovskii, V. Zakharov, and V. Keimetinov, 'Evenskoe skazanie', *Sever*, 1989, 4, pp. 86–95. The Evens numbered 12,523 in the 1979 census, and were 17,199 by 1989, with about 9,000 living in Yakutia. The more southerly Evenks numbered 27,294 in 1979, and 30,163 in 1989. Both have experienced strong 'Yakutisation' and Russification pressures, linguistically, culturally, and demographically.

24 See A. Irving Hallowell, 'Bear Ceremonialism in the Northern Hemisphere,' *American Anthropologist*, 1926, 28, pp. 81–7, 142–75; Boris Chichlo, 'L'Ours Chamane', *Etudes Mongoles*, 1981, 12, pp. 35–112; and B.A. Vasil'ev, 'Medvezhii prazdnik', *Sovetskaia Etnografiia*, 1948, 4, pp. 78–104. See also M.M. Balzer (ed.), *Shamanism: Soviet Studies of Traditional Religion in Siberia and Central Asia* (New York, M.E. Sharpe, 1990).

25 On the Yukagir, see W. Jochelson, *The Yukagir and the Yukaghirized Tungus* (New York: Memoirs of the American Museum of Natural History, Pt. I, 1910, Pt. II–III, 1926), especially pp. 120–215; and V.A. Tugolukov, *Kto vyi, Iukagiry?* (Moscow, Nauka, 1979). On calls for an ecological zone, see the round-table sponsored by A. Shishov, 'Na Perelome', *Sovetskaia kul'tura* (11 February 1989), p. 3; and the Novosibirsk panel discussion 'Rodom s severa', *Sovetskaia Rossiia* (31 March 1989), p. 3. Cf. Z.P. Sokolova, 'Narody severa SSSR: proshloe, nastoiashchee i budushchee', *Sovetskaia etnografiia*, 1990, 6, pp. 17–32.

26 G.N. Kurilov, researcher in the Academy of Sciences Institute of Languages, Literature, and History in Yakutsk, is from a talented Yukagir family of three writers. I heard him speak at a Soviet–Canadian conference in Yakutsk in 1986. See his *Slozhnye imena sushchestvetel'nye v Iukagirskom iazyke* (Yakutsk, Yakutsk. kn. izdat, 1977). See also Z.V. Gogolev, I.S. Gurvich, I.M. Zolatareva, and M. Ia. Zhornitskaia, *Iukagiry (istoriko-etnograficheskii ocherk)*, (Novosibirsk: Nauka, 1975); and N. Graburn and B. Stephen Strong, 'The Decline of the Yukagir' 1, in *Circumpolar Peoples: An Anthropological Perspective* (Pacific Palisades, Goodyear, 1973), pp. 38–49.

27 See E. Tseitlin, 'Iakutskie eskizy', *Druzhba narodov*, 1988, 7, pp. 247–51 on recent Yukagir village life.

28 Two of the best scholars of Siberian shamanism have worked with the Evenk (Tungus): S. Shirokogoroff, *The Psychomental Complex of the Tungus* (London, Kegan Paul, Trench, Trubner, 1935); and A.F. Anisimov, *Religiia Evenkov* (Moscow, Nauka, 1958). Cf. the Evenk writer G. Keptuke (Varlamova) *Imeiushchaia svoe imia, Dzheltula-reka* (Yakutsk, Yakutsk kn. izd., 1989), and *Evenkiiskie geroicheskie skazaniia* told by N.G. Trofimov (Novosibirsk, Nauka, 1990, with record). See also A.F. Anisimov, 'The Shaman's Tent of the Evenks', in H. Michael (ed.), *Studies in Siberian Shamanism*, (Toronto, *Anthropology of the North*, 1963, IV), pp. 84–133; and M. Nowak and S. Durrant, *The Tale of the Nišan Shamaness* (Seattle, University of Washington, 1977), pp. 3–38. For a different interpretation of the origin of the word 'shaman' see R. Austerlitz, 'Shaman', *Ural–Altaic Yearbook* 1986, 58, pp. 143–4.

29 S. Shirokogoroff, *The Psychomental Complex of the Tungus*, e.g. pp. 259, 268; 'What is Shamanism?' *China Journal of Science and Arts*, 1924, 2, pp. 275–371.

30 In 1991, this Evenk shamaness asked the film makers to return. I learned about her in Moscow and Yakutsk, in 1986, from the film makers and others. A 1982 version of the film, titled 'Time of Dreams: Siberian Shamanism', by A. Slapinsh, Director, Riga Film Studia, Latvia (tragically killed in 1991) with E. Alekseev and E. Novik, is in Smithsonian Institution archives.

31 I am grateful to V. Shadrin for data on religion in Yakutia.

32 Alitet Nemtushkin 'Vasha pozitsiia?', *Komsomol'skaia Pravda*, 17 June 1988, p. 1.

33 Alitet Nemtushkin, 'Stoit li mnozhit' oshibki?', *Sotsialisticheskaia industriia*, 28 June 1988, p. 4.

34 Improved sensitivity to the cultural and economic needs of the Even, Evenk, and Yukagir is manifest through their Yakutia branch of the Association of the Peoples of the North; in a new division for them in the Institute of Languages, Literature, and History; and at the Museum of Music and Folklore of the Peoples of Yakutia, founded by ethnomusicologist Aiza P. Reshetnikova. See also P.A. Sleptsov's discussion of northern minorities in *Sovetskaia Rossiia*, 24 June 1989, p. 3.

35 I am grateful to V. Kondakov and two other *oiuun* who prefer western anonymity. See N. Senkina, 'V.A. Kondakov: tselitel' – lish' posrednik mezhdu vysshimi silami i liud'mi', *Molodezh Iakutii* (14 March 1991), p. 5. Re-evaluations of shamanism were evident in many conversations. See A.I. Gogolev, *Istoricheskaia etnografiia Iakutov: Narodnye znaniia, obychnoe pravo* (Yakutsk, Yakutsk. universitet, 1983), pp. 44–73; D.S. Makarov, *Narodnaia mudrost': Znaniia i predstavlenniia* (Yakutsk, Yakutsk. universitet, 1983); A. Mordinov, 'Sakhalarga filosofskai sanaa ufskeehine (The rise of philosophical ideas among the Yakut)', *Khotugu sulus*, 1982, 7, pp. 82–9; 8, pp. 89–101; 11, pp. 80–92. Cf. M.M. Balzer (ed.), *Shamanism*, pp. vii–xviii; M.M. Balzer, 'Doctors or Deceivers?', in L. Romanucci-Ross and L. Tancredi (eds.), *The Anthropology of Medicine* (New York, Praegar, 1983), pp. 54–76.

36 *Sakha Omuk* philosophy and goals are expressed in its journal *Ilin* (Forward), edited by O. Sidorov, and by its leaders A. Borisov and V. Nikolaev. *Kut-Sur* ideals and ideas are explained in the pamphlet *Aiyy yorehe* (God–Spirit–Fate Enlightenment) (Yakutsk, Sakha Keskile, Kut-Sur, 1990) by L. Afanas'ev, A. Romanov, R. Petrov, N. Petrov, and V. Illarionov.

37 Lest some think this story akin to throwing coins in a wishing well, it should be noted that one Sakha friend was embarrassed by the display of what he called naivete and superstition. In 1986 and 1991, I was taken to nine sacred groves where spirit offerings were made.

· 11 ·

The spread of modern cults in the USSR

OXANA ANTIC

The spread of modern cults in the Soviet Union is – in the same way as is the continued existence of the official churches – a convincing proof that the regime did not succeed in extinguishing Soviet people's faith in God. In the face of the extensive system of scientific–atheist propaganda which was systematically conducted in the Soviet Union on a far-reaching scale, the spreading of new religious teachings was a heavy blow to ideological education, since atheist propaganda was one of its most important components. This propaganda was supposed to influence Soviet people from kindergarten to the grave with the aim of freeing them from all 'religious remnants'.[1] To reach this aim, mass persecution of all churches and believers was started immediately after the Bolsheviks came to power in Russia. The official churches – Christian as well as the non-Christian – were subject to heavy persecution, along with the numerous sects which had existed in Tsarist Russia (the Baptists, the Seventh Day Adventists, the Mennonites, the Dukhobors, the Molokans, and others). By the eve of the Second World War, practically all the religious organisations had been destroyed, and the church as an institution had been forced out of public life. Statistics of that time indicate that the Russian Orthodox Church had been reduced to a tiny proportion of its pre-revolutionary strength. The situation of the Russian Orthodox Church and other churches as well changed positively only after Josef Stalin received the hierarchs of the Russian Orthodox Church in September 1943, at the height of combat action, and concluded a kind of concordat with them.[2] About this time, the Jehovah's Witnesses, a US-based religious sect, first came to the Soviet Union. The first Jehovah's Witnesses came following the annexation of the western Ukraine, western parts of Belorussia, the Baltic states, and Moldavia in the 1940s.[3] In spite of the radical persecution of Jehovah's Witnesses, who were not only considered illegal, but also accused of serving the 'foreign enemy, US imperialists', this religious denomination succeeded in surviving and, according to official statistics,[4] still has 378 communities.

About thirty years later, in 1970, another modern cult, the Hare Krishna movement (originally founded in India) arrived in the Soviet Union via the United States. Though the authorities immediately started a campaign against the followers of Hare Krishna, the cult has survived and expanded its ranks. Many other modern cults of eastern origin have also appeared in the Soviet Union, giving the leaders a heavy headache: 'Children of Jesus' walked the streets of Ufa and Irkutsk, the Scientology Church sent its emissaries to the Soviet Union. The 'Children of God' and the 'Family of Love' turned up in Soviet towns; and followers of the painter and philosopher Nikolai Roerich have been reported as sun-bathing in an Altaic village. Soviet press, radio, and television warned in general against the non-traditional religious cults and neo-mysticism, and especially against the leader of the Moonies, the Reverend Sun Myung-Mun. Numerous articles were devoted to exposing the 'black aims' of his 'Unification Church'. Special care was paid to inform Soviet readers about the connection between Reverend Moon and some of the Russian *émigrés*. In an article in the popular journal, *Nedelya*, the political activities of the Moon sect in the United States and France were discussed, as well as its contacts with the *émigré* organisation, Resistance International, headed by Vladimir Bukovsky and Vladimir Maksimov. The Moon organisation, presented as one of the fifty largest private corporations on earth, is supposed to have followers in the Soviet Union. *Nedelya*'s correspondent put it in a veiled fashion: according to him, there was talk among the leaders of the Unification Church that the sect has 'follower-agents' in the Soviet Union and some other socialist countries. But, as the correspondent points out, that fact was not advertised.[5]

Indeed, this could be the explanation why the Soviet media attacked the Reverend Sun Myung-Mun regularly for decades. In a Soviet television programme, the Reverend was presented as 'a prominent figure of the new Christianity', who preaches that there will be no communism in the future of mankind.[6] Soviet media even used Chinese anti-Moon propaganda, which was far more outspoken. In an article in the newspaper, *Tonyir Sinbo*, for example, Reverend Moon is called a 'beggar', who invented a 'black plan' to avoid work and so created a new church. Now, according to the article, the history of the movement is covered by blood and crime.[7]

The growing interest of the youth in eastern religions gave the authorities cause for serious concern, since this phenomenon signaled not merely the failure of the atheist propaganda, but also the general crisis of the spiritual world of Soviet reality. The vacuum created by the totalitarian Marxist–Leninist ideology, which claimed to know the answers to all the questions, became obvious in an alarming way, since *glasnost* and *perestroika* made it possible for publicists, writers, and journalists to study the spiritual world of young people more objectively. Dozens of articles warning against the 'infatuation of the youth with eastern religions' and describing 'the negative effects of religious cults and neo-mysticism upon the mental health and the life in general of young people are regularly published in the Soviet press. The names of the newspapers show how far the spread of modern cults has advanced in the Soviet Union: *Sovetskaya Belorussiya* attacked followers of modern cults in Belorussia, *Pravda Ukrainy*, *Sovetskaya Estoniya*, *Moskovskii Komsomolets*, *Sovetskaya Kirgiziya*, and *Pravda Vostoka*, appearing respectively in Ukraine, Estonia, Russia (Moscow), Kirghizia, and Uzbekistan, participated in the campaign against religious cults and their followers. The leading atheist journal *Nauka i religiya* dedicated a series of eleven articles in 1983–5 to the story of 'Scientology' and its founder, Lafayette Ron Hubbard.[8] Philosophers, writers, and publicists strongly decry the increase of interest in astrology, spiritualism, yoga, extrasensory perception, parapsychology, telepathy. The criticism of the modern cults in the mass media had frequently a political coloring: Radio Moscow said in a programme in summer 1987, that 'not only Radio Liberty/Radio Free Europe but also the Voice of America and the BBC have activated the propaganda of ideas concerning liberty of religion in the Soviet Union. Thereby, these radio stations allegedly advertise not only the traditional religions, but also various sects, now fashionable in the West, radical religious groupings, which propagate hate of life and radical anti-Communism.'[9] The press also published, on a regular basis, letters by the parents of young people under the influence of modern cults. All of these stories were very tragic: the parents described the negative changes which took place in their children after they got interested in a religious teaching – be it Hare Krishna or a 'starets' from a small village, a Russian guru.

A round table talk between two scientists – Vladimir Kornev, a senior scientific employee of the Institute for Oriental Studies of the Academy of Sciences of the USSR, and Evgeni Balagushkin, a senior scientific employee of the Institute of Philosophy of the Academy of Sciences of the USSR – showed the search of Soviet authorities responsible for ideological education of the Soviet people, for the reasons why some young people in the USSR tried to escape from life. The question these two experts discussed had essential meaning: is the current religious revival a 'renaissance of the faith' or a 'change of idols'?

The participants of the discussion mentioned the fact that the revival and rapid development of young people's interest in religion was, to a large extent, a reaction to the negation of religion by official atheism, the argumentless destruction of the objects of criticism which ranges from the physical destruction of churches to categorical accusations of religious writers and philosophers to be ignorant and obscurant. Such open admission of serious mistakes in ideological education was rare even in the days of *glasnost* in the press. 'As a result', *Komsomolets Tadzhikistana* commented, 'a distorted acceptance of religions takes places'. That, according to the Tadzhik paper, was the reason why eastern and European mysticism was spreading in the Soviet Union, with more than 100 such groups functioning in Moscow alone.[10] The hippie worldview, deeply penetrated by religious and occult/mystical elements, is symbiotically related to this phenomenon.

A. Fain, a senior teacher of the Higher Trade Union School of Culture, describes the history of Soviet hippies. According to his research, the 'flower children', who turned up in Moscow, Leningrad, and the capitals of the Baltic republics as early as the beginning of the 1960s, were the forerunners of today's hippies. The latter now constitute a kind of movement, which has produced a 'manifesto' along with other documents. Fain underlines that Soviet hippies, by contrast with hippies in the West, categorically reject the use of narcotics. Not only in the 'manifesto', but also in a number of other programmatic documents, Soviet hippies have rejected drugs as being dangerous and compromising.

This serious and surprisingly objective article analyses the ideals of the hippies, their use of psychological measures borrowed from non-confessional religions, mostly of eastern origin. Fain stresses the creativity of hippies by stating that they created, and continue to create, a great number of works of art in various fields: poetry, prose, music, painting, theatre, photography. He writes that he knows at least ten hand-written journals regularly published in various cities, which contain poetry, literature, and plays, of doubtless value.[11]

There have been articles which testify to the spread of the 'Children of God' to the USSR. In January 1988, for example, *Komsomol'skaya Pravda* reported that emissaries of that cult, from abroad, were trying to influence Soviet young people, and criticised converts in Moscow.[12] David Berg, the US leader of the Children of God, was described as a totally amoral man, and his teachings, as an exhortation to young people to free love, unnatural love, and prostitution. Adherents, in

Moscow, of the Children of God were accused of parasitism, refusal to serve in the Soviet army, and other crimes.[13]

Other articles criticised *stilyagi* (latterday zootsuiters), jazz musicians (*labukhs*, in Russian slang), beatnicks, punks, rockers, adherents of heavy metal, practitioners of yoga, Hare Krishnas, etc., betraying the fact that, for some Soviet writers, there was little difference between adherence to a religious cult and immersion in the rock scene.[14]

However, under the influence of *glasnost*, the Soviet readers began to reject the official propaganda and to ask for objective information. A reader of the series 'Scientific Atheism' from Kiev complained in his letter to the editor that, in spite of the fact that 'many of our journals and newspapers' were now writing about the 'International Society of Krishna Consciousness', he found it impossible to learn the truth about this teaching since these publications contradict each other and do not seem very convincing. The reader objected to the fact that most of these publications stressed only the negative sides of the Hare Krishna teaching, and suggested that a serious work should be written about this movement.[15] This letter showed that some of the Soviet anti-religious propaganda not only fell on stony ground, but that the people were not afraid any longer to protest against brain-washing of that sort.

Gorbachev's policy of *glasnost* and *perestroika* doubtless facilitated the spread of unofficial religious bodies and groupings. Since the authorities could not apply any longer the so-called 'administrative methods' – oppression and persecution – to check them effectively, other ways had to be found. The journal *Nauka i Religiya* seemed to give an answer to the question, in which way did the Soviet authorities plan to deal with all those who were interested in eastern teachings? The journal, which was the most aggressively atheist journal since its beginning in September 1959, recently started to publish neutral and objective information on religion. The September 1988 issue was devoted to a large degree to problems of eastern religions. There is an article on Tibetan medicine, its history and prospects, written in objective and informative style, followed by an essay 'Kung Fu: The Truth Behind the Myth'. Under the column: 'Encyclopedia of *Nauka i Religiya*', there is information on 'Buddha's Tooth. Vajra', but the most intriguing story ('The Smile of the Immortal Old Man') deals with the mummified corpse of a Vietnamese Buddhist monk who died 300 years ago during meditation. The Soviet journalist, who visited the temple where the mummy reposed, wrote an article full of understanding for Buddhist teachings. The author was obviously deeply impressed by the meeting with the mummy, and described enthusiastically that it was not prepared in the same way as old Egyptian mummies had been, and would not decay in the hot and humid climate of Indonesia.[16]

In November 1988, *Nauka i Religiya* reported triumphantly about a festive formation of the 'Vivekananda' Society for the Study of Indian Culture in the Soviet Union. The meeting took place in the House of Friendship with the Peoples of Foreign Countries (in Moscow). Svami Lokeshvarananda, present at this event, was described by *Nauka i Religiya* as one of the leading religious figures in India and a follower of the important religious movement, Mission of Ramakrishna. Lokesh-varananda's interview with *Nauka i Religiya* occupied four pages in what used to be the leading atheist journal of the Soviet Union.[17] The next issue of the same journal featured a scientific article on the art of yoga breathing exercises (with illustrations), written by Soviet academician Boris Smirnov.[18]

The situation of the followers of the modern cults remained abnormal in the Soviet Union: Hare Krishna meetings were systematically disturbed 1988–90, although the mass persecution of believers ceased. Suppressed and persecuted for dozens of years, some of these religious groups may, now that they can expect to gain more freedom, play an important role in the religious life of the Soviet Union.

Jehovah's Witnesses

As already mentioned, the Jehovah's Witness movement, which originated in the United States in the late nineteenth century, took roots in the Soviet Union following the annexation of the western areas of the Ukraine, Belorussia, the Baltic states, and Moldavia in the 1940s. Since then, the movement has spread to many other parts of the USSR. According to reports of Jehovah's Witnesses' activities that appeared in the Soviet press, the main centres of the movement are in Belorussia, Moldavia, Zakarpatskaya Oblast, and the Ukraine, but in search of remote areas where they hoped they might face less persecution, groups of Jehovah's Witnesses have also settled in the Far East and in Kirghizia, and may also be found in Transcarpathia and Kazakhstan.

The Soviet press constantly accused Jehovah's Witnesses of subservience to orders and instructions emanating from the movement's headquarters in Brooklyn, which, it claimed, was engaging in a crusade against the socialist countries, trying to discredit Marxism–Leninism, and conducting active anti-communist propaganda. It was charged that the 'apoliticism' of the Jehovah's Witness publications, *Watchtower* and *Awake!* was in fact a specific political line serving the forces of reaction and harming the cause of peace and freedom of peoples. The main indictment was, however, that 'the authors of Jehovist tracts' incite Soviet citizens to disregard their civic obligations, in particular to refuse to serve in the ranks of the Soviet Army, and to commit other 'punishable offences'.

From time to time, republican newspapers published accounts of trials of Jehovah's Witnesses. One such report appeared in 1982 in *Sovetskaya Kirgiziya*.[19] A truck driver, Vladimir Zhitnikov, had been stopped by the police for 'committing a serious traffic violation'. In the truck the police found several hundred copies of *From the Lost to the Regained Paradise*, a book printed in Brooklyn, and some zinc printing plates not on open sale in the USSR. The account stated that Zhitnikov was charged under Article 217 of the Kirghiz Criminal Code, which prescribed the penalties for 'acquisition or sale of property known to have been criminally obtained'. The sentence he received was not mentioned.[20]

Jehovah's Witnesses in the Soviet Union refused to register with the authorities as a religious group and were subjected, as an illegal association, to especially severe persecution. It was claimed in the Soviet press that the Jehovah's Witnesses were free to register their association and 'satisfy their religious needs in complete accordance with Soviet law'. This was reiterated by a people's court in the town of Torez in Donetsk Oblast at the trial of five leaders of communities of Jehovah's Witnesses in January 1983, all of whom were sentenced to five years in confinement.[21] But the Jehovah's Witnesses, like many other illegal religious communities in the Soviet Union, long considered that it would be a betrayal of their faith even to register legally with what remains an atheist state. The trial of the five Jehovah's Witnesses in Torez in 1983 was accompanied by a strident campaign in the press. A special correspondent of *Pravda Ukrainy* provided reports from the courtroom three days in a row, and the *Argumenty i fakty* bulletin of the 'Znanie' Society also published his article about the trial.[22]

In early 1985, western news agencies reported that a group of eight Jehovah's Witnesses had been brought to trial in Khabarovsk and sentenced to terms of between four and five years in either ordinary or strict-regime camps. The court also ordered that the property of one of the defendants be confiscated. The eight had been arrested in late autumn 1984. It was also reported that seven other Jehovah's Witnesses had been arrested in Kuibyshev, Moscow, and Leningrad. At least seven Jehovah's Witnesses were sentenced in 1984. In 1985, the aggressive press campaign against the religious movement continued. One of such articles, entitled 'Retribution', and intended primarily, it must be assumed, for women readers, described how the four children of a woman who belonged to a community of Jehovah's Witnesses left her, one after the other, to go to their father.[23] Another, entitled 'Self-Styled Prophets', contained the standard charges about the dependence of Jehovah's Witnesses on their American headquarters, and the 'anti-state and anti-social attitudes of the extremist leaders of the sect', but also revealed some details of activities that are rarely publicised in the press. Among other things, it described a pamphlet entitled *Tidings (Terrible and Joyful) to All Kingdoms, Peoples, and Tribes from the God of the Holy Prophets*, made out of 'pages from an ordinary notebook, carefully stitched with white thread'. In fact, this is a reproduction of a pamphlet originally published in 1890, and it would seem hard to believe it would contain anti-Soviet propaganda. N. Sidirov, the author of the article, describes how Jehovah's Witnesses drop copies of this hand-made pamphlet into mailboxes:

These underground agitators are forced to grope their way around other people's backyards in the dead of night, with dogs barking at them, always on the lookout, to drop their 'tidings' into other people's mailboxes.[24]

But the campaign lost energy as the process of restructuring relations between state and church gathered speed. In October 1989, *perestroika* bore fruit on the official level: TASS reported that the leader of the European part of Brooklyn Centre, Willi Pohl, had arrived in the USSR on the invitation of the Council of Religious Affairs. He spent three days in Kazakhstan, investigating the life of the Jehovah's Witnesses there. In an interesting departure, Pohl said that the organisation now considered legal registration with the Soviet authorities to be necessary. After his meeting with representatives of the Council for Religious Affairs, Pohl said that the question of building prayer houses was now under discussion.[25] The official visit of a high-ranking representative of the Jehovah's Witnesses to the Soviet Union must be considered to have been a sign that the Soviet authorities were ready to grant full legal rights to what had been one of the most suppressed and persecuted religious denominations. With the collapse of the Soviet Union at the end of 1991, the Jehovah's Witnesses suddenly found themselves, like other citizens, in entirely new political circumstances.

The Hare Krishna movement in the Soviet Union

Among some of the modern cults which reached the Soviet Union via the West, the Hare Krishna movement occupies a very special and most prominent place. Soviet Hare Krishnas grew in number in spite of the systematic persecution to which they were subjected. In the late 1980s, they made efforts to defend their rights and to develop religious activities in public places. In Moscow and Kiev young Krishnas sang and prayed in the streets in 1989[26] and several groups of Hare Krishnas visited editorial offices of newspapers to talk to the journalists and to complain about what they called false and slanderous reports written by these journalists.[27] Hare Krishna teachings have attracted, as a rule, young and educated Soviet specialists, members of the technical intelligentsia class. The Soviet regime considered Hare Krishna devotees to be ideological enemies, and developed an extensive and scrupulous campaign of harassment against them. Hare Krishna followers were arrested and sentenced to long prison terms, their houses were searched, their property confiscated. Some of them were confined to psychiatric hospitals, some were tortured. Two young Hare Krishna devotees died in confinement.

The persecution of Hare Krishnas until spring 1988 was accompanied by a vigorous campaign of the Soviet press. A number of important central newspapers, including *Literaturnaya Gazeta*, *Sovetskaya Kul'tura*, and *Komosomol'skaya Pravda*, regularly published highly negative articles about this religious teaching and its 'demoralizing effect upon young people'. Followers of Hare Krishna were described in these articles as young, intelligent, and kind people who had become, under the influence of Hare Krishna teaching, rude to their parents, asocial, lazy, and mentally disturbed. The republican newspapers – *Sovetskaya Estonia*, *Sovetskaya Kirgiziya*, *Pravda Ukrainy*, *Komsomol'skaya znamya Ukraina* – reported over the years about trials of Hare Krishna followers which took place in their republics. The young people in the defendant's dock were usually described either as hard boiled criminals or as sentimental young people, with illusions, who had been led astray. Numerous articles were published in the form of letters written by the parents of Hare Krishnas, who complained about the tragic changes in the lives of their children since they had become interested in this movement. Efforts were made to ridicule some aspects of the teaching by describing how Hare Krishnas recited the mantra 1,728 times a day, or how Soviet Hare Krishnas had washed the 'lotus-like' feet of a guru from the United States and then had drunk the water, believing that it would 'enlighten' them.[28] Hare

Krishna communities were accused of trying 'to poison young minds', 'to nurture passivity', and to encourage 'a negative attitude to reality'. Some of the anti-Hare Krishna articles explained that those who fell under the Krishna spell could not return to their normal lives without psychiatric treatment. In view of the fact that Soviet authorities were using special psychiatric hospitals for the confinement of religious and political dissenters, this threat was a very serious one.

A special place in the anti-Krishna propaganda campaign in the press was occupied by accusations that Hare Krishna followers were under the influence of western anti-Soviet clerical organisations and the CIA. In an article 'When the ratio is asleep' with the sub-title: 'New forms of clerical diversions of imperialism', the author, a candidate of philosophical sciences, explained that in the West hundreds of organisations and centres undertake great efforts to create the impression that there is a 'religious opposition' in the Soviet Union. A 'psychological warfare' was being waged against the Soviet Union by imperialist powers for this purpose. The imperialist reaction was using the teaching of Krishnaism in this 'psychological warfare', continued the author. He depicted the Hare Krishna movement as an anti-Soviet, anti-social sect.[29] Representatives of the Hare Krishna movement rejected the accusations of anti-Sovietism. 'They also charge us with being agents of the CIA', said a Krishna follower, Alexander Gromov at the first press conference of the Hare Krishnas in Moscow in April 1982. 'All these charges are false. We don't do anything against the law and we are not afraid of anyone.'[30]

The first Hare Krishna group was founded in Moscow in 1971 by Anatoli Pinyayev, a technician. Born 13 May 1941, he has a tragic biography. He has been persecuted since he met the spiritual leader of the Hare Krishna movement, Bhaktivedanta Swami Prabhupada in 1971. Prabhupada was invited for a visit to the Soviet Union by the Moscow Academy of Sciences.[31] He had several talks with representatives of the Academy and officials dealing with religious problems, and made efforts to explain the value of the Hare Krishna teachings and the common principles it shares with Soviet ideology: refusal of alcohol, negative attitude to consumers' mentality, strict moral behaviour . . . But for obvious reasons his efforts to establish some contacts with the Soviet authorities failed. He met, however, some young men, and one of them, Anatoli Pinyayev, became his devoted follower. For ten years he travelled through the Soviet Union, spreading the teachings of Hare Krishna. During these years he was hospitalised seven times in psychiatric hospitals for short periods of time. In April 1982 Pinyayev was arrested, but he escaped in May 1982 and was able to hide until May 1983, when he was rearrested. Pinyayev was tried on 7 June 1983 and found guilty of 'infringement upon the person and rights of citizens in the guise of performing religious rites' under Article 227 of the Criminal Code of RSFSR, which was applied to Hare Krishna followers. The court found Anatoli Pinyayev to be mentally ill and – instead of sentencing him to a prison-term – decided to confine him to a special psychiatric hospital for an indefinite period of time. Pinyayev was reportedly treated with neuroleptic drugs in a psychiatric hospital in Smolensk. In 1986 he was moved to a hospital of the same kind in Oryol.[32] Dozens of Hare Krishna followers were confined by court rulings to forced 'hospitalisation' in psychiatric hospitals. The press in turn portrayed the religion as a kind of mental illness which must be cured in a psychiatric hospital, since those involved could not, allegedly, return to their former normal life without such help.[33]

The fact that this movement spread in a relatively short time to various parts of the Soviet Union, with Hare Krishna groups forming not only in the Russian Republic, but also in Armenia, Kirghizia, the Ukraine, and the Baltic Republics, and that it attracted young and educated people is certainly the reason why the Soviet authorities used such brutal force against the sect. Not only did adherents receive, as a rule, long prison terms, but they starved in prisons, since they were refused vegetarian food and were not permitted to receive money and parcels sent by relatives and friends. Some of the prisoners developed serious diseases like tuberculosis as a result of malnutrition.

The arrest of the Hare Krishnas on a large scale started in 1982. The article 'The Yogi with Blue Eyes, or The True Face of Krishna Preachers', published in *Sotsialisticheskaya Industriya* in January 1982 served as a sort of signal for the start of the persecution campaign. The article contained attacks against the Krishna group which sprang up in the Palace of Culture in Krasnoyarsk and its leader, Evgeni Tretyakov. Ten Krishna followers from the group were named in the article, most of them engineers from the same town, but also Anatoli Pinyayev from Moscow, who was accused of having influenced Evgeni Tretyakov to become a follower of the Krishna movement. The article ended with the statement that Tretyakov had been sentenced for 'parasitism', which would mean a prison term of up to one year.[34] In April 1982, Candidate of Physical and Mathematical Sciences, Vladimir Kritski, and an architect, Sergei Kurkin, were arrested in Moscow. A series of house searches was carried out in Moscow in connection with this arrest. The Kalinin District Court in Moscow heard the case of Kritski and Kurkin from 2 to 7 December 1982, and simultaneously tried Anatoli Pinyayev *in absentia*, since he was in hiding after having escaped in May 1982 from Psychiatric Hospital No. 5, where he had been sent for examination. The accused were found guilty under Article 227 of the Criminal Code of the RSFSR. Kritski was sentenced to four years in labour camps and confiscation of property, and Kurkin to two-and-a-half years in camps. At the trial, the court also announced a private ruling to bring proceedings against Alexander Korablev from Moscow and five other Krishna followers.[35]

In the second half of 1984, Kritski was released conditionally, with the obligatory induction to labour, and sent to work on a construction site. There, however, he was rearrested and charged with the same article of the Criminal Code as before. Kritski was sentenced to five years in a strict regime camp in conjunction with the remainder of his first uncompleted sentence, which meant about six years in camps.[36]

Other trials followed. The Krishna group in Sverdlovsk was liquidated; its leader, Valeriya Sukhova, a physiotherapist, was sentenced under Article 227 to four years in general regime camps. Two teachers at the Sverdlovsk Pedagogical and Polytechnical Institute and several students received an official 'warning' about their liability under Article 190 of the Criminal Code of the RSFSR (Dissemination of Knowingly False Fabrications Discrediting the Soviet State and Social System).[37] The arrests and trials continued after the new leader, Mikhail Gorbachev, came to power. In 1985 six arrests of Hare Krishnas took place, in 1986 this figure doubled: twelve arrests were reported, and, at the end of 1986 – thirty-four Hare Krishnas were in prisons, camps, and psychiatric hospitals.[38] But in 1987 some positive changes took place. No arrests of Hare Krishnas were reported. Representatives of the movement started efforts to defend their rights. In spring 1987 three letters, signed only 'Soviet believers of the Hare Krishna movement' went to General Secretary Mikhail Gorbachev, the participants of the Vienna CSCE Review Conference, and academician Andrei Sakharov.[39] In the letters, the difficulties faced by the members of the movement over the past seven years were described. In the letter to Gorbachev, the Hare Krishna followers explained the ancient nature of the teaching and described the various methods of persecution applied to members of the sect in the Soviet Union. They denied the accusation that Hare Krishna followers were encouraging Soviet citizens to refuse to take part in activities for the benefit of the society, and that the Hare Krishna movement in the Soviet Union was initiated and controlled by the CIA. The authors of the letter appealed to Gorbachev to end the persecution campaign and to allow them to confess their faith freely. If that would not be possible, the Hare

Krishna followers said they were willing to emigrate to countries
where they can live according to their religious convictions.

In the letter to the Vienna conference, the Hare Krishnas repeated
the history of their movement in more detail. They also mentioned the
sustained efforts by the authorities to force the Hare Krishna
adherents to recant and to condemn 'foreign intervention' in their
support. The participants of the conference were asked to support the
Hare Krishnas' appeal to the Secretary General and to help the dozens
of prisoners who had been deprived of their freedom, and of all their
rights, for their desire to live according to their faith. In the letter to
Andrei Sakharov, the Hare Krishna believers expressed their joy at his
release from exile in Gorky, reported to him about the sufferings of the
members of their religious movement, and asked him to support their
appeal to Gorbachev and to the Vienna Conference.

Six members of the movement travelled in April 1987 from all parts
of the country to Moscow to hold the first Hare Krishna conference.
Representatives from Moscow, Leningrad, the Ukraine, the Baltic
Republics, and the North Caucasus met in what a western press
correspondent described as 'a cramped apartment on the outskirts of
Moscow'. A statement was signed by forty-six Hare Krishnas and
addressed to 'all the religious and non-religious world organisations to
please support us in getting a legal position'.[40] The conference was
characteristic of the changes in the political atmosphere in the Soviet
Union. On the one hand, the fact that this conference could take place
was a positive result, because up to then the Hare Krishna devotees
had been reluctant to talk to western correspondents. On the other
hand, it was revealed during the conference that, despite the general
relaxation toward religious practice, the authorities continued to har-
rass Hare Krishna followers and refused their requests for official
registration.

In May 1987, reports about the first releases of imprisoned Hare
Krishna followers reached the West. In 1986, Yevgeni Lerner was
released from camp after having written a letter to the newspaper
Izvestiya, expressing repentance. At the end of March 1987, Armen
Sarkisyan was released from a regular psychiatric hospital in the city of
Erevan.[41] But, in the middle of June 1987, at least a dozen Hare
Krishnas were detained by militia men as they sang prayers at an
outdoor shopping mall. According to eyewitnesses, twelve to fifteen
young people from the Hare Krishna movement were taken away in a
van. A peaceful demonstration of activists of the Hare Krishna move-
ment in the centre of Moscow was broken up by militia in August.
Western correspondents reported that about eighty people had parti-

cipated in the demonstration, which had been under way for only a few minutes before the militia moved in and dragged about twenty young people onto a militia van. The demonstrators were demanding official recognition of the Hare Krishna movement as a religious group.[42]

Two months earlier, in June 1987, a group of Hare Krishna devotees in Riga had been refused registration as a legally recognised religious community. The plenipotentiary for religious affairs of the Latvian Council of Ministers told Hare Krishna representatives that their community 'contains non-religious features'.[43] In December 1987 two important events took place, both typical of the difficult situation of unofficial religious communities in the Soviet Union: Sarkis Ogadzhanvan, twenty-three years old, arrested in January 1986 in Armenia for his participation in the Hare Krishna movement, died in prison only a few weeks before his expected release. Malnutrition, and tuberculosis resulting from it, might have caused his death. His vegetarian diet allowed him to eat only bread in camp and the authorities in Sol-Iletsky, near Orenburg, where he served his sentence, refused to give him parcels of vegetarian food and the money relatives and friends sent to him. Another Hare Krishna follower, also an Armenian, Martik Zhamkochyan, died in November 1986 in a psychiatric hospital in Erevan, after forcible treatment with drugs and force feeding. But the initiator of the movement, Anatoli Pinyayev, was released from the psychiatric hospital after he had spent three-and-a-half years there.[44]

In the West, remarkable efforts were made to support the cause of the Hare Krishnas in the Soviet Union. For years representatives of various religious and human rights organisations staged demonstrations and appealed to the Soviet government to stop the persecution of the Hare Krishnas. At a demonstration for their sake on United Nations Day, 26 October 1986, hundreds of people were participating in a procession in the streets of Stockholm, carrying torches, banners, placards, and flags. They were chanting and playing religious music. On the banners were the words: 'Free the Soviet Hare Krishnas' in English, Russian, and Swedish. A solemn ceremony was held, at which flowers were offered on an altar on behalf of the thirty Hare Krishna followers, prisoners in the Soviet Union. The names, biographies, and circumstances of individual persecutions were read aloud. The demonstrators appealed to Mikhail Gorbachev to intervene and to ensure that the human rights of Hare Krishna followers be respected. Similar demonstrations took place in various West European cities in 1987: in London, Paris, and Stockholm, people demanded freedom for Soviet Hare Krishnas.[45]

By the end of the 1980s, it appeared that the sufferings and the moral integrity of the Hare Krishna devotees had borne fruit. In June 1988, the sensational news reached the West that the Hare Krishna group in Moscow had been registered, on 20 May 1988, as an officially recognised religious community. Though this move of the Soviet authorities was doubtless a great change, the speaker of the movement expressed his concern about the fact that the registration covered only the Moscow group, and that six Hare Krishna followers were still in jail.[46] As if to confirm that that concern was not without some basis, a Ukrainian newspaper published an aggressive attack on the Soviet Hare Krishnas (in June 1988), covering four pages. All the old accusations against the movement were repeated: Hare Krishna faith was teaching asocial behaviour, parasitism, spiritual self-isolation, etc. American leaders of the movement were described as totally amoral people, whose 'earthly deeds' and 'all their teachings' were soaked by hypocrisy and falseness.[47] This article could certainly be just an automatic continuation of the old Hare Krishna campaign in the press, but it could also be interpreted more specifically as a demonstration that the authorities had not changed their attitude toward this religious group.

The following events support this theory. In summer 1988, several *kirtans* (a *kirtan* is an outdoor singing of spiritual songs) were broken up. On 2 July 1988, a *kirtan* was broken up in a park in Tbilisi (Georgia). The same day, Krishnaites were holding a *kirtan* at the Bolshoi Theatre in Moscow. Police asked them to move on and they went to Pushkin Square. At 8:00 p.m. a *kirtan* began at the 'Smolenskaya' metro station. The militia asked the participants to stop. Seven people were detained and taken to the police station. On 6 July 1988, the flat of a Krishnaite believer, Gocha Chigvadze, in Tbilisi was raided by militia men and the Krishna followers assembled there were taken to the police station. In July 1988 three Krishnaites were detained on the beach in Riga while they were holding a *kirtan*. They were taken to a militia station, where Krishna follower Valentin Yaroshchuk came to help. He was searched, beaten, and locked in a cell. But, in several towns, Hare Krishna followers have held *kirtans* without any official objection: in Dnepropetrovsk, Moscow, Vilnius (Lithuania), and also in Sukhumi (Abkhaz ASSR) and in Riga (Latvia).[48] The last three Krishnaites were released from prison in winter 1988–89.[49]

In early 1989, a group of Soviet Krishnaites was permitted to travel abroad. That was the first such occasion in the history of Soviet Krishnaites. A group of 59 followers of Krishna from the USSR went to India for several weeks. 'Thank you Gorbachev, thank you *glasnost*' read a banner carried by the group as they marched through the streets of Calcutta on 22 February 1989. At a press conference, the group members (49 men and 10 women) said that the International Society for Krishna Consciousness had been virtually banned in the Soviet Union until 1988. The speaker of the group, Olga Kiseleva, a Moscow teacher, said that there were then about 450 initiated Krishna devotees in the Soviet Union, and at least 10,000 Hare Krishna followers. Upon returning home, the group was welcomed by the press and once again lauded the process of *perestroika*: Sergei Zuev, chairman of the Moscow Krishnaite Council, when asked about his impressions of the trip to India, stressed the friendly reception there, and the fact that this pilgrimage was only possible because of *perestroika*.[50]

Perestroika has, indeed, changed the political climate in the Soviet Union in such a manner that now voices are raised in the press, defending the Hare Krishna movement. The most stirring example of this development was the comment of a deputy department head of the Council for Religious Affairs, Yevgeni Chenetsov. He criticised a recent television programme entitled 'Warning', which, as he pointed out, mendaciously depicted Hare Krishnaites as linked to narcotics, weapons, criminal circles, etc. Chenetsov remarked bitingly that the Soviet journalists were inclined to present the problem of Hare Krishnaites in the Soviet Union in a sensationalist way, adorned with 'cheap revelations'. He wrote that the Council for Religious Affairs had examined Hare Krishna literature and how they practised their faith, and had found that many aspects of their teaching had been portrayed in an exaggerated or distorted way. Their prayers take up between one-and-a-half and two hours daily, their moral code forbids premarital sex and abortion, they abstain from all stimulants, and their food is not meagre or monotonous. Chenetsov ended his article by criticising the television programme on the Krishna Society as unobjective and superficial, and reminded the readers that Krishna devotees enjoy the constitutional right to religious freedom.[51]

In the wake of *glasnost*, Krishna devotees occupied a notable place in the Soviet press. The chair of the Moscow community, Sergei Zuev gave interviews to press organisations in spring 1989. He discussed the organisation of the Moscow community, which is the largest of the Soviet Krishna groups. It is headed by a three-man council which is elected at a general meeting. The council controls the observance of the chapter, protects the cult property, and takes responsibility for the budget. There is also an auditing commission, supervising all financial activities. And a publishing and international department is also in the making. The Moscow community now issues an information bulletin, *Skayatanya world.*[52]

The Krishnaites in Moscow asked the authorities for a prayer-house, but subsequently turned down several suggestions made by the Council for Religious Affairs. In April 1989, they agreed to take the building of a former school. 'This decision,' Zuev said, 'reflects in the same way as the official registration of the Krishna Society those changes in the relations of church and state which have taken place in the course of the democratisation of the country. That is the human-isation of all sides of Soviet society.'[53]

Conclusion

The Hare Krishnas and other sects in the former USSR will share the fate of other believers as the diverse peoples and regions struggle to cope with mounting social, political, and economic chaos. Despite the new religious freedom, it is conceivable that groups such as the Hare Krishna Society will never enjoy anything like the prerogatives avail-able to the Russian Orthodox Church. Culturally and socially, these groups remained on the margins of post-Soviet society.

Notes

1 Oxana Antic, 'The Promotion of Atheism in the Soviet Union Today', *Radio Liberty Research* (8 November 1977).
2 Oxana Antic, '40th Anniversary of Stalin's Meeting with Hierarchs of the Russian Orthodox Church', *Radio Liberty Research* (2 September 1983).
3 Trevor Beson, *Discretion and Valour: Religious Conditions in Russia and Eastern Europe.* Rev. edn (Philadelphia, Fortress Press, 1982), p. 97.
4 Konstantin Kharchev, 'Garantii svobody', *Nauka i religiya*, 11 (November 1987), p. 21–3.
5 N. Bykov, 'Ot tyur'my Rebibbiya do Sekty Muna', in *Nedelya*, 1 (January 1988), pp. 14–16.
6 Soviet Television (Moscow), 12:15 GMT, 21 May 1987.
7 *TSTAK* (Pkhenyan), 3 August 1987.
8 L. Timoshin, 'Saientologiya: fantastiku – v bisiness', in *Nauka i religiya*, 7 (July 1982); 9 (September 1982); 11 (November 1982); 1 (January 1983); 2 (February 1983); 9 (September 1983); 10 (October 1983); and 1 (January 1985).
9 Radio Moscow, 31 May 1987, 3:30 p.m.
10 *Komsomolets Tadzhikistana* (5 April 1989), pp. 1–2.
11 A. Fain, 'Lyudi sistemy? – mirooshchushchenie sovetskikh khippi', *Sotsiologicheskie issledovanniia* (1989), 1, pp. 85–92.
12 *Komsomol'skaya Pravda* (1 January 1988), p. 2.

13 *Ibid.*

14 See Yu. Kus'mina, 'V kol'tse otreshennosti', *Nauka i religiya*, no. 12 (December 1987), pp. 12–14; Yu. Kus'mina, 'Skitayas' tikho po Rossii', *Nauka i religiya*, 4 (April 1988), pp. 12–14; and A. Georgiev, 'Deti andergraunda – pod solntsem Kryma', *Semya* 49 (December 1989), pp. 11–14.

15 Aleksandr Shamaro, '*Russkoye* tserkovnoye sodtchestvo', series 'Nauchny ateizm', in *Znanie*, 10 (1988), p. 63.

16 I. Lisevich, 'Ulybka "bessmertnogo startsa" ', in *Nauka i religiya*, 9 (September 1988), p. 55.

17 S. Barsukov, 'Obshchestvo imeni Vivekanandy', in *Nauka i religiya*, 11 (November 1988), pp. 40–3.

18 B. Smirnov, 'Ioga', *Nauka i religiya*, 12 (December 1988), p. 49–51.

19 *Sovetskaya Kirgiziya* (7 January 1982).

20 The prescribed penalties for the offence are corrective labour for a term not to exceed one year or a fine not to exceed 100 rubles. If, however, the offence is committed on a commercial or large scale, the penalty is deprivation of freedom for a term not to exceed five years with or without confiscation of property. *Kirgizskaya SSR. Ugolovnyi kodeks* (Frunze, Kirgizskoye gosudarstvennoye izdatel'stvo, 1964), p. 272.

21 Deutsche Press Agentur (DPA), 25 January 1983; and Reuter (25 January 1983).

22 M. Derimov, 'Svidetely Iegovy v bruklinskikh setyakh', *Argumenty i fakty*, 20 (1983), p. 7; and *Pravda Ukrainy* (21 January 1983), (22 January 1983), and (23 January 1983).

23 *Sovetskaya Kirgiziya* (30 March 1985).

24 *Komsomolets Kirgizii* (15 January 1985). See also Oxana Antic, 'Religious Chain Letters in the USSR', *Radio Liberty Research* (8 November 1979).

25 TASS (5 October 1989).

26 *Sovetskaya kul'tura* (18 February 1989), p. 6; *Komsomol'skaya Pravda* (19 February 1989), p. 4; and Yuri Sverdlov, 'Ekh, Arbat', *Chelovek i zakon*, 5 (May 1989), p. 10.

27 *Komsomol'skoye znamya* (10 January 1988), p. 3.

28 Oleksandr Rushtchak, 'Kudi vede lotosostopii bog?', *Ranok* (June 1988), pp. 10–13.

29 *Pravda Ukrainy* (15 June 1986), pp. 3–4.

30 UPI (27 April 1987); and *Washington Post* (21 May 1987).

31 Wybo Nicolai, 'Hare Krishnas in the Soviet Union: the Attraction of Eastern Religions', in *European Background Brief*, 35 (April 1987), pp. 6–7.

32 *Vesti iz SSSR/USSR News Brief*, 15/19; 12/20, 1986.

33 *Komsomol'skaya Pravda* (22 March 1986), p. 4, and (15 May 1986), p. 4; and *Sotsialisticheskaya industriya* (19 August 1987), p. 4.

34 A. Motsov and S. Sadoshenko, 'Iog s golubymi glazami', in *Sotsialisticheskaya industriya* (24 January 1982), p. 3.

35 *Vesti iz SSSR/USSR News Brief* (1982), nos. 23/24–33. See also Julia Wishnevsky, 'Persecution of the Hare Krishna Movement in the Soviet Union', *Radio Liberty Research* (14 November 1985).

36 *Vesti iz SSSR/USSR News Brief* (1984), nos. 13–14; (1985), nos. 18–24.
37 *Arkhiv Samizdata*, Radio Liberty, no. 4905; and *Trud* (28 August 1983).
38 *Los Angeles Times* (30 August 1987); and AP (17 August 1987).
39 *Keston News Service*, No. 270 (5 March 1987), p. 11.
40 *Washington Post* (2 May 1987), and (15 May 1987).
41 Press release, *USSR News Brief* (15 May 1987).
42 AP (17 August 1987).
43 *Keston News Service*, No. 278 (25 June 1987), p. 19.
44 *Ibid.*, No. 292 (21 January 1988), p. 17.
45 Press Release, The Committee to free the Soviet Hare Krishnas, Stockholm (28 October 1986); AFP (11 September 1987); and Reuter (15 September 1987).
46 AFP (8 June 1988); and *Komsomol'skaya Pravda* (2 February 1989).
47 Rushchak, 'Kudi vede', pp. 10–13.
48 *USSR News Brief*, editor Cronid Lubarsky (1988), nos. 14–24.
49 *Keston News Service*, No. 318 (2 February 1989), p. 16.
50 AP (23 February 1989); and *Trud* (11 May 1989), p. 4.
51 *Moscow News*, No. 28 (10 July 1988), p. 7.
52 APN (Agentstvo pechati novosti), 21 February 1989.
53 TASS (20 April 1989).

PART V

The world of Christianity

12

The Russian Orthodox Renovationist Movement and its Russian historiography during the Soviet period

ANATOLII LEVITIN-KRASNOV

The renovationist schism was founded on 12 May 1922, at the time of the arrest of Patriarch Tikhon when, in Moscow in the Troitsk parsonage, he signed an order for the transfer of church authority to Metropolitan Yaroslav Agafangel and for the formation in Moscow of the Supreme Church Administration, headed by Bishops Leonid and Antonin.

However, a few years before this there had begun in various places in Russia the formation of renovationist groupings which found their expression in literature. So, even as early as 1918 in Penza, there was founded a group of opposition clergy led by the local archbishop, Vladimir Putyat, who had been deprived of office by Patriarch Tikhon for sins against the Seventh Commandment (adultery). Under the banner of a renovated church, he raised a revolt against the Patriarch, a revolt known as the Vladimirshchina.[1] The schism dried up before 1925. Its characteristic history of drunkenness was detailed in an unpublished manuscript by Master of Theology Nikolai Pavlovich Ivanov, *Raskol arkhiepiskop Vladimira – Vladimirshchina* (The Schism of Archbishop Vladimir – Vladimirshchina). This work was written in 1956 in Moscow. It was circulated among church people, and was known to His Holiness Patriarch Aleksii and Metropolitan Nikolai.

Far more important was the so-called Lebedyan incident, also reflected in the literature. The chief initiator of this incident appears to have been a priest, Father Konstantin Smirnov. An educated, well-read man who left his aristocratic family, Father Konstantin produced a series of decisive reforms in holy services. Shortly thereafter, like the local church authorities, Patriarch Tikhon forbade him from performing priestly duties. He circulated an open letter to the Patriarch, which soon was published separately and circulated widely in Russia.[2]

It must be said that, even before the revolution there appeared works by future *choir-masters* of renovationism, providing a foretaste of their activity. One of these was an article by Aleksandr Ivanovich Vvedenskii, 'Causes of Unbelief of the Russian Intelligentsia', printed in the magazine *Strannik* (Traveller) in 1911. This article reflected the views of a small circle led by Vvedenskii, at the time still a student at Saint Petersburg University; he had the support of the liberal newspaper *Russkoe slovo* (Russian Word).

In 1917 and 1918 there were articles by Vvedenskii in the Petrograd Left-church magazines *Golos Khrista* (*Voice of Christ*), *Bozhya Niva* (*Field of God*), *Sobornii razum* (*Synodal Reason*) and *Vestnik truda* (*Herald of Labour*). The most well known of these pieces was 'The Divine Liturgy and Ioann of Kronstadt'.[3] The founding of a co-operative publishing house by Father Yevgenii Belkov also dates from this time. *Sobornii razum* publishing house was set up at the end of 1917 in Petrograd, on the Ligovka. It printed a series of pamphlets expressing the views of the Left clergy, including the next pamphlets of Vvedenskii: *Paralich tserkvi* (*Paralysis of the Church*), *Sotsializm i religiya* (*Socialism and Religion*) and the richest of all in content, *Anarkhizm i religiya* (*Anarchism and Religion*).[4]

In *Paralich Tserkvi*, Vvedenskii uses a saying by Dostoyevskii on changing the Christian clergy into fighters against inertia and conservatism in the life of the clergy. In his pamphlet on socialism Vvedenskii gives voice to the idea of Christian socialism and supports the foundation of a Christian–socialist party. (It was founded, and contested elections to the Constituent Assembly. It came in fourth in Petrograd, as the Worker–Peasant Socialist Party).

One should also mention Vvedenskii's characteristically pregnant *Khristianstvo i anarkhizm* (*Christianity and Anarchism*). In the first part, the author highlights the relationship between anarchism and subjective idealism: 'If Kant compares himself with Copernicus, then anarchists are able to claim for themselves yet more glorious wreaths, since Kant conquered for theoretical thought, and they attempt to change concrete fact.'[5] From the Russian anarchists, Vvedenskii cited F.K. Sologub (in 1905–08 this poet presented himself as a mystical anarchist), Shatrov, Grav and others. Analysing their views, Vvedenskii ascertains the existence of a relationship between the Christians and the anarchists in their acknowledgement of the infinite value of each human individual, and cites in this regard the words of Saint Afanasii the Great: 'Christ becomes incarnate in order that we may worship.'

Further, the priest Vvedenskii notes the complete opposition between the methods of anarchism and those of Christianity:

Christianity never says: as much dynamite as possible! It discovers another demand: as much love as possible! Love – may this be that dynamite which explodes all untrue social reality! Love – may this be the fire which burns down all impediments to the original, true, divine freedom of Man! Then on the Earth, not only will rule the 'justice' and 'freedom' of which the anarchist Grav dreams, but it will be Paradise.[6]

At the same time, a few other works were issued by ideologues of renovationism. A particular impression was made on student youth by the 1918 work of the priest Father Ioann Fyodorovich Yegorov, *Pastyr tserkvi* (*Pastor of the Church*) and *Nelzya molchat i zhdat* (*It is Forbidden to Keep Silent and Wait*). He expressed his opinion against the neutrality of the clergy in the class struggle. Everywhere a pastor is required to be a rifleman in the struggle for truth, for the liberation of the orphaned and the poor from eternal oppression. A further fundamental work of his, *Pravoslavie i zhizn v nyom* (*Orthodoxy and the Life in It*) (Petrograd, 1918), is devoted to the problems of instructing the law of God. Father Ioann Yegorov speaks with great strength of the necessity for the church to be in the thick of life, always and everywhere to defend righteousness. He foresees the appearance of a great ecumenical movement, which would appear spontaneously among the masses and embrace the whole world. He speaks heatedly of happiness as being the forerunner of religious renovation and human regeneration. He died in 1920 of typhus, leaving behind a separate current, Religion in Union with Life, which existed until 1927. Its founder guaranteed himself a shining memory in future generations, who discover and raise his name to eminence.

In 1918, Sobornii razum Publishing House issued a book by Aleksandr Ivanovich Boyarskii, *Tserkov i demokratiya: Sputnik Khristianskikh demokratov*. Boyarskii was not only one of the founders and best-known leaders of renovationism, but the only renovationist leader who died a martyr. He was arrested in 1934 and disappeared without a trace – it is clear that he was shot in 1937. *Tserkov i demokratiya* distinguishes most of all the practical approaches to social questions. It begins with a review of the situation of the church before the Revolution, that it was in the position of an oppressor, perverted in service to the ruling class, isolated from the struggle for the interests of the mass of the people. It pointed out that the church profited from its vast authority with the people. Therefore, the church is obligated to take an active part in constructing the new life. 'Without Christ, there has not been and will not be a true freedom, equality, brotherhood.'[7]

The political platform was developed by Father Boyarskii in his fourth work, *Sovremennye politiko-ekonomicheskie voprosy pri svete khristianskogo tserkovnogo soznaniya* (*Contemporary Politico-Economic Problems in the Light of the Christian Church Confession*). 'The church of Christ', begins a chapter, 'maintains to all that the Eternal Truth of Christ must not destroy itself by sinking to the level of a political party.'[8] 'However, the church confession has its opinion on urgent questions, and this opinion perhaps is expressed in the following 13 points.'[9] There followed an explanation of the political programme of Father Aleksandr Boyarskii.

In these thirteen points, Father Boyarskii praises the confiscation of factories, plants, and estates for their use as social property. Special emphasis is given to Point Eight, 'Treasure and Poverty'. Here Boyarskii argued that the true Christian cannot be rich. In support of this assertion he provided quotations from the Gospels. Father Boyarskii remarks cleverly that, if any capitalist whatsoever would choose to follow Christian norms, he would be ruined in just two days.

Father Boyarskii was widely known by the nickname the Workers' Father. He served in the workers' settlement in Kolpin, near Petrograd, and was very popular among the workers of the Izhovskii plant. In essence, his programme coincided with that of the Socialist Revolutionary Party or the Left Social Democrats. Differences between their programme and that of Father Boyarskii appear solely in his thirteenth point, 'Methods of Struggle with Evil'. In substance, this point can be stated in one phrase: 'exclusively peaceful methods'.[10]

Another authoritative leader of the Left church movement was one of the major church writers and scholars, Bishop Antonin Granovskii. Here we must keep in mind primarily his dissertation, *Kniga proroka Barukha* (*The Book of the Prophet Baruch*),[11] defended by him before a session of the council of the Kiev Ecclesiastical Academy on 18 December 1902. The use of facts makes it a book of world-wide exegesis, not only Russian.

It is well known that the book of the prophet Baruch came down to us in Greek translation and, therefore, does not belong to the canonical books of the Old Testament. Attempts by the German exegetes Frankel and Pressner to reproduce the Hebrew original by analysis of the Greek text had no positive results. It was to this problem that Antonin addressed himself. Not limiting himself to the Greek text, he enlisted texts in Syrian–Pushtun, Syro-Cuneiform, Arabic, Ethiopian, Armenian, and Georgian. From these texts – in his opinion more ancient than the Greek and therefore closer to the original – Antonin restored the ancient Hebrew text, which he placed at the end of his work. This method of restoration of ancient originals produced a sensation, not only in Christian circles, but also in Jewish ones.

The church schism, in its life, gave rise to a river of appropriate literature. For a few months before the schism, when the problem of aid to the starving in the Volga region was discussed in the columns, not only of the Soviet, but also of the world, press, in Moscow the magazine *Zhivaya tserkov (Living Church)* began to be published. This magazine later gave its name to one of the radical schismatic groupings, and subsequently to the whole movement, beginning in 1922. In any event, nobody now remembers who invented the term.

In a work I wrote together with Vadim Shavrov, one can find the account of the arrival in Moscow of the future members of the Supreme Church Administration Vvedenskii, Krasnitskii and Belkov, who carried out the ecclesiastical revolution. We found that,

It was easy for all of them to bring themselves to agree with S. Kalinovskii, Father Superior of the Grebnevskaya Church, which was on the Lubyanka. Several months before he took off his holy orders and transformed himself into an antireligious lecturer, he told his interlocutors that the first issue of his magazine, *Zhivaya tserkov*, was about to be printed. He had already corresponded about this with the Petrograders, so then and there they decided to call the new movement the Living Church. It is somewhat symbolic that this title, so powerfully compromising and fraught with consequences, was thought up by a renegade – actually, the renovationist movement officially bore this name not for long, but the epithet 'Living Church' as a shameful blot was attached to the renovationists for good.[12]

That the foreign reader may comprehend the sense of the preceding part, one must add that this group was the first to open the way of the Russian clergy to the GPU–KGB in the capacity of agents.

However that may be, from May 1922 to August 1923, *Zhivaya tserkov*, published in Moscow, was the official organ of this schismatic church. It came out monthly, and altogether there were sixteen numbers. Its editors were the priests Sergei Kalinovskii and Zinovii Belkov. It printed articles by the leading activists of the renovationist (Living Church) movement. Although, understandably, biased, it illuminated in great detail the church life of the time and, because of this, is of paramount importance for historians of this period.

In those years, interest in the church was almost universal, manifesting itself in the relative abundance of church magazines. Beside the central organ, *Zhivaya tserkov*, a local edition was published in Kiev. Here the Living Church was beginning to fight on two fronts, not only against the supporters of the old church, but also against the label 'Lipkovshchina', the private term for a group of Ukrainian priests who placed themselves totally in the service of the uncanonical 'Metropolitan' Lipkovskii, who defended the idea of Ukrainian separatism. Only a few numbers of this magazine came out.

In Leningrad in 1923, the church journal *Sobornii razum* was revived. A collision occurred at once. If *Zhivaya tserkov* in Moscow reflected the point of view of Krasitskii, who fought the interests of the White clergy in his struggle with the episcopacy, *Sobornii razum* reflected the opinions of the Boyarskii–Vvedenskii group. Vvedenskii soon moved back to Petrograd, was injured by a fanatic's rock to his head at the time of the trial of Metropolitan Vanyamin, and was pushed out of participation in the Supreme Church Administration.

Sobornii razum demanded deeper church reforms. Fundamentally, it was interested in ideological questions, and blamed the administrative methods which motivated the Moscow group (in its limited contact with the GPU) and, primarily, Krasitskii.

At the same time, in Samara the *Samarskie Eparkhalnye Vedomosti* (*Samara Eparchial Newspaper*) began appearing. The publisher and chief editor of this paper was a renovationist bishop, the future Metropolitan Aleksandr Anisimov.

In Vologda, the renovationist magazine *Tserkovnoye znamya* (*Church Banner*) began publication and issued a few numbers. Here the authority of the Living Church supported it, the Vologda Eparchy being headed by Archbishop Aleksandr Nadezhdin, a pre-revolutionary appointee.

In 1925 in Vologda a church journal, *Tserkovoye zarya* (*Church Dawn*), was issued under the editorship of a priest, Father Rafail Burichka.

Archbishop Anisimov's magazine enjoyed a certain popularity. The archbishop was a man with an odious reputation, but he was talented. His *Samarskie Eparkhialskie Vedomosti* cast light on church life in the Volga area. Three issues of a comparable magazine were published in Ulyanovsk, where a renovationist eparchy disputed with the intelligent and enlightened Bishop Ioann Nikolskii. It presented its own peculiar appearance, and even its name, *Ulyanovskii Eparkhialnii Listok* (*Ulyanov Eparchial Leaf*), was original. Besides editorial articles, it sported garish slogans: 'In unity is the spiritual strength of the church', 'If you yourself want the good of the church, go to the Holy Synod', etc.

In 1924, in Vladimir, one thousand copies were printed of *Tserkovnaya zhizn* (*Church Life*), under the editorship of Archbishop Serafim Ruzhentsov. In 1925 in Tula, the *Tulskie Eparkhialnye vedomosti* (*Tula Eparchial Newspaper*) was issued under the editorship of V.M. Nikolskii. However, the principal newsorgans of the church were produced in Moscow and Ryazan.

In Moscow, after the events of 1923–4 (the liberation of Patriarch Tikhon from confinement, the reorganisation of the Supreme Church

Administration in the Holy Synod of the Russian Orthodox Church and the coming to power of Metropolitan Yevdokim), a multi-paged and beautifully produced journal, *Vestnik Svyashchennogo Sinoda Russkoi Pravoslavnoi Tserkvi (Herald of the Holy Synod of the Russian Orthodox Church)*, was issued almost to the end of 1930. When it first appeared, Vvedenskii, because of his repulsive personality, had been largely eased out of the leadership, and his articles and speeches were published with considerable trepidation on the part of the publishers.

However, in 1925 there began to be issued a new magazine in Ryazan, *Tserkovnoye obnovleniye (Church Renovation)*, under the leadership of Archbishop Mikhail Popov. It was considered to be the official organ of the Ryazan Eparchial Council, but its importance spread far beyond the local stage. Considered today, after sixty years, it must be said that the journal retains interest for the contemporary reader. In large part, this is due to the contributions of two people: the local renovator, Mikhail Popov, and Metropolitan Aleksandr Vvedenskii.

Regarding Mikhail, he appears to be one of the most enlightened and broadly educated representatives of the clergy. With a master's degree from the Petersburg Ecclesiastical Academy, Mikhail Popov was known from the beginning of the century as the author of the fundamental research, *Tserkov vo vremya Velikoi Frantsuzkoi revolyutsii (The Church at the Time of the Great French Revolution)*. Exceptionally modest and plain, he was very talented in literature. He guided *Tserkovnoye oblovleniye* splendidly, and wrote a great deal of topical and historical material. Among other things, he wrote various pieces on Georgii Gapon, his comrade at the Ecclesiastical Academy.

As to Metropolitan Vvedenskii, he here published not only his essays devoted to practical questions, but also his philosophical researches.

In his time, Vvedenskii was carried away by the works of the French philosopher Henri Bergson, whose philosophy of the vital impulse and intuitionism he considered to be the foundation of twentieth-century theology. Building from this, he propagandised it in his statements during his disputes with Lunacharskii.

This magazine appeared for two years, 1924 to 1926, but its memory deserves to be preserved among church people.

There is much writing on the renovationist schism by official publicists. The chief specialist at that time is reputed to be a certain Mikhail Gorev, who worked at *Izvestiya*. Here I cannot resist the temptation to quote my work on the renovationist schism. Recounting the removal of church valuables, allegedly for the use of the hungry, I wrote:

When people in leather jackets entered churches to remove silver and gold chalices, the mass of believers rushed to the defence of the valuables, and a wave of incidents swept the country. In newspaper columns appeared thunderous articles against church people, and the arrest of priests began. The entire church was in motion. Careerists and opportunists, as always, heated the atmosphere even more, rushing back and forth lest they not earn this political capital. A certain Mikhail Gorev bent over backwards with articles filled with cries to lynch the clergy. His contributions were never absent from the columns of the central press. Those who read his pieces, malicious and scathing, probably would have been very astonished to learn that just four years before, the anti-religious declaimer himself had been a priest. Moreover, the priest Galkin, writing after the Revolution under the pseudonym of Mikhail Gorev, was in his time on familiar terms with Metropolitan Pitirim and a constant companion of the 'God-fearing monk' Rasputin.[13]

In 1927 this former priest wrote an interesting piece of research on the last days of the Tsarist regime, *Poslednii svyatoi* (*The Last Saint*), a history of the 1916 canonisation of Saint Ioann of Tobolsk. This book, written in the style of a breezy, sensationalist novel, was published in 1927 in *Ogonëk* (*Bonfire*) magazine and later in a separate edition. This sensationalist wrote pieces on the church schism in *Pravda* and *Izvestiya*, including bombastic statements by the active schismatics he tracked down.

Much has been written, in a more decorous tone, on the schism by the old Bolshevik, Skvortsov-Stepanov, then working in the capacity of editor of *Izvestiya*.

At that time there were various books devoted to the church upheaval. First forward in this field appeared the well-known church historian, Professor Boris Vladimirovich Titlinov. Before the Revolution, he was a professor at the Saint Petersburg Ecclesiastical Academy, a doctor of church history whose specialty was the seventeenth and eighteenth centuries. He had the reputation of a liberal. Because of that, after the Revolution he became a church activist, close to the 'revolutionary' chief prosecutor V.N. Lvov. He appeared also as one of the organisers in 1917 of the Union of Democratic Clergy and, in 1917 and 1918, as a member of the Local Assembly of the Russian Orthodox Church.

Titlinov's book, *Novaya tserkov* (*The New Church*), being printed in 1922, was one of the first responses to the church schism. Objectively, with scrupulous neutrality, Titlinov explains the course of events. Speaking of the situation of the church in Russia, he does not conceal its difficulty. He ends on a pessimistic note: 'Slowly but surely the church in Russia comes to its complete downfall.'

Later on, Boris Vladimirovich was a professor at the renovationist Theological Institute in Petrograd. At that time, the State Publishing House dared to issue a few books on his specialty: *Politicheskaya borba molodyozhi v dukhovno-uchebnykh zavedeniyakh* (*The Political Struggle of Youth in the Ecclesiastical Educational Institutions*), 1926, and *Tserkov vo vremya revolyutsii* (*The Church at the Time of the Revolution*), 1927, reminiscences of the 1917–18 Synod. They also issued one book, in a large edition, *Pravoslaviye na sluzhbe samoderzhaviya* (*Orthodoxy in the Service of the Autocracy*), in which was contained a chronicle of the counter-revolutionary activity of the church in the twentieth century.

One must consider the glorification in the 1920s of the 'eloquence' – as it was called by its worshippers – of the renovationist Metropolitan Vvedenskii. His first published work in the 1920s was the small but clear *Tserkov i revolyutsiya* (*Church and Revolution*), Petrograd, 1923. This appears to be a stenographic transcript of a speech given by the celebrated Petrograd orator at the Tauride Palace on 4 June 1922, the Feast of the Trinity. The speech displays his magnificent artistic skills. It resounds even in the transcript. It called for a regenerated, renovated Christianity. Clearly and with bright brushstrokes, the author describes the tragedy of Christianity, unveiling the spiritual spring in humanity, and subsequently the usurpation and defilement of the spiritual forces of the world. The flaming orator improvised:

The church of Christ, the church of the Lord, goes before us as a young, beautiful girl in dawn-coloured clothes with white lilies in her hand, with a look so serene, and the fire of love in her deeds. We see that this is a victorious procession of the young bride of Christ. The church of Christ entered the world so that from the cavern, from the saloon, it can enter the shining palace of eternal truth . . . You see, in essence, the undertaking of the Apostles – we shall speak in the language of humanity – their purpose, was idiotic: twelve fishermen, semi-literate, casting their nets in the calm Galilean waters, leave for universal nets to catch all humanity. Before them was proud Rome, before them were the cultured Athenians; against them was all civilisation, all Plato and his achievements, all the beauty of ancient culture, all the power of the Roman state and, finally, each luxurious, mystical bouquet and its heresies and sects, which were tumultuously flooding the Roman state at the moment of the appearance of Christianity.

What kind of new word would Christianity be able to tell the world? What kind of new truth would these twelve dirty, uneducated Galileans be able to represent? And do you understand that word with which the Lord of Truth came into the ancient world and the face of Pilate. See how against Pilate stands Truth, that very Truth which is written in flaming letters. But the skeptical, cold mind, thinking much and seeing much but with no faith, the Roman coldly flings: what is Truth? And not waiting for an answer, Pilate turned away in order to judge Christ. We were not then present when the foundations were laid, when students of this one Truth, of course without an end to weakness, saw this Truth speak not only to Pilate, but all Pilates, all antiquity. Then antiquity must finally have turned back to those Galilean fishermen and asked: what is truth? We see how the Roman state, throne by throne, made one attempt after another to suppress Christianity, and they ended in failure. We see Domitian and Diocletian with gleaming swords cutting down highly-opinionated madmen, and we perceive from the depths of the ages that ringing, tragic and terrible, as the swords fall from the hands of Domitian and Diocletian. Who extracted that sword? Which new sword compares Christianity invidiously with that force of paganism? It is that very same truth. For if the apostles were purged as men, if they were sometimes simply illiterate, they were, therefore, those who believed in truth, acted for truth, possessed truth, and this truth won the world. This was the truth of love. They hurled at the world the blessed name of the Incomprehensible God – Love. It is just that simple. It is just that simple and that difficult; it is just that difficult and that joyous; it is just that joyous and that captivating; which the whole world verified – and toward the Fourth Century we see prone at the feet of Jesus Christ the entire world . . . So it was. And further? It happened further that the fateful, the inevitable inevitably arrived, for in history nothing is by chance. This we all know, both the powerful and the powerless. We see how to the Church of the Lord came the flatterers, the sly ones, coming to the Church of Jesus not because they cared, but only to say: I love you. Oh, how beautifully did one Christian teacher remark: 'To the Church of the Lord they came, not pleased by her beauty, but pleased by her dowry.' The church became such a huge force, that the Byzantine emperors came to see in the church, not an opposition, but at first allies, and later . . . prisoners. The state claimed the church, and the snow-white clothes of the bride of the Lord – pay attention! – were surrounded by shackles and flails. To the church of the Lord there came all those Byzantine, Lombard and Frankish monarchs, they bought booty – gold and silver – obtained by military force in unjust battles, they gilded her cupolas, they jewelled her walls, they gave her endless quantities of land and slaves, but . . . look, if you do not see that whenever an emperor attempts to place a pious kiss on the hand of the bride of the Lord, he also places on her hand more shackles and flails of gold . . . The church falls into the captivity of the state. The church keeps on welding its own cage. Yes. This cage is massive and so large that it is possible to pretend that it does not exist. Yes, the shackles, chains and flails, they are not iron or steel so that this indecency was not immediately obvious. Perhaps they are more like a fine web of golden thread, but it still is metallic and holds strongly.

So she came upon the Lord's dove in the hands of humanity, but was not able to ascend on its wings, was not able to soar further above the earth and to announce truth to the world.[14]

The effectiveness of the church schism more than a little soaked in oratorical splendor, while they were leaning on the GPU, to which topic I shall return.

The next landmark in the work of Vvedenskii was a speech to the Renovationist Synod in 1923, published also as a separate brochure, *Za chto lishili cana Patriarkha Tikhona* (*Why Patriarch Tikhon was Deprived of Rank*) (Moscow, 1923).

When you read Vvedenskii's report, it seems that you are always turning from one end of the telescope to the other: so much in this report is great and true, and at the same time there is so much here which is petty, empty, mendacious . . .[15]

What was said above about the appearance of Vvedenskii at the Tauride Palace applies in a large degree to his speech at the Synod. At the beginning of the report, where the orator with burning words discloses the untruth of life – these are pages of genius. The second part of his speech, where he kicks the helpless and imprisoned Patriarch Tikhon and demands that he be deprived of rank – this produces a horrible impression and sounds like an official Soviet document: 'There is only one face more vile than the executioner's: that is the servant of the executioner.' These words belong to Stalin, and appear in one of his notes to the Yugoslav regime in 1950. Since the chief executioner did not much respect his assistant, his 'executioner's servant', the victory of Vvedenskii at the Synod could perhaps be called Pyrrhic.

In some measure, the year 1923 was the summit of Vvedenskii's creativity. In particular, this refers to two of his books, published in large editions: *Tserkov patriarkha Tikhona* (*The Church of Patriarch Tikhon*) and *Tserkov i gosudarstvo* (*Church and State*). The former was published in an edition of 5 thousand, the latter of 8 thousand.

Tserkov patriarkha Tikhona appears to develop the bases of the schism which occurred. The introduction contains a sharp polemic against Tikhon's supporters. Having been written before the renovationist Synod, the preamble makes clear that the book was delayed in being published. As a pupil of Petersburg University, Vvedenskii is sufficiently objective to explain the point of view, the allies of the imprisoned patriarch:

A lesser impression is given to the reader by these pages [i.e., on the church schism]. But I fear that reading these pages many – perhaps very many – will not find in the church of Patriarch Tikhon anything such as may have terrorised them, may have morally killed them. For many, the figure of Patriarch Tikhon assumes exaggerated dimensions and my book may have the effect of rendering these readers captives of the legend of Tikhon. I want to be frank, I want to point out how unexpected may have been this result of the work. I contrast the church of Patriarch Tikhon with the church of Christ the Savior. And nevertheless, Tikhon is a hero? Yes, if you wish! And even sufficiently large. But for those, there is no cause of Christ and His original church.[16]

In this lugubrious book the author argues that the Synod of 1917–18 and its election of Tikhon as patriarch was a reaction of the state's church, supporting the monarchist state of mind in the Russian revolution, both the February revolution and the October revolution. One important chapter of the book presents a section of the steno-graphic report of the Synod, and is of great interest to the church historian, since nothing else has ever been published.

The basic idea of the book is that the Russian Church was always deeply monarchist. To a certain extent, the way of the Orthodox ruler blinds him to the way of Christ. Therefore, the church revolution of 1922 manifests a lawful Christian revolution against the monarchist forces in the church. Such is the dilemma: either with the church of Tikhon against the church of Christ, or with Christ against Tikhon.

Vvedenskii displayed his main historical work in *Tserkov i gosudarstvo* (Moscow, Izd-vo Mospolitgrafa, 1923), an outline of Russian church–state relations from 1918 to 1922. This book was distributed widely and was cited often during the 1920s and 1930s in publications devoted to this theme, since this collection contained very comprehensive materials on the subject. Characteristically, this was the only Vveden-skii book to be found in the closed 'special collections' of libraries, and is not given to readers in the Lenin State Library, the Public Library in Leningrad or the Library of the USSR Academy of Sciences.

In its introduction, the author formulates its main task. It is like that in *Tserkov patriarkha Tikhona*: to show the counter-revolutionary attitudes and militant monarchism of the Russian Church. In the conclusion, he describes the consequences of the necessity for the church revolution:

The church was a bulwark of the monarchy; when the monarchy fell, the church was left hanging in midair. The ideal job of the church – to realise on the earth the teaching of Christ – was long forgotten by the church, because of her responsible leaders. The monarchy no longer exists. The Revolution crushed it. What then to do? See how in the spring of 1917 the church dreams. The best (not very numerous) forces of the church wish to place it in a friendly, not hostile, position toward the liberated people. But dark reaction was strong in the church. It was concealed. But it quickly raised its voice. As the Revolution's measures developed, all the reactionary forces joined around the church. And quickly the church counter-revolution sank into the abyss, the delicate little boat of the original evangelical tradition. The church rushed to restore in Russia its former national glory and power. From this point of view they managed all the pre-Synod work, with hopes that the pre-Synod council, and the Synod itself, would be church-political, and not purely religious.[17]

For the period covered by his research, Vvedenskii, with his characteristic talent and lustre, exposes the unnatural alliance of the church with the autocracy in the pre-revolutionary years. He writes much on Rasputin, on his enormous influence on the church and on what happened because of this compromise of the church. He also tells of the small group of those who wanted to renovate the church, and of the celebrated preacher, Father Grigorii Petrov, and how the church harassed him. Further, the author describes the publications produced by the church after the February revolution.[18]

The second chapter is entitled, 'The Church in the Period from the February Revolution to the Synod of 15 August 1917.' Here, he tells of the outbreak of clerical progressivism. In particular, he refers to the foundation of the Union of Democratic Clergy:

Only a small current of clergy and laymen, united in the aforementioned All-Russian Union of Democratic Clergy and Laymen, spoke of the necessity of destroying the capitalist order, of the liquidation of capital in the name of Christ. For the great majority this was stupid, unnecessary, harmful, threatening. Lenin already was working, and for these progressives he was a symbol of lying and of that which must not be. Thus the progressive church publicist Sokolov on 25 May, speaking of 'harmful' church leaders, labels them 'Lenins in churches'.[19]

Remembering the dispute with Prince Yevgeni Nikolaievich Trubetskoi, a church liberal and well-known philosopher, Vvedenskii expresses very radical views which he hardly would have expressed twenty years later, at the time of the Patriotic War, when he was in a very patriotic frame of mind:

Many church people acknowledged at that time the necessity of preserving the conquests of the Revolution by organising resistance to its enemies . . . The motherland *for a Christian is nonsense and nothing because he is a citizen of the world. The nation for a Christian is nothing because he is part of no nation, but of humanity.* Therefore, national and state tasks for the Christian, as such, do not exist. Furthermore, these tasks are for him foreign, political. In the meantime, Trubetskoi [oh, how this afterwards will be often repeated! – A. L-K.] conspired with other clergymen, quasi-clergymen, political clergymen, state clergymen.[20]

In actuality, at this time, the summer of 1917, Vvedenskii was a member of the Republic Soviet (the Pre-Parliament), where he attached himself to the socialist wing and strove toward founding in Russia a Christian–Socialist party.

Vvedenskii also mentioned the opening of the Synod of the Russian Orthodox Church. Here was begun an historical chapter, which has not been written about by a single historian of the church because the basic protocols were never printed. They are of major significance to the history of the church.

In 1963, fifty years after Vvedenskii wrote his book, Metropolitan Nikodim Rotov spoke to me about it, intending to write his master's thesis on the 1917–18 synods of the Russian Church. He informed me that he profited greatly from those protocols, and indicated a stack two metres high. Since then, a quarter of a century has passed. Metropolitan Nikodim wrote his thesis on an entirely different theme, Pope John XXIII, and died thirty years ago. Vvedenskii's book remains the sole source for our knowledge of the Synod, learning about the restoration of the Patriarchate, and at the same time about an event outside the Synod, the firing upon a religious procession in Penza, on the life of the church during the Civil War – all told clearly and beautifully. This man had an amazing talent: whatever he wrote, whatever he spoke, was remarkable. Here he already presents himself as an historian of the recent past, in an attractive, lively book, like a novel. Concluding the book is a topical chapter, wherein the church revolt of 1922 is recounted.

Vvedenskii's main creative exploits in the 1920s were contributions to the anti-religious disputes. These disputes were quite elementary. Except for official approbation, they literally sank. From Moscow and Leningrad, from Siberia to the Caucasus, from the Ukraine to Central Asia, they expired everywhere.

Vvedenskii was the main opponent everywhere, beginning in the capital, where he was the chief antagonist of A.V. Lunacharsky, and ending in the provincial cities, where his opponents were professors of dialectical materialism and old Communists. Vvedenskii usually stepped forward as the main disputant. Of course, along with Vvedenskii, other activists came forth: Bishop Antonin Granovskii, Boyarskii, Krasnitskii, Bishop Iiarion Troitskii, but the major figure in the dispute always was Vvedenskii. These debates remained in the minds of the people. Even Vvedenskii's irritated enemies acknowledged his power and worth. 'People who came to a debate with a desire to see how they would throw the priest in a puddle, left arguing with each other, wrote Archpriest Father Konstantin Ruzhitskii, rector of the Moscow Ecclesiastical Academy, in 1962.

These debates were written of in fictional literature. In particular, Vvedenskii's approach was written about by the well-known writer N.K. Chakovskii in his novel *Yunost* (Youth):

The priest was very lean, tall, thin, stooping, displaying some strangeness – a red, young, non-Russian face. Armenian or Greek? The pointed, trimmed, short beard was extraordinarily dark. A hooked, bent nose, very thin, swarthy cheeks, very green eyes with an extraordinary gleam . . . black, climbing hair from under the grey hat. 'Our purpose is a concordat', said the priest, 'and they will go for it'.[21]

In the writings of the then-popular Olga Forsh, arranging for the debates also was very colourful:

The windows were dark. Excited, curious soldiers' faces, bearded Old Believers next to sailors in Budyonni-style caps. The entire hall was sighing, agitated. Here and there, exclamations. Outside is the 'liberal father' [Boyarskii, of course]. A woman calls out, 'Cross yourself Father, the Holy Father will start his speech by crossing himself'. Trying to keep his hair out of his face, smiling, is the rebaptised workers' priest . . . The main one [Vvedenskii] speaks in a black cassock and white shoes. The cross peeks out on its white chain, a little like a trinket. Revolutionary, no, the meeting speaks of the exclusion of bonds, of Black Hundred propaganda, of the Synod in Karlovtsy, where White generals proposed to the clergy the restoration of the house of Romanov. He was very fast, throwing his hands in the air and dropping them, his vestments flapping, his voice so penetrating that it hurt the ears. By the end of the speech he conquers, the majority led astray by his hysterical whirlwind . . . The archpriest concluded his speech. Suddenly, victoriously, he exclaimed, 'What ruin, what emptiness there is in the soul without Christ!' Appearing to sway, for a minute appearing forgetful and about to fall. No, he got to the point. He settled down suddenly and smiled pityingly. The smile, helpless and exhausted, immediately made him resemble one of the apostles of Vrubel.[22]

A very talented sketch of Vvedenskii also is contained in Varlam Shalamov's book, *Voskresheniye listvinnitsi* (*Resurrection of the Larches*), Paris, YMCA Press, 1985. The son of a Vologda renovationist clergyman, Shalamov conversed in his youth many times with the renovationist Metropolitan Aleksandr. He saw him both in Vologda and Moscow, and observed him while he served. (He correctly notes the ecstatic and mystical character of Aleksandr's service). He also saw his manner of living. He disputed with some of the leading orators of the time: Trotskii, Bukharin, Lunacharsky. Shalamov also correctly points out that Vvedenskii, in their opinion, must have been the most famous.

Unfortunately, we have few portions of the stenographic reports of Vvedenskii speeches in these debates. But even so, such material that we do have bears witness to his talent. Such is the book, *Disput s Lunacharskim na temu: 'Iisus ili Khristos?' po povodu knigi Anri Barbyusa* (*Dispute With Lunacharsky on the Theme: 'Jesus or Christ?' Regarding a Book by Henri Barbusse*) (Moscow, 1924) and *Religiya i kommunizm* –

stennogrammy dvukh disputov s Lunacharskim mitropolita Vvedenskogo (*Religion and Communism – Stenographic Report of Two Disputes with Lunacharsky by Metropolitan Vvedenskii*) (Leningrad, 1927). The latter was published in a large edition.

From this debate we realise, among other things, that the censorship permitted the issuance of a major work, *Apologetika* (*Apologetics*), but at the last minute it was sequestered. It was preserved in manuscript by Professor V.Z. Belolikov, an instructor at the renovationist Ecclesiastical Academy, but was seized when he was arrested in 1934 and disappeared into the depths of the NKVD.

Only in the magazines *Tserkovnoye obnovleniye* and *Vestnik svyashchennogo sinoda* may we read the separate philosophical lectures of Metropolitan Aleksandr, rector of the renovationist Academy.

As mentioned above, Vvedenskii was a student of Henri Bergson. His point of view was of mystical biologism. For him, everything in the world was composed of currents of impulses. The vital impulse lies at the foundation of the world. At that time, Vvedenskii belonged to the non-Platonists. For him, number was the most important reality. The vital impulses receive a command from the centre the way nerves do in the human body. God exists, in such cases, simultaneously as a divine number, the Trinity, and as the Centre, from which issue impulses. Christ is a manifestation of the Supreme Impulse. In Him is Truth, Life, and Beauty. Metropolitan Aleksandr developed these thoughts in all his speeches and appearances.

However, in 1929 a black curtain was drawn over his creative works. Not one of his works could be published. After his death on 25 July 1946 in Moscow, his widow kept a major philosophical work, *Dialektika bytiya* (*Dialectics of Existence*). I learned this in a conversation in Yaroslavl on 25 March 1966 with Archbishop Sergei Larin. He bought it from the late widow, Anna Pavlovna Zavyalova, because he wanted to use it in his doctoral dissertation. However, Archbishop Sergei died soon thereafter, in September 1967, and the present whereabouts of this work is unknown to me.

The great religious reformer, Bishop Antonin Granovskii, died on 14 January 1927, having spent the end of his life in seclusion. He was alienated from the official Orthodox church, and quarrelled with Tikhon and the renovationist hierarchy. He argued with the Union for Church Renewal, which was founded at the Zakonospasskii Monastery in Moscow, and had under its jurisdiction a few parishes and provinces. Two of his works remain: *Trudy pervogo Vsyorossiiskogo syezda ili Sobora Soyuza tserkovnogo vozrozhdeniya* (*Works of the First All-Russian Congress or Synod of the Union for Church Renewal*) (Toropets, 1925) and

Bozhestvennaya liturgiya, retsenzovannaya po chinom drevnikh liturgii mitropolitom Antoninom (*The Divine Service, Reviewed from the Beginning of Ancient Liturgies by Metropolitan Antonin*) (Moscow, 1923; 5 thousand copies).[23]

Both of these works manifest great historical interest. At Antonin's funeral, his follower, Archpriest Smirnov, stated that Antonin's immediate heritage, the Union for Church Renewal, died with him. He spoke the truth. The Union collapsed after a few months. Nevertheless, the ideas of Antonin revived and live in the precincts of the Ecumenical Church. It must be said that the reforms of Popes John XXIII and Paul VI in all respects recall the reforms of Antonin. There is literature of the contemporary Catholic Church which is a word-for-word repetition of Antonin. So is the democratisation of the clergy, though at the same time without the bigamous vulgarisation, episcopal marriage or the casting out of monasticism.

In the final analysis, the path of the Universal Church is the path of Antonin.

We have traced all the major written works connected with the renovationist Russian Orthodox Church.

It is well-known that renovationism, such as the Union for Church Renewal, did not outlive its founders. July 25, 1946, the day the renovationist Metropolitan Aleksandr Ivanovich Vvedenskii died, also was the day renovationism died.

Recently, however, interest in renovationism has risen again. There have been a number of works devoted to it. Among these works, many are preserved thanks to the fiery energy of my brother and friend, Vadim Mikhailovich Shavrov (1924–83).

What are the basic points of our work?

The conclusion to our book ends with the following words: Do not lie! Speak the Truth, the whole Truth and nothing but the Truth, however bitter and difficult. And have faith in God!

With these words, written twenty-eight years ago, permit me to conclude my modest work.

Appendix: Literature on the renovationist schism

Besides the ones mentioned in the text, the following are the leading recent books.

1. Archbishop Sergei Larin, *Obnovlencheskii raskol* (*The Renovationist Schism*) (Leningrad, Ecclesiastical Academy). An unpublished doctoral dissertation.

This work uses a large amount of previously unknown material. However, the author's conception does not deserve serious attention: according to Larin, Patriarch Tikhon and his circle were 'Soviet men', and renovationism manifested characteristics of a provocation, with the aim of causing a quarrel between Tikhon and the Soviet regime. All the Renovationists were morally unscrupulous people with one exception: the author himself, who praises his own 'noble trustworthiness'.

2. The work by the anti-religious writer Shishkin, *Prisposoblenchestvo Tserkovnikov v 20-ye gody* (*Time-Serving Churchmen in the 20*), (Kazan, 1973). The usual Soviet agitation. Of no scientific interest.

3. Lev Regelson, *Tragediya russkoi tserkvi* (*The Tragedy of the Russian Church*) (Paris, YMCA Press, 1975). A biased book. The author examines the events of the 1920s and 1930s from the position of a catacomb church. All activists of the Russian Orthodox Church of this period he regards indiscriminately as time-servers. Moreover, he is not very concerned that the Russian Church's going to the catacombs might have led to its physical destruction, and the church in Russia might not exist. There might be only unco-ordinated, ignorant groupings and extremely reactionary people. At one time I put to the author this rhetorical question: It is interesting to speculate where you yourself might have been christened in 1963, had there not been an official church – might the ones in the catacombs, catching sight of a young Jew and suspecting that he was a provocateur, have run so fast that you could not see their feet?

They say that, in 1943, because of pressure from Roosevelt, Stalin might have recognised the catacomb church, but for Metropolitan Sergii. Nothing more ridiculous could be conceived. Stalin was never in a position in 1943 wherein Roosevelt could dictate to him. He never would have agreed to the legalisation of an openly anti-Soviet organisation.

4. Vladimir Rusak. *Svidetel Obvineniya* (*Witness for the Prosecution*), 1987. Our review of this book appeared in *Kontinent*, 56 (1988), pp. 291–305.

At that time the father deacon was in custody, and we had to give our opinion in greatly attenuated form. It is different, now that he lives in freedom. Now I am able to say that all his facts are mixed up, and the author has added mere rumour and apocryphal reports, such as the 'information' from Metropolitan Nikolai of a meeting between Stalin and the hierarchy in September, 1943. This is valueless. We may hope that now that Father Rusak is free, he will become acquainted with the historical conditions of the 1920s and 1930s and will rework his book.

Translated from Russian by George E. Rennar

Notes

1 Roughly, 'the frightful actions of Vladimir'. (Tr.)
2 K. Smirnov. *Otkritoye pismo patriarkhu Tikhonu* (Open Letter to Patriarch Tikhon) (Lebendyan, 1923).
3 *Bozhya Niva*, 3–5, 1917, pp. 37–47.
4 *Sobornii razum*, Petrograd, 1918.
5 *Ibid.*, p. 21.
6 *Ibid.*, p. 47.
7 *Ibid.*, p. 14.
8 *Ibid.*, p. 17.
9 *Ibid.*, p. 31.
10 *Ibid.*, p. 32.
11 Reproduction, Saint Petersburg: 1902.
12 Anatolii Levitin and Vadim Shavrov, *Ocherki po istorii russkoi tserkovoi smuti* (*Sketches of the History of Russian Church Disturbances*), (Kusnacht, Institut 'Glaube in der Zweite Welt', 1978), I, p. 79.
13 *Ibid.*, p. 58.
14 *Ibid.*, pp. 4–5.
15 Levitin and Shavrov, *Ocherki*, II, p. 85.
16 *Ibid.*, p. 95.
17 *Ibid.*, p. 3.
18 *Ibid.*, p. 7.
19 *Ibid.*, p. 39.
20 *Ibid.*, p. 40. Emphasis added.
21 N.K. Chakovskii, *Yunost* (Leningrad, 1930), pp. 128–9.
22 O. Forsh, 'Zhivtsi' (The Living) in *Letoshnii snyeg* (Summer Snow) (Moscow–Leningrad, 1925), p. 113.
23 The latter was reprinted in Levitin and Shavrov, *Ocherki*, III, pp. 309–34.

13

The re-emergence of the Ukrainian (Greek) Catholic Church in the USSR

MYROSLAW TATARYN

In April 1945, Joseph Stalin ordered the arrest, trial, and imprison-ment of all the bishops and thousands of priests, monastics and laity of the Greek Catholic Church of Ukraine (today known in the West as the Ukrainian Catholic Church). The then primate of the church recalled:

> On April 11, 1945 I was arrested together with all the other bishops. Within a year more than 800 priests followed us into imprisonment. From the 8th to the 10th of March 1946 the illegal synod of Lviv was convened and under atheistic pressure announced the 'reunion' of the Ukrainian Catholic Church with the Soviet controlled Orthodox Church.[1]

Within a year the largest non-Roman, Catholic Church was officially liquidated. A church with ten bishops, 3,470 clergy, 1,090 nuns and over four million faithful became the largest illegal Christian com-munity in the world.[2] For almost forty-five years Greek Catholics were forced to hide their religious convictions, or feign Orthodoxy, or endure arrest, fines, even imprisonment. On 1 December, 1989 that persecution officially ended with the announcement by N. Kolesnick, chair of the Ukrainian Council for Religious Affairs, that Greek Catholic communities would be allowed to register with the authorities.[3]

The change in Soviet policy towards the Greek Catholics is indica-tive of the depth of transformation in the policies of the USSR. For years the Greek Catholics were not tolerated because of their ties with the Vatican, their nationalism, and their religious beliefs. In the 1980s Soviet attitudes to all of these have changed dramatically, with pro-found consequences to the resurgent Greek Catholic Church. Perhaps the most important cause of these changes is the historically unique moment of having a reformer at the head of the Soviet state, and a Slav as Pope of Rome. In a 1979 letter to the primate of the Greek Catholic

Church, Josyf Slipyj, Pope John Paul II wrote, 'I think now that the primary necessity of the moment is to guarantee the right to existence and to citizenship of Ukrainian Catholics in their homeland'.[4] Two years earlier at the Helsinki follow-up conference in Belgrade the Vatican delegate stated: 'There exists still another large wound, which we hope to see resolved and healed. This is a matter of concern for the Catholic Church, the status of certain communities of faithful of the Eastern rite, who were once flourishing in their religious life . . . who in the new juridical–political post-War situation have lost their official right to exist.'[5] This policy became a cornerstone of Vatican policy in the 1980s.[6] In the period 1987–9 the various speculations concerning a potential papal visit to the USSR were often met by the Pope's response that such a visit would have to include a pastoral visit to his Greek Catholic brethren in Ukraine. The very possibility of a papal visit to the Soviet Union may be the clearest sign of the reforms of M. Gorbachev. Acceding to the post of General Secretary of the CPSU in 1985 and later to the Presidency of the USSR, Gorbachev single-handedly made such a papal visit not just conceivable but probable. Wishing both to reform the state internally, as well as to make the USSR a more acceptable member of the international community, he has influenced the thinking of Soviet policy makers. The Vatican is no longer the strange foreign power to be kept at a distance; Ukrainian nationalism is now to be tamed, not silenced; and religion, no longer the opiate of the masses, is viewed as a force for reform in the ex-USSR. It is within this atmosphere that the Greek Catholic Church in Ukraine emerged from official non-existence.

Josef Stalin decided to physically obliterate the Greek Catholic Church in 1945–6.[7] His unofficial declaration of war against this community meant that all but two of the original bishops died in the camps. Thousands of clergy and faithful were condemned to a slow death in the Siberian Gulag. Even those who were granted an amnesty by Khrushchev were forced into menial and demeaning tasks. Although a small group of Catholics, under duress, agreed to stage a so-called re-union with Orthodoxy at the pseudo-Synod of Lviv, in 1946, this 'Initiative Group' never gained any popular support. Years later Josyf Slipyj wrote:

Our priests were given the choice of either joining the 'Church of the Regime' and thereby renouncing catholic unity, or bearing for at least ten years the harsh fate of deportation and all the penalties connected with it. The overwhelming majority of priests chose the way of the Soviet Union's prisons and concentration camps.[8]

In the post-Stalin period repression eased in comparison with the Stalinist terror, yet the church's life continued to be threatened. The consistent official position of the Soviet government and the Russian Orthodox Church was that the Greek Catholic Church no longer existed – it had 'voluntarily dissolved itself'. As a result of international pressure, in 1963 the church's primate, Josyf Slipyj was sent from his Siberian labour camp into exile in the West. In 1972 his successor, Archbishop Velychkovsky, was also exiled to the West. News concerning the life of the church was limited to occasional private correspondence smuggled out of the USSR, creating the impression of a church struggling to survive: an ageing clergy, monastics forced to live privately or in pairs, and a laity which remained faithful to their church, some attending clandestine services, others becoming increasingly accustomed to attending Orthodox services.[9] Circumstances did not allow the formation of a more detailed picture.

The 1980s radically transformed this description. On 9 September 1982 an 'Initiative Group for the Defence of Believers and the Church in Ukraine' was created. Its founding members were: Josyp Terelya, the chairman; the Studite priest–monk Hryhorij Budzinsky, the priests Dionisij and Ihnatij and Stefania Petrash-Sichko. Fr Budzinsky's membership was significant since this tied the group to the church hierarchy and to the historical struggle with the Soviet government.[10]

The Initiative Group published its programme in which it called for the legalisation of the Greek Catholic Church under the following circumstances:

(a) a referendum is to be held in the eparchies of Western Ukraine to decide which properties should remain in Orthodox hands and which should be returned to the Catholic Church;

(b) where Catholics are in the minority they should be allowed to build new churches;

(c) the return of Catholic seminaries in Lviv and Uzhorod;

(d) to allow 50 theology students to study in the Vatican and 10 students each in Vienna, Warsaw, and Munich;

(e) to return the printing houses of each of the five eparchies;

(f) to study the crimes of the security organs against the church;

(g) to study the criminal use of psychiatry in the repression of church activists;

(h) the church agrees to be a law-abiding member of Soviet society; and

(i) the Church's ultimate head is the Pope of Rome and not Soviet power.[11]

The Group also began publication of the 'Chronicle of the Catholic Church in Ukraine', modelled on the very successful Chronicle of the Lithuanian Church.[12]

The government's response was far from tolerant. On 29 September 1982 a twenty-eight-year-old nun, Maria Shved, was shot to death by the militia on the streets of Lviv. In 1984 another nun was beaten to death at the Lviv railway station by 'hooligans'. Priests continued to be arrested and often exiled. On 24 December 1982, J. Terelya was arrested. During his one year in prison the 'Initiative Group' was led by Vasyl Kobryn. Both men were arrested in 1984. On 22 March 1985, Kobryn was sentenced to three years imprisonment and, in August, Terelya was sentenced to seven years hard labour and five years exile. Nevertheless the life of the church was not destroyed.

In these years the church's life became increasingly public and more fervent. Initiative Group members continued to publish the Chronicles even after Terelya's imprisonment. Reports reached the West concerning an underground seminary. At a 1985 synod of the Ukrainian Catholic Church in the Vatican, Cardinal Lubachivsky reported that there were ten bishops functioning clandestinely in Ukraine.[13] The famous Furov Report spoke of 'uniates' among candidates to the Russian Orthodox priesthood from Western Ukraine.[14] Religious congregations, especially among women, were able to find postulants to bolster their members.

Although the Initiative Group had distinct ties with the church it was not known whether it was functioning with the blessing of the hierarchy. In fact, evidence would seem to indicate that the group tried to straddle the middle ground between a solely religious organisation and a secular human rights group. In a conversation between Group leader J. Terelya and Transcarpathian Party authorities, documented in Chronicle 6, Terelya calls his group the 'Helsinki Initiative Group in Defence of Believers and the Church',[15] suggesting the group is heir to the tradition of the Ukrainian Helsinki Monitoring Group. All the lay members of the group had a history of membership or co-operation with the Helsinki Group. The Initiative Group therefore, marked an historic coalescence of religious and secular human rights workers. Human rights activists were impressed by the examples of courage and suffering given by Greek Catholic clergy. Consequently prominent dissidents spoke out in defence of the church's rights. In 1979 the historian, Zinovij Krasivsky, mid-way through a seventeen-year term of imprisonment stated: 'I wish to declare that along with other problems I am most troubled by the state of the Greek Catholic Church in Ukraine. I will never leave this matter alone, I will take up this matter and show the entire world that its banning is not only anti-constitutional but inhuman – an evil.'[16] In private conversation Josyp Terelya verified that Krasivsky, a co-founder of the Ukrainian National Front in 1967, became an active supporter of the rights of the church after his release from prison.

In the mid-1980s the Soviet government was faced with the reality of former dissidents defending with increasing outspokenness the rights of the church. A legalised Greek Catholic Church in Ukraine became the cause célèbre of a rejuvenated patriotic movement in Western Ukraine. Similarly the Chronicle of the Catholic Church in Ukraine touched upon not only questions of religion, but also of human and national rights.[17]

Nothing seems to have galvanised movements for change in Ukraine as much as the disaster in Chernobyl in 1986. Although the connection is not direct, ostensibly Chernobyl helped bring about a radical rethinking among faithful supporters of the old Communist party line. After this great tragedy leading personages such as Oles' Honchar, Boris Olijnyk and others stepped forward to criticise the centralist policies of Moscow. Chernobyl became a symbol of Ukraine's inability to shape its own destiny.

Not only were Ukrainians now becoming more outspoken in their demands upon *glasnost* and *perestroika*, the media, both Soviet and non-Soviet, became more aggressive in their search for the truth. More questions were being asked about the fate of the Greek Catholic Church and the old answers no longer sufficed. Although many Orthodox hierarchs still contended that the Greek Catholic Church no longer existed, others began to answer more honestly.[18] In May 1986, the Russian Orthodox Metropolitan of Kyiv,[19] Filaret, made an indirect admission of the renewed strength of the Greek Catholics when he stated: 'The reactivation of the Union in recent times has caused apprehension among Orthodox Churches.'[20] It quickly became obvious that the greatest opposition to a resurgent Greek Catholicism would come from the Russian Orthodox Church.

Finally in 1987 the hierarchy of the Greek Catholic Church began to emerge from the underground. On 9 May 1987 an appeal of the episcopate and lay committees of the Greek Catholic Church was sent to the participants of the Vienna follow up conference to the Helsinki accords. The letter stated that in the four years since the Madrid conference of 1983 nothing had altered in their status. They wrote, 'the USSR has no intention of fulfilling the obligations it has entered into the area of human rights: the right to choose where one lives and the right to religious freedom'.[21] Nonetheless, changes were occurring.

During that year most prisoners of the conscience were being released from Soviet camps: Josyp Terelya was prematurely released in January. Then in April, an eleven-year-old girl, Maryn Kizyn, revealed that she had seen the Mother of God on the chapel dome of the closed church in Hrushiv, near Lviv. Streams of pilgrims came from all over the Soviet Union to 'see' the Mother of God. Tens of thousands of people congregated on the village, reports were broadcast over Soviet television and the whole affair was condemned as a 'work of the Vatican' by the Soviet press.[22] A Kyivan intellectual reflected upon the effect of the apparition: 'Whether it is a miracle or not – the apparition has done its work. It has not only mobilised a heretofore unique number of faithful, but has once again demonstrated that the need for faith, for a higher power, cannot be suppressed by "atheistic museums" or by "courses in atheistic materialism".'[23] Hrushiv became a forum at which Catholic activists could remind people of their ancestral faith.

Finally, in August 1987, the church hierarchy resolved to take a chance on Gorbachev's *glasnost*. On 4 August 1987 a letter was penned to Pope John Paul II and through him to the Supreme Soviet of the USSR calling for full legalisation of the Ukrainian Catholic Church. The letter was signed by 174 laypersons, 36 religious, and, for the first time since the church was declared illegal, two bishops. The two signatory bishops were Pavlo Vasylyk of Ivano-Frankivsk and Ivan Semedi of Uzhorod. After their signatures they added 'in consultation and with the blessing of the other Catholic bishops in Ukraine'.[24] The document was a signal that the church's hierarchy was now going to play a more public role in the resurgence of the church's life. On 6 August, two members of the Sister Servants of Mary Immaculate from Lviv took the initiative to officially send a declaration to M. Gorbachev calling for the recognition of their constitutional rights to freedom of religious expression.[25] Then, on the Feast of the Dormition of the Mother of God, an unprecedented event: a public Divine Liturgy celebrated by Bishop Vasylyk and five priests at the pilgrimage cite in Zarvanytsya, Western Ukraine. Over 3,000 people attended under the watchful, but inactive, eye of the militia. After the service Bishop Vasylyk was fined and those still at the site in the village were violently dispersed, however there were no mass arrests. One month later, Josyp Terelya, who had been threatened with re-arrest owing to his public agitation for the legalisation of the church, was exiled from the Soviet Union. His exile was interpreted by some as a sign that Moscow was finally willing to compromise on the issue of the Greek Catholic Church.[26]

Further progress towards a settlement of the problem was taken when the primate of the Greek Catholic Church resident in Rome declared, on 6 November 1987, that he extended his 'hand in forgiveness, peace and love to the Russian people and the Moscow Patriarchate'.[27] Although it did not receive an official response from the Russian hierarchy, it did help pave the way for greater reconciliation between the Orthodox and Catholics in their mutual struggle for religious rights.

In December of that year this co-operation was displayed in a press conference convened by Alexander Ogorodnikov, editor of 'The Bulletin of the Christian Community' and long time Russian Orthodox dissident. Ogorodnikov hosted the conference in his Moscow apartment to present the struggle of the Greek Catholic Church for legal rights. Present at the meeting were Ivan Hel', the new head of the Committee for the Defence of the Greek Catholic Church, and other committee members. With the expulsion of the Committee chair Josyp Terelya, Hel' took over his responsibilities and also added new people to the group. Among the new members was Ivan Margitych, reportedly a priest from Transcarpathia, but soon to be revealed as a clandestinely consecrated bishop. At the press conference representatives of various western media were presented with the case for legalisation of the Greek Catholic Church. By the end of 1987 the issue of the continued repression of the church was a major point of discussion between the Soviet Union and various western governments.[28]

Gradually it became apparent that the authorities' commitment to repression was waning. Although clergy were still arrested, detained, fined, and some were even given forced labour for up to six months in the Chernobyl area, there were no mass arrests, no waves of repression. *Glasnost* was slowly reaching Ukraine, and the local powers seemed unsure of the implications for their relations with the Greek Catholic Church.

The church activists however were certain of their strategy: they had, by the beginning of 1988, collected over 10,000 signatures on a petition calling for legalisation; they continually passed information on to the West describing their struggle; they were persistently decrying the 'lack of *glasnost*' in the area of religious rights; and perhaps the boldest step was that they began to publicly defy the ban on church activities by increasingly holding public services. From the late summer of 1987 the Greek Catholic priest, Fr Petro Zelenyukh, openly celebrated services in the village of Kalynivka.[29] Although in January 1988 the church was officially opened by the civil authorities for the Russian Orthodox Church, Fr Zelenyukh continued to celebrate the

Liturgy in the village and pay the constant fines given him by the courts. In June 1988 a public memorial service was conducted by Greek Catholic priests in Lviv's Lychakiv cemetery with over 6,000 people in attendance. In July some 6,000 Catholics attended a public Liturgy in the village of Hoshiv, and over 20,000 participated in a similar service in Zarvanytsya. Popular pressure was building for recognition by the authorities of the Greek Catholic Church's right to exist.

Official attitudes in Moscow were beginning to change as well. In September 1988, Yuri Smirnov, a member of the Council for Religious Affairs, declared that the status of the Greek Catholic Church was 'highly charged politically' and could only be resolved by an understanding between that church and the Russian Orthodox.[30] This changed atmosphere also influenced Orthodox Metropolitan Filaret of Kyiv, who, in an 'Ispania' interview, finally admitted that a 'few thousand' Ukrainian Catholic believers do exist in Western Ukraine'.[31]

Local officials were slow to appreciate these changes however. The Catholic churches in Hoshiv and Kalynivka, which had become functional by the actions of the villagers and local priests, were taken and handed over to the Russian Orthodox Church. Clergy who celebrated public liturgies were harassed and fined.[32] In February, 1988 the wife of one such priest wrote to Catholics world-wide:

Despite the changes in our country the local authorities have in recent times taken to my husband and ruined our family by constantly imposing fines. In the last few months alone, my husband has been fined 40 times! Many faithful from the village of Kalynivka help us as best they can, but they, too, no longer have the means to cover the fines imposed on their priest.[33]

Pressure on the Soviet government increased in June of 1988. A Vatican delegation to the Russian Orthodox celebrations of the Millennium of the Christianisation of Kyivan-Rus' added an unexpected meeting to their agenda. On 10 June, while in Moscow, Cardinals Agostino Casaroli, Secretary of State for the Vatican and Johannes Willebrands, head of the Secretariat for Christian Unity, met privately with two bishops and three priests of the still illegal Greek Catholic Church. It was essentially an occasion which allowed the underground church leaders to personally present their concerns to the Vatican representatives. The symbolic value of the meeting was unquestionable: the Vatican stood wholeheartedly behind the struggle for legalisation. Subsequently, three days later Cardinal Casaroli presented Gorbachev with a private letter from the Pope along with a memorandum.[34] In this latter document the entire second section is devoted to the 'Catholic Church of the Byzantine Rite'. After discussing the history of this church, including the illegality of its forced liquidation, the Vatican document restates the Vatican's unequivocal support for the church's right to exist. 'The Holy See has repeatedly defended the right of the Ukrainian Church to exist before the Moscow Patriarchate. The Holy See feels that to raise this problem is in harmony with the spirit of the ecumenical dialogue begun during the Second Vatican Council.'[35] It was made clear to the Soviets that future strengthened relations with the Vatican would depend in large measure on the improvement in the status of the Greek Catholic Church. Similarly, the Russian Orthodox were informed that the Vatican would not accept their insistance that the Ukrainian Church's existence was a stumbling block to ecumenical dialogue.

That very dialogue was developing so successfully that the Russian Orthodox felt mounting pressure to come to some form of accommodation with the Greek Catholics. A series of International Catholic – Orthodox agreements meant that in 1987 the serious question of 'Uniate Churches' could be tackled by the International Theological Commission.[36] Although initially reluctant to discuss with the Vatican the specific question of the Ukrainian Church, Filaret of Kyiv was finally forced by the evolving situation within the Soviet Union to accede to such discussions.[37] A sub-commission of the Joint International Commission was established to study the ecclesiological and practical implications of the Greek Catholic Churches. The commission's meetings were compelled to go beyond the superficial. Growing numbers of Russian Orthodox activists, theologians, and even a bishop spoke out demanding that their hierarchy accept a legalised Greek Catholic Church.[38] International pressure was also added when during his Moscow summit, while visiting the Danilov monastery, President Reagan called for the legalisation of the Greek Catholic Church.[39]

No decision was being made to resolve the situation by either the Soviet government or the Russian Orthodox Church, but Greek Catholics continued to press their case. In October 1988 two separate delegations of Greek Catholic Bishops and clergy presented their demands for legalisation to Soviet authorities.[40] On 17 November 1988 a delegation of the church met an inter-parliamentary committee of Soviet and American officials. The next day the delegation met the deputy to the Austrian ambassador, this time receiving a letter of support from Austrian president Kurt Waldheim.[41] Petitions delivered to the Supreme Soviet now numbered in the tens of thousands. Millennium crosses were erected by Greek Catholics throughout Ukraine to mark not only the millennium, but the revival of the church. At the close of 1988 an observer noted:

Although it struggled unsuccessfully for legalization during the past year, the Ukrainian Catholic Church did at least manage to secure a semi-official status. Priests and bishops now celebrate openly and receive stiff fines for doing so. But, as one young priest from Lviv explains: 'the authorities know that we are living in an interregnum. *De facto*, the old laws are no longer in force, and nobody knows the new ones.'[42]

Expectations soared for 1989.

The first changes noticed in 1989 related more to the Russian Orthodox Church than the Greek Catholic. In 1988 the Soviet authorities had demonstrated their continued support for the Russian Church with the return of over 800 church buildings, a number of monasteries and permission to open new seminaries. However, the Russian Orthodox hierarchs had been reluctant to embrace the new policies of *glasnost*.[43] In fact it was only in January 1989 that the hierarchy announced that they had accepted a proposal to study the available materials concerning victims of Stalinism.[44] Furthermore, Orthodox activists who were critical of the hierarchy were beginning to receive Soviet media attention.[45] Finally, in February significant cracks began to develop on the grass-roots level within the Russian Church. On 26 February a Greek Catholic and Russian Orthodox priest celebrated a memorial service together in Lviv, with over 20,000 attending. Meanwhile in Kyiv another Orthodox priest announced that he was supporting the restoration of an Autocephalous Ukrainian Orthodox Church.[46] The Russian Orthodox Church continued its half-hearted policy of Ukrainianisation, instituted in 1988, without success: it announced the use of Ukrainian in services, courses would be given in Ukrainian in the Odessa seminary and the Ukrainian Exarchate's organ, *Pravoslavnyj Visnyk*, would have a larger press run.[47]

Greek Catholics however were now poised to launch their most sustained campaign for legalisation. In May 1989 a delegation of Bishops – Kurchaba, Dmyterko, and Vasylyk – along with three priests travelled to Moscow in order to meet the Deputy Head of the newly elected Supreme Soviet.[48] The delegation presented a letter requesting legalisation to President Gorbachev, signed by four bishops and ten priests. Included among the signatures for the first time was that of Archbishop Volodymyr Sternyuk, senior prelate of the Greek Catholic Church in Ukraine. The delegation received all kinds of assurances from Yuri Khristoradnov, then Vice President of the

Supreme Soviet and soon to be head of the Council for Religious Affairs. After their departure Bishop Ivan Margitych arrived to present a petition from the Bishop of Mukachiv Ivan Semedi, his clergy, and faithful requesting legalisation. However, because of the delays in the meetings and the lack of concrete results many faithful and clergy came to Moscow and began a rotating hunger strike. The hunger strikers gathered on Moscow's Arbat and conducted public services and distributed literature. In the heady days of the first session of an elected Congress of People's Deputies the Greek Catholic demonstrators were not given much attention by western media. Their presence was felt nevertheless by Soviet reformers and media. At the 28 May rally in support of reformer Borys Yeltsin, in Luzhniki stadium Fr Ivan Lesiv was asked to speak about the concerns of Greek Catholics. Throughout the summer hunger strikers and demonstrators kept the issue of the church before the citizens of Moscow. Their compatriots joined them in huge numbers throughout Western Ukraine. Mass rallies of 10 and 20 thousand became the norm. On 6 August a reported 50,000 gathered at the village of Pidlyssya for a pilgrimage commemorating the birthday of national folk hero, Fr Markian Shashkevych.[49] Perhaps the most striking development was that finally the Greek Catholics were getting a sympathetic hearing in the reform-minded Soviet media. Beginning with a photo and caption in the 11 June 1989 issue of *Moskovski novosti* (*Moscow News*), the issue of the legalisation of the Greek Catholic Church was being objectively presented in the Soviet press. In the July 30th issue the same newspaper printed a letter from Metropolitan Filaret of Kyiv critical of this coverage, however it followed the letter with an article from Sergei Filatov of the US and Canadian Institute. The latter article wholeheartedly championed the Greek Catholics and derided the Russian Orthodox Church's complicity in the destruction of this church. In a similar vein the Ukrainian Writers' Union newspaper, *Literaturna Ukrayina* published an article by Oles' Honchar in which he also spoke out in defence of the Greek Catholic Church.[50] Finally in its August 13th issue, *Moskovski novosti* published an interview with Greek Catholic Archbishop Volodymyr Sternyuk. In the article the senior prelate defended the church's right to exist, calmly refuted allegations that the church was a supporter of the Nazis during the Second World War and called for reconciliation with the Orthodox.[51] The issue of the legalisation of the Greek Catholic Church was finally open for public discussion.

Sensing the growing sentiment in favour of the church's legalisation, the official Soviet position began to alter. In July Yuri Smirnov of the

Council for Religious Affairs suggested that the long awaited new law on religions would allow for the registration of Greek Catholic communities.[52] At an August 27 rally for *perestroika* in Lviv, leading non-Party and Party figures publicly supported calls for the legalisation of the Greek Catholic Church. At this same rally Metropolitan Volodymyr issued a pastoral letter in which he spoke with optimism about legalisation.[53] When Ivan Hel', chairman of the increasingly vocal Church Defence Committee appealed to Lviv city authorities for permission to hold a rally in September calling for legalisation, the city mayor threatened to resign if the rally was forbidden.[54] When the rally finally occurred on 17 September 1989 over 150,000 people participated. Popular support for a legalisation of the Greek Catholic Church was undeniable, while official sympathy for the cause was increasing.

However, the issue was not simply decided on the streets of Western Ukraine. Although village churches were slowly proclaiming themselves Greek Catholic and hundreds of thousands now supported legalisation, the decision to legalise the church was to be made on the highest levels in Moscow. It would soon become apparent that it was in fact a bargaining chip in a higher game. Mikhail Gorbachev sincerely wished a Papal meeting: for the Pope and the head of the Soviet Union to meet amicably, head to head, would be another feather in his domestic and international cap. It was on this level of interstate relations that the issue was to be decided.

Speculation concerning a Papal–Gorbachev summit had been in the air since 1987. However as recently as June, 1989 Cardinal Cassaroli stated that a Papal visit to the USSR was 'still very far away',[55] the reason: being the continued illegal status of the Greek Catholic Church. In October 1989, the Pope once more raised the issue of the legalisation of the church. This time, in addressing the Ukrainian Catholic Bishops' Synod, he made two startling appeals: first to the Russian Orthodox Church to support their 'brother Catholics who are suffering' and, secondly, to the Soviet authorities to demonstrate their 'good will and recognise the sad socio-political events of the past and in so doing resolve the problem of the recognition of the rights of the Ukrainian Catholic Church . . . Without the legalisation of the Ukrainian communities the process of democratisation will never be complete.'[56] On the eve of the announcement of a Papal–Gorbachev summit the Pope reiterated his unequivocal support for the legalisation of the Greek Catholic Church.

It is likely that a decision to allow registration of the Greek Catholic Church was made sometime in the late summer or early fall of 1989.[57]

This decisive factor in confirming Papal interest in a summit with President Gorbachev was ostensibly communicated to the Vatican in early October. One final complicating factor remained: the Russian Orthodox Church.

During the summer the Orthodox hierarchs began an intense campaign to prevent Greek Catholic legalisation. In August a delegation of the Moscow Patriarchate visited the Vatican and called upon the Pope, in the name of ecumenism, to instruct the Greek Catholic faithful to choose between the Roman Catholic Church and the Russian Orthodox Church.[58] In the beginning of October, when an irenic letter of the Ukrainian Catholic Bishop's synod, meeting in Rome, was sent to the Moscow Patriarchate, it was totally ignored.[59] At the end of the month the Russian Orthodox hierarchy levelled a new weapon at the Greek Catholics. When on 29 October the Lviv parish of the Transfiguration declared itself Greek Catholic, the Orthodox charged the Catholics with orchestrating a violent takeover.[60] Even though a Canadian network's television crew broadcast the events of that Sunday, and no acts of violence or aggression were witnessed, the Orthodox maintained their story. A Vatican delegation arriving in Moscow on 2 November to discuss the resolution of the thorny issue of the Greek Catholic Church was sidetracked into a discussion of 'acts of violence' by Greek Catholics. The delegation had to settle for a declaration restating a desire for collaboration in the spirit of Christian charity, which excludes any act of violence. The statement concluded: 'This spirit must also inspire the believers of the two churches in the delicate and complex evolution of events in the situation of Catholics of the eastern rite, above all in Western Ukraine.'[61]

This development was nothing more than a minor irritant in the growing *rapprochement* between the Vatican and Moscow, however. Two weeks prior to the Gorbachev–Papal meeting the Chairman of the Department for External Church Relations of the Moscow Patriarchate was removed. On 20 November 1989 Archbishop Kirill of Smolensk and Kaliningrad was appointed to head the Department. Archbishop Kirill was perceived as a 'new thinker' more in step with Gorbachev's policies of *glasnost* and openness,[62] than outgoing Metropolitan Philaret of Minsk. This change in the senior levels of the Patriarchate was the reason given for the postponement of a meeting between Vatican and Orthodox officials, although Metropolitan Juvenalij of Krutitsy suggested that it had more to do with the Catholic seizure of the Transfiguration Church in Lviv.[63] But none of these events prevented President Gorbachev's visit to the Vatican. Finally, when on 1 December, 1989 Mikhail Gorbachev met Pope

John Paul II, it was not unexpected when the Council for Religious Affairs in Ukraine issued a statement declaring:

The Council for Religious Affairs states that under the condition of an unequivocal adherence to the constitution of the Ukrainian SSR and the law on religions Greek Catholics may benefit from all the laws established for religious groupings in the Ukrainian SSR.[64]

Although not resolving the outstanding issues of church property, the church's right to own property, and the settlement of disputes with the Russian Orthodox Church, the statement of the Council did ultimately recognise the Greek Catholic Church's right to have its communities officially registered. Within hours the primate of the Greek Catholic Church Myroslaw Ivan Cardinal Lubachivsky issued a statement greeting the development and calling upon his faithful to avail themselves of the new right. Archbishop Sternyuk repeated this appeal. By the end of the year over 300 parishes were already functioning as Greek Catholic, 650 had applied for registration, and over 200 formerly Russian Orthodox priests had joined the Greek Catholic Church.[65]

1990 brought further unforeseen developments. The Greek Catholic Church continued to grow and some might even say flourish. Christmas and Theophany celebrations were held joyously and with large crowds gathered at all Greek Catholic Churches. On 23 January 1990 a synod of Greek Catholic bishops of Ukraine was held, with the participation of 7 bishops and over 200 priests. The church was beginning to stand on its own feet and plot out its own direction into the future.

However both Moscow and the Vatican clearly desired, for their own purposes, to gain control over the situation. Developments in the USSR in 1989 placed the ongoing Roman Catholic–Eastern Orthodox dialogue in jeopardy. On 12 January 1990 a Vatican delegation arrived in Moscow to re-open talks concerning the 'Western Ukrainian situation'. Although the delegation was scheduled to travel to Lviv and there meet Greek Catholic hierarchs, the itinerary was changed at the insistence of the hosts and the Greek Catholics were summoned to Moscow.[66] In Moscow the delegation from Lviv was quickly plunged into the middle of a thorny diplomatic session where they were immediately placed upon the defensive. An attempt was made to have them sign a statement condemning the violence of 'Uniates' in Western Ukraine. Clearly they would not do this and the meetings adjourned with a nebulous commitment to continue discussions in an attempt to resolve the problem.[67] The development of a

split between the Vatican position and the position of the Greek
Catholic bishops of Ukraine was clear: the former sought to achieve
peace by diplomacy, whereas the latter felt the priority should be given
to justice (allowing the people of Ukraine to decide for themselves the
church of their allegiance). Later in the month on the 26th, the sub-
commission of the International Catholic–Orthodox Dialogue group
met in Vienna and the meeting was almost aborted until a compromise
'Press release' was issued, not a common statement as had been the
normal practice. The bone of contention was the status of the Greek
Catholics within the Roman Catholic communion and recent events in
Ukraine. The Orthodox held firm to their official position that 'the
abolition of Uniatism and the incorporation of the members of the
Uniate Churches either in the Latin Roman Catholic Church or in the
Orthodox Church' should be demanded.[68] In the same release both
sides 'declared that on no account should forceful methods be used to
solve any problems whatsoever between the Churches', a comment
clearly aimed at the Greek Catholics whom the Orthodox had continually accused of 'acts of violence'. This meeting seemed to re-establish
dialogue on the highest Catholic–Orthodox levels. However, it had
nothing but a negative influence on the Greek Catholics. Lviv felt more
and more isolated from both Moscow and the Vatican.

This isolation/independence of the Lviv-centred Greek Catholic
Church reached its apex in March. Political and religious events
coalesced to effectively divide the Greek Catholic Church leadership in
Ukraine from the Vatican and from many Greek Catholic bishops in
the West. On 28 February 1990 the Vatican representatives were
named for the upcoming meetings of a Quadrapartite commission
representing the Vatican, the Greek Catholic Church, the Moscow
Patriarchate, and the Russian Orthodox Church in Ukraine, since the
beginning of the month called the Ukrainian Orthodox Church. The
Vatican representatives were to be two Greek Catholic prelates from
the West: Archbishop Myroslav Marusyn, a senior Vatican official
and Archbishop Stephan Sulyk, Ukrainian Catholic Metropolitan of
Philadelphia (USA). Although this selection seemed to be a sign from
the Vatican that Greek Catholics would be allowed to speak for themselves and direct the talks in the direction they wished, this was not to
be the case. Although Greek Catholic, the Vatican representatives
chose to follow the traditional diplomatic approach of appeasing
Moscow and avoiding confrontation, an approach which would soon
put them at odds with the local Greek Catholic hierarchy.

When the Quadrapartite Commission met in Kyiv on 6 March 1990
the conditions of the meeting were once more unacceptable to the

Greek Catholic bishops of Ukraine. The church's senior prelate, eighty-three-year-old Archbishop Volodymyr Sternyuk was brought a telegram by his old nemesis, Yuri Reshetylo, head of the Lviv Council of Religious Affairs instructing him to come to Kyiv that very evening (March 6th) for the Commission's meeting.[69] Sternyuk, was totally surprised since he had earlier been told that the meetings would take place in Lviv. When he arrived in Kyiv he was informed at a four-party meeting that the commission had begun deliberations a day earlier and had already prepared a preliminary statement in which recommendations were to be made how to 'regulate the situation in the churches seized by Catholics of the eastern Rite without the agreement of the given communities'.[70] Sternyuk refused to accept this statement although it was made public over state radio. On March 8th the Commission moved its meetings to Lviv. Dissatisfaction was growing among the Greek Catholic bishops of Ukraine, the clergy, and faithful. Schedules were rearranged by the Orthodox with the compliance of the Vatican representatives. Archbishop Sternyuk's repeated demand that the return of the historic cathedral and centre of Greek Catholicism, St George's Sobor, to his jurisdiction be placed on the table was ignored. Finally, on 13 March Archbishop Sternyuk withdrew from the negotiations protesting the Moscow Patriarchate's refusal to address the issues of St George's Sobor and putting a stop to the accusations of Greek Catholic violence. The Greek Catholic representatives of the Vatican were shocked, no less surprised were Vatican officials in Rome – the Greek Catholic bishops in Ukraine were not going to blindly follow the Vatican position, they were rather willing and able to establish an independent and unique approach to inter-church relations in the USSR.[71]

This independence of the Greek Catholic bishops of Ukraine was further bolstered as a result of the local elections on 4 and 18 March. In these elections Democratic Bloc candidates swept into office in the three Western Ukrainian provinces where the Greek Catholic Church was strongest. The provincial and municipal governments throughout Lviv, Ternopil and Ivano-Frankivsk provinces were now in the hands of sovereigntists or even independentists, most of whom were very sympathetic to the Greek Catholic Church. (Ivan Hel' former head of the Committee in Defence of the Church was now elected vice-chair of the Lviv provincial government.) The Greek Catholic bishops of Ukraine now had a local government which clearly supported them in their struggle with the Russian Orthodox Church and was in fact quite sympathetic to the bishop's establishing an approach to the problem independent of the Vatican.

Emboldened in this manner all the Greek Catholic bishops of Ukraine met in Synod on 17 March and issued a 'Statement of the Hierarchy of the Ukrainian Greek Catholic Church in Ukraine Regarding Talks of the Quadrapartite Commission'. In their statement they distanced themselves from the work of the commission and said that no further discussions could take place until 'the Russian Orthodox Church is ready to recognise the Ukrainian Greek Catholic Church as a Church, an institution and a juridical body', and 'until the fundamental questions of full legalisation and rehabilitation of the Ukrainian Greek Catholic Church are settled'.[72] The clear message of the fourteen point statement was that the Greek Catholics wanted to be treated as equal partners in any discussions, whether that be with the Soviet government, with the Moscow Patriarchate, or even with the Vatican.

From March formal discussions with the Moscow Patriarchate stopped. Greek Catholics began to press their case with local civil authorities in an attempt to regain 'from the state' that which the state had taken from them in 1946. With the death of Patriarch Pimen in May the situation within the Moscow Patriarchate itself became increasingly problematic. By the summer of 1990 all reports indicated that although the Russian Orthodox continued to complain about the Greek Catholics their own position in the three western provinces of Ukraine was increasingly weak. Statistics supplied to the author in June by local government officials clearly placed the Russian Orthodox Church (now called Ukrainian Orthodox) in third place numerically in the western provinces. The new contender for dominance in this area was the Ukrainian Autocephalous Orthodox Church.

Added signs of the fact that in 1990 the Greek Catholic Church had become well-established in Western Ukraine were the return of St George's Sobor in late August, and the establishment of three seminaries (two Eparchial and one for the Basilian Order). The June 25–26 meetings of the Greek Catholic bishops of Ukraine with the Pope and their western counterparts in Rome proved that the government of the USSR would no longer stand in the way of the external contacts of the Greek Catholic Church. Both these events signalled to the populace of Western Ukraine that the Greek Catholic Church in Ukraine was now not only recognised by the government, but also, and perhaps more importantly, by the Pope of Rome.

The church which re-emerged from its clandestine activity on 1 December 1989 was in many ways strong, but also greatly burdened by its forty-four years in the underground. It was surprisingly vibrant in numbers and popular support, as the previous summer had demonstrated. The church arose with eight publicly acknowledged bishops, approximately 1,000 priests and 1,200 nuns. It had a number of religious congregations which had survived more or less intact: among the male orders there were Basilian Fathers, Redemptorists and the Studites; whereas the female orders included Sister Servants, Basilian Sisters, Sisters of St Vincent, and Josephite Sisters. The church was inevitably plagued by division and dissension inherent to its situation as an illegal church. Already during the years in the catacombs the 'Pokutnyky' sect had formed. This group claimed to represent a more penitent, purer form of Christian life. Yet more profound divisions lay within the church's mainstream. In the 1930s the Greek Catholic Church had developed a number of trends: a more Latinising position was defended by many Basilian priests, others, often Studites and Redemptorists, supported a more Easternising tendency, while still others tried to maintain a middle ground. Although Metropolitan Sheptycky strove to hold a moderate position, he was often strongly criticised for his 'Easternising' policies. These divisions became commonplace in the underground church. Easternisers willingly used the formula 'all you Orthodox Christians' in the Liturgy; Latinisers rejected this formula. The latter wished to draw as sharp a line as possible between themselves (the 'true church') and the 'atheistic' Russian Orthodox. These differences divided Greek Catholics in the catacombs, heightened by the fact that many clergy and faithful lacked the theological formation to discuss adequately the issues involved. Further, the church's isolation during and after Vatican II meant that few Greek Catholics were aware of the radical changes going on in the Catholic Church. Still less were they aware of their own church's post-Vatican self-awareness which demanded a re-acquaintance with the historical traditions of the church, especially those which unite East and West. Re-emergence from the catacombs occasioned a re-emergence of old wounds.

A valuable insight into the Greek Catholic Church can be garnered by even a brief overview of the various groupings which are surfacing in the now legalised church. Within this church there are many groups; to mention only a few: the high Catholic grouping, predominantly made up of the Basilian Order and their supporters; there is the crypto-Catholic grouping which has, over the past forty years, attended more or less regularly the Russian Orthodox Church; there are the middle-of-the road people who served in the catacombs but were more or less sympathetic to the crypto-Catholics, and there are many Catholics who are presently served by the Ukrainian Autocephalous Orthodox Church.

The group which has been termed high Catholic, represents sincere Christians who have interpreted their survival in the catacombs as a sign of their being members of the one church of Jesus Christ. They believe that they are the true remnant: they have maintained the customs, practices, and faith of the church through the years of persecution. They do not seek any form of reconciliation with the Orthodox because the latter served the atheistic regime. Nor are they sympathetic to the crypto-Catholics who attended the official church over the years. In their eyes this group also has compromised itself. Being defenders of the 'true, Catholic faith' they oppose the liturgical use of the term 'all you Orthodox Christians', arguing that they are not Orthodox and never were. They further insist that St Volodymyr accepted the Catholic (as opposed to Orthodox) faith in 988. Theirs is an all too exclusivistic view of Christian and Catholic teaching. Unfortunately, they have been extremely vocal and aggressive. In the past clergy in this group forbade attendance at any Orthodox services[73] and challenged the validity of Orthodox sacraments. Their supporters have publicly disrupted Catholic services over the issue of the term 'all you Orthodox Christians'.[74] After the transfer of the Church of the Transfiguration to the Greek Catholics one Basilian priest even suggested that the parish's pastor Fr Chuknij was not Catholic since he 'must first serve profound penance for his years of service in the Russian Orthodox Church' and then he must be ordained by a true bishop![75] There have in fact even been unsubstantiated rumours that 'truly Catholic' bishops have been consecrated in order to have a hierarchy free of any taint of Orthodoxy. They have rebaptised persons baptised by Orthodox priests and re-ordination of Orthodox priests is also quite common. This group clearly verges on Donatism.

The next group of interest to us are the crypto-Catholics, those that maintained their Catholic faith in secret while overtly attending the Russian Orthodox Church. Without doubt this would be the largest group and the promoters of the transfers of churches to the Catholic side in the last months of 1989. This is the group which today wishes to cleanse itself of its Orthodoxy, but is at times unsure of what is Orthodox and what is Catholic.[76] Further in their desire to discard their Orthodoxy they sometimes err in charity. During the memorial services surrounding the internment of Vasyl Stus, held in Kyiv on 19 November 1989 the pastor of the Russian Orthodox Church in which the body was resting was forbidden to join the service by his own parishioners, they said he was unworthy of joining the Catholic priests in prayer.[77] Members of this group also tend to distinguish between the hierarchy and the people of the Russian Orthodox Church. The hierarchy is said to have betrayed the people and destroyed the church, making it a servant of the state. As a result, representatives of this group would say that the Russian people do not really have their own church, it has been usurped by the hierarchy which makes of it what they will.[78] Such views, though understandable are nonetheless uncharitable. It is too simple a solution to say that the Russian Orthodox hierarchy has totally destroyed Russian Orthodoxy. Certainly there were many who willingly served the state, but many others worked honestly in difficult conditions to guarantee the preservation of the Orthodox Church. It is to be hoped that good pastoral leadership and the open preaching of the Gospel will assist this group in coming to extend its hand in forgiveness and love to the Russian Church.

The third group to which we turn our attention is a moderate grouping which although working steadfastly in the underground maintained ties with those Catholics who outwardly joined the Orthodox Church. The grouping is dominated by the clergy of the Redemptorist and Studite orders and predominates in the Archeparchy of Lviv, although some of its number are also working in the central Ukrainian regions. Both its spiritual and ecclesiastical superior is Metropolitan Volodymyr Sternyuk of Lviv. The group consciously promotes the policies and attitudes which are engendered in the tradition of Metropolitan Andrei Sheptycky and Patriarch Josyf Slipyj. They supported the latter's attempts to establish a Ukrainian Catholic Patriarchate, and believe such a Patriarchate would have eased the process of re-establishing the Greek Catholic Church in the USSR. Perceiving themselves in continuity with the Easternising traditions of the past two Metropolitans of Lviv they also feel that their church can serve as a bridge between Orthodoxy and Catholicism – a bridge which demonstrates the viability of an Eastern Church in union with Rome. As a result they are somewhat more sympathetic to the Orthodox themselves and have supported the overtures made by Greek Catholic hierarchs in the West towards the Moscow Patriarchate. In general, this group is much more conciliatory and accepting of the Russian Church than the others.[79] Further this group defends the use of the term 'all you Orthodox Christians', on two grounds: firstly, this is the proper historical liturgical usage and, secondly, the Greek Catholic Church is in fact an Orthodox Church in union with Rome.[80] All this makes members of this group most open to the crypto-Catholics who are returning to the Catholic Church since the announcement of 1 December, 1989. They are most able to engage in a dialogue with the clergy of the Russian Orthodox Church who contemplate such transfers, and consequently they are the most able to engage in a true dialogue of charity with the Russian Orthodox Church. They are also willing to make accommodations with the Ukrainian Autocephalous Orthodox Church: Archbishop Sternyuk has repeatedly proposed sharing churches in villages, rather than allowing the church to be the cause of sometimes even violent disputes. This group, perhaps numerically the smallest to be discussed, is conceivably the most prepared for a 'normalised' church life within the new, pluralistic realities of the Soviet Union, and the most open to the changes in the post-Vatican II Catholic world.

The final group to be discussed is that of the Catholics who today find themselves members of the Ukrainian Autocephalous Orthodox Church. This church began its renewal in central Ukraine in the early part of 1989, as a movement of laity desirous of a truly Ukrainian Orthodox Church. However, the movement of renewal began in earnest with the declaration on 19 August 1989 by the pastor of Sts Peter and Paul Church in Lviv, Fr V. Yarema, that he was withdrawing his parish from the jurisdication of the Moscow Patriarchate. Fr Yarema had already in February 1989 noted his dissatisfaction with Russian Orthodoxy and Greek Catholicism in a letter to Kyivan Exarch, Metropolitan Filaret,[81] but it was not until late summer that he made his intentions public. In effect, by re-establishing an Autocephalous Ukrainian Orthodox Church, the supporters were attempting to establish a uniquely, Ukrainian ecclesial reality which could nurture the best of both Orthodox and Catholic traditions. As in the 1920s experiment[82] the most important element was that of complete independence (autocephaly). Since the summer of 1989 aggressive propagandising was launched by leaders of the autocephaly movement. The basic thrust of the campaign has been to paint the Russian Church as an agent of the Soviet government and, repeating the jargon of early anti-Uniate campaigns, to paint the Greek Catholics as agents of the Vatican. Reports reached the West that priests leading the autocephaly movement called their church the 'blue and yellow' church, unequivocally referring to the national flag of an independent Ukraine. As a result, many historically Catholic communities were willing supporters of autocephaly. However this support was not based on religious conviction or theological argument, rather it was simply a desire to have 'our church open'. Further, it must be noted that many autocephalous Orthodox considered becoming openly Catholic, but finally decided against it because of two factors: anti-Orthodox sentiment among, what has been termed above, the high Catholics and, secondly, Vatican opposition to a Greek Catholic married clergy in the West and its denial of Patriarchal status to the church.[83] Even Fr Yarema was reported to have decided conclusively for Autocephaly because of a vehemently anti-Orthodox homily given by Bishop Paul Vasylyk at Pidlyssya, near Lviv on 6 August 1989.[84] In mid-1990 bishops, priests, and laity of the Autocephalous Church met in Synod in Kyiv and elected Metropolitan Mstyslav (Skrypnyk) Patriarch of their Church. Metropolitan Mstyslav had been the leader of the *émigré* Ukrainian Autocephalous, and was a resident of the United States. In late October 1990, he returned to Ukraine to be enthroned in Kyiv as Patriarch of the Ukrainian Autocephalous Orthodox Church, on 18 November. Although his title is Patriarch of Kyiv and all Ukraine, this church continues to exist almost exclusively in the three Western Ukrainian provinces which suggests that its strength lies with disaffected Catholics, who have joined it in response to its strongly nationalistic slogans.

Conclusion

The survival and re-emergence of the Greek Catholic Church is truly one of the great stories of the perseverance of the human spirit. The total number of persons who died in the name of this church is unrecorded and will probably never be known. However the courage, faith, and love which allowed the church to survive is now recognised. Finally, in 1989 these virtues were crowned with the legalisation of the church. The form that the legalisation would take, the difficulties which lay in the future, and the effect of legalisation on the life of the church and the life of the USSR could not be calculated. But certainly the very legalisation was a compelling argument for acknowledging the radical nature of the transformation initiated by Mikhail Gorbachev.

It is a credit to both Gorbachev and Pope John Paul that legalisation occurred with a minimal disruption by the Russian Orthodox Church. By far the greater loser in the legalisation of the Greek Catholics, the Russian Orthodox continually threatened both Gorbachev and the Pope. Gorbachev was threatened with civil strife should the Catholics be legalised, whereas the Pope was threatened with an end to the ecumenical dialogue. Both these threats proved empty. The Russian Orthodox were historically dependent on government favours, and so were in no position to make serious threats. Secondly, they could ill afford an end to ecumenical dialogue at a time when their relations with Constantinople were at a low and government pressure on them to embrace *perestroika* was mounting. At best the Russian Orthodox could accept legalisation and determine an advantageous compromise, but they failed to see this as an option.

Now the Greek Catholic Church of Ukraine has entered into the religious life of the world as an honoured member. But in so doing it has to transform itself from an underground, persecuted church to a vibrant, lively church able to function in an increasingly pluralistic and materialistic society. It will have to come to grips with its own inner contradictions and dissensions. It will have to regain a sense of corporate direction and ecclesiastical harmony. It would not be an overstatement to say that the road ahead may be no less difficult than the road already travelled.

Notes

1 Cardinal Josyf Slipyj in his address to the Congress of 'Kirche in Not', 28 July 1980, Königstein, West Germany. Published in *Mirror*, 2 March 1981 (Königstein, Kirche in Not), p. 5.

2 These figures represent the church's status in 1939. Zinkevych, Osyp and Lonchyna, Taras R. (ed.), *Martyrolohiya Ukrains'kykh Tserkov*, II (Toronto, Baltimore, Smoloskyp, 1985), pp. 49–50.

3 'Zayava Rady v spravakh relihiyi pry Radi Ministriv Ukrainskoi RSR', 1 December 1989. A copy is available in the 'St Sophia' Religious Association (Canada) archives.

4 *Blahovisnyk*, 21:1–4, 1985, p. 42.

5 'Memorandum of the Holy See', *Visti z Rymu*, 24:3, 3 (414), 1989, p. 10.

6 See Ivan Hvat, 'The Ukrainian Catholic Church, the Vatican and the Soviet Union during the Pontificate of Pope John Paul II', *Religion in Communist Lands*, 11:3, 1983, pp. 264–80.

7 See Bohdan R. Bociurkiw, 'The Uniate Church in the Soviet Ukraine: A Case Study in Soviet Church Policy', *Canadian Slavonic Papers*, 7, 1965, pp. 89–113. The Soviet media itself has finally admitted to the government's role in the so-called Synod of Lviv, see Georgiy Rozhnov 'Tse my, Hospody', *Ogonëk*, 38, September 1989, reprinted in a Ukrainian translation in *Zhyttya i Slovo*, 13 November 1989, pp. 6–7 and 20 November 1989, pp. 6–7.

8 Cardinal Slipyj's address cited above, p. 5.

9 An interesting underground document giving an overview of the church's life in the 1970s can be found in *Religion in Communist Lands*, 11:3, 1983, pp. 280–90.

10 Fr Budzinsky was a member of the church's official delegation to Stalin of 1944 which attempted to reach a modus vivendi with the Soviet authorities. *Martyrolohiya*, II, p. 67.

11 *Martyrolohiya* II, pp. 664–5.

12 For an overview of the first eleven issues of 'The Chronicle' see, Andrew Sorokowski, 'The Chronicle of the Catholic Church in Ukraine', *Religion in Communist Lands*, 13:3, pp. 292–7.

13 *Il Tempo*, 2 October 1985, p. 19.

14 'The Furov Report', *Religion in Communist Dominated Areas*, 20:4–6, 1981, p. 53.

15 The conversation was translated and excerpted in *Church of the Catacombs*, 7 March 1986, p. 20. (A monthly bulletin published by St Sophia Religious Association (Canada).)

16 From Anna Halja Horbatsch, 'Relihijni aspekty pravozakhysnoho rukhu v Ukraini'. An unpublished paper available in the St Sophia (Canada) archives.

17 For example much of the sixteenth issue of the Chronicle is devoted to the fate of Helsinki Group member Mykhajlo Horyn, who was in the mid-1980s imprisoned in the death camp, Kuchino, 36–1 and near death on a number of occassions, due to a heart condition.

18 See my article 'Russian Orthodox Attitudes towards the Ukrainian Catholic Church', in *Religion in Communist Lands*, 17:4, 1989, pp. 313–31.

19 I am using the transliteration of the city's name from Ukrainian rather than the more common form Kiev, which transliterates from Russian. This is a practice which is in accord with the Ukrainian SSR's language law of January 1, 1990.

20 *Ukrainian Press Service* (Canadian edition) (*UPS*), 12, 1986, p. 12.

21 *UPS*, 9:21, 1987, p. 2.

22 'Marian Apparitions in Hrushiv', *UPS*, 9:21, 1987, pp. 7–10.

23 'Marian Apparitions', p. 10.

24 'It is pointless to remain underground', *UPS*, 9:21, 1987, p. 5.

25 *UPS*, 10:22, p. 2.

26 Desmond O'Grady, 'Byzantine Rite to be Recognized in U.S.S.R.?', *Our Sunday Visitor*, 22 November 1987, p. 3, and 29 November 1987, p. 4.

27 Myroslaw Ivan Cardinal Lubachivsky speaking at the *Kirche in Not* Congress, Rome, 6 November 1987.

28 The importance in this development of the US State Department's report 'Soviet Repression of the Ukrainian Catholic Church', January 1987, cannot be underestimated.

29 Fr Zelenyukh's report can be found in *UPS*, 3:27, 1988, p. 12.

30 *Keston News Service*, 311, 20 October 1988, p. 7.

31 *Ibid.*, 299, 28 April 1988, p. 20.

32 An interesting report of 'A day in the life of a Ukrainian Catholic priest' can be found in *UPS*, 9:33, 1988, pp. 5–6. The report dates from 20 April 1988.

33 *UPS*, 7–8:31–32, 1988, pp. 2–3.

34 The text of the 'Memorandum of the Holy See' was published in Ukrainian translation in *Visti z Rymu*, 24:3 (414), 1989, pp. 4–10.

35 'Memorandum', p. 10.

36 'Russian Orthodox Attitudes', pp. 315–16.

37 Felicity Barringer, 'Russian Orthodox to Meet Vatican about Ukrainians', *New York Times*, 5 June 1988, p. 1.

38 'Russian Orthodox Attitudes', 323, pp. 326–28.

39 'Excerpts from Reagan Talks to Dissidents and at Monastery', *New York Times*, 31 May 1988, p. 8.

40 2 October 1988 delegation see: *UPS*, 10:34, 1988, p. 2; 25 October 1988 delegation see: *UPS*, 11:35, 1988, pp. 3–5.

41 *UPS*, 12:36, p. 4.

42 K. Horbatsch, 'Ukraine in 1988', *UPS*, 12:36, 1988, p. 3.

43 The demise of Konstantin Kharchev as head of the Council for Religious Affairs was plainly a result of his attempt to force the church to embrace *glasnost* and *perestroika*. *Keston News Service*, 325, 11 May 1989, pp. 6–7 and *Ibid.*, 349, 30 November 1989, pp. 16–18.

44 *Ibid.*, 317, 19 January 1989, p. 3.

45 *Ibid.*, 317, 19 January 1989, p. 19.

46 *Ibid.*, 320, 2 March 1989, pp. 7–8.

47 *Ibid.*, 320, 2 March 1989, p. 9.

48 For details see *UPS*, 5:41, 1989, pp. 1–4.

49 Details are available in *UPS*, 6:42 – 9:45, 1989.

50 Oles' Honchar, 'Vypravdaty Spodivannya', *Literaturna Ukrayina*, 26, 29 June 1989, p. 1.

51 'Nelegalnaya Tserkov', *Moskovski Novosti*, 33, 13 August 1989, p. 13.

52 *Ibid.*, 331, 3 August 1989, p. 7.

53 Copies of both documents are in the St Sophia (Canada) archives.

54 'Events preceding the mass demonstration of September 17', St Sophia Press Release, dated 17 September 1989.

55 *UPS*, 24:7–8 (418–19), p. 9.

56 *UPS*, 24:10 (421), p. 3.

57 Already on 22 November 1989 while having discussions with the Prime Minister of Canada, Soviet Foreign Minister E. Shevernadze said that the Greek Catholic Church would soon be legalised, a statement repeated during a Foreign Ministry press briefing on the same day. St Sophia Press Release 27/89, 22 November 1989.

58 Valerij Senderov, 'Katolyky vostochnoho obrayada i deputat Filaret', *Russkaya Mysl'*, 3 November 1989.

59 A copy of the letter is in the St Sophia (Canada) archives.

60 Francis X. Clines, 'At Newly Freed Parish, Priestly Skirmish Rages', *New York Times*, 11 December 1989.

61 Press Communiqué of the Holy See, 4 November 1989.

62 *Ibid.*, 346, 14 December 1989, pp. 8–9.

63 'Orthodox Leader meets with Pope', *New York Times*, 28 November 1989.

64 'Zayava Rady v spravakh relihiyi pry Radi Ministriv Ukrainskoi RSR', 1 December 1989.

65 St Sophia Press Release, 22 December 1989.

66 Keston College News Release dated 23 January 1990.

67 One of the bishops present recounted that what most set him off balance

was the pressure for such a statement which was coming from certain members of the Vatican delegation!

68 Press release in my possession and issued by the Pontifical Council for Promoting Christian Unity.

69 Reportedly, Archbishop Marusyn had left Rome without Archbishop Sternyuk's address, and so turned to Metropolitan Filaret in order to call Sternyuk to Kiev. Filaret, in turn contacted the Orthodox Bishop of Lviv, who called upon Reshetylo to take the telegram to Archbishop Sternyuk.

70 Ukrainian Press Bureau (Rome) press release dated 12 March 1990.

71 An interesting report on the events at the commission meetings and subsequent to them was made by the Chancellor of the Lviv Metropolitanate, Fr I. Dacko (resident in Rome). This report was made by him to the Aid to Church in Need Congress held in Königstein, Germany, 26 March 1990. Fr Dacko arrived in Lviv on 14 March and was instrumental in 'picking up the pieces' after the commission meetings fell apart. The document is available in the St Sophia (Canada) archives. It is valuable to contrast this report with the report made public on 27 March by Archbishop Sulyk who seems to suggest that in fact the commission was in its final session anyway when Archbishop Sternyuk walked out. This 'less dramatic' account does not however reflect the consternation which witnesses to the commission meetings in Lviv comment on, nor does it concur with reports of general anger in Greek Catholic circles with the conduct of Archbishop Marusyn, the senior Vatican delegate at the meetings. This report is also available at St Sophia (Canada) and was published in *Postup*, 8 April 1990.

72 The full text of the statement is available in the St Sophia (Canada) archives.

73 Joseph Terelya's support of this viewpoint was mentioned in the autobiography of Fr Mykhailo Havryliv, who also seems to support it. Mykhailo Havrlyiv, *Kozhna lyudyna – tse persh pz vse istoriya*, (Rome, Ukrainian Press Bureau, 1987), p. 151.

74 This was recounted by an eyewitness during a video-taped conversation with Metropolitan Sternyuk in August 1989.

75 This was recounted to me in Lviv, during my visit there 25–8 November 1989.

76 In a conversation with two formerly Russian Orthodox priests who joined the Catholic Church, I was told by both that they weren't completely sure how the Catholic Church's teaching was different from the Orthodox, they simply knew that their families were traditionally Catholic and so they rejoined the Catholic Church at the first opportunity.

77 St Sophia Press Release 36/89, 13 December 1989.

78 Iryna Kalynets. Rukh Meeting, Lviv, 27 August 1989.

79 In Metropolitan Volodymyr's pastoral letter of 27 August 1989, he called for understanding and reconciliation. Aware of the danger of the persecuted becoming the persecutor he said: 'Let us not say that we were persecuted so therefore we can now persecute. In that case we will be no better than those who persecuted us.' A copy is available in the St Sophia (Canada) archives.

80 Metropolitan Volodymyr's pastoral letter of 26 November 1989. A copy is available in the St Sophia (Canada) archives.

81 A copy is available in the St Sophia (Canada) archives.

82 Bohdan R. Bociurkiw, 'The Ukrainian Autocephalous Orthodox Church, 1920–30: A Study in Religious Modernization'. Dennis Dunn (ed.), *Religion and Modernization in the Soviet Union*. (Boulder, Colo, Westview Press, 1977), pp. 310–47.

83 These opinions were expressed to me in conversation with a number of priests during a visit to Ukraine in November 1989.

84 This was related by an acquaintence of Fr Yarema who spoke to the priest a number of times in the days before his announcement.

· 14 ·

Protestantism in the USSR

WALTER SAWATSKY

By the summer of 1990 Soviet Protestant church leaders were heard to say that they often felt literally torn apart by persons coming to them from all sides to ask questions about faith. A villager, for example, would ask the evangelicals in a nearby city to visit his village, bring along a group of singers and a speaker. Vice-President Alexei Bychkov and editor Vitali Kulikov of the Baptist Union found themselves invited to give ten minute sermons on Moscow radio on a monthly basis. When in June 1990 the Baptist Union called a national consultation of evangelists, pastors from all over the Soviet Union reported invitations they were receiving to speak to university professors, or to their classes, to lecture on Christianity at nearby institutions of higher learning. When many of them expressed their insecurity at addressing the educated of society, Nikolai Kolesnikov responded by reminding them of the intent of those invitations. Those inquirers knew that these poorly trained pastors or simple church members claimed to have a personal relationship to Jesus Christ, and that was what they wanted to hear about, not a scholarly dissertation on the nature of transcendance or proofs for the existence of God. Their task was to explain what difference their faith in Christ made in their lives.

The process of evangelisation was in essence a becoming acquainted with the nature of the Gospel; all Christian confessions were involved in explaining their faith to seekers. Many of the converts were individuals who now chose to make public their earlier secret belief; others responding with requests for baptism to the Christians that they met. Statistically speaking, a minority of the population was converting, and, of these, the vast majority became Orthodox. Soviet evangelicals, however, were the most systematic in outreach and received disproportionate assistance with literature and even personnel from abroad. In October 1990 the Lausanne Committee for Evangelism conducted a congress in Moscow for Soviet evangelists, of

319

whom the majority were Protestants. The influx of new members was already sufficiently large to create initial anxiety about the capacity of these Protestant congregations to adapt themselves culturally to such new members.

There are essentially two stories and two sets of issues for Protestants in the USSR. On the one hand it is the story of Protestant believers settling in the Russian Empire as early as the 1760s as foreign colonists with special privileges of religious freedoms,[1] supplemented by other Protestants added through political annexation, particularly in Estonia and Latvia during the imperial period and after the Second World War. On the other hand, it is the story of the rise of popular education and the spread of Bibles, newly translated into the vernacular during the nineteenth century. In the way that the Bible in the vernacular was a key *raison d'être* for the rise of Protestantism in Habsburg Europe, so now the Bible in modern Russian (finally completed in 1876) triggered the rise of a Slavic Protestant sectarianism.[2] In terms of the issues, it is helpful to distinguish the churches of the Magisterial Reformers (Lutheran and Calvinist) from those of the Radical or Left-Wing of the Reformation (Anabaptists). Indeed, the intellectual origins of Slavic Protestant sectarianism are more complex than the standard literature on the Reformation would suggest, since the First or Hussite Reformation has tended to have a renewal impact on the thought of Soviet and East European Protestantism, especially during the twentieth century.

In what follows it will be impossible to devote adequate detail to each of the churches normally subsumed under the rubric 'Protestant'. The term embraces formerly established Lutheranism in Latvia and Estonia; German Lutherans and German Mennonites once living in separate colonies in South Russia, in the Saratov region (Volga) and along the expanding frontier east of the Ural and Caucasus Mountains, who had developed in considerable isolation from the surrounding population. It includes Evangelical Christians (related to the Open Brethren) and Baptists (Russian, Ukrainian, Latvian, Estonian and German) who formed the largest and most dominant church union in 1944, the All Union Council of Evangelical Christian–Baptists (AUCECB). It includes Pentecostals and Adventists, both of which are divided into a moderate and officially registered group (part of the Pentecostal wing joined the AUCECB in 1945) and an independent union.

There has also been an Estonian Methodist Church since the late nineteenth century, twentieth-century missionary efforts by Methodists in Siberia having been swallowed up into the subsequent Evangelical Christian–Baptist (ECB) structure. A small number of Hungarian speaking Reformed Churches still exist on the south-western border regions (Transcarpathia). Little is known of them, although they received a small gift of Bibles in 1988.[3] Even less information is available about New Apostolic Christians (Neutaeufer) whose co-religionists in other East European countries have led a precarious existence largely owing to their pacifism. The Jehovah's Witnesses are treated separately in another chapter, they will not be covered here except to note that the difference between them and other neo-Protestants is more keenly felt than might be true in America. In a modified way 'Protestant' should include uniquely Russian groupings like the Molokany and the Dukhobortsy. To the degree that they shared the common experience of faith under stress they are included in this treatment, but it is not possible to do them justice on the basis of the available information. We will seek instead to sketch the broad outlines of a common historical experience and to illustrate the major issues from those denominations who sensed them most deeply.[4]

Decade of growth and subjugation 1917–1929

Two somewhat contradictory themes dominated the first period of Protestantism under Soviet power. For sectarian or Neo-Protestantism it was both a decade of growth and of submission (under considerable administrative pressure) to the new Soviet authorities. For Lutherans and Mennonites the first decade represented the final loss of privilege, an uncertain status as a foreign ethnic element, and then the breakdown of the colonist system of life through the dekulakisation campaign and the collectivisation campaign that followed. The breakdown was aggravated by a major out migration to North and South America.

Statistics for church membership throughout the Soviet era have always been problematic. Scholars accept that in 1905 there were approximately 105,000 Baptists and Evangelical Christians, their number having risen to 150,000 by 1917, then increasing rapidly to about 350,000 by 1920, and to over 500,000 by 1929.[5] Adding the non-baptised family members, then the latter figure of 500,000 would suggest over three million persons identifying themselves as either Baptist or Evangelical Christian. Pentecostalism, which had begun in America in 1901, entered the Russian Empire a few years later, largely through the influence of Ivan Voronaev. A gifted organiser, his wing of the Pentecostals claimed 17,000 members in 350 assemblies by 1928.

For Lutherans and Mennonites on the other hand, the first decade of Soviet power became an uncertain one, portents of the loss of independence and privilege coming through the anti-Germanism during the war. Approximately one fourth of the 100,000 Mennonites had been permitted to emigrate to Canada, Paraguay, and Brazil by 1929 when that possibility ended.[6] Lutherans had experienced a longer process of attrition, as far as the church (rather than German culture) was concerned, which was only partially reversed through the impact of regional conferences and participation in the general Protestant revival movement in the mid-twenties. Loss of leadership through emigration and death was severe for both Mennonites and Lutherans. As far as total adherents were concerned, of the 1.35 million Lutherans in 1923 (of which 1 million were Germans), there were only 900,000 left in 1926 (540,000 of them Germans).[7]

Common persecution and collapse 1929–1939

The second decade of Soviet power was characterised by experiences common to all religious bodies. The excesses of administrative persecution and the atheistic propaganda of the League of Militant Godless left an indelible mark. To speak of the commonalities of Soviet Christianity today is to acknowledge the degree to which church institutions and church practice stopped and had to start over fifteen years later.

The details have been widely covered in the literature, although we have recently been witnessing an astonishingly candid Soviet re-examination of the record. For our purposes the basic outline shall suffice. There was, first of all, the decision taken by the Communist Party in April 1926 to foster atheism aggressively in all spheres of education and culture.[8] This was followed by the Law on Religious Associations of April 1929 which had the effect of drastically curtailing religious activity. All those activities for expansion that the evangelicals had engaged in were now expressly forbidden (especially Article 17) and massive closures of churches quickly followed. Within a year, the evangelicals had dropped to one fifth of their previous number. A series of governmental actions (such as high taxation) culminated in the wholesale arrest and imprisonment in labour camps of clergy and other leaders. Of those taken during the wave of arrests in 1937–8, many never returned. After 1930 it became increasingly difficult to communicate with fellow believers abroad, all contact ceasing after 1935. By that year the Baptist Union was no more, and the Evangelical Christian Union now ceased to exist except for one congregation in Moscow. The Pentecostal leaders were all in prison, with Voronaev never to return from his second imprisonment in 1937. The Lutheran church collapsed in 1937–8, experiencing only a brief revival during the German occupation 1941–3, as did the Mennonites in the Ukraine.

Rise of Soviet Protestantism

The rather sudden and surprising national congress of leading Evangelical Christians and Baptists in Moscow in October 1944 to announce their unification into one church union marks the birth of Soviet Protestantism. In August 1945 Pentecostals officially joined what came to be known as the All-Union Council of Evangelical Christian–Baptists (AUCECB). The Smorodintsy wing of the Pentecostals also joined for a few years, and in 1963 the majority of Mennonite Brethren began joining that evangelical union. Official recognition of independent Pentecostals, Mennonites, Lutherans, and Adventists did not come until the late sixties and early seventies.

This union of Soviet evangelicals now began to shape a Soviet form of Protestantism, in which the historic traditions were a dim memory and a closely watching unfriendly state was not. The early leaders had been active in the Baptist, Evangelical Christian, and Pentecostal Unions before their collapse, but they were not necessarily the primary leaders of earlier days, since most of those had perished in prison.[9] Many of the delegates were released from prison to attend the congress of 1944. Thus for many years members harboured suspicions that these leaders had compromised their faith in order to be released, and that this explained their cautious leadership, their counsels of restraint to energetic pastors, and their loud public pronouncements on behalf of Soviet peace policies.

Although there was a continuing effort at a balance of representation between Baptists and Evangelical Christians, it is safe to say that the union came about through the adoption of Baptist polity by the less rigid Evangelical Christian leaders who provided the dominant leadership. The Pentecostal presence was to be a persistent problem. The August Agreement spelled out in twelve points what boiled down to Pentecostals agreeing to abandon their distinctive emphases (except in private worship).[10] The evidence points to a state policy to allow one national structure for Orthodoxy and one national Protestant church structure. If the Pentecostals wished to be legalised, then they must subordinate themselves to the AUCECB; otherwise they would remain illegal and subject to harassment. Major conflicts with the Pentecostals developed in 1949, 1957, 1972, and 1979, and in each case the AUCECB reasserted the need to adhere to the terms of that August Agreement. As a result, up to one half of the Pentecostals left the AUCECB and chose to remain independent and unregistered.

A major task of the union leadership initially was to assist in rebuilding a church structure by appointing regional superintendants and facilitating the registration of local congregations. By 1949 such registration was no longer possible, leaving about two thirds of the worshipping groups unregistered. The leadership also sought to obtain Bibles and songbooks, finally managing a small printing of 10,000 New Testaments in 1956. It became increasingly difficult to hold conferences of the leadership. As a result the overall leadership became entrenched and increasingly authoritarian. After 1955 the AUCECB leaders began travelling abroad to defend Soviet peace themes and claims for religious liberty. In 1958 the AUCECB joined the Christian Peace Conference (Prague) and in 1962 it joined the World Council of Churches. These have come to be very important and helpful international connections, but seemed politically contrived initially since the broad membership did not get to vote on these decisions, and many of the rank and file members have remained decidedly suspicious of the ecumenical movement.

Impact of Khrushchev's anti-religious campaign

Although there was some ebb and flow in the church–state relationship between 1944 and 1958, for our purposes the next major stage of development was the concerted state effort (1959–64) to eradicate religion from society as it sought to take a major step toward full communism.[11] It began with an announced increase in atheist education and propaganda, but the campaign soon turned to administrative measures. Unauthorised religious services were stopped, local vigilante bands broke up authorised meetings, and the organisers of religious groups were arrested. In 1960 the authorities pressured the central church leadership (of both the Orthodox and Evangelicals) to restrain and reduce religious activity by issuing new governing church statutes more in line with state legislation on religion.[12] The 1929 Law on Cults had been drastically amended secretly, but only in 1962 after the new restrictions on religious practice were already in force.[13] Charges brought against a growing list of local pastors and church activists concerned violations of this secret law.

The AUCECB leaders watched how Metropolitan Nikolai lost his position and soon died in suspicious circumstances when he ventured to resist the state pressure. That cowed them into arbitrarily issuing a new statute (without approval by a congress of elected delegates) and sending it to the regional superintendants with an accompanying secret letter of instructions on enforcing it.[14]

This letter precipitated a split in the evangelical union. By August of 1961 an Initiative Group had formed to challenge the Moscow church leadership. Led by A.F. Prokofiev, G.K. Kriuchkov and G.P. Vins, this group dispatched letters across the Soviet Union, calling for sanctification of the church. The use of Samizdat as a means of communication was a key factor in informing the broader church public and marshalling opposition to the instructions from Moscow.[15] Particularly shocking to many were such phrases in that letter of instruction as 'harmful missionary tendencies' and the assertion that the chief goal of worship services was 'not the attraction of new members but satisfaction of the spiritual needs of believers'. The Initsiativniki, as the reformers were soon called, quickly labelled the letter an 'anti-evangelical document'.[16]

Initial efforts at dialogue with Alexander Karev, the Evangelical Union's general secretary in Moscow, and with other leaders proved fruitless. The Moscow leaders saw no possibility to obtain permission to convene a national congress. Instead they tried to get the reformers, most of whom had only recently been exposed to the nature of the restrictions under which the AUCECB had been permitted to exist since 1944, to be realistic. The reformers then turned to the member churches, appealing for disciplinary action against those leaders who were co-operating with the state's anti-religious programme. Having formed an organising committee (Orgkomitet) in February 1962, they drafted a revision of the 1960 statute, called for a day of prayer and fasting for 6 May 1962 so that the leaders in Moscow might repent, then in June 1962 they issued Protocol No. 7 in which 27 persons were declared excommunicated, which included most of the central leadership. They also declared the Orgkomitet as temporary leading organ until a congress of the Evangelical Christian–Baptist congregations had been held. State authorities meanwhile had arrested numerous local leaders who supported the reformers, and the AUCECB leadership had also responded to the dissenters by arranging for the dismissal or excommunication of local reformers.

What made the reformist movement a significant problem for the authorities was the concerted actions. There was the very effective and widespread distribution of written summaries of discussions and actions through the laborious and dangerous methods of Samizdat. Arrests of believers stimulated the dissent movement, a result of the reduced atmosphere of fear after the short de-Stalinisation phase. By 1962, there were 94 evangelical activists known to be in prison, including one of the key leaders, Prokofiev. In early 1964, relatives of these prisoners met to form the Council of Prisoners' Relatives (CPR) and prepared a list of known prisoners, which included the names of five persons who had died in prison or exile. Since those beginnings, the CPR has regularly produced a Bulletin, on an average six times per year, filled with details about arrests, trials, and treatment of prisoners. This organisation, led by women, attained a reputation for reliability of information and has made it possible for more information to be known about this group of Baptists, than any other religious group.[17]

Support for the Reformers grew steadily, reaching a peak in 1966 when perhaps one half of the evangelicals supported them.[18] In September 1965 the Reformers announced the formation of their own national church union called the Council of Churches of Evangelical Christian–Baptists (CCECB). Two months later they issued their own statute. Although permitted to hold one national congress by state approval, they never succeeded in securing state recognition so their leaders were forced to work clandestinely.

Already in 1963 the AUCECB was permitted to respond to the Initsiativniki challenge by calling a national conference and submitting for approval, to a body of delegates, a revised church statute which borrowed extensively from the Initsiativniki proposal. These reforms did not go far enough, but the changes registered at a second congress in 1966 turned the tide. By the 1969 congress this rejuvenation was nearly complete. Perhaps most important, was the radical revision to the church statute in content and tone into a more clearly congregational polity with an increasing affirmation of the centrality of witnessing to the Gospel.[19]

Following the ouster of Khrushchev in 1964, the anti-religious programme was reviewed and modified in order to focus more on education, although the number of religious prisoners continued to rise until 1968. Gradually a pattern of policy set in whereby the registered AUCECB with its member churches received state concessions to engage in religious practices with less state interference, whereas the CCECB and its churches were subjected to the brunt of state pressure. That included surveillance of leaders, reporting on worship services, and reporting to schools the names of children at church services. It also included threats to deprive parents of parental rights, in several cases actually removing children to state orphanages. There were also many cases of physical abuse, a few leading to death.

Thanks to Samizdat and the increased travel to the Soviet Union under the era of *Détente*, this conflict between church and state became more exposed to world public opinion. In 1974, when Georgi Vins was caught (having worked in secret since 1970) and put on trial, a major international campaign developed to appeal for his release and for increased religious rights. That included public letters, statements, and appeals by a number of ecumenical leaders, in contrast to the more muted voice of the WCC after 1961 when the Soviet churches had become members. In 1975 the legislation on Cults was revised.[20] Although the legislation was still very restrictive, this marks the beginning of a period of stabilisation in the church–state relationship that lasted until the recent era of *perestroika*.

Denominationalism and stabilisation 1975–1985

Only after the retirement of the long-time chairman of the Council of Religious Affairs Vladimir A. Kuroedov (in office 1960–1984) did his successor, Konstantin Kharchev publicly acknowledge that the churches and religious beliefs were not likely to disappear in the immediate future.[21] Therefore a *modus vivendi* had to be found that went beyond grudging toleration of this 'pernicious vestige' of the past, to find ways that Communist and Christian citizens could coexist in this world and co-operate on mutual concerns. That is one of the indicators of the most remarkable change in the church–state relationship under *perestroika*.

Normal or stable relations between church and state – true for both Orthodoxy and Protestantism – involved a relationship of hostile state supremacy over the churches, the declarations of separation notwithstanding.[22] That involved clearly established limits to the extent of religious activity, basically understood as the satisfaction of the need for religious ritual within the confines of a specially designated building.[23] For example, it assumed the need for the local congregation in question to submit an application for state registration that assumed a readiness to abide by state legislation. The understandings included permission for regularly stated worship in a prayer house that met health and safety standards and did not violate zoning considerations. For evangelicals this was usually two hours of worship three times on Sunday and three evenings in the week. Locally licensed pastors and regionally licensed superintendants were free to work within their jurisdictions, but needed permission from the plenipotentiary of the Council of Religious Affairs (CRA) to exercise their office outside that jurisdiction. The CRA was usually informed about baptisms and ordinations. Sometimes that required a list of names (certainly with regard to ordination candidates) and sometimes only the number of persons involved.

Stabilisation also involved a slow but steady granting of small concessions. Every year a few more congregations were registered, and
permission was given to renovate a few church buildings. In most
cases these approvals came through after years of appeal. The number
of copies of the journal *Bratskii Vestnik* increased from 3,000 to 5,000
copies, to 8,000 and to 10,000 copies at the beginning of *Perestroika*. A
small literature plan became evident as the AUCECB secured permission to publish several thousand Bibles, or New Testaments, then a
song book, then a licence to import some Bibles, then again the right to
print a few thousand, and so on. It gave the membership, or at least
the broader leadership that knew about the negotiations, a sense of
small but steady progress. Throughout the decade the expectations
and demands of the membership grew. By 1979 they were asking the
central leadership for a special department for the needs of younger
believers. Five years later they were more articulate in requesting
religious educational materials for children. In this way the *de facto*
religious activity of the AUCECB churches stretched well beyond the
limits of the legislation on religion, state authorities giving tacit
approval or else granting special permission for very specific activities.

These concessions need to be understood in light of the two-prong
policy toward religion. Although it had emerged sooner, after 1975
there were explicit statements in popular literature indicating that
registered churches (and approved central church organisations) were
free to practice their religion, but specifically named churches were
illegal and their leaders must be prosecuted.[24] These illegal churches
included the Initsiativniki (or CCECB) whose General Secretary
Georgi Vins was in prison (until 1979 when he was deported to
America in exchange for a Soviet spy) and whose President, Gennadi
Kriuchkov, was living in hiding. Other illegal churches whose activities were to be suppressed were dissident wings of the Adventists and
of the Pentecostals, and the Jehovah's Witnesses sect as such. These
latter groups began developing their own *Samizdat* which gave them
more recognition in world public opinion, but their key leaders
remained in prison. Pentecostals in particular began demanding the
right to emigrate for reasons of religious freedom. This was dramatised
by seven Pentecostals from Siberia who gained an extended refuge in
the American embassy (1978–83), before the authorities gradually
permitted their departure.[25]

For these illegal Protestant churches, the second half of this period
(1979–84) became a major time of persecution. With the ouster of Vins
in 1979, the number of Baptist prisoners began to climb again from its
low of 33 persons, eventually reaching 150. These groups also suffered

as a result of the new cold war and the fact that Soviet authorities turned away from cultivating public opinion in the West by easing up on dissent, as had been true under *détente*. This was the period when most of the dissident movements were crushed through the imprisonment of leaders, the forced emigration of others, and the more frightening technique of incarceration in psychiatric hospitals including the injection of drugs to induce behaviour modification. KGB interrogation was brutal, and the majority of prisoners returned with their health broken owing to prison conditions. It meant that the network of co-operation between dissident and human rights movements was shrinking, an atmosphere of resignation and hopelessness became apparent.[26]

Authorities began further differentiation by granting registration to locally autonomous congregations. Some of the CCECB leaders began suggesting such registration of their congregations, particularly since the authorities were not insisting on strict adherence to the law on cults, provided a minimum of normalisation through registration was achieved. Kriuchkov opposed all such adaptations and developed a very authoritarian leadership style. Owing primarily to this latter feature, and the lack of systematic leadership from Kriuchkov living in hiding, nearly all of the original members of the CCECB were ousted over the course of the decade, or left of their own accord. In 1983 such churches formed a very loose association on the basis of a memorandum of agreement of principles. They are now known as the Autonomous ones (*Avtonomnyi*) or Autonomous ECB churches.[27]

After the war, Soviet Lutheranism had been reintroduced by virtue of the annexation of Estonia and Latvia, republics that included large national Lutheran churches. Their church life was permitted to continue, but controlled by means of ensuring a church leadership selection acceptable to Soviet authorities.[28] The German Lutherans and Mennonites had a more unique experience. After all Germans were forcibly resettled to Siberia and Central Asia in September 1941, as a response to the Nazi invasion, a special administration of these deported nations was established, known as the *Spetskomandatura* or Deportation Regime.[29] Following the war, 280,000 forcibly repatriated Soviet Germans were added to these settlements making a total of 1,250,000 people living under a special command that functioned like forced labour camps. The Soviet Germans lost all civil rights and had to report their location monthly to a special command. This Deportation Regime dealt a debilitating blow to German culture and religion. It was long estimated that up to 80 per cent of the Soviet Germans would emigrate if they could, and popular discrimination against them as fascists was fostered by the Soviet press till the mid-eighties.

Soviet German Lutherans were in a sorry state, with only two pastors, Eugen Bachman in Tselinograd (1957–72) and Johannes Schlundt in Prokhladnyi (1971–73), to provide services.[30] Both of them were able to emigrate in the early seventies. After considerable negotiation by the European Secretary for the Lutheran World Federation, Paul Hansen, the CRA granted permission in 1980 for a Latvian pastor, Harold Kalnins of Riga, to visit the Central Asian German Lutherans and function as their superintendant. During the period from 1957 to 1985 around 250 congregations were registered, and permission to import a few thousand German Bibles and songbooks were secured. Finally, under Gorbachev, it became possible to consider the possibility of a separate organisation for Lutherans in Central Asia, with a few ordinations, but thus far not a single German Lutheran has been sent for theological study to the Baltic.[31]

Mennonites attempted to worship wherever they could. Some of them were exposed to the religious revival in the post-war years, but the major religious renewal came in 1956 with the dismantling of the Spetskomandantura and the return of ordained ministers from the camps. The rebuilding of the Mennonites as a denomination proved to be difficult. The Mennonite Brethren came to be the larger wing, owing in part to many new converts being baptised by immersion (the Baptist way) and fitting in to the general ECB milieu. The Church Mennonites (Kirchliche) retained the more traditional form of baptism of adults by effusion, a form that the ECB churches refused to recognise. Hence it became necessary for the Church Mennonites to organise their own churches, once the disregarding of denominational difference that had characterised the initial post-war religious revival movement had passed. Certainly, many of the returning clergy from the prisons came with a sharper sense of denominational identity than was true of the average believer.[32]

It was obvious to these leaders that some intra-church structure was necessary for dealing with the task of establishing regular contact with the scattered groups. Several Kirchliche leaders did meet in Solikamsk (Urals) in 1957 to form a Mennonite Church union, but the authorities stopped it by arresting the leaders.[33] All that remained was that individual ministers and elders (bishops) such as Heinrich Voth, Johann Penner, Hans Penner and Aron Thiessen made private visits, secretly baptising and conducting communion, as well as giving encouraging counsel.

After the Khrushchev era these independent Mennonite congregations gradually emerged into the open and applied for local registration. The first congregations to receive registration were in Karaganda, Novosibirsk and Tokmak (1967). Others were granted a filial status as a part of an ECB registered congregation that met in the same building at different hours. A similar arrangement developed with accommodating Methodist and Baptist congregations in Latvia and Estonia. By 1980 most of these congregations had obtained their own meeting house and separate registration, or, in the case of the Baltic, the Mennonite contingent had dissolved due to emigration to West Germany. There were also several instances where a local congregation was technically ECB, but included German Lutherans and Mennonites, all of them agreeing to recognise each other and to include certain traditional distinctives, as in the manner of conducting communion.

Social demographic aspects

If the Protestants in the Soviet Union included both lower- and middle-class strata originally, this had changed after the Second World War. Although officially all citizens were now either workers or peasants, the discriminations toward all religious persons ensured that adherents were almost invariably the least advantaged in society. Soviet Protestantism as a whole does not differ significantly from the overall demographic picture of religious concentrations. The western border regions have continued to be the most active religiously. One half of all evangelicals (whether AUCECB, CCECB or autonomous) are located in the Ukraine, with the western half of the Ukraine preponderant in membership and number of churches. Another 30 per cent are scattered across the vast RSFSR, again with certain identifiable pockets of concentration. These are the regions around Moscow and extending south to the Ukraine, and on to Rostov and the Caucasus, the Volga region, the Novosibirsk and Altai regions. A very active movement developed in the twenties in the Far East owing to the exile system and active missionary activity. Much of that went underground, congregations re-emerging after Stalin's death in a much more restrained climate than in the central USSR. At that time a major contingent of independent Pentecostals moved to the Far East. Over 5,000 of their number have succeeded in leaving the Soviet Union since 1987.[34]

Soviet scholars maintained that the rapid growth of Protestant sectarianism during the first decade of Soviet power came largely from the Kulak class of peasants, an argument that supported the claim that the sectarians were an opposition movement to the Communists.[35] The initial growth spurt in the post-war years was interpreted as a response to the general social and economic crisis occasioned by the ravages and traumas of the war. The usual concluding projections for such treatments of the evangelical movement, which provided a theoretical explanation for the active role of younger persons in the Initsiativniki or CCECB, was that it was only a matter of time until secularism would quash the latter, for it was only an alarmist response by backward-looking leaders seeking a following.

Then came the researches of new regional field studies in the mid-seventies that forced three inescapable conclusions.[36] Regional studies now showed that evangelical congregations were primarily urban, and such urban evangelicals were very active proselytisers, relying on religious education in the home (Mennonite families apparently being most active in this sphere) and music ensembles for youth or other special events to attract young adherents. During the late sixties and early seventies families of atheists were the major source of new members. In short, during the seventies the number of male members increased more rapidly than did that of females; the number of younger persons, and persons with middle-level education (high school and trade school graduates) increased, and this growth occurred primarily in urban congregations.[37] These conclusions resulted in renewed theoretical work to develop new explanations for the persistence of religion.

That included a stronger emphasis on the role of historical tradition in producing sectarian loyalty, an obvious answer for the retention of children of believing families, once those children reached adulthood and must initiate baptism for themselves. Further, the pace of modernisation of Soviet society was seen to contribute to the emergence of new sects who sought a more satisfying religious experience to compensate for the strains of keeping pace with progress. One increasingly prominent sociologist of religion (D.M. Ugrinovich) began drawing on Weberian typologies applied to American denominationalism in order to differentiate among the diverse Protestant sects, and to locate them along a spectrum between church and sect types.[38]

No major work on sectarianism has appeared since 1980, but there have been further developments in sociological theory. Ugrinovich began examining the psychology of religion, allowing for the religious personality type.[39] The political goal of bringing all tolerated Protestants under the umbrella of the AUCECB appears to have been abandoned, although that church organisation is undeniably the most important alternative religious sub-culture for Soviet citizens drawn to Christianity for other than national reasons.

Religious *perestroika* begins with millennium celebrations

Between the death of Brezhnev (November 1982) and the election of Gorbachev (March 1985) there were uncertainties about the future of the churches. It appeared that there might be a new anti-religious drive as part of an effort to rejuvenate communist ideology.[40] Another disturbing sign was the growing number of cases where a religious prisoner was re-sentenced on a new charge before completing the current term. The appointment of Kharchev as chairman of the CRA (1984) sounded positive, but the first signs of a more friendly policy to religion were little things like the publication of Aitmatov's novel in spite of the positive image of a believer in it, or Yevtushenko calling for broader access to the Bible as necessary for understanding world literature. In his bestseller, *Perestroika . . .*, appearing on the eve of his visit to America, Gorbachev quoted at length a letter from a Lithuanian Catholic who promised to pray for him. By then, Gorbachev's position seemed increasingly secure, and expectations for applying *perestroika* to religion grew, with preparations for the millennium of Christianity in Rus now gaining state support.

The celebration of the millennium continued throughout the year, producing precedent after precedent.[41] It began with the opening of the Danilov Monastery as Orthodox headquarters and publishing centre, including permission to publish 100,000 Russian Bibles. The Protestants received permission to import 100,000 Russian Bibles, 10,000 German Bibles for Mennonites, 5,000 for Lutherans, 8,000 Latvian Bibles and permission to publish a new translation of the Bible in Georgian. The AUCECB also received 5,000 sets of the 15 volume New Testament Commentary by William Barclay in Russian. Almost on its heels came the permission for the Orthodox to receive 10,000 copies of the Lopukhin Study Bible (3 vols.), and then a further order for a staggering 150,000 copies. These amounts had nearly doubled the total number printed or officially imported since 1945.[42] Then the AUCECB senior presbyters for the Ukrainian and RSFSR republics began submitting requests for literature. That included approvals to import 100,000 Ukrainian Bibles, 20,000 songbooks (Ukrainian) and 50,000 Concordances in Russian. Surprising too was the permission to import 50,000 copies of a children's Bible story book. When all this literature was tallied (not counting what was sent privately in the mails) it became evident that in 1987 and 1988 a total of 2.1 million Bibles and New Testaments had been sent or printed.[43]

Whereas the Soviet press and television provided quite amazing coverage of the Orthodox millennium celebrations in Moscow and

Kiev, there were numerous celebrations in many cities organised by all the religious groups. For the Protestants this included inviting foreign radio evangelists who spoke to large crowds in public squares. There were riverside baptismal services attended by thousands, with 50 to 70 persons baptised at a time, and often more than 100 new converts as a result of such an open meeting. Such events happened in numerous locations and usually included the co-operation of several churches, even AUCECB and autonomous Baptists sharing the preaching. In one instance the evangelicals in Tallinn rented the sport palace (ice arena) seating 10,000. This filled within a few minutes. Leaders then invited the believers in the crowd to step forward onto the ice (covered by a carpet) in order to make room for more of the unbelievers eager to get in. After 2,000 had stepped forward, the authorities opened the doors and allowed more people to stream in.[44]

The 'process of evangelisation'

It was common in 1989 for Soviet church leaders to preface their remarks about the situation by saying that the Soviet Union was now in the 'process of evangelisation'. In the first place, this had to do with Bibles and other literature. After that initial inundation of 1988, people from all levels of society were now demanding a copy of the Bible to read for themselves. That is, such new readers were experiencing their first ever confrontation with the Evangel, and from those reactions everything else flowed. Soviet Evangelicals, especially the loosely organised group of Autonomous ECB churches and often in local or even national co-operation with the AUCECB organised preaching missions. That included foreign speakers such as Luis Palau, James Irwin the American astronaut, and Bill Bright of Campus Crusade. But there were many more less famous speakers who preached in rented stadiums and arenas, or to large masses of people in the open air, inviting the tens of thousands of listeners to respond to a Gospel invitation. Gospel tracts or even New Testaments were distributed in massive numbers, and still the appeal for more literature would not let up. Mass baptisms became common throughout the summers of 1989 and 1990.

In April 1989 the Soviet postal authorities removed the restrictions on individual persons receiving packets from abroad containing religious literature. Very quickly the warehouses in the West containing Russian language literature were depleted. After August of 1989 it was no longer necessary to secure special permits to import religious books. One mission society, for example, long associated with the ECB fellowships, started sending one three ton truck of literature a month. Visitors to church headquarters in Moscow or Kiev found all available staff in a nearly constant state of perspiration as they hurried to unload the literature shipments, tried to find storage space in corridors, or in and around the church pews, and then reloaded the literature into cars or suitcases for the persons from other cities sent to pick up their supply.

Protestants and nationalism under *perestroika*

Glasnost and *perestroika* have encouraged new thinking among Protestants. Most surprising has been the Rebirth and Renewal movement among Latvian Lutherans.[45] Following the death of Archbishop Matulis in March 1986, before his successor Eriks Mesters had been consecrated, a Latvian Lutheran theology student named Maris Ludviks who was having difficulty being ordained, apparently because of his religious activism with young people, asked the Lithuanian Lutheran Bishop Kalvanas to ordain him. When a Latvian newspaper attacked Ludviks in print, calling him a black marketeer and former juvenile delinquent, the rector of the Lutheran correspondence seminary, Propst/Dean Modris Plate (aged thirty-six) and four other leading clergymen handed in a letter of protest to the newspaper. They argued that the attack was not in keeping with the new thinking and openness advocated by Gorbachev. The response was that the Latvian Council for Religious Affairs (CRA) pressured the consistory and Archbishop Mesters to dismiss Plate.

At first the consistory asked the CRA to reconsider, since Plate was very popular and respected both in the seminary and in the congregation he was pastoring where, in the space of four years, the number of communicants had increased from 400 to 1,200. In March 1987, the consistory did suspend him, whereupon open letters of support for Plate were sent to the Archbishop. One letter was signed by 19 clergymen, another by 5, both praising Plate's qualities as pastor and teacher. The signatories included the seminary rector, four lecturers, and three deans. In spite of this response on behalf of Plate by many other persons, the consistory bowed to CRA pressure and reconfirmed his dismissal as both dean and pastor.

In June 1987, Modris Plate and fourteen other leaders (which included the seminary rector Dr R. Akmentins and two other deans) formally founded a group named 'Rebirth and Renewal' with the declared aim 'to defend openly the right of Latvians to lead a Christian life'. They presented 'a few points' to the Archbishop and the consistory, asking them to propose the following revisions to the Latvian Law on Religious Associations. They included

the issue of alternatives to military service for religious believers, religious instruction for children, legal rights for the church, the possibility of religious radio and television programs, the publication of more religious literature and the authorisation of religious activities in hospitals and old people's homes.[46]

Further, they explained their activities as an effort to halt the further decline of the Latvian Lutheran Church. From a pre-war membership of over one million, it had declined to 350,000 in 1980, of which, the Rebirth and Renewal Group claimed, only about 25,000 were regular communicants. A crucial problem was the shortage of clergy. Since this movement also participated in the national demonstrations against the annexation of Latvia or to commemorate Latvians deported by Stalin to the camps, the consistory refused to identify with it, opting for stringent measures instead. Plate was now dismissed as lecturer also, as well as pastor; the rector was dismissed, and another dean, Reverend Aivars Beimanis, was deprived of his position. To forestall further protests by faculty and students, courses were temporarily suspended. By now the movement had become known through samizdat, so that in addition to the pressure from local clergy and the CRA, there was pressure from Lutherans abroad, including a visit from the General Secretary of the Lutheran World Federation, Dr Gunnar Staalstett, to discuss the matter.

The change began in January 1988, when Modris Plate was permitted to resume his duties as pastor. The stern reprimand of the rector, Dr Akmentins, was withdrawn, and Plate was permitted to resume lecturing, although he was not restored as dean. Somewhat later, a sympathiser with the Rebirth and Renewal Movement was appointed 'pastor of the youth movement' of the Latvian Lutheran Church, a position that was still illegal according to the old law on religion.

Finally in April 1989 the General Synod of the Latvian Lutheran Church voted the entire consistory and Archbishop Mesters out of office, replacing them with Karlis Gailitis as new Archbishop and a consistory of eight persons, all from the Rebirth and Renewal movement. They included Plate and Akmentins. Archbishop Gailitis soon thereafter placed an advertisement in the newspaper inviting young people interested in the pastorate to apply for a new intensive six-month theology course intended for pastoral assistants.[47] Still another action of the Synod was a resolution to the Latvian government, based on the Christian conviction of overcoming evil with good, to permit conscientious objectors to military service to do an alternative social service. It is a fascinating story reminiscent of the goals and actions of Orthodox and Baptist dissent during the sixties, but where the apparently positive outcome now being signalled is due to the appeals to *Glasnost* and New Thinking. Indeed, the newly appointed plenipotentiary for Religious Affairs, Alfred Kublinskis gave an extended speech where he indicated that the media were to become available to the church, stating that 'religion is a social necessity'. He concluded his address by apologising for all the injustices that the state and his office had done to the church, promising not to interfere in church affairs anymore.[48]

Rebirth and Renewal was closely linked to the revival of Latvian nationalism. Those linkages made possible the organisation of the Latvian Christian Mission as an ecumenical service agency. Volunteers were soon working in hospitals and prisons as visiting chaplains. A newly appointed director of Sunday School education for children was able to spell out her vision for religious education in the national newspaper. As the *de facto* independence of Latvia grew, the churches received back confiscated church buildings and the liberty to organise church schools.

The Estonian Lutheran Church did not experience quite as much drama, nevertheless, at its most recent synod 12–13 June 1990 major changes were undertaken in contrast to the previous years of regimented and controlled debate, and excessive state controls.[49] Presiding was not only the Archbishop Kuno Pajula, but also Propst Einar Soone of Tallinn. The newly elected consistory had only two former members left in it. The 90 pastors had conducted 7 times as many baptisms and confirmations in 1989 as in 1988. Pastors were now no longer paying the higher income tax rate. The Synod decided to undertake the preparation of a new church statute without waiting for a new state constitutions to guide them. The Peace Fund, for which the state had insisted on voluntary donations, was now redirected to church purposes with each local congregation able to determine how funds were to be applied. Now they were able to go directly to the printing house to print religious material, without checking with a censor – only paper was in short supply. The Estonian Lutheran Church is now visible and audible in the media with a Sunday morning prayer on radio 8:45–9:00, plus church news every second Sunday, and the television was carrying a series on 'The Book of Books'. In addition they had now organised worship services in hospitals, counselling in senior citizen homes and the first national Estonian Christian youth gathering (June 1990) since 1939.

On 13 November 1988 Harald Kalnins of Riga was ordained as

bishop of the 250 registered German Lutheran congregations (for the approximately 250,000 practising German Lutherans out of 1.2 million ethnic Germans, most of whom are located in the Asiatic part of the USSR).[50] Kalnins had officially begun a ministry as superintendant for these German congregations in 1980. He was not, however, planning to move closer to his flock (he now resides in Riga) and at age 78, was no longer young. Perhaps more significant than this personal honour was the fact that twenty preachers received some supervisory rights which could lead to more networking between locally registered associations.[51] Yet these promising changes came too late for many Soviet Germans. The change in official attitude and policy toward the emigration of Jews, Germans, and other groups, which began in February 1987, produced a major new wave of emigration. Churches that had grown in membership rather rapidly during the early 1980s were suddenly reduced to less than half their size. New converts among the Soviet Germans temporarily replaced those who had emigrated, but pastors found themselves baptising and marrying couples who were already packed to leave for West Germany. The renewed sentiment among Soviet Germans to obtain a German autonomous republic was of little interest to those Soviet Germans who were actively religious, whether Catholic, Lutheran or Mennonite. Observers (Soviet and western) tended to agree that the trauma of the Spetskomandantura was still too recent a memory for them to join in the rebuilding of Soviet society.

Soviet Mennonites also appeared to have begun their final emigration after February 1987. Over 35,000 of their number had left by the end of 1990. Many of their strongest independent churches in Central Asia were reduced to a remnant. The independent Mennonite Brethren church of Karaganda, with over 1,000 members in January 1987, had only several hundred members left, with only about 20 families not already in the process of applying for emigration. Yet, at the same time, this church illustrated what was happening elsewhere. The key leaders who remained were young (under 40), with some professional training in industry, and full fluency in the Russian language. These now chose to organise mission and service projects for the society around them, and in the process were adding more Russian language character to their churches, thus making it easier for non-Germanic converts to join.

In August 1989 Soviet Mennonites organised officially approved celebrations of their Bicentennial, receiving positive coverage in the national press. Instead of merely recounting their two-hundred-year history, these celebrations were converted into evangelistic events involving closer co-operation with other evangelicals than had been the case heretofore.

Perestroika of structure

Much of what has just been described went well beyond what the legislation on religion would allow. Indeed, since the summer of 1987 a revision of that legislation had been expected. The longer it was delayed, the more the expectation grew that it would be a major revision, an expectation confirmed by reports of a consultation with religious leaders in March 1988, where authorities were urged to abandon the 1929 law as part of discredited Stalinism, in favour of a shorter statement of principles similar to the 1918 separation decree. In his interview with the press during the millennium celebrations in June 1988, which received front page coverage, then President Gromyko freely acknowledged that a revision was in process, but that there were strongly opposing views.[52] Council of Religious Affairs officials began speaking at the end of 1988 as if the old legislation had been abrogated, indicating, for example, that increased charitable work would be part of the activities granted to believers by new legislation, soon to be announced. The worldwide response of assistance after the Armenian earthquake also became a further stimulus to permitting religious organisations (local and foreign) to become involved in the rebuilding effort. There was also strong resistance to liberalising the law, and it should be remembered that at the time of writing there are still local regions where the plenipotentiary for religious affairs still functions as if *perestroika* has changed nothing.[53]

Soviet evangelicals also submitted their recommendations for new Soviet legislation on religion. By the time the new law was printed for public discussion (June 1990) and then approved by the Supreme Soviet (1 October 1990) the focus had shifted. If in 1989 they were regularly saying that none of the changes could be regarded as achieved until they had been anchored in law, Baptist and Adventist leaders, for example, now stated that the new law seemed acceptable for this time of transition, but they were already looking to the time when the need for special legislation on religion would have withered away. For most churches, including the Protestant groups, the new religious legislation of 1990 meant the following:

1 The right to provide religious education for children, also by designated persons, but not in public school facilities.
2 All religious institutions from a congregation with a minimum of 10 members to regional and central unions, monasteries, seminaries, etc. whose statute was legally registered, received full rights of juridical personhood.

3 Such institutions had the right to hold property, usually tax free, and the right to engage in business, but then subject to normal taxation.

4 Religious bodies had the right not only to conduct religious services on their own premises, but also in hospitals, homes for seniors, etc. if that was requested, and suitable scheduling was worked out with the administration; public meetings should be arranged according to normal procedures for organising demonstrations and use of buildings.

5 Religious bodies received unrestricted right to produce, distribute, import, and export religious literature and supplies.

6 Religious bodies had the right to engage in charitable activities as a religious body, or as part of a charity society.

7 Relations with religious bodies abroad (individual or group) were permitted, plus travel and study abroad.

8 Persons working on salary in a religious institution should now be paid according to a contract, the worker able to join a union, and such workers (including clergy) became part of the national health and pension system.

9 The powers and obligations of the council for religious affairs are spelled out – here there do not appear to be any significant changes.[54]

Even before this new legislation that appears to simplify and depoliticise the registration process, registration of churches was proceeding at great speed, about 2,900 churches (mainly Orthodox) having been registered 1985–9.[55] That points to another prime concern of the Protestants as well as the other confessions. Alexei Bychkov of the AUCECB reported in October 1988 that their union had contributed 750,000 rubles to ten or more local congregations engaged in church building projects. Whereas the architecture of evangelical prayer-houses has been more than simple, there is a noticeable shift to erecting buildings that are visually attractive.[56] Hence the Soviet evangelicals are now under great financial strain to carry out local renovations and new building projects while feeling the need to employ more evangelists and teachers.

In February 1990 the largest of the neo-Protestant churches, the AUCECB met for its regular national congress.[57] As expected, that congress restructured itself extensively. In keeping with the decentralisation theme of *perestroika*, as well as recognising the *de facto* shift to more regional and local independence, the All-Union Council now became a Union of Evangelical–Christian Baptists (UECB).

Abolishing the office of general secretary, the UECB elected forty-five-year-old President Grigori I. Komendant (a Ukrainian) as chief executive officer, assisted by Vice-Presidents for Theological Education, for Evangelism and Service, and for Financial Administration. Senior Presbyters of republics were renamed President of regional unions of ECB churches. There was much talk of evangelism and training, but the financial report showed an eroding financial base, and the official statistics for membership, after subtracting the Pentecostals who had left in June 1989 and the Germans who had emigrated, this union that many have claimed had 550,000 baptised members now claimed only 204,156. Throughout the spring and summer the UECB conducted training sessions for leaders, nationally, then regionally, in order to be able to launch a systematic programme of Sunday School instruction for children in September 1990.

The Pentecostals had always chafed under the restrictions of the August Agreement of 1945 whereby they were brought into the AUCECB. Many of their number left soon after, more left the AUCECB during the past decade in order to register as autonomous Pentecostal congregations. A conference of representatives of unregistered Pentecostal fellowships meeting in Zagorsk, 17 September 1988, with 150 representatives failed to agree on a common position toward registration.[58] Finally in June 1989 a separation agreement with the AUCECB was worked out and the CRA agreed to recognise the Pentecostals as a separate denomination. Since then, under the leadership of B.I. Bilas, until then key Pentecostal spokesperson in the AUCECB leadership, they have sought to establish an independent structure, in which both former AUCECB Pentecostals and the independent and unregistered were participating, though not with full support of all. Bilas has also been a member of the European Council of the Assemblies of God since 1987. They too are engaged in organising a Bible school. Progress has been hampered, however, by the loss of valued leaders to the emigration (mainly to America) that has affected them in increasing numbers since 1987.

After years of illegal and semi-legal existence, the Adventists of the Soviet Union reached an understanding with the authorities to regularise the relationship. The negotiations of the Adventist world body were helpful, as was also Kharchev's visit to its headquarters near Washington DC. In October 1987 Adventists in America and the USSR published a joint issue of a magazine entitled 'Is There Faith in God in Russia?', with 35,000 copies printed in Russian. This included the announcement that a theological course by correspondence was to be started in September 1988. In the meantime, permission had been received to obtain a building in Zaokski (Tula region) to serve as headquarters for the RSFSR. Negotiations started for beginning a publishing house as a joint-venture company, 51 per cent of the stock owned by the Soviet government, 49 per cent by Review and Herald Publishing Association. This was to serve the 32,000 Adventists, now led by 178 ordained ministers.

The Soviet Adventist programme in Zaokski has quickly become a praiseworthy model. Their administrative and educational complex erected in the village of Zaokski, complete with red-brick student dormitory and greenhouse have attracted up to 1,000 visitors a month. Graduates of their seminary with its well-stocked library return to their home areas with enough practical training to assist in establishing vegetable and fruit farms so they can fight hunger directly. By the end of 1988 the prisoners of conscience had been released, and the Adventist leaders claimed to be in dialogue with the unregistered body.[59]

Perhaps a bigger challenge right now is the issue of Soviet Baptist unity after so many years of rivalry. Since 1960 there had been two ECB unions (AUCECB and CCECB), but after 1976 the number of autonomous ECB churches gradually increased. Rejecting the authoritarian leadership of Gennadi Kriuchkov, and feeling that a policy of negativism toward the AUCECB did not do justice to the presence of many respected Christians active in that union, nor did it conform to Biblical admonitions to reconciliation, these churches decided to remain autonomous after they had been rejected by the CCECB. They soon met with AUCECB leaders for unity talks, but without the intention of joining that union – rather to indicate acceptance of each other in Christian fraternity. By 1988, this movement had grown larger than the CCECB, one knowledgeable visitor reporting that they numbered around 115 congregations with about 20,000 members, compared with 15–18,000 CCECB members in about ninety congregations.[60] At the CCECB congress in July 1989, Kriuchkov, who made a dramatic appearance to address the delegates before returning to hiding, indicated that they would continue to reject registration until new legislation would provide guarantees against state interference.

Thus far the autonomous ECB churches have resisted forming a competitive union, feeling a deep suspicion of hierarchical structure. In 1980 several of their leaders met in consultation and reached a Fraternal Agreement (*Bratskoe soglasie*). A second meeting 12 November 1983 produced a statement of common principles. Here they elected five spokespersons for maintaining intra-church contacts. They were, in alphabetical order: Bondarenko, Josef D.; Nazaruk, A.G.; Shaptala M.T.; Shumeiko F.A.; Iakimenko, P.Ia. Another major figure in the movement is Nikolai K. Velichko, pastor in Kiev, with 960 members the largest of their churches.

It has been this group of Independent ECB churches that have shown the greatest creativity and initiative in responding to the opportunities of *perestroika*. They were the ones to invite several foreign radio evangelists, including also astronaut and Christian preacher James Irwin. They have been open to fellowship with both sides, but still feel that the AUCECB is maintaining too close a link to the state. Indeed, in terms of their approach to the state, the list of leading names should indicate that these are all former members of the CCECB who still believe in the principles that prompted the original movement, but who wanted a different structure more suited to changing times.

It is no surprise therefore, that the most recent effort at a new ECB unity comes from their circle. On 17 October 1988, M.T. Shaptala and F.A. Shumeiko drafted a new 'Fraternal Proposal' addressed to all staff members of the ECB unions and associations, and to 'all persons who love the brotherhood and are zealous for revival and the unity of the children of God in our country'.[61] The writers developed a six-point proposal for a new unity that would be more in the form of a facilitating federation, than the strong administrative offices now in place. As a start they called for the creation of a working group consisting of representatives from the AUCECB, the CCECB and the Independents[62] who would collect and then work through suggestions coming from the broad membership of the church. Having done so, this working committee would convene a congress to form a new union with a new constitution and newly elected leaders. The writers wanted to restore unity in order to tackle the major tasks of evangelism, religious education, and literature production jointly, but they also insisted on rejection of the Pentecostals and any contacts with the WCC and 'other religio-political organizations'.[63]

The CCECB leadership, on the other hand, has remained rather quiet during the time of *perestroika*. Its leader Kriuchkov continued to work from hiding. Leaders of that union in Kazakhstan recently elected to keep aloof from joint evangelistic efforts because they feared that some of the evangelists were too indiscriminating in cooperating with Orthodox and Pentecostal believers. In other words, they appear to see their task as keeping free of entanglements by being separatist.

Protestants and the *perestroika* of society

In June 1988 it was announced that members of the Patriarch's parish had been invited to offer voluntary care at a nearby hospital. At the same time about fifty members from the Moscow Baptist church began volunteering at the central psychiatric hospital (Kashenko). In October Dr Vladimir Kozyrev, the chief psychiatrist, and several colleagues attended an evening service at the church where the doctor delivered a 25-minute speech of warm affirmation of the need to combine chemical science and love, the latter a specialty for the church volunteers. There were numerous other beginnings at involving religious people in charitable work. Kozyrev and three of his staff, for example, came to America in October 1990 as part of an exchange of mental health professionals sponsored by Mennonites and Baptists.

Approximately 100 mission or charity societies had been organised by Soviet evangelicals and Protestants by 1990. Their statutes or stated programmes were quite inclusive. For example, the Latvian Christian Mission (in which Lutherans, Baptists, and Pentecostals cooperated) was sending volunteers to visit or provide care services at 7 hospitals and 3 children's homes, were providing meals on wheels for 200 persons daily, were visiting 6 prison camps, began a Sunday morning newspaper, and had secured land on which to establish a Christian centre that would include a 400 bed polyclinic, children's home, rehabilitation centre for offenders, home for seniors, and a hostel.[64] Other groups became involved in organising charity societies to assist the handicapped.

Protestants took part in the politicisation of society, but were not as prominent in seeking electoral office as were the Orthodox. But everywhere they kept in touch with politicians working for social change to offer their views on legislative changes or to assist in finding funding (also from abroad) for worthy charity projects.

The new opportunities to organise co-operatives also resulted in numerous new attempts to begin publishing operations. One of the first was Protestant, an inter-denominational association that began publishing a monthly newspaper in 1988. When it failed to get AUCECB endorsement, it continued on its own, selling a few thousand copies by subscription; the remainder of their 25,000 copies being sold by vendors in a few cities. Licensed as a branch of another co-operative company, they were able to obtain buildings, paper, and equipment in order to establish a publishing company selling books and other print products for profit. By 1990 there was no longer only the bimonthly AUCECB journal called *Bratsky Vestnik*, but also a well-designed and edited monthly paper entitled *Khristianskoe Slovo*. The editor, Viktoria Mazhurova, was also the main force behind a Christian farmers' collective which secured property rights to land near Riazan. The Russian and Ukrainian ECB union each produced a magazine, and numerous local church papers began to appear. Often the new mission societies or co-operatives were the organising unit for new Bible schools by extension, working in close partnership with a mission society from abroad.[65]

Soviet Protestants, though not expecting to become the dominant Christian culture, nevertheless were behaving as if they belonged, and had a great deal to offer citizens seeking a road that led to a church.

Notes

1 Roger P. Bartlett, *Human Capital: The Settlement of Foreigners in Russia, 1762–1804* (Cambridge, Cambridge University Press, 1979).

2 Surprisingly, Jeffrey Brooks, in his *When Russia Learned to Read: Literacy and Popular Literature, 1861–1917* (Princeton, Princeton University Press, 1985) ignores religious literature.

3 Fritz Peyer-Müller, 'Reformierte Ungarn in der Sowjetunion. Eine Minderheitenkirche in der Karpato-Ukraine', in *Glaube in der 2. Welt* 11 (1987), pp. 21–30. There are 80,000 believers in 90 parishes with only 21 pastors headed by Bishop Pal Forgon.

4 Recent basic monographs on the different Protestant groups, that provide more detail and bibliographic aid, are: Wilhelm Kahle, *Die lutherischen Kirchen und Gemeinden in der Sowjetunion – seit 1938/1940* (Güterloh, Güterloher Verlagshaus Gerd Mohn, 1985); Walter Sawatsky, *Soviet Evangelicals since World War II* (Scottsdale, PA., Herald Press, 1981); William C. Fletcher, *Soviet Charismatics: The Pentecostals in the USSR* (New York, Peter Lang, 1985); Marite Sapiets, 'One Hundred Years of Adventism in Russia and the Soviet Union', in *Religion in Communist Lands*, 12:3 (Winter 1984), pp. 256–73; *Istoriia evangel'skikh Kristian–baptistov v SSSR* (Moscow, Izdanie Vsesoiuznogo soveta Ev. Khristian–Baptistov, 1989); A.T. Moskalenko, *Ideologiia i deiatel'nost' khristianskih sekt* (Novosibirsk, Nauka sibirskoe otdelenie, 1978) – a relatively theoretical treatment of chiliastic groups among which he includes Pentecostals and Jehovah's Witnesses.

5 Where not otherwise indicated, more detail can be found in my *Soviet Evangelicals*: in this case, pp. 27–54.

6 J.B. Toews, *Czars, Soviets and Mennonites* (Newton, KS, Faith and Life Press, 1982); and Frank H. Epp, *Mennonite Exodus* (Altona, Manitoba, D.W. Friesen, 1963).

7 Wilhelm Kahle, 'Die kirchlichen Gemeinden und die nationale Identität der Deutschen. Unter besonderer Berücksichtigung der Zeit zwischen den Weltkriegen', in Andreas Kappeler, Boris Meissner and Gerhard Simon

(eds.), *Die Deutschen im Russischen Reich und im Sowjetstaat* (Cologne, Markus Verlag, 1987), pp. 104–5.

8 The most recent general survey is Dimitry V. Pospielovsky, *A History of Marxist–Leninist Atheism and the Believer* (New York, St. Martin's Press, 3 vols, 1987–88). See also P.S. Fateev and V.V. Korolev (eds.), *O Emel'iane Iaroslavskom: Vospominaniia, ocherki, stat'i* (Moscow, Politizdat, 1988), pp. 199–240.

9 See my *Soviet Evangelicals*, pp. 78–104, for an extended treatment.

10 Fletcher, *Soviet Charismatics*, pp. 92–3; and Sawatsky, *Soviet Evangelicals*, pp. 93–5, 286–8, 476–7.

11 The literature is extensive, but there is no definitive treatment yet, the latest undertaking by Pospielovsky – *History of Marxist–Leninist Atheism* – being too focused on Orthodoxy. For one competent recent review of state policy that provides a guide to some of the literature, see Bohdan R. Bociurkiw, 'The Formulation of Religious Policy in the Soviet Union', in *Journal of Church and State*, 28:3 (Autumn 1986), pp. 423–38.

12 Metropolitan Filaret (Minsk) acknowledged this openly at the Sobor in June 1988. The speeches and documents of the Sobor appeared in Novosti's monthly news service, *Religion in the USSR*.

13 Walter Sawatsky, 'Secret Soviet Handbook on Religion', in *Religion in Communist Lands*, 4:4 (Winter 1976), pp. 24–34. The most relevant parts of the handbook were published in German translation with annotations as: Otto Luchterhandt, *Die Religionsgesetzgebung der Sowjetunion* (Berlin, Berlin Verlag, 1978).

14 See Sawatsky, *Soviet Evangelicals*, p. 139; also Michael Bourdeaux, *Religious Ferment in Russia* (London, Macmillan, 1968), for extensive citation of documents covering 1961–6.

15 *Samizdat* refers to self-published materials to escape the censor. Much of the early Baptist *samizdat* is available in the publication series, *Arkhiv Samizdata* (Munich), especially volumes 14, 15, 16, and 19.

16 The Initsiativniki version of these events was recently republished by Friedensstimme, *25 Jahre auf dem Weg*. (Gummersbach, Missionswerk Friedensstimme, 1987).

17 The CPR was dissolved in September 1987, and the Bulletin became part of a CCECB Department of Intercession.

18 G.S. Lialina, *Baptizm: Illuzii i real'nost.* (Moscow, Politizdat, 1977), p. 51.

19 English translations of the successions of states and revisions are printed in the appendices of Bourdeaux and Sawatsky, respectively (as cited in note 14); see also *Istoriia* AUCECB, pp. 238–49, for the official AUCECB version of these events.

20 Walter Sawatsky, 'The New Soviet Law on Religion', in *Religion in Communist Lands*, 4:2 (Summer 1976), pp. 4–10.

21 As reported by Father Taska, participant in the 1987 NCC Pilgrimage Tour (June 1987).

22 I am following the language of Otto Luchterhandt, in *Der Sowjetstaat und die*

russische Orthodoxe Kirche (Cologne, Verlag Wissenschaft und Politik, 1976), pp. 244 and 253.

23 To compare this to regulated prostitution in designated areas and buildings as practised in some western countries is a fair approximation of the attitude.

24 G.R. Gol'st, *Religiia i zakon* (Moscow, Iuridicheskaia literatura, 1975), p. 42.

25 The Siberian Seven story has been retold most recently in Kent R. Hill, *The Puzzle of the Soviet Church: An Inside Look at Christianity and Glasnost* (Portland, Multnomah Press, 1989), pp. 15–72.

26 Ludmilla Alexeeva, *Soviet Dissent: Contemporary Movements for National, Religious, and Human Rights* (Middletown, Conn., Wesleyan University Press, 1985).

27 *Samizdat* copy in author's possession.

28 Kahle, *Die lutherischen Kirchen . . . seit 1938/1940*, pp. 27–37, plus special chapters on each national body. The Latvian and Estonian synods of 1989 and 1990 stated this publicly.

29 Ingeborg Fleischhauer and Benjamin Pinkus, *Soviet Germans: Past and Present* (London, C. Hurst and Co., 1986), especially pp. 66–91, 103–11. Over 100,000 were placed in a labour army (*trudarmiia*).

30 Johannes Schleunig, Peter Schellenberg, and Eugen Bachman, *Und Siehe, Wir Leben*, 2nd edn (Erlangen, Universitäts Verlag, 1982).

31 Gerd Stricker, 'German Protestants in Tsarist Russia and the Soviet Union', in *Religion in Communist Lands*, 15:4 (Spring 1987), pp. 32–53.

32 See Walter Sawatsky, 'From Russian to Soviet Mennonites, 1941–1989', in John Friesen (ed.), *Mennonites in Russia* (Winnipeg, CMBC Publications, 1989), pp. 299–337. See also Gerd Stricker and Walter Sawatsky, 'Mennoniten in der Sowjetunion nach 1941', in *Kirche im Osten*, 27 (1984), pp. 57–98, appearing in an abbreviated form in English in *Religion in Communist Lands*, 12:3 (Winter 1984), pp. 293–311.

33 V.F. Krestianinov, *Mennonity* (Moscow, 1967), p. 78.

34 John Pollock, *The Siberian Seven* (London, Hodder and Stoughton, 1979). More recently, the so-called Siberian Seventy from Chuguevka received extensive publicity, started emigrating in 1987, with the last of their leaders arriving in Germany in October 1988. See Hill, *The Puzzle*, pp. 15–72.

35 Lialina, *Baptizm: Illuzii*, pp. 60–72.

36 See volume 24 of *Voprosy nauchnogo ateizma* (1980), a special issue on sectarianism with D.M. Ugrinovich apparently writing much of the general text.

37 Summarised and analysed in more detail in my 'Evangelical Revival in the Soviet Union: Nature and Implications', in Dennis J. Dunn (ed.), *Religion and Communist Society* (Berkeley, Calif., Berkeley Slavic Specialties, 1983).

38 See also his *Vvedenie v religiovedenie*, 2nd expanded edn (Moscow, Mysl', 1985), pp. 142–3.

39 D.M. Ugrinovich, *Psikhologiia religii* (Moscow, Politizdat, 1986).

40 Paul Steeves, 'The June Plenum and the Post-Brezhnev Anti-religious Campaign', in *Journal of Church and State*, 28:3 (Autumn 1986), pp. 439–58. In the same issue, Jerry Pankhurst argued for a longer-term view that Soviet society needed the churches for community building. See his 'Soviet Society and Soviet Religion', pp. 409–22; similarly, Walter Sawatsky, 'Soviet Evangelicals Today', in *Occasional Papers on Religion in Eastern Europe*, 4:2 (March 1984), pp. 1–20.

41 For extended descriptions, see Michael Bourdeaux, *Gorbachev, Glasnost and the Gospel* (London, Hodder and Stoughton, 1990), pp. 42–64; and Jim Forest, *Religion in the New Russia: The Impact of Perestroika on the Varieties of Religious Life in the Soviet Union* (New York, Crossroad, 1990), pp. 6–35.

42 See my 'Another Look at Mission in Eastern Europe', *International Bulletin of Missionary Research*, 11 (January 1987), pp. 14–15.

43 Mark Elliott, 'New Openness in USSR Prompts Massive Bible Shipments to Soviet Christians in 1987–1988. A Statistical Overview', *News Network International* (20 March 1989), pp. 24–31. Elliott also presents a chart showing a total of 5,915,000 Bibles/New Testaments for importing or printing in 1989, all of it legally approved.

44 Viktor Hamm, 'Marvellous in Our Eyes. Report on a Visit to the Soviet Union', in *Mennonite Brethren Herald* (14 October 1988), pp. 7–9.

45 I am relying here on the helpful reconstruction of events by Marite Sapiets, ' "Rebirth and Renewal" in the Latvian Lutheran Church', in *Religion in Communist Lands*, 16:3 (Autumn 1988), pp. 237–49.

46 *Ibid.*, pp. 242–3.

47 *Keston News Service*, no. 324 (27 April 1989), p. 2; and no. 325 (11 May 1989), p. 5.

48 Report by Johannes Baumann, Osterholz-Scharmbeck, Germany (20 April 1989), made available to the author by Dr Gerd Stricker.

49 German language report by Th. Hasselblatt, Hannover, kindly made available to the author by Dr Gerd Stricker.

50 *Frankfurter Allgemeine* (22 October 1988) claims 590 congregations, half of which are smaller groups of 20–70 persons.

51 Gerd Stricker reports that Kalnins described this function with the words, 'as if you are deans (*Pröpste*)' in a letter to him of 14 November 1988. I am relying on Stricker's data, supplied privately to correct the published reports.

52 The reception of church dignitaries and the interview questions and answers were given extensive verbatim coverage in *Pravda* (11 June 1988).

53 For an up-to-date summary of the background, see John Anderson, 'Drafting a Soviet Law on Freedom of Conscience', *Soviet Jewish Affairs*, 19:1 (1989), pp. 19–33; also Bourdeaux, *Gorbachev, Glasnost and the Gospel*, pp. 65–74.

54 Based on the draft, as published in *Pravda* and *Izvestiia* (6 June 1990).

55 Bourdeaux, *Gorbachev, Glasnost and the Gospel*, p. 57; and *Keston News Service*, no. 323 (13 April 1989), based on *Moscow News* (9 April 1989).

56 I am relying on private talks during my visit to the Soviet Union in October 1988, and that of a Mennonite World Conference delegation a week later.

57 Bourdeaux, *Gorbachev, Glasnost and the Gospel*, pp. 119–20, 127–8 offers a brief analytical summary. He mistakenly describes Dukhonchenko of Kiev as having been 'elected' president of the union in December 1989 by the council of the union (which would have been a violation of their statute anyway) when he was merely 'nominated' for election at a congress of delegates in February 1990. Here he withdrew his candidacy in favour of his deputy, Komendant.

58 Bourdeaux, *Gorbachev, Glasnost, and the Gospel*, p. 131.

59 On the latter, see Marite Sapiets, *True Witness: The Story of Seventh Day Adventists in the Soviet Union* (Keston, UK, Keston College, 1990).

60 Bourdeaux, *Gorbachev, Glasnost and the Gospel,.* pp. 128–29 argues for 40,000 members as logical deduction from the number of delegates at its congress in July 1989; that figure is considered too generous by knowledgeable persons who have been discussing this with Soviet evangelicals in the past two years.

61 Copy in author's possession.

62 A label they seem to prefer for themselves.

63 Copy in author's possession (same as note 61).

64 *Khristianskoe Slovo* (January 1990).

65 In addition to 10 such regional centres begun by UECB churches in 1990, other such projects involved independent Baptist and Pentecostal churches working with agencies such as Slavic Gospel Association, Logos, East Europe Seminary (Vienna).

· 15 ·

Epilogue: after the collapse

SABRINA PETRA RAMET

In August 1991, on the twenty-third anniversary of the Soviet invasion of Czechoslovakia, a group of Soviet hardliners arrested Gorbachev, and attempted to set up a restorationist regime that would roll back the reforms of the previous six years, and restore the system as it had existed under Brezhnev. The coup lasted scarcely four days. It was defeated on the streets of Moscow, where a defiant and courageous Boris Yeltsin stirred the population in leading the resistance to the coup. Ultimately, the coup's leaders, though including Gorbachev's vice president, the head of the KGB, the head of the Soviet military, and the Minister of the Interior among its members, lacked even sufficient support to effect basic orders: when, for example, they ordered KGB units to storm the parliament building where Yeltsin was trapped and kill the defiant Russian leader, KGB officers refused. The coup was doomed. Its ringleaders either committed suicide or were arrested. Their supporters were removed from responsible office. Yeltsin emerged as the hero of the New Revolution, and Gorbachev returned to the Kremlin physically drained and politically weaker.

Yeltsin took immediate steps to accelerate the de-communisation of the country, and Gorbachev, left without any alternative, resigned his post as General Secretary of the Communist Party. Meanwhile, the fissiparous forces unleashed during the coup accelerated. The Baltic Republics declared their independence once and for all, and now, in the transformed atmosphere after the coup, quickly won diplomatic recognition from fellow European states as well as from other countries, including the United States.

Gorbachev's draft Union Treaty, which he had been promoting on the eve of the coup and which was one of the chief factors that provoked the hardliner coup, had become a dead letter in the meantime, as not only the Baltic republics, but also Ukraine, Belorussia, Georgia, and Armenia now declared their intention to secede from the moribund union. Boris Yeltsin now sponsored an alternative treaty of union, and before the end of the year, was able to offer his plan for a new Commonwealth of Independent States to the Soviet public. Where Gorbachev's plan had fallen on deaf ears, Yeltsin's plan quickly won support in ten republics, and an eleventh (Ukraine) accepted the plan after a short delay. Only the Baltic republics of Estonia, Latvia, and Lithuania, together with the Caucasian republic of Georgia, chose to remain outside the new Commonwealth, even if its rules of order remained, at that stage, vaguely defined.

The collapse of the old USSR was thus total and complete before the end of 1991. But if the death of communism in the republics of the former USSR was clear by then, it was vastly less clear whether the new 'Commonwealth' could succeed in establishing a stable order. It faced gargantuan challenges in the deteriorating economy, the acceleration of interethnic hatred, and the gathering momentum in the drift toward ever greater social, political, and economic chaos. As historians know all too well, in times of chaos, it is always difficult, and sometimes impossible, to create political order.

In such conditions, all sectors of the society are transformed, forced to redefine themselves in fluid conditions. For the religious faiths of the former USSR, the new conditions of chaos, deprivation, expectation, and fear of deeper impoverishment force the religious organisations to assume more prominent roles. The self-evident power vacuum reinforces the liberalisation of the Gorbachev era in making such a heightened social and political role possible. Meanwhile, the republics assume ever more nationalistic stances, ethnic chauvinism is on the rise, and the churches can scarcely escape this vortex, even if they wished to. Inevitably, thus, the religious organisations are drawn into the nationalist vortex and take up the 'national' cause, however it may be defined. In this way, the churches actually contribute to the deterioration of relations between peoples of different ethnicity and different religious faiths.

For now, the religious organisations of the ex-USSR exist in a kind of legal limbo, enjoying legal guarantees and assurances which, in some cases, may prove transitory. Even before the dust had settled from the Soviet collapse, for example, Islamic fundamentalists in Central Asia, some of them associated with the illegal Party of Islamic Renaissance, registered demands that the entire region be united into an Islamic Turkestan, and declared an Islamic republic, with its civil laws based on the shariat.[1] Islam would be the state religion, and other religions would be, at most, tolerated, but within the framework of Islamic law. Nor can it be excluded that Christian churches may also

try to establish themselves as official state religions, much as the
Catholic Church in Poland briefly attempted to do in 1990, and as the
Georgian Orthodox Church showed some inclination to do, at least as
long as Zviad Gamsakhurdia was Georgian president. But the abolition of church–state separation means privileges for some, and
deprivation for others. As a political solution, it is certain to offend
minorities whether of other faiths or non-believers.

The decision of the Russian Orthodox Church to canonise Grand
Duchess Elizabeta Fiodorovna, a member of the last tsar's family, is a
sign of things to come. In fact, church elders betrayed their intention
to follow this step by canonising the entire slain family of the last tsar –
a move redolent of political meanings.[2]

In conditions of political vacuum and social chaos, it is not surprising that the churches seem to possess a unique claim to institutional
legitimacy, to the point of appearing as the ultimate arbiter of the
nation's conscience. It was surely in this spirit that Boris Yeltsin, at
the height of the August coup, sent an urgent appeal to Patriarch
Aleksii II of All Russia 'to use your authority among all religious and
believers, as well as the influence of the Church'. Yeltsin closed his
appeal with the telling words, 'Believers, Russian people, the whole of
Russia awaits your words.'[3] Within hours, the patriarch replied with a
public statement calling for President Gorbachev to be allowed to
address the country and make his position known.[4] (The coup leaders
had claimed that Gorbachev was retiring for reasons of health.) Even
before these developments, CPSU Central Committee member Vadim
Zagladin had praised Vatican encyclicals *Rerum novarum* and *Centesimus
annus* for their 'influence on the progress of humankind'.[5] *Rerum novarum*
was, of course, Leo XIII's seminal critique of both pluralism and
socialism, in which he called for an alternative to both.

Alongside this process of re-engagement of the traditional religious
organisations in ethnic politics, there is a second parallel, but counter-
vailing, process: a sudden upsurge in the membership of nontradi-
tional religious groups, including groups best viewed as sects and
cults. Protestant fundamentalists from America have come to Russia
in recent months in search of converts, only to find a receptive
audience in people close to despair of this world. 'We are seeing the
movement of God in Russia', said Virginian evangelist Rev. Dennis
Pisani of his work in Moscow. 'Now is the time for us to win millions
and millions of Russian souls for Jesus Christ.'[6] The Baptists alone
doubled their Russian membership in three years, claiming a figure of
600,000 members by late 1991.[7] What the Protestants offer their brethren is less mystery and more lay participation. Responding to this

competition, the Russian Orthodox Church has lately seen an increase in grass roots religiosity in its ranks, reflecting elements of what St Petersburg historian Vladislav Arzhanuhin has called the 'Protestantisation' of the Russian Orthodox Church.[8]

For the time being, the religious organisations enjoy an accelerating surge of concessions. Taxes have been eased,[9] alternative service introduced,[10] and new guarantees of the equality of believers of different faiths, as well as of nonbelievers, enshrined in law.[11] In July 1991, Russian Lutherans were able to hold their first synod since 1924,[12] while Moscow even played host the following month to an unprecedented conference on 'The Islamic Factor in the East European Processes', with invited clergy and other guests from Bulgaria, Romania, Yugoslavia, Turkey, and other countries.[13]

The churches have also had to come to terms with their own past. This has involved, among other things, the removal of senior clerics who collaborated with the KGB from responsible posts in the Russian Orthodox Church[14] and in the Islamic community.[15] The churches are also becoming aware, at least to some extent, of the need to purge their mindset of the operative assumptions and behavioural habits needed to survive in the communist order. The Holy Synod of the Russian Orthodox Church put it very succinctly in a public message issued in late August 1991. In this appeal, the Synod asked, 'May there be a transformation of our minds, and may they be freed from the totalitarian kind of consciousness that has made millions of people participate in lawlessness, whether willingly or not.'[16]

Like all of post-Soviet society, the religious organisations are confronting a serious overload of simultaneous challenges and tasks, most of which are urgent. At this writing, any of a number of scenarios seem conceivable for the near future, including general chaos, civil war, widespread political gangsterism, a relapse into authoritarian rule whether of the left or of the right, and just maybe – although it seems the least conceivable – the eventual attainment of a stable democracy. In fluid conditions, the role that the churches will play can only be enhanced, and, mirroring those conditions, likewise fluid.

Notes

1 *New York Times* (11 October 1991), pp. A1, A4.
2 Interfax (Moscow), 8 July 1991, in Foreign Broadcast Information Service (FBIS), *Daily Report* (Soviet Union), 9 July 1991, p. 45.
3 *Vladivostok Domestic Service* (20 August 1991), trans. in FBIS, *Daily Report* (Soviet Union), 20 August 1991, pp. 57, 58.

4 TASS (20 August 1991), in FBIS, *Daily Report* (Soviet Union), 21 August 1991, p. 20.

5 *Süddeutsche Zeitung* (Munich), 25/26 May 1991, p. 6.

6 Quoted in *New York Times* (7 October 1991), p. A1.

7 Vladislav Arzhanuhin, 'The Russian Orthodox Church in the USSR Today', Lecture at the University of Washington, Seattle, 2 December 1991.

8 *Ibid.*

9 Re. Turkmenistan, see *Izvestiia* (20 July 1991), p. 1.

10 Re. Moldova, see *Ibid.* (11 July 1991), p. 3.

11 Re. the Uzbek religious law, see TASS (2 July 1991), trans. in FBIS, Daily Report (Soviet Union), 5 July 1991, p. 92.

12 Interfax (29 July 1991), in FBIS, *Daily Report* (Soviet Union), 30 July 1991, p. 57.

13 *Izvestiia* (12 August 1991), p. 1; and All-Union Radio Mayak Network (Moscow), 13 August 1991, trans. in FBIS, *Daily Report* (Soviet Union), 14 August 1991, p. 31.

14 *Süddeutsche Zeitung* (21/22 September 1991), p. 9; and *Argumenty i Fakty* (Moscow), no. 36 (September 1991), p. 7, trans. in FBIS, *Daily Report* (Soviet Union), 19 September 1991, p. 24.

15 *Komsomol'skaia Pravda* (9 July 1991), p. 1; and Interfax (12 July 1991), in FBIS, *Daily Report* (Soviet Union), 16 July 1991, p. 103.

16 TASS (31 August 1991), trans. in FBIS, *Daily Report* (Soviet Union), 3 September 1991, p. 87.

Appendix

Religious groups numbering 2,000 or more in the USSR (All figures are from 1990, unless otherwise stated.)

ORTHODOX	
Russian Orthodox	50 million
Ukrainian Orthodox	unknown
Belorussian Orthodox	unknown
Georgian Orthodox	5 million
Armenian Apostolics	4 million
Old Believers	3 million
True Orthodox	unknown
Innozenti	2,000[4]
MUSLIMS	44–50 million (nominal)[1]
CATHOLICS	
Greek Catholics in Ukraine	3–5 million
Roman Catholics in Lithuania	2 million
Greek Catholics in Belorussia	1.8 million
Roman Catholics in Latvia	500,000
Roman Catholics elsewhere in the USSR	500,000 (est.)
JEWS	1.5 million[2]
PROTESTANTS	
Baptists (all)	247,000
Lutherans	230,000
Pentecostals	100,000
Hungarian Reformed (Transcarpathia)	80,000
Seventh Day Adventists	35,000
True Adventists	32,000
Mennonites and Independent Mennonites	25,300
Reformed Church of Lithuania	10,000
Methodists	2,200

OTHER CHRISTIANS
Jehovah's Witnesses   10–20,000[3]
Molokans   10,000[3]
New Apostolics   unknown

BUDDHISTS   590,000[2]

HARE KRISHNA   100,000

BAHAI   4,000[5]

1 = 1983
2 = 1988
3 = 1980
4 = 1984
5 = 1982

Data compiled by Sabrina Petra Ramet and Walter Sawatsky from various sources. For a listing of some of these sources, see Sabrina Ramet, 'Politics and Religion in Eastern Europe and the Soviet Union', in George Moyser (ed.), *Politics and Religion in the Modern World* (London, Routledge and Kegan Paul, 1991). pp. 73–4.

Index